ॐ Meaning and Representation in History ॐ

MAKING SENSE OF HISTORY
Studies in Historical Cultures
General Editor: Jörn Rüsen, *Institute for Advanced Studies in the Humanities, Essen,*
Alon Confino, *University of Virginia, Charlottesville,* Alan D. Megill, *University of Virginia, Charlottesville* in Association with Angelika Wulff

Volume 1
Western Historical Thinking: An Intercultural Debate
    Edited by Jörn Rüsen

Volume 2
Identities: Time, Difference, and Boundaries
    Edited by Heidrun Friese

Volume 3
Narration, Identity, and Historical Consciousness
    Edited by Jürgen Straub

Volume 4
Thinking Utopia: Steps into Other Worlds
    Edited by Jörn Rüsen, Michael Fehr, and Thomas W. Rieger

Volume 5
History: Narration, Interpretation, Orientation
    Jörn Rüsen

Volume 6
The Dynamics of German Industry: Germany's Path toward the New Economy and the American Challenge
    Werner Abelshauser

Volume 7
Meaning and Representation in History
    Edited by Jörn Rüsen

Volume 8
Remapping Knowledge: Intercultural Studies for a Global Age
    Mihai Spariosu

Volume 9
Cultures of Technology and the Quest for Innovation
    Edited by Helga Nowotny

MEANING AND REPRESENTATION IN HISTORY

Edited by
Jörn Rüsen

Berghahn Books
New York • Oxford

First published in 2006 by
Berghahn Books
www.berghahnbooks.com

© 2006, 2008 Jörn Rüsen
First paperback edition published in 2008

All rights reserved. Except for the quotation of short passages for the purposes of criticism and review, no part of this book may be reproduced in any form or by any means, electronic or mechanical, including photocopying, recording, or any information storage and retrieval system now known or to be invented, without written permission of the publisher.

Library of Congress Cataloguing-in-Publication Data

Meaning and representation in history / edited by Jörn Rüsen.
 p. cm. — (Making sense of history ; v. 7)
Includes bibliographical references and index.
ISBN 978-1-57181-776-1 (hbk) 978-1-84545-262-9 (pbk)
 1. History—Philosophy. 2. Memory—Social aspects. I. Rüsen, Jörn.
II. Series.

D16.9.M298 2006
901—dc22

2006040244

British Library Cataloguing in Publication Data

A catalogue record for this book is available from the British Library.

Printed in the United States on acid-free paper.

Contents

List of Illustrations   vii

Preface to the Series   ix
    Jörn Rüsen

Introduction: What does "Making sense of history" mean?   1
    Jörn Rüsen

Part I: Meaning

Chapter 1: Memory—Forgetting—History   9
    Paul Ricoeur

Chapter 2: How Meaning Came into the World and What Became of It   20
    Günter Dux

Chapter 3: Sense of History: What does it mean? With an Outlook onto Reason and Senselessness   40
    Jörn Rüsen

Chapter 4: "The Meaning of History": A Modern Construction and Notion?   65
    Jörn Stückrath

Chapter 5: The Meanings of History: Enacting the Sociocultural Code   89
    Johan Galtung

Chapter 6: The Three Levels of "Sinnbildung" in Historical Writing   108
    Frank R. Ankersmit

Chapter 7: The Reality of History 123
David Carr

Chapter 8: Language and Historical Experience 137
Frank R. Ankersmit

Part II: Representation

Chapter 9: Flights from History: Reinventing Tradition between
the 18th and 20th Centuries 155
Aleida Assmann

Chapter 10: Memory and Identity: How Memory Is Reconstructed
after Catastrophic Events 169
Alessandro Cavalli

Chapter 11: The Material Presence of the Past: Reflections
on the Visibility of History 183
Detlef Hoffmann

Chapter 12: Ruins: A Visual Expression of Historical Meaning 209
Moshe Barasch

Chapter 13: Three Versions of Wallenstein: Differences of Meaning
Production between Historiography, Biography, and Novel 223
Eberhard Lämmert

Chapter 14: The Arts of Jewish Memory in a Postmodern Age 239
James E. Young

Bibliography 255

Notes on the Contributors 267

Index of Names 271

List of Illustrations

Figure 11.1 "Nothosaurus giganteus on a coral-reef" 186

Figure 11.2 "Reconstructed bone find of a Nothosaurus" 186

Figure 11.3 Karl Jauslin, *Pfahlbausiedlung* (Pile Village) 188

Figure 11.4 Wislaw Smetek, "Die letzen Tage des Ötzi" (Ötzi's Last Days) 189

Figure 11.5 "Reconstruction of Ötzi" 190

Figure 11.6 "Traces of a Saurian, 135 million years before Christ" 191

Figure 11.7 Windsor MacCay, "Gertie der Dinosaurier" (Gertie the Dinosaur) 192

Figure 11.8 Burnt-out chariot from the 1948 War of Independence 192

Figure 11.9 Lifesize reconstruction of the battlefield of 1948 193

Figure 11.10 The Pompeian dog 194

Figure 11.11 Albrecht Dürer, *Hiob wird von seinem Weib verspottet* (Job scoffed by his wife, 1500–1505) 197

Figure 11.12 Hilmar Pabel, *Soldat* (Soldier, 1944) 198

Figure 11.13 Bedrich Fritta, *Theresienstadt* (between 1942 and July 1944) 199

Figure 11.14 Bookcover *Denk ich an Deutschland* (Thinking of Germany) 200

Figure 11.15 Horst Strempel, *Gefangen* (Caught, 1946) ©VG Bild-Kunst, Bonn 2006 200

Figure 11.16 Melancholic gestures from *Vorwärts* 201

Figure 11.17 Herbert Sandberg, "Die Überlebenden" (The Survivors, 1963) ©VG Bild-Kunst, Bonn 2006 203

Figure 11.18 Alfred Kantor, *"Birkenau,"* from *Das Buch des Alfred Kantor* 204

Figure 12.1 Bamberg Apocalypse, Bamberg, Staatliche Bibliothek, Msc. Bibl. 140, fol. 45r 213

Figure 12.2 Beatus Manuscript, Morgan Library, Ms. 6434, fol. 176v 214

Figure 12.3 Belleville Breviary, Bibliothèque national de France, Ms. Lat. 10483-4 216

Figure 12.4 Rogier van des Weyden, *Die Anbetung der Könige* (Adoration of the Magi) St. Columba Altarpiece. Bayerische Staatsgemäldesammlungen, Alte Pinakothek, Munich 219

Figure 12.5 Albrecht Dürer, Paumgärtner Altarpiece, Bayerische Staatsgemäldesammlungen, Alte Pinakothek, Munich 221

Preface to the Series

Jörn Rüsen

At the turn of the twenty-first century the very term "history" brings extremely ambivalent associations to mind. On the one hand, the last decade has witnessed numerous declarations of history's end. In referring to the fundamental change of the global political situation around 1989/90, or to postmodernism or to the challenge of Western dominance by decolonization and multiculturalism, "history"—as we know it—has been declared to be dead, outdated, overcome, and at its end. On the other hand, there has been a global wave of intellectual explorations into fields that are "historical" in their very nature: the building of personal and collective identity through "memory," the cultural, social, and political use and function of "narrating the past," and the psychological structures of remembering, repressing, and recalling. Even the subjects that seemed to call for an "end of history" (globalization, postmodernism, multiculturalism) quickly turned out to be intrinsically "historical" phenomena. Moreover, "history" and "historical memory" have entered the sphere of popular culture, from history channels to Hollywood movies. They also have become an ever more important factor in public debates and political negotiations (the discussions about the aftermath of the wars in the former Yugoslavia, European unification, or the various heritages of totalitarian systems, to name a few). In other words, ever since "history" was declared to be at its end, "historical matters" seem to have come back with a vengeance.

This paradox calls for a new orientation or at least a new theoretical reflection. Indeed, it calls for a new theory of history. Such a theory should serve neither as a subdiscipline reserved for historians, nor as a systematic collection of definitions, "laws," and rules claiming universal validity. What is needed is an interdisciplinary and intercultural field of study. For, in the very moment when history was declared to be "over," what in fact did abruptly come to an end was historical theory. Hayden White's deconstruction of the narrative strategies of the nineteenth-century historicist paradigm somehow became regarded as historical theory's final word, as if the critique of the discipline's claim to rationality could set an end to the rational self-reflection of that discipline—as if this very critique were not a rational self-reflection in itself.

Nevertheless, in the late 1980s the "critical study of historical memory" began to substitute historical theory. What has been overlooked in this substitution is the fact that any exploration into the ways of historical memory in different cultural contexts not only crosses into the field of critical studies, but also contains the keystones for a more general theory of history. Each analysis of even a simple instance of historical memory cannot avoid questions of the theory and philosophy of history. And vice versa: the most abstract thoughts of philosophers of history have an intrinsic counterpart in the most secular procedures of memory (for example, when parents narrate past experiences to their children, or when an African community remembers its own colonial subordination and its liberation from it). As long as we fail to acknowledge this intrinsic connection between the most sophisticated historical theory and the procedures of historical memory most deeply imbedded in the culture and the everyday life of people, we remain caught in an ideology of linear progress, that regards cultural forms of memory simply as interesting objects of study instead of recognizing them as examples of "how to make sense of history."

The series "Making Sense of History" aims at bridging this gap between historical theory and the study of historical memory. Its contributions, from virtually all fields of cultural and social studies, explore a wide range of phenomena that can be labeled "making historical sense" *(Historische Sinnbildung)*. The series crosses the boundaries between academic disciplines as well as those between cultural, social, political, and historical contexts. Instead of reducing historical memory to just another form of the social or cultural "construction of reality," its contributions deal with concrete phenomena of historical memory: it seeks to interpret them as case studies in the emerging empirical and theoretical field of "making historical sense." Along the same line, the rather theoretical essays intend not only to establish new methods and theories for historical research, but also to provide perspectives for a comparative, interdisciplinary, and intercultural understanding of what could be called the "global work of historical memory." This does not imply the exclusion of critical evaluations of the ideological functions of historical memory. But it is not the major aim of the series to find an ideal, politically correct, ideology-free mode or method of how to make sense of history. It rather intends to explore the cultural practices involved in generating historical sense as an extremely important realm of human thought and action, the study of which may contribute to new forms of mutual understanding. In an age of rapid globalization that manifests itself primarily on an economic and political—and, much less so, on a cultural level—finding such forms is an urgent task.

This is why—in contrast to the German version of this series—the English edition, addressing a much broader international audience, sets out with a volume documenting an intercultural debate. This volume questions whether or not the academic discipline of "history"—as developed at Western universities over the course of the last two hundred years—represents a specific mode or type of historical thinking that can be defined and differentiated from other forms and practices of historical consciousness. The following volumes represent it as a genuinely interdisciplinary field of research. Historians, anthropologists, philosophers, sociologists, psychologists, and literary theorists, as well as specialists in fields such as media and cultural studies, explore questions such as: What constitutes a specifically historical "sense" and meaning? What are the concepts of "time" underlying different historical cultures? Which specific forms of "perception" inform these concepts, and which general problems are connected with them? What are the dominating strategies used to represent historical meaning?

Ranging from general overviews and theoretical reflections to case studies, the essays cover a wide range of contexts related to the question of "historical sense," among them topics such as collective identity, the psychology and psychoanalysis of historical memory, and the intercultural dimension of historical thinking. In general they indicate that historical memory is not an arbitrary function of the cultural practices used by human beings to orient themselves in the world in which they are born, but that such memory covers special domains in the temporal orientation of human life. These domains demand precisely those mental procedures of connecting past, present, and future that became generalized and institutionalized in the West as that specific field of culture we call "history." The special areas of human thought, action, and suffering that call for a specifically "historical thinking" include (1) the construction and perpetuation of collective identity, (2) the reconstruction of patterns of orientation after catastrophes and events of massive destruction, (3) the challenge of given patterns of orientation presented by and through the confrontation with radical otherness, and (4) the general experience of change and contingency.

In accordance with the general aim of the series "Making Sense of History" to outline a new field of interdisciplinary research (rather than to offer a single theory), the volumes are not designed to establish those general domains and functions of historical remembrance as keystones for a new historiographical approach. Instead they explore them further as subfields of the study of "historical cultures." One focus, for instance, is on the notion of collective identity. General theoretical aspects and problems of this field are considered, most importantly the interrelationship between identity, otherness, and representation. But case studies on the construction of gender identities (especially of women), on ethnic identities, and on different forms and politics of national identity are also included. The essays on this subject point out that any concept of "identity" as being disconnected from historical change not only leads to theoretical problems, but also eclipses the fact that most modern forms of collective identity take into account the possibility of their own historical transformation. Thus the essays suggest that identity be regarded not as a function of difference, but as a concrete cultural and ongoing "practice" of difference. Therefore they try to prove that the production of "sense" is an epistemological starting point as well as a theoretical and empirical research-field in and of itself.

Another volume focuses on the psychological construction of "time" and "history," analyzing the interrelation between memory, morality, and authenticity in different forms of historical or biographical narration. The findings of empirical psychological studies (on the development of temporal and historical consciousness in children, or on the psychological mechanisms of reconstructing past experiences) are discussed in the light of attempts to outline a psychological concept of historical consciousness around the notions of "narration" and the "narrative structure of historical time."

A special volume is dedicated to specifically psychoanalytical approaches to the study of historical memory. It reconsiders older debates on the relation between psychoanalysis and history and introduces more recent research projects. Instead of simply pointing out some psychoanalytical insights that can be adopted and applied in certain areas of historical studies, this volume aims at combining psychoanalytical and historical perspectives, thus exploring the history of psychoanalysis itself, as well as the "unconscious" dimensions underlying and informing academic and nonacademic forms of historical memory. Moreover, it puts special emphasis on transgenerational forms of remembrance, on the notion of trauma as a key concept in this field, and on case studies that may indicate directions for further research.

Cultural differences in historical thinking that arise from different time concepts are the subject of another volume. With a view to encouraging comparative research, it consists of general essays and case studies written with the intention of providing comparative interpretations of concrete material, as well as possible paradigmatic research-questions for further comparisons. In the light of the ongoing success of ethnocentric world-views, the volume focuses on the question of how cultural and social studies could react to this challenge. It aims at counteracting ethnocentrism by bridging the current gap between a rapid globalization manifesting itself in ever increasing economic and political interdependencies of states and continents, and the almost similarly increasing lack of mutual understanding in the realm of culture. The essays illustrate the necessity of intercultural communication about the common grounds of the various historical cultures as well as about the differences between them. Such communication seems not only a possible, but indeed a necessary presupposition of any attempt to negotiate cultural differences on a political level, whether between states or within the increasingly multicultural societies in which we live.

The special emphasis the series puts on the problem of cultural differences and intercultural communication shows the editors' intentions to aim beyond the realm of mere academic interest. The question of intercultural communication represents a great challenge, as well as a great hope, to a project committed to the general theoretical reflection on the universal phenomenon of "remembering the past." Despite the fact that "cultural difference" has become something like a master phrase of the 1990s, this topic is characterized by a paradox quite similar to that underlying the current fate of the notion of "history."

The past fifteen years have witnessed intensified interventions and pursuit of interest by the industrialized states in the political and economic affairs of the rest of the world, as well as an increased (if sometimes peculiar) appropriation of modern economic and political structures in the developing countries, and in the formerly or still officially "communist" states. But this process of mutual rapprochement on the political and economic level is characterized by a remarkable lack of knowledge of, or even interest in, the cultural and historical backgrounds of the respective nations. Thus, the existing official forms of intercultural communication, so often required in public discourse, lack precisely what is "cultural" about them, leaving the themes and problems analyzed in this book series (identity, memory, cultural practices, history, religion, philosophy, literature) outside of what is explicitly communicated; as if such matters would not strongly affect political as well as economic agendas.

On the other hand, the currently dominant approaches of cultural theorists and critical thinkers in the West either claim the general impossibility of an intercultural communication about the common grounds of "cultural identities"—based on the assumption that there are no common grounds (the hypostatization of "difference")—or they politicize cultural differences in such a way that they are relegated to mere material for the construction of cultural subject-positions. Despite their self-understanding as "critique," these intellectual approaches appear to correspond to the exclusion of "culture" on the level of state politics and economic exchange alike. Thus, cultural theory seems to react to the marginalization of culture by way of its own self-marginalization.

The series "Making Sense of History" intends to challenge this marginalization by introducing a form of cultural studies that takes the very term "culture" seriously again, without dissolving it into identity politics or a hypostatized concept of unbridgeable "difference." At the same time it wants to reintroduce a notion of "historical theory" that no longer disconnects itself from historical memory and remembrance as concrete cultural practices, but seeks to explore those practices, interpreting them as different articulations of the universal (if heterogeneous) effort to "make sense of history." Thus, the series relies on the idea that an academic contribution to the problem of intercultural communication should assume the form of a new opening of the academic discourse to its own historicity and cultural background, as well as a new acknowledgement that other cultural, but nonacademic, practices of "sense-formation" are equally important forms of human orientation and self-understanding (in their general function, in fact, not much different from the efforts of academic thought itself).

Such a reinscription of the universal claims of modern academic discourses into the various of cultural contexts, with the object of providing new starting points for intercultural communication, is an enterprise that cannot be accomplished or even outlined in a series of a few books. Therefore, "Making Sense of History" should be regarded as something like a first attempt to circumscribe one possible field of research that might prove to suit those general intentions: the field of "historical cultures."

The idea of the book series was born in the wake of the successful completion of a research project on "Making Sense of History: Interdisciplinary Studies in the Structure, Logic and Function of Historical Consciousness—an Intercultural Comparison." This project took place at the Center for Interdisciplinary Studies (ZiF) of the University of Bielefeld, Germany, in 1994/95. It was partly supported by the Kulturwissenschaftliches Institut (KWI) Essen im Wissenschaftszentrum Nordrhein-Westfalen (Institute for Advanced Study in the Humanities at Essen in the Scientific Center of Northrhine Westfalia). Included in the project a selection of contributions to a series of conferences and workshops forms the core of the different books of this series. The constellating, editing, and completion of the different texts occupied the next several years, and the first volume came out in 2002.

I would like to express my gratitude to the staff of the Center for Interdisciplinary Study at the University of Bielefeld and of the Institute for Advanced Study in the Humanities at Essen. I also want to thank the editors and co-editors of each of the volumes in this series and, of course, all the contributors for the effort and patience they expended to make these books possible. Finally, my thanks go to Angelika Wulff for her engaged management of this series, and to my wife Inge for her intensive support in editing my texts.

INTRODUCTION

What does "Making sense of history" mean?

Jörn Rüsen

> Man wird sich nicht mehr auf die Suche nach der verlorenen Zeit begeben, sondern auf die Suche nach dem verlorenen Sinn für die verlorene Zeit.
>
> Botho Strauß[1]

History is not a simple fact. It is not here in the way that I am here, sitting at my desk writing this introduction. It has to do with the past, and the past consists of real things, which happened at a certain time and in a certain place, for certain reasons and in a context of other facts. But a summary of what happened in the past is not history. Before we call them history, past happenings must possess a certain quality; a connection of the past with the present.

Those who discuss the question of what history is about have agreed upon a constructivist conception. In its fundamental hypothesis, it says that history is made by people in the present through their way of looking at the past—that is, by their making sense of the past. Therefore history is understood as a "construction," even as an "invention." This understanding has become dominant today despite the fact that this "constructed" or "invented" history is based on facts or information about "what really happened,"[2] about what was actually the case.

This thesis of the constructive character of history is one-sided. It overlooks a special fact: Those who work on the meaning of the past called history, whose interpretations give the past a specifically historical meaning, are determined and conditioned by the circumstances of their work, which in turn are results of past developments. The past has already been effective in the cir-

---

Notes for this section begin on page 5.

cumstances and mental attitudes of those who relate themselves to it. It has a "constructing" power over its own construction as history.[3]

Thus the meaning of history is a very complex matter: it is already there in the cultural preconditions of historical thinking, but it is only impending as a potential, a condition, a need for orientation. It is incorporated into cultural life, it is a real element in human life, but at the same time it is a task, an objective, an aim of mental activities. It is a product, a result of creative processes of the human mind.

History has always been an issue of time, and time has dimensions both external and internal: the change of things in the world, and the intentionality of the human mind. If time seen as change is related to human life, it does not simply happen but at the same time is accompanied by human activity and suffering. This temporality of human life constitutes the double nature of history, its relatedness to the reality of the past and to the activities of the human mind in the present. History is the course of time in the real world and, at the same time, a meaningful interpretation of this course. Philosophy of history has made a clear distinction between the two: Facts are juxtaposed to fiction as evidence and information are to interpretation and representation. "History" in its proper meaning is a synthesis of both. If we want to understand what historians do—what the subject matter of their work is, and what role the representation of the past plays in present-day human life—we have to overcome the one-sidedness; we can no longer abide the contradiction of materialism versus idealism, realism against constructivism, empirical evidence against poetic creation, but must look instead at this synthesis.

In order to do this, we should start by looking at the function of historical thinking in social life. Concentrating on the social and cultural reality of the human mind, we should inquire into the part of the symbols that define what people take as the reality of their world and themselves. In cultural life we can find a broad variety of relations to the past that play an essential role in orienting people to undergo the temporal change of their of present-day lives. In the cultural framework that places human life in the course of time, the past is relevant for the present and its future perspective. The features of this relevance vary. It may be the realm of accumulated experiences without which no human orientation in real life is possible. It may "teach" a lesson about the modes and consequences of human behavior. It may be a powerful tradition of life form. It may horrify people and push them into promising future-perspectives (or into the compulsion of repetition). It may be felt as a loss that is agonizing to those who feel committed to it.[4] But regardless of its many shapes, it is this relevance that attributes to past events the character of history. Past "becomes" history in the above-mentioned double sense: by being effective in the conditions and circumstances of present-day life and, at the same time, by being seen as having importance to those who look back at the past in search of some orientation for their future.

Thus history is always more than only the past. It is a relationship between past and present, that has a realistic nature as a temporal chain of conditions and at the same time an "idealistic" or symbolic nature as an interpretation that bears meaning for the purposes of cultural orientation and charges it with norms and values, hopes and fears.

What keeps these two sides of history together? And what decides upon the role of facts and norms, of experience and evaluation, in the interrelatedness of past and present? It is the unifying and synthesizing forces of sense and meaning.

The contributions to this book are dedicated to the general question of what makes sense in history. This question has a twofold direction: What importance does the past have for the present—what is its power over the minds of people? And what is the power of the human mind over the past—what do people think about the past, what do they attribute to it, when they relate themselves to it?

Memory is the most fundamental of the human mind's procedures that constitute history. It is elementary and universal. Therefore every discussion about the sense of history has to look at the mental procedures of human memory: What happens there with the past? How is it actualized, and what principles are decisive for this transference of the past into its commemorative meaning for the present? Memory is related to the past. It is the door of the human mind to experience. At the same time it transforms the past into a meaningful and sense-bearing part of the present. Here the future plays an essential role that is very often overlooked in the discourse on memory. Human time-consciousness has two basic intentions: memory and expectation, *retention* and *protention*,[5] which are substantially and fundamentally interrelated. So the relatedness of memory to the past is always a matter of future perspective as well. Therefore the sense of history synthesizes all three time dimensions in a specific way, namely, the interpretation of the past serves as a means for understanding the present and expecting the future.

This complex interrelationship of time in the human mind as it constitutes history is the subject of the contributions in this volume. They ask for "sense" as the synthesizing principle in this interrelationship or "meaning" as the result of this interrelatedness in the human mind. By doing so they open the perspective of a broad field of historical culture in different times and places. The outlook is universalistic, but nevertheless interested in understanding the variety of cultural manifestations, of historical changes and developments, and of paradigmatic case studies.

The first part of the book treats the modes of transforming the past into history. It looks at the specific "historical" qualification of the past, its relatedness to evidence on the one hand, and the creative role of the human mind in symbolizing and interpreting on the other—and, of course, at the interrelatedness of both. Paul Ricoeur explicates the anthropological basis of historical consciousness—memory and its counterpart, forgetfulness, which both constitute the historical realm of the human mind. Günter Dux approaches the question of sense-generation from a comprehensive evolutionary perspective, which emphasizes the general transformation of sense from subordination to objective spiritual forces to subjective human responses to the challenges of nature. Jörn Rüsen analyzes the logic of historical sense generation by referring to the cultural practice of story telling. Jörn Stückrath reflects on the historical conditions under which the issue of "sense of history" has become dominant in philosophy of history. Johan Galtung presents a universal typology of cultural codes of sense criteria, thus inspiring intercultural comparison. Frank R. Ankersmit presents in his two contributions a critical overview of the recent development of philosophy of history, ending in a new approach to historical experience. With this approach he claims a definitive transgression of the radical subjectivism of postmodernism in history. The necessity of recognizing reality as a dimension of historical thinking is underlined by David Carr. He keeps up the narrativistic tradition of philosophy of history but gives it a thought-provocative realistic turn, thus bringing the ground of social reality under the feet of the historians.

The second part of this book discusses the manifestation of the meaning and sense of history in cultural life. It sheds light on cultural practices that keep or make the past present, which works on their significance. Most of the contributions analyze nonverbal manifestations, thus going beyond the usual emphasis on texts in theory of history. By doing so the space of historical meaning is substantially widened and the symbolizing force of the human mind acquires a more complex dimension.

Aleida Assmann thematizes tradition as a powerful presence of the past in its specific modern form and emphasizes its dynamics and fungibility. Alessandro Cavalli presents a case study of memories that are related to experiences of catastrophes. Detlef Hoffmann takes the visibility of history into general consideration as a powerful way of keeping or making the past alive and effective in the minds of people. Moshe Barasch concretizes the visibility of history in a case study of the importance of ruins in the imaging of the past. Eberhard Lämmert's contribution is dedicated to the literary representation of the past in the intersection between historiography and fictional narratives. Finally, James E. Young analyzes case studies of Holocaust representations by relating them to postmodernist modes of sense generation.

All these articles underline the importance of attitudes and practices in making sense of the past, which renders them essentially different from historical studies. They allow instructive insight into the wider field of historical culture as an important part of humans' efforts to come to terms with their world and themselves. They reveal in a broad perspective the manifold strategies and procedures by which the past is shaped into the form of history. The scope of this variety can in turn help to contextualize the work of professional historians and delimit their place in the realm of historical culture. The essence of this professionality—the cognitive modes of sense generation, conceptualization, and methodization in the process of making sense of history—is a different issue worthy of separate treatment.

This book's indebtedness of to Western culture and tradition may be looked upon as a limitation of its scope (with the exception of Johan Galtung's text). Yet its theoretical contributions to our understanding of what history is about can serve as methodical tools of intercultural comparison. The case studies and historical investigations born of the Western tradition may engender a new approach to history[6] by disclosing the variety of historical cultures on the level of constitutive time concepts and related sense-criteria. This will be the subject of another book in this series.[7]

Notes

1. Botho Strauß, "Wollt ihr das totale Engeneering?," *Die Zeit* 52.20 (December 2000): 59–61, cited p. 61. (It's not the search for the lost time that will be pursued but the lost sense of the lost time instead.)

2. These are the famous and often quoted words of Leopold von Ranke, who simply wanted to show "Wie es eigentlich gewesen" (Leopold von Ranke, *Geschichten der romanischen und germanischen Völker von 1494–1514, Sämtliche Werke,* vol. 33 [Leipzig 1855], p. VIII).

3. The most convincing example I know is the generational position of historians or other interpreters with respect to the Holocaust. Cf. Saul Friedländer, ed., *Probing the Limits of Representation: Nazism and the "Final Solution"* (Cambridge 1992); Jörn Rüsen, "Holocaust memory and German identity," in idem, *History: Narration—Interpretation—Orientation* (New York 2004).

4. Cf. Frank R. Ankersmit, "The sublime Dissociation of the Past: Or How to Be(come) what one is no longer," *History and Theory* 40 (2001): 295–323.

5. Edmund Husserl, *Vorlesungen zur Phänomenologie des inneren Zeitbewußtseins,* ed. Martin Heidegger, 2nd ed. (Tübingen 1980).

6. A first step in this direction is discussing the Western way of historical thinking from the perspective of non-Western historical traditions. See Jörn Rüsen, ed., *Western Historical Thinking: An Intercultural Debate* (New York 2002).

7. Jörn Rüsen, ed., *Time and History in the Variety of Cultures* (New York, forthcoming).

Part I
MEANING

CHAPTER 1

Memory—Forgetting—History

PAUL RICOEUR

Perhaps I might be allowed to begin with an observation that puzzled me and that inspired me to reflect on the topic of memory and forgetting in history. It has to do with the spectacle offered by the post–Cold War period and the problem of difficulty of integrating traumatic memories from the totalitarian era. Among some, especially in the West, one might well deplore a *shortage of memory* and an *excess of forgetting*. Among others, for example in the Balkans, one would be more inclined to complain of an *excess of memory*, since events connected with past greatness or former humiliations are so resistant to being forgotten.

I.

Before tackling the problem of forgetting directly, I asked myself how it is that the history as written by historians operates as a critical authority capable of distinguishing between an excess and a shortage of memory. The first step in our inquiry involves resituating the entire sequence—memory/forgetting/history—against the background of a wider dialectic, that of historical consciousness. Here, the term *historical* does not designate a particular discipline, but rather the fundamental condition of humanity, commonly known as its "historicity." Why extend the framework of discussion in this way? Because the three terms of the triad in question all concern the past, and the past acquires its double sense of having been and no longer being only in relation to the future. In this respect, I shall adopt the conceptual framework proposed by Reinhart Koselleck in *Futures Past,* in particular the fundamental polarity between "space of experience" *(Erfahrungsraum)* and "horizon of expectation" *(Erwartungshorizont)*.[1]

Notes for this section begin on page 18.

Space of experience implies the totality of what is inherited from the past, its sedimentary traces constituting the soil in which desires, fears, predictions, and projects take root—in short, every kind of anticipation that projects us forward into the future. But a space of experience exists only in diametrical opposition to a horizon of expectation, which is in no way reducible to the space of experience. Rather, the dialectic between these two poles ensures the dynamic nature of historical consciousness.

II.

Let us consider now the relation between memory and the history of the historians, which completes, corrects, and sometimes contradicts the memory of survivors, their ancestors, and their descendants. The privilege that history cannot take away from memory is that of, on the one hand, preserving—and even, in the Husserlian sense of the term, of constituting—the relationship with the past, and also, on the other hand, of bringing out clearly the dialectic between space of experience and horizon of expectation. This dialectic tends to be obscured by history, which focuses on the events and human beings of the past methodically and with, as it were, a gaze that is professionally sharpened to such a degree that we might well be led to believe it possible to have an interest in history that is cut off from any connection to the present and the future. It is only memory, which turns again, and in a renewed way, to the future, that restores the link between the work of the historian and historical consciousness.

The relation of history and memory can thus be analyzed in three steps. First, memory establishes the meaning of the past. Second, history introduces a critical dimension into our dealings with the past. Third and finally, the insight by which history from this point onward enriches memory is imposed on the anticipated future through the dialectic between memory's space of experience and the horizon of expectation. We shall examine each of these three moments in turn.

1.

The original link between consciousness and the past is to be found in memory. This has been known, and repeatedly stated, since St. Augustine: memory is *the present of the past*.[2] However, this simple and in a certain sense undeniable observation is not unproblematic. If history is to be able to engage critically with memory one needs to give a meaning to the notion of *collective memory*, proposed by Maurice Halbwachs in an unfinished work posthumously published in 1950.[3] This is no small problem, given that nationalism, the excesses of which we deplore, sets great store by the shared recollections that endow an alleged collective entity with its distinct image—an ethnic, cultural, or religious identity. People do not remember in isolation, but only with help from the memories of others: they take narratives heard from others for their own memories, and they preserve their own memories with help from the commemorations and other public celebrations of striking events in the history of their group.

These are all well-known phenomena, aptly described by Halbwachs. But to move from these reflections to the assumption that there exists a collective subject of memory, thus going directly against the idea of an individual proprietorship or "mineness" of memories, is a more problematic step to take, for it would imply that the collective memory of a group exercises the functions of conserving, organizing, and evoking that were formerly attributed to individual memory. Halbwachs appears to take this step when, in a sentence that reminds us of Leibniz, he writes that "each memory is a viewpoint on the collective memory."[4] My preference, on the contrary, is to use the idea of collective consciousness as a working rather than as a substantive concept. The way that Husserl develops the concept of "personalities of a higher order" at the end of the fifth of his *Cartesian Meditations* is instructive in this regard.[5] By dint of this concept he gives an intersubjective basis to a network of relationships. We objectify this network only if we forget the process by which it was constituted.

It is important not to conflate, carelessly, the legitimate idea of the objectification of intersubjective relations in collective entities with the idea of alienation or reification.

It is only by analogy with individual consciousness and its memory that collective memory can be described as assembling together in a unity the traces left by momentous events in the history of the group concerned. This same analogy attributes to collective memory the ability to bring these common memories to life again in public anniversaries, rituals, and celebrations. Once this analogy is acknowledged, nothing prevents us from regarding these "personalities of a higher order" as subjects with inherent memories. Nor is there any barrier to speaking of their temporality or historicity. In short, one extends by analogy the "mineness" of memories to the idea that "we" collectively possess collective memories. This is enough to give historians a starting point for investigating the existence, as phenomena, of groups: the historian of "mentalities" and "cultures" asks for nothing less—and nothing more.

2.

We take a step forward in the dialectic between memory and history when we bring in history as a critical authority that is able not only to consolidate and to articulate collective and individual memory but also to correct it or even contradict it. To understand this critical relationship between history and memory one must introduce the linguistic medium of narrative, which memory and history share.

What interests me here is the difference in epistemological status between what might be called *memory narratives* (individual or collective) and *historical narratives*. Memory narratives circulate in conversation and belong to everyday discourse. Admittedly, memory narratives are not devoid of critical second thoughts, since during conversation a play of question-and-answer introduces into a concrete public space an exchange of narratives. But criticism, here, is not raised up to the level of an authority standing above the living exchange of memories.

In contrast, in the case of historical narratives this does happen. Historical narratives break with the discourse of memory on three levels. First and most obviously, they do so in the process of establishing the facts, a level that might be labeled "documentary." Second, historians search for explanations. They do so in two respects: on the one hand they search for causes (more or less as do natural scientists and practitioners of some of the other human sciences), and on the other hand they look for the motives and justifications out of which deeds arose. Even in this second type of explanation the critical spirit of history emerges—from the procedure itself. As Max Weber showed in his discussion of the work of E. Meyer, the historian first assumes, in imagination, the absence of the presumed cause, and next asks himself what the probable course of historical events would have been, as compared to what actually happened.[6] This process of "singular causal imputation" highlights the divergence between historical explanation and the "uncontrolled" explanations of ordinary conversation.

The divergence between history and memory becomes greater still at the *compositional* level—the level of vast tableaux, such as those we find in authors like Michelet, Burckhardt, Braudel, and Furet. In his *Narrative Logic: A Semantic Analysis of the Historian's Language,* Frank Ankersmit puts forward the thesis that these great narrative frescoes, which he dubs *"narratios,"* are unique entities that are exempt from the logic of falsification, a logic that, in his view, the work of the historian defeats on the documentary level and even, to some degree, also on the explanatory level (whether it is a matter of explanation by causes or explanation by reasons).[7] *Narratios* arise, rather, on the field of controversy, where each *narratio* competes with others on the basis of its ability to give an arrangement to established factual knowledge as well as to "middle-range" explanations.

Briefly put, a *narratio* asserts itself on the basis of its breadth of view and breadth of significance. Discussion among specialists and among an educated readership will assign to a large *narratio* a high degree of plausibility and probability. Already by virtue of its purely probable character, the *narratio* plays a critical role with respect to collective memory. Perhaps, in establishing this distinction between memory and history, one should go further, by denying to history the capacity for the reenactment of the past that Collingwood attributed to it.[8] Far from abolishing temporal distance, history deepens it by making absence the essential sign of the "pastness" of the past, as Michel de Certeau suggests in his *L'Absent de l' histoire.*[9]

The most noteworthy consequence of the critical intervention of history into the forming of memory (both collective and individual) seems to me to consist in a kind of splitting of memory into two divergent modes of functioning. To help clarify this cathartic effect of history, I would like to draw attention to a distinction proposed by Freud in a clear and very noteworthy essay of 1914, "Remembering, Repeating and Working-through."[10] The starting point of Freud's reflection here is his attempt to define the basic obstacle hindering the "work of interpretation" as it seeks to recover traumatic memories. He designates this obstacle, which he attributes to "repression resistances," by the term "repetition compulsion" *(Wiederholungszwang)*. According to Freud, a repetition compulsion consists in a tendency to proceed toward action *(Hang zum "Agieren")* that gets substituted for memory. The patient reproduces the forgotten fact "not as memory, but as an action: he repeats it, without, of course, knowing that he is repeating it."[11]

In addition to this clinical observation, Freud makes two therapeutic suggestions that, in view of the traumatic state of memory of some nations today, are of the greatest importance for us. The first suggestion is addressed to the analyst, the second to the patient. To the analyst, he advises showing a great deal of indulgence when dealing with repetitions appearing under cover of "transference." Freud asserts that such transference creates, by its operation, an intermediate space between illness and real life: one can consider it a "playground" where a compulsion is allowed to expand in almost total freedom, and where the subject's underlying pathology thus has the possibility of openly manifesting itself. But something is also demanded of patients: they must stop complaining and stop disguising their true condition from themselves, they must "find the courage to direct [their] attention to the phenomena of [their] illness," and they must move away from thinking of their illness as something contemptible and instead come to consider it a worthy opponent. This doubled handling of resistances, which concerns both the patient and the analyst, is what Freud calls "working through" *(Durcharbeiten)*. Hence it becomes possible to talk about memory itself as a form of work, the "work of recollection" *(Erinnerungsarbeit)*.[12]

Is it not clear that this little text by Freud offers moralists and politicians a sort of scaled-down model of the pathology of historical consciousness and of its cure?

The discrepancy between an excess of memory and a shortage of memory, mentioned at the beginning of this essay, can be reinterpreted in terms of the categories of resistance, repetition compulsion, transference, working through, and, finally, "the work of recollection." Following along this line, we can say that excess of memory resembles repetition compulsion, which Freud tells us puts a turn to action in place of the genuine memory through which the present and the past could be reconciled with each other. How much violence throughout the world is equivalent to an "acting out," instead of a remembering! With regard to such festivals of death we can speak of a repetition-memory *(wiederholendes Gedächtnis)*. Following this train of thought, however, one needs to add that repetition-memory is resistant to criticism, while recollection-memory *(Erinnerungsgedächtnis)* is a fundamentally *critical* memory. If this interpretation is right, then a shortage of memory can be interpreted as follows: some people take a sick pleasure in cultivating the repetition-memory from which others flee with a bad conscience. The former like to lose themselves in it; the latter are afraid of being swallowed up by it. But both suffer from the same critical deficiency, failing to achieve what Freud called the work of recollection.

The work of recollection, with its necessary phase of distancing and objectification, can contribute to the interrogating of history. In the end, it is at the "probabilistic" level of large *narratios* (as Ankersmit calls them) that historians offer the most powerful alternatives to that "official history" into which the grand narratives of collective memory tend to congeal. These controversial *narratios* first of all teach us to see the events of the past simply as "other," and then they teach us how to narrate them from another standpoint, from another perspective. This exercise can lead us even so far as to narrate our own history from the standpoint of the memories of people belonging to other groups, and even to other cultures, than our own. But one must also allow for the two therapeutic suggestions given by Freud. True political wisdom is to be derived from the advice that we ought to exercise patience toward compulsive outbursts in the fictive playground of transference: some peoples need symbolic satisfaction of their fears and hatreds. Great tolerance is required of communities to whom history has given great real satisfaction, or who are far enough advanced along the path of mourning the "lost object" of their past psychic investments. But this advice, offered to those to whom history has given a place comparable to the position occupied by the therapist, does not excuse anyone from Freud's advice to the patient. It is work *on oneself* that induces "repetition compulsion" to give way to "the work of recollection." Critical history can make a contribution to this healing of collective memory.

3.

I do not wish to leave the last word to written history as opposed to collective memory. Memory asserts its priority over history not only because it ensures a consciousness of, respectively, continuity between past and present and a feeling of belonging, but, on the contrary, also because it maintains the dialectical connection between what, following Koselleck, we have called space of experience and horizon of expectation. But this dialectic involves an apparent discrepancy, with repercussions for the function of history in relation to memory. The discrepancy is the following: the past, so it is said, cannot be changed, and in this sense it appears determinate; the future, by way of contrast, is uncertain, open, and in this sense indeterminate. If, in reality, events are ineradicable—if one cannot undo what is done or make what has happened not happen—on the other hand, the *meaning* of what has happened is not fixed once and for all. Apart from the fact that past events can be interpreted differently, the moral burden attached to the debt that is owed to the past can be increased or lightened, depending on to whether an accusation imprisons a guilty party in a painful sense of irreversibility, or a pardon opens the prospect of a deliverance from debt that is equivalent to a transformation of the actual meaning of the past. This phenomenon of reinterpretation, on both the moral plane and on a simple narrative level, can be considered a case of retrospective action by the expectation of the future on the apprehension of the past.

Memory reinterpreted by this kind of retrospective action serves as a model of historical knowing. Such an instructing of history by memory goes directly contrary to the underlying orientation governing the mode of work of the academic discipline of history. By its nature this work is pure retrospection; it defines itself as the science of human beings in the past. It consequently proceeds by abstracting out "the historical" from the three temporal dimensions of past, present, and future.

Nonetheless, the lessons of memory, as retrospectively transformed by the expectation of the future, are not entirely inaccessible to the historian. After all, it is given to the historian to go back imaginatively to any moment in the past as something that was once present—that is, as it was lived by the people of that time, as the present of their past and the present of their future (evoking Augustine again). Like us, people of the past were subjects with the gifts of retrospection and prospection. The epistemological consequences of this consideration are striking. Knowing that the people of the past expressed expectations (predictions, desires, fears, plans) means breaking up historical determinism and retrospectively reintroducing contingency into history. Here we revert to a persistent theme of Raymond Aron in his *Introduction to the Philosophy of History* (1938), namely, his struggle against "the retrospective illusion of fatality." His general consideration of historical causality leads him to link the reaction against this retrospective illusion of fatality to a comprehensive conception of history, defined by "the effort to resurrect, and, more precisely, an attempt to get back to the moment of the action, to become a contemporary of the actor."[13]

However, I would like not only to consider the implications for epistemology and the philosophy of history of this critique of the retrospective illusion of fatality, but also to indicate the therapeutic possibilities that it yields. Past human beings projected a determinate future for themselves, but their actions had unintended consequences that contradicted their expectations and disappointed their most cherished hopes. Thus the temporal gap that separates the historian from these past human beings appears as a graveyard of unfulfilled promises. To awaken and reanimate these unfulfilled promises is no longer the task of the professional historian, but it is certainly a task for those who might be called mentors of the public sphere—a group among which historians also ought to be numbered. In view of the apparent pathologies in the historical consciousness of some nations following the end of the Cold War, this resurrection of the unfulfilled promises of the past takes on a therapeutic significance.

It is a matter of the engagement of people with their own traditions and with what these traditions teach concerning their founding events and heroes. Above all, it is in relation to these traditions that we find the value of the above-mentioned recommendation that we should learn how to narrate in another manner, and that we should become acquainted with the history of others—history as it is written by historians of other nations and cultures.

III.

So far, nothing has been said about *forgetting*, at least not explicitly. Let us first make explicit what is implicit. Speaking about memory necessarily means speaking about forgetting, because one cannot remember everything. A memory with no gaps would be an unbearable burden; it is a cliché to say that memory is selective. Narrative structure, which memory and history have in common, confirms this law of the necessity of forgetting. A narrative always consists of only a limited number of events, selected in the operation of narrative composition. The methods of academic history merely raise this necessary selectivity to the level of a strategy for, respectively, understanding and explanation.

More significant for the analysis of forgetting is a distinction between two forms of memory that critical history brings to the fore—repetition-memory and what we call, with Freud, "the work of recollection." One might be tempted to say that there are also two kinds of forgetting, passive and active, although it is less a matter of two distinct phenomena than of a continuum between two extremes, with much overlap between them. At the "passive forgetting" end of the continuum one finds what we designated above by the concept of repetition compulsion, where the patient "acts out" instead of remembering. As we have already suggested, the collective memory of some groups, peoples, and nations seems to have fallen victim to this sort of pathology, which resembles Freud's "substitution discharges" and which is accompanied by forgetting.

More interesting in the present context is how passive forgetting manifests itself as soon as it appears as a shortage of active memory. It is a matter here of *escapist forgetting*—and of bad faith, a strategy of avoidance, that for its part is guided by an obscure desire not to know, not to be informed about, and not to inquire into atrocities committed in one's own neck of the woods. To the extent that this shortage can be considered a shortage of active memory, it might also be classified as passive forgetting. However, as an unacknowledged strategy of avoidance, evasion, and flight, it is in the final analysis an ambivalent form of forgetting, as much active as passive. Its active side brings down upon itself the same kind of accountability as do other acts of negligence or omission.

At one end of its range, escapist forgetting turns into active forgetting. Here we first of all encounter the selective forgetting that we have already said belongs to the work of recollecting, and also to the work of history. This form of forgetting becomes subject to criticism when it is practiced by "official history," which is essentially the history of the greatness of peoples, the history of what Hegel called "world-historical individuals"—in short, the history of the conquerors. Even when it is methodologically guided by historical criticism, this forgetting boils down to a forgetting of the victims. It then becomes the task of memory to correct this systematic forgetting and to encourage the writing of the history of victims.

We move a step further along the spectrum of active forgetting if, like the author of the second *Untimely Meditation,* we dare to offer up a hymn of praise to forgetting.[14] In actual fact, Nietzsche in this famous text was not directly concerned with the work of the historian but was concerned rather with the burden imposed by an excess of history on historical consciousness. One should not forget the title: "On the Uses and Disadvantages of History for Life." It is not a question of epistemology, but of behavior within time. What is at stake is life itself, which is threatened by the "abuse of history." This is another way of speaking of the excess of history already referred to. However, what is at issue here is no longer repetition compulsion, but rather the pressing burden of a purely retrospective knowing. The target here is academic historical culture seen as a "consuming fever of history." In the face of this abuse—abuse rather than excess—it is good to listen to an "untimely" statement that wishes on the reader the happiness that derives from an ability to feel, for a time, "unhistorically." "Forgetting," Nietzsche writes, "is essential to action."[15] Here we diagnose a sickness we have not yet named—"historical sickness"—and detect a poison—the excess *(Übermaß)* of the historical, which consists in a perversion of the relationship between past and future at the expense of the latter. *History* (Geschichte) is endangered precisely to the extent that it is interested in the past alone. The teaching of the second *Untimely Meditation* is that memory, and in its wake history, are first of all and always lifeworks, and only secondarily operations of pure knowledge.

At the other end of the spectrum of active forgetting is forgiveness. Here we must be very cautious. In one sense, forgiveness is the opposite of forgetting, at least of passive forgetting (whether this be a traumatic forgetting or escapist forgetting). In contrast to passive forgetting, forgiveness requires additional engagement in the "work of recollection." Yet despite this, it simultaneously consists in a sort of active forgetting that concerns not events themselves—on the contrary, the traces of these must be carefully protected—but the burden of guilt that paralyzes memory and, by extension, also paralyzes the capacity for a creative orientation toward the future.

Unlike escapist forgetting, forgiveness does not remain enclosed in the narcissistic relationship of the self to itself: it always assumes mediation by another consciousness, the victim's, which alone is entitled to forgive. Those who bear responsibility for events that have wounded memory can only ask for forgiveness and may have to face the possibility of a refusal. To this degree forgiveness must always know the unforgivable, the unredeemable debt, the irreparable wrong. Nevertheless, although this is far from obvious, forgiveness is not without a certain inner purpose, which has to do with memory. Its intention is not to extinguish memory: on the contrary, the goal it has of canceling the debt is incompatible with that of canceling memory. Forgiveness is a way of healing memory and of completing its period of mourning. Delivered from the weight of guilt, memory is liberated for great projects. Forgiveness gives memory a future.

This should not be taken to imply that forgiveness has a place only in the religious dimension of existence. Admittedly, in the Judeo-Christian culture of the West forgiveness has the same significance as grace, and grace is the prerogative of the one who, since he can read our hearts, can forgive to the extent that he can also punish. But the warm glow of forgiveness can extend outside the religious sphere, in the form of an "economy of the gift," where the logic of superabundance outweighs the logic of just equivalence. Such an economy of the gift has considerable juridical and political implications.

It would not be straying too far from Nietzsche to say that these juridical and political forms of forgetting are components of a therapy that would calm the spirit of revenge, which once conferred upon justice an aura of the sacred. This is the lesson of Greek tragedy. The whole of the *Oresteia* revolves around this enigma of a right of revenge that never comes to rest, in which we can recognize a repetition compulsion that makes an authentic memory impossible. The vicious circle is broken in the tragedy by the conversion of the Furies into the *Eumenides*. Here, on the political as well as on the private level, to forget revenge becomes a sign of grace. It is good for the health of our societies and thus for life itself that crimes that cannot be considered genocide or crimes against humanity should be subject to a statute of limitations. It is not an absurdity to assert that this kind of forgetting is a strict corollary of the critical memory that we have tirelessly opposed to repetition-memory.

Translation revised by Allan Megill

Notes

1. Reinhart Koselleck, *Futures Past: On the Semantics of Historical Time,* trans. Keith Tribe (Cambridge, Mass. 1985).
2. Augustine, *Confessions,* trans. R.S. Pine-Coffin (Baltimore 1961), Book XI, 254ff.
3. Maurice Halbwachs, *The Collective Memory,* trans. Francis J. Ditter, Jr., and Vida Yazdi Ditter (New York 1980).
4. Ibid., 48.

5. Edmund Husserl, *Cartesian Meditations: An Introduction to Phenomenology*, trans. Dorion Cairns (The Hague 1977), 132ff.

6. Max Weber, "Critical Studies in the Logic of the Cultural Sciences" in idem, *The Methodology of the Social Sciences,* ed. and trans. Edward A. Shils and Henry A. Finch (New York 1949), 113–188.

7. Frank R. Ankersmit, *Narrative Logic: A Semantic Analysis of the Historian's Language* (The Hague 1983).

8. R. G. Collingwood, *The Idea of History,* rev. ed., with *Lectures 1926–1928,* ed. Jan Van der Dussen (Oxford 1993), 282ff.

9. Michel de Certeau, *L'Absent de l'histoire* (Tours 1973), 174.

10. Sigmund Freud, "Remembering, Repeating and Working-through" (1914), in idem, *Standard Edition of the Complete Psychological Works,* ed. and trans. James Strachey, in collaboration with Anna Freud, assisted by Alix Strachey and Alan Tyson (London 1953–1974), vol. 12: 126–136.

11. Ibid., 150.

12. Ibid., 153.

13. Raymond Aron, *Introduction to the Philosophy of History: An Essay on the Limits of Historical Objectivity,* 2nd ed., rev., trans. George T. Irwin (Boston 1961), 232.

14. Friedrich Nietzsche, "On the Uses and Disadvantages of History for Life," in idem, *Untimely Meditations,* trans. J.P. Stern (Cambridge 1983), 59–123.

15. Nietzsche, "Uses and Disadvantages," 60.

CHAPTER 2

How Meaning Came into the World and What Became of It

Günter Dux

Meaning as the Distinguishing Feature of Human Existence

In the wake of the three revolutions that led up to modernity—the revolutions in natural science, industry, and politics—the world has become a different world. We ourselves have become different, and we must learn to understand ourselves differently. As always, controversy surrounds just how the human life form is to be understood. Nonetheless, certain basic presuppositions can be established.

One indisputable presupposition involves an evolutionary understanding of the organizational forms of human life, regardless of how one goes on to define the mechanisms of evolution. Such an understanding recognizes that within the continuity of evolution there are discontinuities, marked by the emergence of new forms of organization. It is decisive to understand "evolution" through a process-oriented logic and "new" in a very strict sense: the new form of life that develops cannot have been already implicit in the form of life that preceded it.[1] The mind-based sociocultural form of human existence must be understood as one such new form in the long chain of forms in the evolution of the species. In the effort to define this form of life, an array of capabilities can be used: thought, language, the use of tools, the ability to love, to name just a few. None of these can be defined without making recourse to meaning.

Therefore, it makes sense to understand meaning as a basic form of human existence that pervades all the others. And what is meaning itself based upon? What defines it?

Notes for this section begin on page 37.

There are advantages to approaching this topic in terms of the evolutionary process out of which the human form of existence emerged. For one it allows a examination of questions whose answers provide a sound foundation for clarifying what is meant by the concept of meaning. The question can be raised as to what conditions enabled the development of the specifically human form of life and, along with it, meaning.

Admittedly, raising the question of the conditions of possibility has been part of the epistemological strategy of the human sciences since the beginnings of modernity, and later of the social sciences as well. Kant introduced it, and social scientists of our day follow him, Luhmann for instance. Whereas the former takes as his ultimate point of reference a transcendental consciousness of the subject or transcendental apperception, the latter takes the social system as subject and seeks to find the conditions for the creation of meaning in the double contingency of a communicative encounter of two black boxes.[2] Both make claim to faculties of an intellectual life form, which has first to be developed and explained. The evolutionary understanding of human life imposes a much more radical epistemological strategy upon us: we start by presupposing nature and let mind and thus meaning be constructed. The question, therefore, is: What is it in the anthropological constitution of humankind that enables man to develop a form of existence in which life is conducted in a meaningful and, as far as possible, in a senseful fashion?

Apparently, in an evolutionary understanding of humankind anthropology becomes some kind of a foundational science. It must be noted, though, that anthropology takes on a different status here than it previously enjoyed. It is no longer a matter of inquiring into the essence of the human lifeform, but instead, one of defining the starting conditions for the formative process of a sociocultural organized form of life.

The Ontogenetic Turn

The evolutionary perspective alone does not enable us to develop a reconstructive strategy for understanding human existence in its symbolically organized sociocultural forms, particularly with regard to the constitution of meaning. This becomes apparent when we regard the most common hypothesis for its generation, still put forward today: the hunting hypothesis. According to it, the cooperative form of hunting creates the basis for the takeoff of the development of the mind. Hunting, however, does not provide an explanation. For either cooperative hunting has a biological basis, as in wild dogs, for example, or the competence presupposes logically the prior existence of a communicative competence, if hunting is to be possible at all. Hence, the only way to reconstruct the formative process of meaning as the organization that emerges from natural history seems to me to take up a finding of anthropology manifest to each and every individual: *The basic sociocultural constitution of the human form of existence is formed in the early ontogenesis of each and every member of the species.* This has been so at all times and in all places, also so at the outset of the history of homo sapiens of our type. If we want to know how and why it was at all possible for sociocultural life forms to develop, and how and why they actually did, as they did, then we must focus on the early ontogenesis of the members of the species, and thus on children.

This methodological strategy is promising, but finds itself subject to a stereotypical objection: children develop the competence of the mind within the forms of sociocultural existence only under the direction and influence of adults who already possess these competences and life forms. Surely! Nonetheless, as important as the contribution of adult others is, they only provide support in a process that assigns the role of constructor to the new members of the species. It would make no sense to tell a child in the first two years of its life to learn to act meaningfully. It would be equally senseless to try to convey to it the category of constancy and permanence of an object by patiently having it look for its rattle and straighten out its blanket. A child has to have its own experiences and learn to control its motor activities by means of these experiences. That is the beginning of action and the beginning of meaning as well, for action is action with meaning. *The basic forms of the intellectually based, sociocultural form of human existence have to be developed by the new members of the species themselves.* This holds for action, thought, and speech, for morals and for love. With reference to the basic forms of language, Andrew Lock has termed this constructive process a "guided reinvention."[3]

In the present context it is not possible to explain in greater detail why the reconstruction of the formative process of the intellectually organized, sociocultural forms of life on the basis of early ontogenesis also has to hold for the phylogenetic process of hominization that took place in two million years of hominid development. It will have to do to note that even in the primates most closely related to us, chimpanzees, we can observe an interaction potential in early ontogenesis between mother and child that suffices as precondition for the takeoff of the enculturation process in the phase of hominization.

The Pragmatism of the Intellect

The first, and extremely important insight into the sociocultural mode of existence as a whole that we gain from reconstructing its formative process in terms of the early ontogenesis of each member of the species is the answer it provides to the question of why this mode of existence forms at all, and why it, as an intellectually based, sociocultural, and thus meaningful organizational form, defines human existence in all of its forms of manifestation. It need not be that this mode of existence should have arisen. The reason that it nonetheless did is clearly manifest in the structure and situation in which the newborn finds itself: it has to achieve the competence to act. But it can only achieve such competence if it constructs the world in a way that action comes to terms with it. The newborn brings along neither of these two qualities, neither action competence nor world in an organized fashion; both have first to be constructed via thought and (later) language. Thus the intellectually organized, sociocultural form of human existence has a firm pragmatic foundation. It is of defining character for the entire process of development. It also defines the developmental process of history.

The compulsion that accompanies the acquisition of the competence to act—that of first having to organize the world in which one acts—can be understood as the basic condition of human existence. The acquisition of action competence is the point of takeoff in the development of a sociocultural form of existence. The demiurgic process can succeed only if knowledge of the world is acquired, for only by acquiring knowledge is it possible to learn how to control unformed motor activity so that it can cope with an already preexisting reality. It is this form of constructive realism[4] that enables us to define a succinct concept of mind without having to presuppose the existence of intellectuality or spirituality in the universe: *Mind is the competence, which enables man to win an insight into the world and to use it to construct the organizational forms of existence.* In this definition, pragmatism apparently is inherent in the intellectual, sociocultural form of human existence without reducing intellectuality to that which the pragmatic deems useful.

Meaning in Meaningful Action

The structure of action differs from that of animal behavior. The latter is tied to certain definite and comparatively simple components and situations in the animal's environment that can be accomplished through learning. Once genetic programming has been replaced by the complex organizing capacity of the brain, interaction with the always preexisting external world cannot be reorganized by the same form of organization. Learning especially is different within the construction of the human world than it is in the organization of animal behavior. In the structure of the human world though there is no naturally defined situation within which one could act, and there are no situational components to which specific action routines could be tied. The action routines themselves are not given in organized form. In order to be able to act, it is necessary to construct an all-comprehensive world and then to determine, in terms of knowledge of this world, the way in which one should act. This is only possible if the competence to control motor activities is developed. One has to become conscious of what one is doing. Whoever acts has to be in the position to choose to act one way or the other. It is precisely this mechanism, whereby one becomes conscious of one's own competence to act, that is acquired by coping with the experience of dealing with the external world.

This consciousness, both of action and of self, develops in a characteristically reflective form in conjunction with the competence to act. The reflective form of action is what we call the sense or meaning of action. It is what defines the genuinely constituent element in the development of subjectivity. This allows us now to say how meaning came into the world: *Meaning is the structural form that organizes action. Therefore, in its elementary form it is the meaning of action—that which the subject intends to do in a world open for action.* Meaning as the meaning of action and world are developed in correlation to one another.

Meaning has still another defining quality, not referring to the organizing form of action but tied to the construct of the world. The construction of the world can only be carried out via a practically infinite partialization of objects, events, and their traits. This is possible only via the resources of language and thus on the level of symbolic constructs, which are created through difference. For this reason, one can ask what an individual word means (the word "digital," for example) or what the meaning of a sentence in a book is.

What then is the meaning of the meaning apart from the meaning of an action? Meaning referred to as meaning of a word, a sentence, a discussion, or a book must be determined relationally, in terms of the interrelations into which the *explanandum* is integrated. The meaning of a word is defined in terms of the references of its semantic field, while the meaning of a sentence is defined in terms of the context of a text, that is, a discussion or book, and this meaning refers to the knowledge of a comprehensive community of communication.

Admittedly, this form of meaning might be understood as a variant of the meaning of action. Anything said is something said by someone seeking to state something, whose intention included that this statement be understood. In this sense, every distinction in the world does in fact have a relation to the element of meaning in action. Yet, anyone who says something makes use of the terminology of a given communicative community in order to define what the statement refers to. However, it can prove difficult to define these references, for (a) no one can take into view everything that a statement refers to, (b) the degree to which these references are defined varies according to context and they are thus often undefined, and (c) every statement that does not remain within purely conventional limits creates new references that must first be defined. To cite a well-known example: What is the meaning of the arrest scene at the beginning of Kafka's *The Trial*? Did Kafka even know what it was? Hardly likely.

The Communicative Genesis of Meaning

A new member of the human species can acquire the competence to act only in interaction with other, always more competent members. Also, language—despite our assumption that its structures are genuinely constructed anew by each and every member of the species—can only be developed communicatively. The truth of these statements is obvious, but: why is it so? Why, for example, can the competence to act only be acquired communicatively? This question is anything but resolved.

It seems reasonable to start from the presupposition of nature, that is, a baby's anthropological constitution. The needs of the newborn member of the species make it dependent upon others who are always more competent. However, these needs and the care it elicits do not explain of the part played by others in the formative process of action competence. Three very distinctive conditions can be established that both on their own and in concert are practically constitutive for the acquisition of this ability: (1) Experiences must be had in doses in order to be transferred into competence. It is completely impossible for a child to gain the competence to act in direct, unmediated dealings with the objects and events of nature. (2) Even well-dosed experiences constantly lead to frustration. The latter has to be counterbalanced by the emotional support of a communicative and interactive relationship. Otherwise, that which is inherent to the reflexivity of action will not emerge: self-confidence, the awareness of being successful at all in the world.[5] (3) Finally, there is a social mechanism involved in the process of acquiring action competence that can confidently be viewed as the key to becoming human: the care-providing reference person—as representative of all significant others within the child's field of activity—ties his or her action to that of the child and holds the child, on the basis of the emotional bond between the two, in the interaction in a way that compels the child to accommodate its motor activities to the care provider's demands. In the end, the social construction of the world as well as the social construction of the action system is highly important because only by the bond between the child and the significant others a bond to the world can be build up. The intimacy by which the bond is founded becomes also highly important for the subsequent sexual relationship.[6]

The Genesis of Language and Its Significance for Meaning Formation

Much less obvious than in the case of cognition is why language can only be generated communicatively. If the genesis of language were clear, it would not have been possible for the present mythologization and mysticism of language to be as widespread as it has been in the wake of the linguistic turn.[7] What is self-evident is that language functions communicatively, and that communication can take place only if speaker and listener share a common medium. However, self-evidence of functions should not be confused with explanation. Functions merely demonstrate that something has to be organized in a certain way if it is intended to bring out a certain form or process. They do not show what made it possible to develop the constitutive moment in the systemic organization of forms or processes. Apparently, there was no one in the formative process of language who reflected on what qualities language must possess in order to serve as a medium. An explanation can be gained only by explaining the conditions of the genesis of the structures of language, for its performance capabilities rest upon the latter. In the present context, only one of these structures need interest us: syntax. It alone allows an action to be conceptualized, and it alone also allows the intentionality of meaning to be incorporated into action. The question, therefore, is how is it possible to organize, in the process of enculturation, the structure of syntax.

I have tried to explain that the key to understanding the process of enculturation must be found in the development of action competence in early ontogeny. Ultimately the development of this competence depends upon brain development. We have to assume that the changes in the genome that led to an extension and reorganization of the brain, brought forth the capacity to develop the competence to control motor activity, which then allowed a world to be constructed in which action is relevant. And we must further assume that due to this capacity the previous instinctive adaptations were deconstructed. For a living being that first begins to develop the basic structures of its interaction with external reality by means of self-constructed forms of organization, this process must also have been initiated in the transitional phase of hominids by means of the acquisition of action competence. For this reason we have to assume that, also phylogenetically, the initiation of the process of acquiring action competence preceded that of the development of language competence.

It is not difficult to observe this, from this side of the threshold between hominid and homo sapiens. Children develop an action competence whose structure becomes evident by the end of their second year of life, when language enters into the constructive process. This observation enables us to resolve the riddle of the genesis of syntax: When language starts to be integrated in the development of action competence, the basic structure of the latter can be used for the construction of the syntax. In other words: *Syntax has as its deep structure the structure of action. In the Indo-European language family the structure of action translates itself into a surface structure. This, though, is not necessarily the case. Precisely because the structure of action represents the deep structure of syntax—a cognitive structure—it is possible for the surface structure of word order to take on practically any shape.*[8]

The understanding of this most important structure of language, syntax, leads to a largely new orientation in the understanding of language as a whole. This applies initially with regard to the question of why language was formed at all and why it could only be formed communicatively. The pragmatism that the formative process of the intellect is subject to, is also the basis for the formative process of language. Language is utilized in the process of acquiring action competence, and the construction of external reality is inseparably linked to this competence.

The insight that the construction of the syntax is ontogenetically bound up in the process of acquiring action competence and in the construction of the world provides a suitable vantage point from which to correct a whole series of assumptions that are almost unanimously connected with language today. In our present context, two are of special importance. Firstly, language appears in contemporary philosophical blueprints as the actual constructive agency of the world; it presents itself as "uncircumventable."[9] It is not. Language has its genesis in the process of enculturation, just like every other intellectual achievement. For this reason, it itself as well as its structures is open to explanation.[10] Moreover, within the development of action competence it is only in conjunction with thought that language is capable of defining the constructive process of the world and the action system in it. Besides that, there are good reasons for granting thought preeminence in this process.[11]

The second assumption in need of examination here is that language is integrated in a process of constructing the world that takes place in interaction with a reality that always exists prior to it. Just as in the formative process of cognitive constructs, the structures of language crystallize in this interaction. A purely linguistic language analysis can satisfy itself with the imaginations of the speakers and listeners in order to connect lingual constructs to these conceptions.[12] This results first in a two-dimensional understanding of language. That can, however, be further reduced. One can assert that the human imagination is also made possible first through language. This leads to a one-dimensional understanding of language, in which the world is represented as a monocausal product of language. Reality outside of language is not denied, but it remains outside of the theory. As a consequence, the pragmatics of existence are either made subject to a crude biological determinism or not explained at all.[13] An understanding of language that sticks to its empirical process of formation and thus proceeds in terms of historic-genetic explanation cannot avoid incorporating the preexisting layer of reality into the formative process of language.[14] Reference is the connection between language and reality.[15]

One thing is certain after all of this: Though meaning as the structural form of action develops in conjunction with the competence to control action prior to the formation of language, without the assistance of language that mirrors the structural form of action itself, the aspect of meaning forms only in an incomplete manner. Precisely because the structural form of action is reflective in and of itself, and is acquainted with the relatedness of the subject to itself, it is dependent upon objectification in language. Only when a course of action can be objectified in language—and one part of this is the objectification of the situation in which the actor acts—can one competently act in a meaningful way. Ontogenetically, this process is enacted in the phase that Piaget largely neglected, since for him it represents the phase in which everything is still on a low reflective level. If one takes the development process of children in industrialized countries as one's measure, it is in the preoperational phase between the second and sixth or seventh year of life.[16]

The question of when this reflective form of meaning-relatedness or even meaningfulness developed in a historical sense is more difficult to answer. Should we place it in the hominization phase preceding *homo sapiens sapiens*?[17] Or should it be set in the early phase of *homo sapiens sapiens* himself, that is, in Europe in the Aurignacian era? One thing is certain: every elaborate form of action and interaction, such as we associate with *homo sapiens sapiens,* is only possible on the basis of an operationality on the symbolic level of a linguistically structured reality. Operational competence must, if one is to make sense of comparative cultural studies, have been developed in the earliest human societies at least up to the threshold of concrete-operational competence. Structurally, this corresponds to the threshold of competences of a six to seven year old child in an industrialized society.[18]

Our discussion has laid the groundwork for understanding one of the most peculiar phenomena in human history: the meaningfulness of the cosmos. In its early times, as well as at the zenith of philosophical reflection, the world was a thoroughly meaningful world—even more, a senseful world. And this is precisely the quality that the universe has lost in modernity. The question that we, therefore, have to answer is: What was the basis of the meaningfulness of the world up until modernity? Once again, we must start from the process of world construction in early ontogeny.

The Meaningful Organization of the Cosmos

The circumstance discussed above, namely, that action competence and the construction of the world come about in the basic structures of interaction and communication with others, has far-reaching consequences for the structures involved in the construction of the world. These structures are the result of the conditions under which they are formed, and they represent the transformation of conditions into a result. As we have seen, action competence and world can be attained only via experiences. These experiences, though, are made in the early phase of ontogenesis, primarily in communication and interaction with others who are always more competent. For this reason, the structure of communication and interaction becomes the basic categorical structure in the construction of the world: accordingly, the structures of objects and events are formed in subjective terms.

"Subjective" means here that these structures are built according to the experiences that the growing member of the species has in communication and interaction with the significant others in his or her surroundings. All objects are understood as if they were centered around an internal sovereignty of action of their own; all events, as if they were produced by a sovereign agency. This is just the way in which we find early worlds to be designed: all things are considered living, though to differing degrees. Since subjectivity pervades all structures, the subjective moment increasingly becomes the material logic of the world. I have discussed this structural foundation of early worlds, their material logic, so often that I will simply make reference to these prior discussions.[19] In the present context, there is only one addition at point of interest: Connected to the subjective basis of categorialization each of these worlds is a thoroughly meaningful world. The intellect- and meaning-relatedness of the pristine cosmos is, all told, a consequence of the subjectivist logic in whose terms it is constructed.

This finding is so apparent that one has to wonder why early societies are thought of as incomprehensible, and why their thought is perceived as confused.[20] If the early world is understood in terms of the structures of its formative process rather than via the semantics of its basic terms, then it becomes completely transparent. This also holds for the constructs on the worldview level. If the world as a whole attracts the focus of interest and becomes the object of reflection, then the sole constructive logic available is that of the practice in everyday occurrences. This is evident insofar as "the gods" are held to determine what occurs and especially to the extent that the major religions' gods of creation promote the continued existence of the world and guarantee its prefixed order.

However, philosophy too is bound by this logic. This insight was expressly brought to awareness by Fichte, following the transformation of the worldview of modernity, as structures became reflective.[21] This holds notwithstanding that philosophy has always considered the anthropomorphization of the world-defining powers as a sort of pudendum. Such uneasiness extends up to the present, for example in the effort to refute the charge that the readily apparent logic of action in Aristotelian physics might have animistic origins.[22] But there has never been any doubt in former philosophy about the intellect-based order of the world, and for this reason, also no doubt that it is organized via meaning. Thus, it is stated in Leucippus of Miletus: "Nothing arises without a plan; instead, everything that comes about has meaning and is necessary."[23] One of the most interesting expressions of the meaningfulness of the cosmos in terms of its structural logic is found in Plato's dialogue *Timaeus*.

Meaning in the Best of All Worlds

"Now that which is created must, as we affirm, of necessity be created by a cause. But the father and maker of the universe is past finding out; and even if we found him, to tell of him to all men would be impossible" [28c].[24]

This is the way the dialogue about the creation of the world begins (following upon a discussion of the history of Athens in pristine times). The context and the way in which the question is introduced make it clear that—in spite of the question about the creation of the world [27a]—the aim is not to explain the world in its materiality, but in its preexisting order. Shortly thereafter, in his explanation of why the god of creation was moved to creation, Timaeus expresses this aim clearly in terms of god's desire to bring order into that which was "moving in an irregular and disorderly fashion" [30a]. This motivation also underlies reports on creation in other cultures. "That which always is and has no becoming" is also expressly distinguished from that which has become [27a–27d]. What is striking in terms of structural logic is the self-evident way in which recourse to a god of creation, a demiurge, is taken in explaining that which has become. This recourse was in fact self-evident, for Greek thought, like all other premodern forms of thought, was subject to the subjectivist material logic of the world.

The *Timaeus* is one of Plato's late works. The conception of a veritable story of creation would have aroused less attention and amazement, if it had not been preceded in the theory of ideas by a movement of convergence between the idea of the good and the absolute in the world.[25] The ideas of the good and of the god of creation appear, therefore, to compete as representatives of the absolute. The question that first arises for us is: what at all is the basis of the convergence of the world in an absolute? To take the convergence as self-evident was possible only as long as reflection itself was fixed to this logic. One considerable advantage of our structural-logic–based reconstruction appears to me to be its ability to offer an explanation of this cognitive structure, which defines all of premodern thought: *The form of thinking that makes the world converge in an absolute, if not in its material substance then in its order, is a consequence of the structure of the pristine logic of action.*

But in what sense? The logic of action in pristine thought is bi-relational: whatever occurs begins in a subject or (less definitely) in an agency, which as the veritable beginning becomes the origin. The real form of explanation, however, is different: in the course of explanation, thought starts from the explanandum and traces that which is given back to the subject, in order to view it as arising out of the substance of its creative powers. The logic of origins is thus, in this structural-logic–based sense, also a logic of substance, even if the materiality of the world is not taken from the creator, but is instead considered eternal. That which is produced by the absolute is, according to this logic, already contained within the absolute in eternity. Accordingly, the way in which one conceives of the relationship between the idea of the good and the god of creation would have to be the object of scholarly investigation, despite the impossibility of providing a definitive answer in purely philological investigations. In structural-logical terms, the relationship between the two, as it appears in Plato, is transparent. But let us first clear up how the theory of ideas came into being.

The logic of action is acquainted with a highly significant mode of events: insofar as actions occur according to a plan, they are conceived of, *modi futuri exacti*.[26] They are first conceptualized as thoughts and then transformed into a real occurrence or event. More precisely: the thought runs through the event until the event reaches its goal, at which point it returns to the start and thus to the actor. In exactly the same way explanations for any phenomena in the world proceed from the end of an event and relate it to its origin. The effects are known; the *causa* is sought for in the subject.

Thought on the abstract level of philosophical reflection proceeds in a similar way: it is always compelled to attribute the world or its order back to an origin out of which it emerges, and this origin must be of an allcomprehensive intellectuality. This is why the absolute is conceived of as spirit in all philosophies: "At the beginning stands the spirit," it is stated in the Shatapata-Brahmana.[27] Plato also establishes the need to search for the creator of all that has become, with the causal statement: "Now everything that becomes or is created must of necessity be created by some cause, for without a cause nothing can be created" [28a].

As long as thinking seeks a cause for individual things and individual events, these things and events must be understood as having been first conceptualized within a pure spirituality or intellectuality before they came into being. They emerge out of this origin. In metaphysics the world exists twice, once in the spiritual realm of essences and thereafter in a "corporeal, ... visible and tangible" state [31b]. In fact, the Greek word idea initially designates the visible, external form of a thing. From there it extends—tracing back by means of the logic of action described above—to that realm that has been termed metaphysics ever since. For as R. G. Collingwood correctly noted, metaphysics must be understood not as something that lies outside of the limits of experience, but rather as a realm that forms the basis of the construction of the world as the latter appears in any experience of it.[28] Now the question becomes: What grants the good, among all ideas, the special significance that Plato attributes to it?

The Greek world is a world whose nature as construct has moved into consciousness since the end of archaic times—like a (distant) run-up to modernity. Admittedly, this is something that is particularly true for the social world; since, however, the distinction between nature and the social world is made on the material, rather than the structural level, this consciousness also encompasses the way nature is conceived of. The fact that the world becomes reflective has an effect that is understandable and compelling in structural-logical terms: due to the powers achieved in controlling the social order, the structures developed up until then have to become the object of consciousness. In other words, thought unfolds its own logic. The logic of action, though, as an absolutistic logic, demands that everything ultimately originates from a single source. Each and everything must be part of the absolute, comprised by it prior to the unfolding of its manifoldness. Anything that has already become concrete always proves to be distinct in comparison to other things. Any idea is such an entity; it thus distinguishes itself from all the other ideas that relate to the concrete thing. Moreover, otherness, unity, and being are also understood as ideas; accordingly, every individual idea has to participate in these ideas and thus ideas must present themselves as a plurality within the unity of one.[29]

In this way, though, comparable in structural-logical terms to the mythologies in cultures such as ancient Egypt, there arises the problem of the one and the many.[30] Plato resolves it by conceiving of the good as the one, the absolute, from which all other ideas have their being and essence, as is stated in the parable of the sun in *The Republic*. Just as the sun is the cause of seeing and being seen, the good is the cause of (re)cognition and being (re)cognized: "And so with the objects of knowledge: these derive from the good not only their power of being known, but their very being and reality; and goodness is not the same thing as being, but even beyond being, surpassing it in dignity and power."[31]

The structural-logical reconstruction of the theory of ideas shows that the elevation of the ideas by means of the good is not simply a random notion of Plato's. Instead, it should be understood as the stringent consequence of a logic inherent to the structure of the argumentation. This could also be shown with regard to the question of why, from among the ideas, it is the good that is considered the origin, but I will forgo doing so here; the discussion to this point is sufficient for understanding the myth of creation in *Timaeus*, which at the same time represents the densest of philosophy: from the outset, *Timaeus* is concerned with explaining the ordering principle of the world as a single, all-encompassing, all-comprehending unity or oneness. The only possible way for this to be accomplished is to bring into play the one, the absolute, as origin. Two things must be explained here: what the world is, and how it is what it is. For both, that it exists and how it exists, Plato makes recourse, as if it were self-evident, to the subject as agent. And for Plato it is self-evident, since action logic is, in terms of its genesis, a logic of the subject.

The explanation that Plato finds for the act of creation is fascinating; it makes the *Timaeus* into the foundational document, as it were, of Western philosophy: the creator, he explains, "was good; and the good can never have jealousy of anything. And being free from jealousy, he desired that all things should be as like himself as they could be" [29e]. The idea of the good was thus built into the creator. Since the idea of the good is the basis of all other ideas, it is fair to consider the ideas themselves to be emanations of the god of creation. In doing so, we would be opting for one possible way of relating the creator and the idea of the good discussed in the literature. This interpretation is certainly correct in structural-logical terms, but it is not in keeping with the depiction given in *Timaeus*.

In *Timaeus*, the god of creation lets the world arise by gazing upon the unchangeable, the eternal, that is, the ideas [28a, b; 29a, b]. What is inside is thus outside. This, however, is in pristine logic not difficult to explain; we have encountered it everywhere since the earliest times of humanity: anything the glance is directed toward also takes on substance; it becomes something existing. You can swear to something not only by your own head but by the spirit of your own head. This form of thought is the consequence of the inability in earliest times to distinguish between thought and the object of thought. If thought cannot be detached from the actually existing object, then conversely, that which appears in thought is conceived of as having objective and independent character. This is the basis of the peculiar philosophy of the thing *(res)* that still defined Cartesian philosophy. And though the Greeks knew to distinguish between idea and object, they conceptualized ideas in a substantialized object like form. Thus it is not merely the biographical point in time at which Plato conceptualizes a story of creation that locates the already long-existing ideas outside of the creator. In this way of thinking, the inner is truly the outer. For this reason, Plato need not have wasted time thinking about the relation between the god of creation and the idea of good. And he didn't, either.

Our structural-logical understanding of the theory of ideas in general and of the story of creation in the *Timaeus* in particular explains a specific way of conceiving of creational doctrine that was to define the philosophical understanding of the world for almost two millenia. Arthur O. Lovejoy, who analyzed this problem in an illuminating study especially concerned with the problems that arose in the confrontation between this doctrine and the Judeo-Christian story of creation, termed the doctrine the "plenitude of existence in the great chain of being."[32] At the present, we are interested only in one aspect: in Greek philosophy creation exhausts the substance of the absolute; all ideas are also realized. Not to realize an idea inherent in the absolute would mean to be envious, to use the semantics developed in the *Timaeus:* the creator would be holding something back, which in this way would be withheld from the world [41b].

Incidentally, this argumentation once again demonstrates that the ideas are attributed to the creator himself. The reason for the argumentation is transparent in terms of structural logic: the doctrine of the plenitude of existence realizes one of the two possibilities with which absolute-based thought is acquainted; in this way it also articulates the difference between the philosophical and the theological understanding of the world. All absolute-based thought, theological and philosophical, proceeds by tracing that which is found existing in the world back to an absolute origin, in order to then view it as arising from this source. Nothing can be said about the absolute otherwise. Thought can leave it that way; in this way the absolute is made congruent with existence. *Timaeus* opts for this solution.

It is also possible, though, to emphasize the surplus that must exist in the actor in order to produce the preexisting from within himself: whoever does something, could always do something else. This is the option taken by Judeo-

Christian thought, which consequently has continued to defend the claim of God's unlimited creative power in this way up to the present day. The decision for one or the other option depends upon what the recourse to the absolute is supposed to accomplish. At the beginnings of religiosity, there was certainly great interest in explaining the irregular and the unanticipated. Moreover, nothing was so certain that it could not have been different or become different. Above all, though, a world that was modeled according to an action logic required a constant input of energy in terms of both its permanence and its regularities. The creator had to maintain the world.[33] In terms of its explanatory structure, Greek philosophy is bound to the same subjectivistic logic as theological thought. Yet philosophy deprives the absolute subject of its anthropomorphic traits. It requires, if not a creator, then at very least an Aristotelian unmoved mover only in order to secure, via the lunar spheres, the energetic requirements of the cosmos and thus its order.

The Best of All Worlds

According to the pristine logic, each world becomes an intellect-based world, ordered in terms of meaning. This holds equally for the animistic, the polytheistic, and the monotheistic worlds. Since everything that is and occurs is conceived structurally (!) in terms of the logic of action, everything is conceived of as meaningful in itself. The saying, attributed to Thales, that "everything is full of gods" can thus be understood as "everything is full of meaning." Religious-theological interpretations translate the logic of action into the details of whatever is found existing and occurring in the world. The immanence of meaning in the world continues to be maintained as the philosophy of thought seizes hold of the world. It is well known that Richard Wilhelm rendered Lao-tzu's *Tao* as "meaning."[34] This is unacceptable, since it destroys the sensitive semantics of the *Tao*. Nonetheless, in structural-logical terms it does grasp a basic aspect of the *Tao* as well. In the theory of ideas, as the *Timaeus* shows, Greek philosophy also developed an immanence of the intellectuality of the world.

Admittedly, the ideas per se do not show that the moment of meaning originates from the logic of action, except where they themselves embody an active occurrence. Ideas, though, are always definable only within a mode of thought that understands itself as meaningful. They necessarily converge toward a "subjective spirit." The totality of one's own thought, meanwhile, is always understood in terms of the totality of spirituality in the world. The latter also converges, according to its inner logic, toward a subjective as absolute spirit. Whether and how its subjectivity becomes the explicit object of discussion, i.e., is "thematized," is another question. The point is that in structural-logical terms, the subjectively mediated unity of meaningfulness in the world is always an implicit assumption of thought in metaphysics. Thus the myth of creation merely gives concrete form to something that is already prestructured in the thought of the world, viewed in terms of its structural logic. This occurs in such a way that the creating is linked back to the all-encompassing idea of the good: the creator himself is good [29e], the absolute best [30a], and in his creation he gazes upon the ideas that immanently converge with the good. In their combined totality the outcome is understood as an expression of reason. Related back to the absolute in this way, the world can only be the best of all possible worlds, regardless of the way in which it conceptualizes itself, and regardless of what may occur within this world.

The Deontologization of Meaning in Modernity

If one reconstructs the formative process of an intellect-based, sociocultural world, it then becomes understandable why the early world, and also the early philosophy, had to develop an ontology of meaning: the constructive process did not occur behind the backs of the actors, so to speak; it occurred by means of the actors. It did get enacted, though, in a way that prevented its nature from being understood as construct and thus the authorship of the constructors from reaching consciousness. For this reason, the world necessarily had to appear in the constructs as if it were so organized "on its own." The concept formation and logicity of thought appeared to be a natural part of the ontic substrate. In fact, nature means origin for the Greeks,[35] but an origin that includes all the concepts and conceptualizations that emerge out of it. This meaning is also given expression in *Timaeus*: on the one hand, nature is the still completely unformed, pliable mass that takes on the eternal forms [50b]; on the other, the eternal forms are also nature, precisely because of their originating character. In other words, they are preformed in the origin.

Insight into the basis of the ontology makes clear the reason for its critique at the beginning of modernity. There was only one way for this to happen: man had to recognize himself as the constructor of his world. This insight, though, cannot be gained through pure reflection. The contradictions and problems that arise within the traditional worldview provide no opportunity for overcoming this worldview. How then did it occur?

A given logic can be overcome only if an alternative logic is available, and the latter must first be successfully constructed. By making this assumption about the developmental process of intellect in history, our position stands in sharp contrast to the opinion customarily and tacitly held in philosophy, and also in part in sociology: namely, that the development of a given worldview obeys an, as it were, autochthonous cultivation of thought.[36] It is true that in sociology Marx used the theorem of base and superstructure to subject the top-heaviness of philosophy to ideological critique.[37] However, at best, only the legitimating semantics can be understood as superstructure. The way in which thought already defines and affects the basic organization of the world could only have been grasped by a theory of cognition never achieved by Marx.

Max Weber, taking support from the Neo-Kantian theory of values, also thought that those ideas that determined worldviews, i.e., the cultural values, were autonomous in their development, clearly distinct from all thought based purely on cognition.[38] The problem with the Weberian understanding of history, and especially of Western intellectual history, is not the one-sided focus of his studies, and particularly of "The Protestant Ethic and the Spirit of Capitalism," though they do emphasize only one of the two causative determinants, ideas, to the neglect of the other, interests. Rather, the problem is that he understood both "as equally originary," to make use of the succinct terminology of Wolfgang Schluchter.[39] The fact, however, is that whereas there is an autonomous logic to the structures of thought and the structures of society, an understanding of history, can be gained only by attempting to determine the systemic dependence of development of the structures in the two strata, the cognitive and the societal. The concept of reciprocal affinities, which Weber favors,[40] is totally unsuited for this task. Moreover, Weber also sought to define the development of ideas solely on the material, not on the structural, level of thought. Yet the condition of possibility for the deontologization of meaning has to be sought on thought's structural level.

The process of history in which man gains awareness of his authorship of the world is tied to a process whose internal logic, once again, can be found already in early ontogenesis: the acquisition of action competence gradually produces in the maturing member of the species an awareness of autonomy. This in turn is reflected in the development of a consciousness of rules and norms.[41] The child becomes aware of its sovereignty in shaping communication, though only within the limits of its field of action. This limitation is often overlooked. History must be understood as a continuation, of a constructive process of world formation, that takes up the task where the structures are built up in early ontogenesis left off. This constructive process becomes more intense on the thresholds to new epochs, acquiring in each instance another dimension, resulting in new structural principles in the organization of the social world. At each of these thresholds, the organizational competence of the socialized actors is increased through the further development of organizational forms that had previously determined their lives. With each new societal form, the consciousness of human authorship grows. Following ontogenetic development, we use the term "decentering" to describe that process in which the subject detaches himself from the world, sets himself in opposition to this world, and in precisely this way becomes increasingly aware of his role as constructor.

In history, this consciousness receives its first impetus in the early advanced civilizations in whose wake nature and culture begin to separate from one another.[42] The polis gains its significance from precisely this process: the organization of power in the constitutional state increases, to a previously unapproached degree, man's detachment from the world. Only in these terms does the reflectivity of the constructs of the world observed in *Timaeus* and still more in *The Republic,* and similarly, though in a different way, in Aristotle's *Physics,* become understandable. The reason for the discovery of mind, which Bruno Snell attributes to the Greeks, is found in this process of decentering.[43] The revolutions at the outset of modernity give definitive character to this consciousness of authorship. The change of logic in understanding the world has to generate the insight that the world of man converges toward man himself. In this way, meaning is identified as a human construct and nothing more, hence resulting in the loss of its ontological attribute.

Notes

1. For a more extensive discussion see Günter Dux, *Historisch-genetische Theorie der Kultur* (Weilerswist 2000), 167–174.

2. Immanuel Kant, "Von der Deduktion der reinen Verstandesbegriffe," in idem, *Kritik der reinen Vernunft,* vol. 3, Werke (Berlin 1968), 137ff. Niklas Luhmann, *Soziale Systeme* (Frankfurt/ M. 1984), 148ff.

3. Andrew Lock, *The Guided Reinvention of Language* (London 1980).

4. Cf. Günter Dux, "Die ontogenetische und historische Entwicklung des Geistes," in Günter Dux and Ulrich Wenzel, eds., *Der Prozess der Geistesgeschichte: Studien zur ontogenetischen und historischen Entwicklung des Geistes* (Frankfurt/ M. 1994), 173–224.

5. Instructive in this context are the studies in Margaret Mahler et al., eds., *Die psychische Geburt des Menschen* (Frankfurt/ M. 1989).

6. Cf. Günter Dux, *Geschlecht und Gesellschaft: Warum wir lieben* (Frankfurt/ M. 1994).

7. On the linguistic turn, see Richard Rorty, ed., *The Linguistic Turn* (Chicago 1964); on the mythologization of language, cf. Jean-Francois Lyotard, *Le Différend,* trans. Van Den Abbeele (Minneapolis 1987).

8. For a more extensive discussion of the genesis of syntax see Dux, *Historisch-genetische Theorie der Kultur,* 287–301.

9. Explicitly so in Peter Winch, "Understanding a Primitive Society," *American Philosophical Quarterly* 1 (1964): 307–324; Michel Foucault, *The Order of Things,* trans. A. Sheridan (New York 1970); Lyotard, *Le Différend.*

10. However, even in Noam Chomsky's theory of syntax, the metaphysics of language are translated into a form of genetic naturalism. See Noam Chomsky, *Aspects of the Theory of Syntax* (Cambridge, Mass. 1965). An impressive argument for the circumventability of language is found in Elmar Holenstein, *Von der Hintergehbarkeit der Sprache* (Frankfurt/ M. 1980).

11. As already argued for by Eric H. Lenneberg, *Biologische Grundlagen der Sprache* (Frankfurt/ M. 1972).

12. Thus Ferdinand de Saussure, *Course in General Linguistics,* ed. C. Bally and A. Sechehaye (New York 1959).

13. Cf. the foundational work of radical constructivism: Humberto R. Maturana and Francisco J. Varela, "Autopoietische Systeme: eine Bestimmung der lebendigen Organisation," in Humberto R. Maturana, ed., *Erkennen: Die Organisation und Verkörperung von Wirklichkeit* (Braunschweig 1982), 170–235; see also Maturana, *Der Baum der Erkenntnis* (Bern 1987).

14. Every empirical investigation of language confirms that the formative process of syntax, like that of vocabulary, takes place in terms of an external reality, even if the latter is only vaguely formed at first. Thus, this process requires references in order to reach definitions qua distinc-

tions. As representative, cf. Roger Brown, *A First Language,* 5th ed. (Cambridge, Mass. 1976); Elizabeth Bates, *Language and Context: The Acquisition of Pragmatics* (New York 1976).

15. Michael DeVitt and Kim Sterelny, *Language and Reality* (Oxford 1987), 218ff.

16. Jean Piaget, *The Construction of Reality in the Child* (New York 1954).

17. As does Sue Taylor Parker, "Higher Intelligence as Adaptations for Social and Technological Strategies in Early Homo Sapiens," in George Butterworth, ed., *Evolution and Developmental Psychology* (Whitstable 1985), 83–101; Sue Taylor Parker and Constance Milbrath, "Higher Intelligence, Propositional Language, and Culture as Adaptations for Planning," in Kathleen R. Gibson and Tim Ingold, eds., *Tools, Language and Cognition in Human Evolution* (Cambridge 1993), 314–333; Kathleen Gibson, "Has the Evolution of Intelligence Stagnated Since Neanderthal Man?" in Butterworth, *Evolution and Developmental Psychology,* 102–114.

18. For the concomitant discussion, see my analysis in Günter Dux, *Die Zeit in der Geschichte: Ihre Entwicklungslogik vom Mythos zur Weltzeit* (Frankfurt/ M. 1989); and Dux, "Die ontogenetische und historische Entwicklung des Geistes."

19. Günter Dux, *Die Logik der Weltbilder: Sinnstrukturen im Wandel der Geschichte* (Frankfurt/ M. 1982); Dux, "Die ontogenetische und historische Entwicklung des Geistes."

20. As in Jürgen Habermas, *Theorie des kommunikativen Handelns,* 2 vols. (Frankfurt/ M. 1981), vol. 1, 72ff.

21. Johann Gottlieb Fichte, *Das System der Sittenlehre,* Werke vol. 4, ed. I. H. Fichte (Berlin 1971), 31.

22. Cf. Wolfgang Wieland, *Die aristotelische Physik* (Göttingen 1970), 256ff. On its comprehension, see Ulrich Wenzel, "Dynamismus und Finalismus: Zur Strukturlogik der aristotelischen Naturphilosophie," in Dux and Wenzel, *Der Prozeß der Geistesgeschichte,* 330ff.; further his brilliant dissertation *Vom Ursprung zum Prozess* (Opladen 2000).

23. Hermann Diels and Walther Kranz, *Die Fragmente der Vorsokratiker,* 2 vols., 15th ed. (Dublin and Zürich 1971), vol. 2, B2.

24. The references in the square brackets here and in the following refer to the numbering of the *Timaeus*. The following version was used: Plato, *The Dialogues of Plato,* translated with analyses and introductions by B. Jowett, 4 vols. (Oxford 1953). (*Timaeus* is found in vol. 3).

25. See *The Republic of Plato,* translated with introduction and notes by Francis MacDonald Cornford (London 1945 [1941]).

26. Alfred Schütz, *Der sinnhafte Aufbau der sozialen Welt* (Vienna 1932), 59f.

27. *Upanishaden,* ed. A. Hillebrandt, 27th–30th ed. (Düsseldorf 1975), 36.

28. Robin G. Collingwood, *An Autobiography,* Oxford 1939.

29. Cf. Plato, *Sophist,* 258d; H. Meinhardt, "Idea," in Joachim Ritter, ed., *Historisches Wörterbuch der Philosophie,* vol. 4 (Darmstadt 1976), 55ff., here 57.

30. E. Hornung, *Der Eine und die Vielen: ägyptische Gottesvorstellungen* (Darmstadt 1971).

31. *The Republic of Plato,* 220 (VI, 509b).

32. Arthur O. Lovejoy, *The Great Chain of Being* (Cambridge, Mass. 1966 [1936]).

33. As Hans Blumenberg correctly notes in *Die kopernikanische Welt* (Frankfurt/ M. 1965), 21.

34. Lao-tzu, *Tao te king,* trans. Richard Wilhelm (Düsseldorf 1982). [For a translation into English, the reader is referred to the rendering by Wing-tsit Chou, *The Way of Lao Tzu* (New York, 1963)—trans. note].

35. H. Diller, "Der griechische Naturbegriff," *Neue Jahrbücher für Antike und deutsche Bildung* 2 (1939), 241–257.

36. For a judicious and differentiated view of this problematic, see Blumenberg, *Die kopernikanische Wende.*

37. Karl Marx, "Zur Kritik der Hegelschen Rechtsphilosophie. Einleitung (1844)," in *Marx-Engels-Werke* (Berlin 1969), vol. 1, 378–391; Karl Marx and Friedrich Engels, *Die deutsche Ideologie* (1845), in *Marx-Engels-Werke* (Berlin 1969), vol. 3, 19ff.

38. Max Weber, *Wirtschaft und Gesellschaft* (Cologne 1964), 317ff. ("Religionssoziologie"); Weber, "Einleitung" to "Die Wirtschaftsethik der Weltreligionen," in Max Weber, *Gesammelte Aufsätze zur Religionssoziologie,* vol. 1, (Tübingen 1968), 237–275.

39. Wolfgang Schluchter, *Die Entwicklung des okzidentalen Rationalismus* (Tübingen 1979), 206.

40. Max Weber, "Die protestantische Ethik und der Geist des Kapitalismus," in idem, *Gesammelte Aufsätze zur Religionssoziologie,* vol. 1, 17–206, here 83.

41. Cf. Jean Piaget, *The Moral Judgment of the Child* (Glencoe 1948).

42. Cf. Günter Dux, *Liebe und Tod im Gilgamesh-Epos: Geschichte als Weg zum Selbstbewußtsein des Menschen* (Vienna 1992); Dux, "Die ontogenetische und historische Entwicklung des Geistes."

43. Bruno Snell, *Die Entdeckung des Geistes* (Hamburg 1955).

CHAPTER 3

Sense of History: What does it mean?
With an Outlook onto Reason and Senselessness

JÖRN RÜSEN

"*Sense is a non-existent entity and maintains special relations to nonsense.*"

(Gilles Deleuze[1])

"*The problem is not to know whether or not history has a sense, whether or not we may dare to take sides in it; whatever the case, we are in it up to our necks.*"

(Jean-Paul Sartre[2])

"*History and sense go together. History is therefore a deeply human affair.*"

(Jan Assmann[3])

The Senseless Sense of History

There is hardly anything as outdated as reflecting on the sense of history, let alone twinning it with reason.[4] Both activities have fallen into discredit, so much so that attempts to reinstate them as categories of historical thinking seem pointless, that is, without sense or reason. If there is a rational answer at all regarding the question about the sense of history (that is, whether it is "generally agreeable for good reasons"), it would be a negative one. Sense and reason, it seems, can be rehabilitated only at mutual cost.

Notes for this section begin on page 60.

Historical theory has long been engaged in criticizing as untenable notions of the course of history and of historical knowledge associated with these two categories. *Sense* follows the tradition of the philosophy of history in which historical memory is hermeneutically assimilated by the category of an overarching process implicitly including all cultures and ages; *reason*, meanwhile, refers to the human capacity for cognitive mastery of such a process through cultural assimilation of the human world and self.

"Sense" implies that the temporal extension of the human world is interpreted within the *schema of subjectivity*:[5] changes appear to be brought about by an intention, a goal-oriented will. The concept of sense is closely tied up with intention and goal-directedness, characterizing human action as the activity of a thinking and reflecting subject. Hence, "sense" has a *teleological connotation*. History is understood as goal-oriented; the temporal changes of the past are reviewed and represented in light of a specific directedness to which an ongoing action may intentionally refer. (Insofar as suffering is also determined by sense—say, e.g., by the tormenting question "Why?"—it may, for an answer, refer to that same directedness.) The experience of the past is adapted to a future-oriented intention and vice versa.

History—"the" history,[6] as a temporal universe of the human world spanning past, present, and future—manifests itself as a synthesis of experience and expectation.[7] The future unfolds from the normative impulses of present-day life-practice, which in turn draws on the experience of past life-practice and its world-transforming energy. Time, having solidified—reflected, as it were, in the accumulated experiences of the past—and become part of the corpus of historical knowledge, liquefies again in the volitional impulses of ongoing action, which is enlightened by this very knowledge as to the direction of its future-oriented intentions.

Ontogenetically, this sense is anchored in early fixations of the subject;[8] historically, it has religious roots. Judaism and Christianity charged the inner-worldly contingency of uncontrollable events with the subject quality of a world-ruling God. This divine being then entered the subject quality of a conception of humankind that, on an anthropological plane, constituted the unity of history and the temporal direction of the course of the world in and through human action.

What used to be traditionally meant by "sense of history" *(Sinn der Geschichte)* (and is still meant)[9], was a *subject quality of the temporal change of the human world,* which as one and the same quality throughout has attended the real temporal processes of the human world in the past, the dynamic of intentional action or of contemplative suffering in the present, and the normative orientation towards an anticipated and intended future. This quality was not expressly referred to as "sense," but was described in substantive terms. Theologically, it was called *providentia Dei* or God's will and served the elaboration of complex theories of redemption, such as the theory of aeons or a "typological" reference system of different times.[10]

Anthropologically, it infused historical experience with the notion of a commonly shared human nature or rational quality of human practical life beyond all temporal and cultural differences. On the historical-philosophical plane, it manifested itself as a categorical definition of the temporal universe of the human world, for instance, as *"Idee der Menschheit und der Kultur"* (Ranke),[11] as reason with a temporal extension, as progress, development, dialectical process; or—under the sign of skepsis, doubt, and disappointment—it became charged with negative concepts: collapse, regression, decline. Finally, it appeared in the metaphorical guise of a variety of historiographic key concepts, for example in Ranke's notion of God's "hieroglyph."[12]

Sensefully constructed, in such ways, the world of history was susceptible to claims of domination: it could be assimilated and practically explored by participation, via faith, in its religious substance, or on the secular level, by knowledge. In the name of history, or of one of the world-transforming powers it had been constitutively credited with, it was possible to act, invoking it as a legitimating category in different, even contrary strategic constellations. Having become part of the telos of individual practical life, it imparted to the subjects' self-assertion the cultural force that derives from identification with world-transforming powers.

With this qualification, "master narratives" of historical thought were conceived and organized. They anchored the collective identity of their authors and addressees in the depths of historical development. The constellation of memories, attitudes, experiences, intentions, and normative points of view that determines belongingness was shaped into a congruous picture of a time-transcending historical process in which those affected by it could consider themselves in conformity with the course of the human world. History—"that" history—developed its temporal profile as a long-term extension of a megasubject (Christianity, humankind, nation, Occident, etc.) embedded in an overarching developmental context of past, present, and future. The temporal perspective of self-understanding had always been organized according to universalistic considerations (humankind, reason, freedom, civilization, culture etc.). As its own master narrative had related, the mega-group viewed itself as the center of "that" history. At best, others' otherness was but an adumbration of the individual self, or its opposite: mentally exterritorialized, negative experiences, anxieties, fears that could not be accommodated within the self and were therefore exiled and excluded to beyond the boundary separating belongingness and the foreignness of another world, even a counterworld in extreme cases. (In a lighter vein, otherness could also serve as a projection area for individual desires and aspirations, e.g., the image of the "noble savage").

The term "sense" *(Sinn)* was not used for this efficient and potent subject quality of historical time, however. It became a technical term only when the teleological subject quality of history lost its credibility.[13] Indeed, it reflects this loss. As if it were a question, "sense" takes the place of concepts that used to be its guarantors in historical thought (reason, idea, progress, etc.). In the German history of concepts and ideas, at least, the philosophical expression "sense of history" *(Sinn der Geschichte)* indicates the loss of an idealistic basic trust in the subject quality of history.[14] Ever since then this concept has accompanied the reflection on the achievements, risks, limitations, necessity, and practical application of historical thought and its own role in the cultural orientation of human life-practice.

Historically, this loss coincides with the abdication of philosophy of history, which left the domain of the cognitive assimilation of the past to the historical disciplines and confined itself to thematizing and reflecting on these disciplines as categories representing the sense of this assimilation. But this guarantee could not be given by the disciplines since the traditional sense-quality, which characterized the past as history, is not to be found in the methodological procedures of historical research, but is one of the preconditions of the methodological process itself, thus remaining inaccessible to them.[15] In the cognitional operations of the historical sciences, the sense of history dissolved into concrete factual data of the past that were, per se, no longer identical with their own historical significance for the present, but were endowed with that sense only later, after being charged with significance by the cognizant subject. Having solidified, so to speak, and become part of the source-based corpus of rationally collected and verified data of the past, "that history" assigned its original sense to the hermeneutic competence of cognizant subjectivity. Subject and object of historical thinking separated; historical experience in itself became senseless, with the qualities of sense (thereafter known as "values") required for its interpretation in turn becoming detached from experience.

The exiling of historical sense from the experience of the past and its shift to a welcoming cognizant subjectivity is most evident in Max Weber. The object quality of history is considered by him to be characterized by absolute senselessness. He speaks of an "immense, chaotic stream of events winding its way through time."[16] On the other hand, he believes the "transcendental precondition of any cultural science" lies in the fact "that we are cultural beings possessing the ability and will to take a position vis-à-vis the world and endow it with sense."[17]

When historical sense lost its objectivity, historical thought's claim of rationality also disappeared. This had consisted in identifying and extracting historical sense, on a factual basis, from historical experience in the course of an interpretative approach to the human past. The disciplines could base their own claim of rationality on the intersubjective validity of their truths only at a cost, namely that the normatively charged sense-criteria, which turn the factual data of the past into history, were excluded from their domain of competence and consigned to a metarational category of creative subjectivity.

In the name of a sense-guaranteeing philosophy of history, reason had originally claimed to be able (hermeneutically) to "apprehend" this sense from the past's store of experience, deploying the fully developed tools of the methodological rationality of historical research in the process. Now, it though, degenerated into mere intellect, referring to metarationally pre-given, constitutive sense-criteria of historical knowledge and applying them to the methodological procedures of historical research, but unable to endow them with the same claims of validity that distinguished the scientifically gathered corpora of knowledge of the past. A reason thus reduced to the science-specific, methodological rationality of historical cognition was no longer capable of producing the sense that the past, as history, holds for the present.

A telling admission of this impotence is the thematization of remembering *(Erinnerung)* and memory *(Gedächtnis),* in which the cultural sciences have been engaged for some time.[18] In the helplessness of a rational concept of sense, the cultural sciences have been looking at the "places of commemoration." This approach to the past is totally, and in principle, effected via sense, and as an element of cultural orientation, the past is alive and effective in ongoing life-practice. Remembering and memory, as fundamental and universal cultural practices of existential orientation, seem like the warming glow of a history endowed with sense, but once reviewed with the cold rationality of objectifying historical research, they may look more like a lost paradise.[19] The gaze that surveys the sense-filled stores of the cultural memory is apt to become an empty stare, for scientists claim to know better: The warmth radiating from historical recollection turns cold when its factual content and truth-value are subjected to critical scrutiny, as science demands.

The loss of sense that the demise of a teleologically conceived philosophy of history has meant[20] cannot be easily reversed. After all, this philosophy did not fail because its specialized disciplines proved incapable of categorically assimilating and integrating it into the concepts of historical interpretation; it failed on account of a temporal experience that shattered the teleologically presupposed interrelation of sense spanning past, present, and future. Historical thinking had been stunned by an experience of contingency of catastrophic dimensions, namely the crises of modernization, which since the late nineteenth century had with increasing radicalness generated needs for orientation that the traditional teleological concepts of history found increasingly difficult to fulfil.[21] Doubtless the single most radical experience of this historical hiatus—not to be compared to a mere orientational crisis of modernization—has been the Holocaust.

The critical awareness occasioned by this experience, with which historical thinking now looked at itself, revealed an implication of its traditional conceptions of sense in the very catastrophe that had eliminated them. Historical thinking, which had taken reason for granted and been certain of sense, was identified as an active moment of the same historical development that had challenged it. Philosophy of history, which used to be a source of sense, came to be deployed as a weapon in a power struggle, not yielding, however, the sense it had claimed. Universalistic criteria of reason turned out to be ideologically generalized particularities ("to speak of humankind is to deceive"), and beyond the claim of reason asserted by such universalistic concepts, a will to power manifested itself among particularistic groups that promptly proceeded to generalize their own interests, thereby curbing divergent or opposing interests, or at least keeping them at arm's length more or less forcibly. Cultural diversity and difference were universalistically leveled, and hence the rule of one culture over the remaining others was ideologically completed and cemented.

New Questions about Traditional Sense

What has become of historical sense? Does it make sense at all to keep using the category of sense when dealing with history? Surprisingly, it has not been consumed in the blaze of ideology critique directed at the sense-laden teleological concepts of history, which had been the foundation of modern historical thought, but has tenaciously maintained its ground and made its point, on several levels.

For one thing, philosophy of history has survived its epistemological and disciplinary critique. It has come to manifest itself in new forms in which the teleological substance of the traditional sense-concept can easily be recognized. This is confirmed, for instance, by the interpretation of the epochal turning-point of 1989 as the "end of history,"[22] which, far from being an isolated case reflective of an *a priori* outmoded historical thinking, has triggered a lively debate on the potential of world historical developments for reaching an end or—indeed—an end-fulfilment. With this discussion about the end of history, Hegelian philosophy of history has revealed a surprising contemporary relevance, as has its postmodern variant, in which teleology becomes the telos of its own elimination.[23]

Apart from the Hegelian variant, the Spenglerian one, too, marked by a teleologically inspired historical thinking, has recently been revived. Huntington's account of world history as a "Clash of Civilizations"[24] interprets the temporal progression of the human world using the sense-concept of "cultures" as megasubjects engaged in a mutual struggle for power. Again history manifests itself as a comprehensive temporal interrelation endowed with the subjectivity traits of "civilizations," which can be generally understood and, as an orienting element, related to intentions of individual political action.

These examples of a renewed philosophy of history whose logic is teleologically inspired or based bear out that there have always been experiences of time that are interpreted by appealing to a constitutive subjectivity of historical processes. It seems that, as a cognitive tool of historical interpretations of contemporary experiences, the category of sense in its traditional historico-philosophical form has not yet become obsolete.[25] The question of whether, and to what extent, it will escape unharmed from the ideology critique that has flared over the insight into the logical inconsistency of universalistic sense-concepts and their political applicability as instruments of domination and power, has so far remained unanswered, for the above examples have been flawed by a Eurocentrist perspective of history. But it has by no means been established whether the sense-categories under review have been ethnocentrically conceived in principle and are therefore ideologically capable only of serving as instruments of domination and power, or whether their framework also allows for cultural diversity and difference as conditions of historical sense.

We note a revaluation of the sense-category even where its traditional form is being demolished: in subjectivism, as reflected in the discussion on historical theory after the linguistic turning-point. Having withdrawn from the pre-given entities of experience through which the past *is* present, historical sense has become a merely subjective achievement of the interpretative approach to that past. Historical thinking becomes recognizable as an achievement of the symbolizing process of historical consciousness. Relying on the creativity of linguistic interpretation of the world, it produces the sense-quality that turns the past into history from the perspective of the present. As stated earlier, though, this sense is weak on experience; it represents a cultural quality granted to the past only *post festum* by the ability of contemporary subjects to remember and interpret. Sense thus becomes a "merely" subjective achievement of historical thinking that refers to, and utilizes, the corpus of experiences of the past. Its meta-empirical quality is expressed by the term "fictionality," making clear, of course, that this type of sense is not one that could be called genuinely historical. For if "historical" denotes a quality of experience of sense itself, that is, if it constitutes the opposite of a literary-aesthetic sense-production exceeding the boundaries of experience, then historical sense remains within these boundaries. In this case, it could in fact be considered complementary to the fictionality of aesthetic constructs of sense.

The thematization of remembering and memory mentioned earlier is a step toward this inner quality of experience of historical sense. Undoubtedly, what is at issue here is the integration of real experience into the cultural framework orienting present-day praxis, that is, remembering, and thereby memorizing for the present the importance and significance of an occurrence that has been experienced as important and significant. As much as this importance and significance subsequently tend to adapt events to the interests of those remembering them, it does not in any way render obsolete the quality of the experience of what is being remembered. If the metahistorical claim of the fictional character of this specifically historical significance was realized on a level where human beings must remember what in order to know who they are, and to organize their lives according to a particular directedness of temporal change—

then they would surely consider a memory recognized as merely fictional to be pointless, an illusion to which they would not entrust the reality of their lives.

Another deficiency of the sense-quality attributed to historical thinking in the mode of remembering and cultural memory concerns the cognitive status of a sense-making effected through remembering. Precisely because the experience of the past, driven by specific interests, is charged with sense-qualities for the purpose of culturally orienting the present, the sense-construct of the past remembered as history inspires little confidence when considered in the light of rational cognition's potential for reason. Reason, as the essence of cognitional capacity and its truth-claims, takes a critical position towards the sense claimed by memory. The relation of scientific knowledge to the prescientific historical memory was considered subversive and destructive, a dissolution of the sense of interpreted historical experience that people rely on for orientation.[26]

The need for sense, which science with its critical stance is unable to fulfill, is nevertheless generated by its own scientific inquiry: the current focus on culture as a dominant hermeneutic category of historical research may be understood as a process in search of sense.

Culture is the quintessence of human beings' subjective hermeneutic achievements in living with themselves and their world. It could be said to be virtually identical with the mental process of sense-making, without which human practical life would be impossible. The world must always be culturally interpreted before it can be mastered by action. Sense is precisely what culture brings to human practical life: culture endows the world and human beings with a subject quality without which they could not come to terms with themselves or their world, either as agents or as sufferers.[27] In shifting its scientific inquiry to culture, historical science is reclaiming, as one of the objects of inquiry of its research and historiographic domains, the sense-quality of human life that it had lost sight of while thematizing history as an overarching framework of past, present, and future. Sense is congealing, as it were, forming a fascinating cultural construct of past modes of human life that offer to the present at least a—primarily aesthetic—reflection of sense that can compensate for the absence of sense in present-day experience.

Max Weber's compelling cultural-historical reconstruction of religion as a key condition of the origin of the modern capitalist mode of life has already drawn attention to this type of concern with sense: The terror caused by a sense that has in effect exited from the objective world leads the despairing subject in need of sense to the domain of historical insight, where potent processes of sense-making can be identified in the origin of the subject's own world. Examination of the temporal beginnings of the historical process leading to the subject's own present, leads that subject to remember calls to mind, the universal potency of subjective sense-making, which functions as a counterconcept to the present-day loss of sense: considered in the mirror of time, the cultural crisis of the present is becoming tolerable.[28] Yet, this view of the past remains clouded with despair because the sense-category can no longer impart to the present an inner coherence that would retain the sense-content of the past world as a future-oriented element. On an epistemological plane, this hopelessness is further cemented by the fact that the cognitive potential of disciplinary knowledge and its quality of value-freedom is cut off from the resources of sense inherent in the cultural achievements as reflected in the human efforts to cope with the world and engage in self-understanding *(Selbstverständigung)*.

This constellation of problems provides impulses for further reflections on the problem of sense in history. The continuing efforts of historicophilosophical hermeneutics suggest there is an inundation with experience coupled with a need for orientation that demands alternatives to the traditional definition of the sense of history. The peculiar separation, of a historical experience conceived as a culture endowed with sense-qualities, from the sense-making competence of historical consciousness, inevitably raises the question of whether it is possible to synthesize a historically interpretative subjectivity and the cultural dimension of historical experience. Ultimately, a rigid separation between cultural memory and disciplinary historical knowledge appears untenable. Following scrutiny of the mental dimensions and operations in which historical knowledge itself, as part of collective remembering and cultural memory, has its roots, the question about the rational character of historical sense-making can be asked again in a new way. Based on methodological research procedures, the historical knowledge of the cultural sciences challenges the subservient subordination of experience to the present-day need for orientation as mediated by memory. This critique need not invalidate the sense-laden nature of the remembered past, however; indeed, by acting like a filter, it could make this sense "rational."

The critical control of experience by historical cognition, the rational tool of historical research, could hermeneutically—that is, by "apprehending" the historical sense as deposited in the past's corpus of experience—become a category of reason that synthesizes this sense with the hermeneutic achievement and potential of the subjects of historical thought and the addressees of historiography.

Sense: What does it mean?

Sense is an ensemble of superior criteria defining the cultural orientation of action and suffering in human practical life. "Culture" is not understood here as a counterconcept to "nature," that is, without the broad connotations of a concept that comprises the human world as a whole. Instead, I understand "culture" as a dimension of human life-practice that is distinct from other modes of life (e.g., the economy, politics, society, human ecology). This distinction may be artificial and analytical but, culture-specific and historical though it may be, it has a categorical significance in that it is concerned with exploring experience.

Defined more narrowly in this way, culture summarizes the hermeneutic achievements that have to be realized by human consciousness (including its unconscious dimensions) in its interaction with the world, with nature, and with itself in order to make human life possible. The world must always be interpreted before it can be actively coped with, and before human beings can interact with each other in a way that ensures their survival. By performing this hermeneutic task, human subjectivity asserts itself in the life-practice of human beings sharing in a state of socialization. Culture is thus the "internal" side of human practical life, onto which the external world has to be mapped symbolically or "theoretically" (albeit not as a mirror image, but as a creative achievement, a generation of a world through interpretation) so that it can manifest itself at all as a real world that can be "lived in."

This mental assimilation of world and self occurs via different mental operations. They can be distinguished as perception, interpretation, orientation, and motivation. *Perception* stands for the exploration of the internal and external worlds by the "senses." The *interpretation* of these perceptions serves to explain the world and arrive at an understanding of oneself and others. *Orientation* refers to the application of interpreted perceptions in the intentional control of life-practice. This application occurs on two levels: in the external world—referring to the interpretation of the "object-world"—and in the internal world. In the latter a personal and social self is formed based on interpreted perceptions, an I and a we, and individuality is constituted; that is, human subjectivity is formed on a cultural level. In this process, others' otherness is also determined. Lastly, *motivation* means that the orienting interpretations, via intentions, determine the will, guide volitional impulses, and in doing so perform a canalizing function *(Weichenstellungsfunktion)*, as stressed by Max Weber, in the expression of interests and needs.[29]

More accurately defined, *sense* can thus be understood as an integration of these four operations. It stands for a coherence of perception, interpretation, orientation, and motivation, and an inner relatedness of their different orientations and mental qualities. The "sense-laden construction" of the human world and the human self[30] by these four mental operations, from which self and world derive significance and can be "dealt with" or "lived," can now be thematized in a history-specific context on an anthropologically universal, that is, a highly abstract, level.

In this context, "historical" refers the cultural management of time as manifesting changes in the human world. *Perception* would denote the exploration of the temporal change of internal and external worlds, and *interpretation* is the reading of temporal change by means of specific hermeneutic patterns. In this process, the events of the past become history from the perspective of the present ("history" being understood here in its broadest sense, as the overarching temporal framework of human life). *Orientation* would denote a "historical" orientation of life-practice based on the concepts of the passage of time infused with experience and of the development of future perspectives derived from interpreted experiences of the past. The external human life-practice is oriented by concepts and time flows that correspond with action-guiding intentions. Internal orientation occurs via the formation of a historical perspective of affiliation and exclusivity; transpersonal experiences and interpretations of time are integrated into the temporal concept of the individual self. Finally, *motivation,* in history-specific terms, refers to a determination of the will by sense-laden intentions that originate in experience, to a guidance or directedness of volitional impulses within a framework of time flow concepts, and most importantly, to the mobilization of emotions through a recalling of memories.

All these operations or cultural dimensions of the assimilation of world and of self-understanding *(Selbstverständigung)* are essentially about the symbolic assimilation of time. Ultimately and in principle, they are about coming to terms with temporal contingency (an anthropologically universal experience of time) and translating it into conceptions of the passage of time that make life possible. Historical sense is interpreted time that becomes part of the orientation and motivation of human action, also manifesting itself in the type and extent of human suffering.

Thus, sense has a mediating function that works in several ways: it synthesizes the experience of the past and the anticipated future, which is guided by norms, praxis-related, and based on intentions; the two are combined in such a way that, at the center of the synthesizing context, the present can be understood and the actual life situation coped with on a practical level. Sense is situated beyond the distinction between factuality and fictionality; it is an earlier synthesis of both. This precedent state of synthesis, indeed unity, makes possible the overarching concept of the passage of time peculiar to historical consciousness and, as in a gestational process—that is, in the narrative treatment of the past—becomes history from the perspective of the present. At the synthesizing center of the present, sense connects human consciousness to itself, where self, ego, and we operate constitutively as primary and fundamental dimensions of consciousness in the complex framework of socialization, in turn affecting the perception and interpretation of human practical life. Sense synthesizes "ego time" and "world time." It centers the passage of time on the fundamental self-referentiality of human consciousness, on the subjectivity of agents and sufferers; at the same time, it relates them to the dynamic situations of their lives, affected as they are by varying demands in terms of action and suffering. In this intermediation between subjectivity and the temporally dynamized life-practice, identity is being formed.

In the process of sense-making, this multiple synthesizing achievement is accessible to reason insofar as it manifests itself on both the symbolic and linguistic levels, thus opening up a cognitive dimension in which insight and reasoning are necessary conditions for the success of this achievement.

The Sense-Laden Nature of Historical Narrative

The specifically "historical" orientation of the mental operations and cultural praxis in which sense is formed as the elixir of human existence is reflected paradigmatically by the mental procedure that processes contemporary experiences and interprets self and world as having an orienting and motivating intention, namely: historical narrative.[31] Through narrative, time acquires that sense-laden quality of subjectivity that human beings need culturally in order to live in it. This mental transformation of time into sense is in the widest sense "historical," if and when it occurs in the medium of memory. It is achieved by appealing to the corpus of past experiences, which in the mode of memory is made significant for the purpose of orienting present-day life-practice.

Historical sense evolves in the process of historical narrative through its complex references to subjectivity and experience. I would like to illustrate this by means of an example that, though far removed from the academic complexities of historical cognition, reflects in a simple way the basic elements of what is being discussed here as the "sense of history."

I will analyse[32] the curious story that told by the single picture cartoon "Civilization comes to the New World" in the series "Non sequitur" by Wiley.[33] On behalf of Queen Isabella of Spain, Columbus is about formally to take possession of the land on which he has just set foot (and which we call "America"), but is prevented from doing so by a legal expert dressed in twentieth-century garb searching his file for the necessary legal papers and titles required for the possession.[33] Columbus says: "I claim thee in the name of Queen Isabella, as soon as her ### [sign for cursing] lawyer completes the title search."

This picture makes clear what it means to tell a story, to understand it as a story told, and, by understanding it, to accept it. This kind of understanding and acceptance of a story is what is meant when it is said that the story has meaning or makes sense.[34] What endows this story with sense? Or, to center the question on the specifically historical: What is "historical" in this presentation, and what does it mean to say that this "historical" element has a meaning or makes "sense"?

At first glance, the historical aspect of the presentation seems to be that it depicts an event of the past: Columbus's arrival in the New World. On behalf of Queen Isabella of Spain, Columbus is about formally to take possession of the land on which he has just set foot (which we call "America"), but is prevented from doing so by a legal expert dressed in twentieth-century garb, who is searching his file for the necessary legal papers and titles required for the possession.[35] This particular comic strip refers to a recent debate on the "discovery of America," focused on the self-critique of the West, which came to a head on the occasion of the fifth centenary of Columbus's discovery.

This reference to the past is a necessary, albeit insufficient indication that we are dealing with a specifically historical presentation. The world of comic strips abounds with examples of this kind. The well-known series *Hägar the Horrible* by Dik Browne is obviously situated in the past, but it would not be correct, in strictly historical terms, to call such comics "historical" since they all deal with contemporary problems dressed in historical costume. Mere references to the past do not make a presentation "historical." Only when the past itself, as reflecting a different time, is made explicit, that is, when it is related to other times (including the present), does a presentation acquire a specifically historical quality. An example from the *Hägar* series is Hägar's comment as he marches past a construction site a notice reading "The cult site of 'Stonehenge' will be erected here": "I hate progress!"[36]

To give a presentation a specifically historical character, time must be shown as reflecting a difference in the qualities of time. In the example just mentioned, this difference is expressed ironically through the category of progress. The same goes for the first-mentioned strip, which, by showing a lawyer dressed in a business suit and carrying a briefcase, transplants a figure from its present-day context to the time of the discovery of America. Thus, history is not merely a time past, but the past's relation to a different time, basically to present-day time (though often only by way of a synthesizing operation), in which as past it relates to the present by conveying distance, but owing to this distance acquires a coefficient of present-day significance.

It is precisely this complex relation between past and present that the comic strip "Non sequitur" illustrates. The present is personified by the jurist, who even in those days had an important role in the administration and subsequent development of modern statehood. Being a professional pettifogger, the jurist has to specify and explain the claims of Queen Isabella to ensure that the act of taking possession of the land fulfills the formal criteria. This is a swipe at the bureaucratism and formalism of jurists. The figure of the jurist makes the present come alive in a picture of the past. This presentation of difference and relatedness between past and present in the first comic strip, I would call "narrative." The text—"Civilization comes to the New World"—refers to the complex temporal interrelation of past and present. It is about the civilizing process in general, its beginning in the New World and its end in the present.

What, then, is the sense conveyed by the historicity of this presentation of time, difference, and temporal context? First and foremost, it consists in the fact that I understand the picture.[37] What does this mean? This understanding has three components *(Hinsichten):* (a) First, I understand what is being conveyed, the content. I understand the allusion to Columbus. Thus, it is the *content* that makes *sense.* (b) I also understand the method of the presentation, its *form.* I understand the irony, the specific refractedness of the historical relation between past and present. Here, it is the form that makes sense. (c) Moreover, I understand the subject of the comic strip, its *function.* Here, sense denotes that looking at it and reading it amuses me. I relate to the picture as a recipient; I agree with its culture critique or reject it, or let myself be annoyed by the text.

This "sense" of understandability lies at the surface of the strip. When one looks at it more closely, implications and conditions can be identified that have always been implied by this making-sense-through-being-understandable, without having been explicitly discussed. The special point about this presentation is the way, experience and subjectivity operate in it as constituents of a sense that has been understood. They come into view when the sense of the presentation does not merely consist in the fact that I understand it, but possesses a higher quality, namely, that I agree with what I understand. Commonly, one would say that one considers the presentation to be "true."[38]

What does this mean with respect to the three aspects *(Hinsichten)* of content, form, and function? (a) As for *content,* the strip makes sense in terms of enabling agreement or being true, if its historical allusions are correct. Sense would then consist in a correctness based on experience: it was Isabella and not any other queen in whose name Columbus acted; another name would make no sense. Sense would also be disturbed by inconsistencies in the presentation that have no intended significance and therefore are factual errors. (b) Concerning *form,* one can speak of sense in terms of enabling agreement, if there is a formal consistency, for example of language and picture. In the allusion made to the progress of civilization and the bureaucratism of lawyers, this consistency is imparted by dissonance. The dissonance signals a difference in time, expressed pictorially by having stone slabs serve as table and chair for a bureaucrat in contemporary outfit, that is, donning attaché case and business suit, thus distinguishing him from Columbus's early modern garb. Further tension is suggested by the flag and sword, on the one hand, and the papers emerging from the attaché case, on the other. (c) The sense conveyed by the presentation acquires a specific "depth" when its audience can agree with its critical interpretation of the discovery of America in the light of individual historical judgements regarding the significance this story holds for them. In this respect, sense refers to a judgemental stance, a critical distance vis-à-vis present-day concepts of progress and civilization.

The analysis can be summarized as follows: historical sense comprises three extensions or dimensions, one related to content, one formal, and one functional, all of which need to be consistently interrelated.

1

In terms of *content,* sense of history means that the past that has been transformed into a history for the present is endowed with the *quality of experience:* things must have happened the way they have been reported to have happened. Historical sense lies in the quality of experience of the past, made significant for the present. More is involved, though, than the mere factuality of past events: namely, the far more complex "reality" of divergence and interrelation of times in which the facts have been deposited. In other words, the pure factuality of past events has to be complemented by the factuality of the passage of time, of the change represented (here; the passage from the Old to the New World).

This sense-criterion of the quality of experience of the past made significant for the present can be developed further into a set of empirically valid categories, such as eyewitness accounts, fidelity to sources, intersubjective verifiability, etc. Scientific objectivity is one such elaborated form of this criterion. It is not added to the sense-quality of stories that have an impact on human practical life, but is rooted in a quality pertaining to these stories themselves. To this extent, the methodical approach of a research methodology that objectifies experience does not, in principle and in every respect, extinguish the sense of history tied up with the experiences that are subjected to methodical and critical investigation.

The usefulness of sense-laden historical experience for practical life is not *eo ipso* limited or negated by the truth-claim of empirical correctness, on the contrary: without truth being empirically consistent, this usefulness would itself be at risk. But what, then, does it mean to say that the methodologically based reason of historical research challenges the sense-quality of a history kept alive by remembering it? The risk does not necessarily lie in the recourse to experience as such, but in its relative position vis-à-vis other dimensions of historical sense. Should it become an independent operation, the sense of historical experience would degenerate into a "dead" depository of knowledge.

2

Formally, historical sense consists in a cogent and credible narrative. The chronology, that is, the changes and relations between times, must be plausible. The presentation requires an identifiable reference subject of the passage of time. It should be clear and comprehensible, have a beginning and an end; the various narrative steps should be interrelated and grow from each other within an overall narrative flow. The importance of the *formal dimension* of this historical sense is reflected in the ceremonial and ritual forms by which world-explaining and identity-presenting (hi)stories are transmitted in particular societies. In some cases, a formal violation may bring instant death to the narrator.[39]

With historical representation becoming more prosaic, the significance of this aspect has not declined, but shifted to other modes of narration. For example, the explanatory character of a narrative linkage of particular time sequences may be of crucial importance for the sense-guaranteeing congruity of historical presentation. The sense-criterion would then be the explanatory power of a narrative integration. In view of the significant role of nonnarrative factors, however, it would be wrong to assume that the sense of history is to be found exclusively in the narrative elements of its presentation.[40] Clearly, though, the sense of a history must remain subject to the condition that the experience of the past it represents is interpreted by means of a conception of the passage of time consistent with the logic of the narrative presentation of time.

3

Historical sense has a *functional dimension*. Its addressees use historically interpreted time for orientation of their action and suffering. Understood in this way, sense implies a significance for an addressee's existential orientation, a relevance that the past made significant for the present has for contemporary problems of orientation. Stories and histories must provide answers to questions shared by narrator and addressee alike, if they, the stories and histories, are to have, and make, "sense" within this communicative context. In the example of Hägar the Horrible, these problems of orientation are reflected in the crisis of progress as a dominant contemporary experience. The experience of temporal change presented in the comic strip has to correspond with the recipient's temporal horizon, or at least come close enough to engage, confirm, change, and broaden it—in any case activating its orientation-function. Here, historical sense describes the functional or pragmatic coherence of the past transformed into history for the present.

Historical sense could thus be said to unfold into three components, experience, interpretation and orientation, all of them referring to a past characterized by a mediated temporal distance from the present. Tensions may exist in their relations, which may negatively affect historical sense. Contradiction between them would obliterate it. If one considers each component separately, one can dispense with the heavy emphasis that is placed on the sense-category and the importance on claims of validity often attached to it. If, on the other hand, the focus is shifted to the inner coherence between them, then "sense" seems an adequate term for this coherence, which is in itself essential to the triad's relation. Sense is an integration of all three components. They need to be interrelated, to converge and mutually support each other.

Ultimately crucial for this coherence is the orienting function, the pragmatic coherence of the past made significant for the present in relation to the orientational needs of the present. To this extent, sense constitutes a congruous impact on life-practice via the past transformed into a history for the present, and via a temporal projecting of the present into the past, from which the future will eventually unfold, as a perspective for action. (Or, to formulate it in more precise terms: a congruous, that is, sense-laden history involves the translation of the present into a history for the past just as much as it does the translation of the past into a history for the present.)

This is not to claim a mere functionalism of historical sense. In fact, the relation of experience of historical sense-making has a basic control function vis-à-vis the congruity of life-practice: pragmatism, which is based on what serves practical life, has an in-built critical agency that controls experience and the argumentative agreeability of historical interpretations. Interpretation, too, has its own modes of sense-making that oppose a banal functionalization, for example that of a clarifying role in the narrative presentation of time flows. Moreover, by the aesthetic standards of the historical, presentations are deemed to make sense especially when they do not merely confirm a pre-given temporal horizon of individual life-practice, but alter, criticize, modify, and expand it, that is, stimulate it in such a way that new elements of self-understanding and existential orientation may become absorbed into it.

In practical terms, the integration of the three components is effected and achieved by the narrative operation. In narration, sense is a red thread pursued by history, produced by the pattern of historical interpretation prevailing at the time. Narrative explores, interprets, and articulates the experience of the past and, once endowed with an abundance of experience, becomes part of the orientation of human practical life precisely where such orientation calls for a temporal framework for external regulation of life and internal self-determination.

Constructed or pre-given?

An analysis of historical sense based on the phenomenon of its realization by way of narrative illustrates its constructive character. Only after the past has been transformed into a history for the present does it acquire sense, namely through the mental operation enacting this transformation. But can such reconstructive sense be called sense at all?[41] It should demonstrably draw on sources of human subjectivity, which should themselves be characterized by the quality of experience. "Sense" must have a set of attributes that connote some pre-given entities, an "objectivity" that limits the arbitrariness of creative subjective sense-making, anchoring such subjectivity securely in "earthly" ground. Or, to use the metaphor of the body, this objectivity supports its head, which is creative autonomy, but grounds its feet in reality. Only then can it be plausibly argued that a reconstructive subjectivity is endowed with a pre-given entity of sense that is mediated with the former in such a way that subjectivity's source of sense also provides access to historical experience.[42]

Clearly, the qualifications of meaning that are imposed on experience of the past as it becomes a history for the present have not fallen from a worldless sky of pure subjectivity, but have always existed in the social reality of human practical life.[43] The reality of historical experience does not lie in the pure factuality of source-based data; indeed, this reality appears quite unreal in light of the real experiences of human beings with themselves and their world. Sense has always had a concrete gestalt, as reflected in the cultural configurations of the human life-world. Life-practice has always been oriented, real, and infused with sense in its everyday activities before any reflectively confirmed certainty of authoritative orientations. By the same token, the past has always been first the present before becoming any specifically historical experience, that is, before its distantness as past. After all, present-day living conditions are the result of past developments; through them the past is fully present, namely by conveying sense in the same measure as the sense categories that determined agents and sufferers in the past have been absorbed into real pre-given elements of present-day action and suffering. One could also say that sense is the capacity to determine future-oriented action for connecting with sense itself as it has come to be manifested in present-day conditions.

The human life-world can only be conceived of as one already accessed by sense—how could action and suffering be possible in it otherwise? That it has been accessed in this way becomes evident when we ask how the cultural practices of explicit sense-making became possible, and how the sense referred to and articulated within them could become operative. A brief look at the ontogenesis of human subjectivity illustrates this: Even before the capacity for reflective sense-making can bring itself to bear on the corresponding narrative practices, it must form a pre-given element of the social reality of the subject's life. Only objective pre-given elements of sense enable the subject genetically to make sense; subjectivity is always objectively pre-"formed" or pre-given, as it were.

This is not to say that a subjectivity engaged in sense-making does nothing more than become conscious of these pre-given elements of sense and implement them as they come. As a pre-given entity in life-world reality, sense will always retain the precarious quality of needing subjectivity in the form of a conscious practice of cultural sense-generation that does not stop at "what is the case." An effort is always required for subjects to adhere to the pre-given elements orienting their life-practice. Indeed, an even greater amount of creative subjectivity is demanded of them to transcend these pre-given elements, which in principle they must do in order to be able to culturally assimilate "pre-givens," to the extent that they affect life-practice.

Ultimately, it is the permanence of the experience of contingency that bids us to go beyond everything achieved so far, beyond every orientation of self and world objectified in human practical life, toward the creative freedom of sense-making, itself based on pre-given elements of sense to which it must refer, if sense is to make sense. (Reference may, of course, be in a critical mode.) Historical sense has to fulfill the condition of being capable of genetic linkage, enabling subjective constructions to appeal to objective pre-given elements when interpreting the human past, and unfold in a significant way in relation to those elements and, at the same time, to the needs of the subjects determined by them. Sense has always been apprehended before, yet has to be formed, generated; indeed, it consists in a plausible integration of both apprehending and generating.

This notion also sheds light on the mode of mental activity in which sense occurs. Speaking of the "production" *(Stiftung)* of sense means overlooking the condition of the capacity for genetic linkage. The term "produced" is applicable to sense-conceptions of world and self only, if, and they these radically, and in principle, transcend all pre-given elements of the past. Such radical transcendence of pre-given elements of sense has rarely been observed in history; it is recommended, therefore, that the term "sense-production" *(Sinnstiftung)* be used with the utmost circumspection.[44] Even the histories of the origin of the great world religions, which we attribute to the "sense-production" of particular individuals (Buddha, Jesus, Muhammad), are anything but new, "unlinked" productions when viewed in the perspective of the self-understanding of their "producers."[45] At any rate, the term "sense-making" *(Sinnbildung)* describes much more aptly the complex relation between pre-given elements of sense *(Sinnvorgabe)* and sense-generation *(Sinnschöpfung)*, and from a historical perspective may well be considered to relate more closely to experience.

Two Perspectives: Reason and Negative Sense

Reason has a precarious status when viewed in relation to the sense-making achievements of historical consciousness. Too often it manifests itself as a claim of the human mind to the domination of the sense-qualities of historical awareness and interpretation, and to the orientation of human practical life according to concepts of the passage of time informed by the experience of the past. Moreover, the category of reason entails a cognitivistic conception of historical sense-making, thereby exposing the complex dimensioning of historical sense to the risk of constraints being imposed on it.

To simplify matters, one could say that the manifestation of historical sense in terms of content, forms, and functions unfolds into three areas of cultural practice, which can be described and analyzed as the cognitive, aesthetic, and political dimensions of historical culture.[46] Reason has to do with cognition, and in the cultural framework of modern societies it is characterized as a methodological rationality operative in the cognizant processing of experience. This very rationality constitutes the scientific character of historical cognition and ties historical sense-making to its established criteria. However, in the methodological approach of objectifying rationality, historical experience, having thus been artificially transformed into a source-based store of information, is likely to lose the very quality of sense in question. Reason would then be the quintessence of the mental operations that synthesize this sense-quality with the methodological operations of historical cognition.

The traditional hermeneutic orientation of the historical method accomplished just this, and was "rational" in the sense of having "apprehended" a pre-given element of sense that, after a critical check of sources and empirical verification, could be realized by way of an interpretation of source data aided by a sense-laden hermeneutic pattern of temporal processes. Inherent in these hermeneutic patterns was a categorical conceptualization of historical sense, which assumed a historical universe endowed with subject quality. Accordingly, the methodologically based reason underlying the critical analysis of sources was "rational" in interpretative terms.

What would happen to this claim of rationality, though, if it were no longer connected with this conceptualization of the sense of the historical?[47] To begin with, together with this conceptualization, the claim of knowledge to a dominant place in the entire mode of historical sense-making would have to be abandoned. Historical sense-making would be "rational" only if, after exposing it to the divergence and complex interplay of cognitive, aesthetic, and political aspects, it was left to the free play of whatever authoritative criteria and regulative factors there might be.

Relinquishing the supremacy of the cognitive is but one facet of a new rationality of historical sense-making. Another comes into view in connection with the question of the coherence of these three mega dimensions. What keeps them together? Here precisely lies the central achievement of the category of historical sense. A closer look at the regulative influences of the various dimensions reveals some common characteristics and perspectives that would certainly qualify as "rational": namely, universalistic criteria of methodological rationality, of aesthetic autonomy, and of political legitimacy. The verdict on their theoretical unfolding so far states that an abstract universalism based on the rationality principle and the quality of humanity has failed to ensure a full thematization of what has always been a central issue of the historical relation to the past: particularity (every identity is particular), divergence, pluralism, and diversity.

But such a critique need not imply an abandonment of the traditional criteria of reason pertaining to the universalistic principles of sense-making—on the contrary, this universalism could be developed further to become a sense-criterion of a reciprocal acknowledgement of difference, capable both of mustering an argumentative power based on experience, on methodological rules, and of being aesthetically distinct, especially where the unfolding of human subjectivity within the range of cultural difference is at stake along with the demonstration of that subjectivity's potential to engage in a mediating process about this difference with others.[48] This rational character of historical sense-making[49] has been effectively reflected in the methodological regulative factors operative in historical research, in the multifariousness of historiographic presentations, and in the various modes of reference relating to the political power struggle of the present.

Regardless of what this may imply in detail, one rational condition of historical sense-making must be mentioned, lest the whole enterprise of rehabilitating the category of sense in historical thinking be extinguished through historical experience itself, while the obsolete temporal context of "the one" history is secretly allowed to reenter through the back door together with a rehabilitated sense-category. Only when—spurred on by the horrific experiences of the last century—senselessness has been established and recorded as something that cannot be exceeded, nor ever be part of the cognitive, aesthetic, and political assumptions and claims of historical sense involved in dealing with the past—that is, only in the presence of senselessness—can sense plausibly be shown to be a fundamental category of history. The temporal context linking past, present, and future within the orientational horizon of human practical life needs to acquire counterfactual qualities, that is, a critical potency. Synchronously, in the complex operations of narrative sense-making, contingency can be manifested as both terror and chance. Sense remains uncertain, also and particularly in the operations of historical narrative.[50]

Terror and chance cannot be made to blend into the unambiguousness of a universe of sense that manifests itself on an inner-worldly plane, in other words, of history. Following this release of contingency by historical hermeneutics, the pragmatic orientation of historical sense-making is acquiring a new rational quality: Its corpus of assimilated experiences of the past offers to contemporary human life-practice a set of possibilities that demonstrate that the contingency inherent in the response of agents and sufferers to the conditions of their world and their selves is both a risk and likewise an opportunity. Considered from the perspective historical experience, a "universe of sense" is of merely a fragment, a splinter, a trace, but no longer a plastic manifestation anticipating a corresponding narrative representation. The historical basic trust *(Urvertrauen),* that is engraved in the traditional sense-category of the historical (and is ultimately religiously founded), in the sense-content of contingency, has given way to a more sensitive, both skeptical and optimistic awareness, in which sense is linked to the contingency of temporal developments in a new way whenever the experience of a particular time is interpreted and human practical life oriented by means of hermeneutically gained insight into the temporality of human existence. Similarly, historical narrative itself should generate sense in the form of countersense. Like modern art, it should thematize the absence of sense by referring to its necessity. This kind of *negative* sense, unlike the plain negation of sense—with the attendant emergence of all kinds of substitutes—would offer a thoroughly rational approach.

Translated from the German by Adelheid E. Baker

Notes

1. Gilles Deleuze, *Logik des Sinns* (Frankfurt/ M. 1999), 13.
2. Jean-Paul Sartre, "Antwort an Albert Camus," *Les temps modernes* (August 1952), quoted in Rossana Rossanda, "Sartre und die politische Praxis," in idem, *Über die Dialektik von Kontinuität und Bruch* (Frankfurt/ M. 1975), 155–196, quote on 157.
3. Jan Assmann, *Ägypten: Eine Sinngeschichte* (Munich 1996), 11.

4. I am grateful to Ingetraud Rüsen, Jan-Holger Kirsch, and Matthias Dornhege for helpful criticism and assistance with the writing of the manuscript. Special thanks to Christian Geulen for his help with the translation.

5. On this, cf. Günter Dux, "How meaning came into the world and what became of it," chap. 2 of this vol.

6. For logical reasons I prefer the term "the history," although it is scarcely used in English.

7. Cf. Jörn Rüsen, "History: Overview," in Neil J. Smelser and Paul B. Baltes, eds., *International Encyclopedia of the Social and Behavioral Sciences* (Amsterdam 2001), 6857–6864.

8. On this, cf. Günter Dux, *Die Logik der Weltbilder: Sinnstrukturen im Wandel der Geschichte* (Frankfurt/ M. 1982).

9. One objection that continues to be made to this term is that it is typically German, and that the question addressing it, as a key question of historical theory, smacks of provincialism and is thus hardly generalizable. In my opinion, this objection is unjustified. The English term "sense" may carry a related categorical meaning. In the *Journal of Educational Psychology* (1917), for example, an article asks, "What is the historic sense? How can it be developed?" (quoted in Samuel S. Wineburg, "Introduction: Out of Our Past and Into Our Future—The Psychological Study of Learning and Teaching History," *Educational Psychologist* 29.2 (1994): 57–60, quote on 57; (Original: J. C. Bell, "The historic Sense," *Journal of Educational Psychology* 5 (1917): 317–318). For an additional example see Gaea Leinhardt et al., "A Sense of History," *Educational Psychologist* 29.2 (1994): 79–88. Cf. also the following passages by Donald P. Spence: "the tendency to make sense of one's life to oneself and to one's fellows," "to make sense out of previously random happenings," "make what sense we can from emerging findings"; Donald P. Spence, *Narrative Truth and Historical Truth: Meaning and Interpretation in Psychoanalysis* (New York 1982), 21, 24.

10. On this, cf. Wilhelm Koelmel, "Typik und Atypik. Zum Geschichtsbild der kirchenpolitischen Publizistik (11.–14. Jahrhundert)," in Clemens Bauer and Laetitia Boehm, eds., *Speculum Historiale: Geschichte im Spiegel von Geschichtsschreibung und Geschichtsdeutung (Festschrift Johannes Spoerl)* (Munich 1965), 277–302.

11. ("Idea of humankind and culture.") Leopold von Ranke, *Über die Epochen der neueren Geschichte: Historisch-kritische Ausgabe* of vol. 2 *Aus Werk und Nachlaß*, ed. Theodor Schieder and Helmut Berding (Munich 1971), 80. Another example is Kant's famous article of 1784 "Idee zu einer allgemeinen Geschichte in weltbürgerlicher Absicht" (Idea for a Universal History with a Cosmopolitan Intent). Cf. Jörn Rüsen, "Following Kant: European idea for a universal history with an intercultural intent," *Groniek. Historisch Tijdschrift* 160 (2003): 359–368.

12. Leopold von Ranke, *Das Briefwerk,* ed. Walther Peter Fuchs (Hamburg 1949), 18.

13. At least Ranke, ibid., 518, does refer to a "Sinn jeder Epoche an und für sich selbst" (the sense of each epoch as such and in itself).

14. On this, cf. Jörn Stückrath, "The Meaning of History: A Modern Construction and Notion?," cap. 4 of this vol.

15. On this, see Jörn Rüsen, "Historische Methode und religiöser Sinn—Vorüberlegungen zu einer Dialektik der Rationalisierung des historischen Denkens in der Moderne," in idem, *Geschichte im Kulturprozeß* (Cologne 2002), 9–41.

16. Max Weber, "Die 'Objektivität' sozialwissenschaftlicher und sozialpolitischer Erkenntnis," in id., *Gesammelte Aufsätze zur Wissenschaftslehre,* 3rd ed. (Tübingen 1968), 146–214, quote on 214.

17. Ibid., 180.

18. See the copious literature, e.g., Jacques Le Goff, *Geschichte und Gedächtnis* (Frankfurt/ M. 1992); Jan Assmann, *Das kulturelle Gedächtnis: Schrift, Erinnerung und politische Identität in frühen Hochkulturen* (Munich 1992); Kristin Platt and Mihran Dabag, eds., *Generation und Gedächtnis: Erinnerungen und kollektive Identitäten* (Opladen 1995); Aleida Assmann, *Erinnerungsräume: Formen und Wandlungen des kulturellen Gedächtnisses* (Munich 1999).

19. Alfred Heuß has expressed this view already in his *Verlust der Geschichte* (Göttingen 1959).

20. To mention one symptom: In 1976 a book was published entitled *Vom Sinn der Geschichte.* Only one of the twelve contributions by notable historians addressed the subject—Theodor

Schieder's "Vom Sinn der Geschichte"—and in it the discussion is only about the interest in history: *Vom Sinn der Geschichte,* Otmar Franz, ed. (Stuttgart 1976).

21. Cf. Friedrich Jaeger, *Bürgerliche Modernisierungskrise und historische Sinnbildung: Kulturgeschichte bei Droysen, Burckhardt und Max Weber,* vol. 5 of Neidhard Bulst et. al, eds., *Bürgertum: Beiträge zur europäischen Gesellschaftsgeschichte* (Göttingen 1994).

22. Francis Fukuyama, "The Ende of History?" *The National Interest* 16 (1989): 3–35; id., *Das Ende der Geschichte: Wo stehen wir?* (Munich 1992); Friedrich Balke et al., eds., *Zeit der Ereignisse—Ende der Geschichte?* (Munich 1992); Martin Meyer, *Ende der Geschichte?* (Munich 1993); Perry Anderson, *Zum Ende der Geschichte* (Berlin 1993).

23. Lutz Niethammer, *Posthistoire: Has history become to an end?* (London 1992).

24. Samuel Huntington, *The Clash of Civilizations and the Remaking of World Order* (New York 1996).

25. An impressive testimony to the unbroken strength of a perfectly conceived category of sense of the historical: Hans Graeve, *Die offene Zukunft: Orientierung in der Gegenwart aus den Lehren der Geschichte* (Gräfelding 1996).

26. Cf. Heuß, *Verlust der Geschichte.*

27. In his *Ägypten,* Jan Assmann has elaborated this understanding of culture into the interpretational concept of a "Sinngeschichte" (history of sense), in which, sense is shown to be a cultural production, something human beings have always referred to in their lives. The same applies to any individual historiography, for historiography is part of the history of sense it writes. This leads Assmann to conclude with convincing clarity that historiography has a decidedly ethical function.

28. Jacob Burckhardt's historical thinking is organized along the same lines. Cf. Jörn Rüsen, *Konfigurationen des Historismus: Studien zur deutschen Wissenschaftskultur* (Frankfurt/ M. 1993), 276ff; Jaeger, *Bürgerliche Modernisierungskrise,* 86ff.

29. Friedrich Jaeger, "Der Kulturbegriff im Werk Max Webers und seine Bedeutung für eine moderne Kulturgeschichte," *Geschichte und Gesellschaft* 18 (1992): 371–393, following Max Weber, distinguishes the following functions of culture: motivation and utopia, course setting, disciplination, stabilization, recruitment and stratification, integration, exclusion, and sense (processing of contingency).

30. The relevant works of Schütz and Luckmann are central to the following considerations: Alfred Schütz, *Der sinnhafte Aufbau de sozialen Welt: Eine Einleitung in die verstehende Soziologie* (Frankfurt/ M. 1974 [1932]); Alfred Schütz and Thomas Luckmann, *Strukturen der Lebenswelt,* 2 vols. (Frankfurt/ M. 1979/1984); Peter L. Berger and Thomas Luckmann, *Die gesellschaftliche Konstruktion der Wirklichkeit: Eine Theorie der Wissenssoziologie* (Frankfurt/ M. 1979); Thomas Luckmann, *Lebenswelt und Gesellschaft* (Paderborn 1980).

31. Cf. Paul Ricoeur, *Zeit und Erzählung,* 3 vols. (Munich 1989), 188–91; Jörn Rüsen, *Zeit und Sinn: Strategien historischen Denkens* (Frankfurt/ M. 1990), esp. 153ff; id., "Historisches Erzählen," in idem, *Zerbrechende Zeit: Über den Sinn der Geschichte.* (Cologne 2001), 43–106.

32. I am grateful to Burkhard Gladigow for useful hints on how to understand this illustration.

33. "Civilization Comes to the New World," series *Non Sequitur* by Wiley, *Washington Post,* 10 Oct. 1994.

34. Rather the opposite of claiming or stating sense "defiantly" of which Oskar Köhler has accused me: Oskar Köhler, ed., *Vom Sinn und Unsinn in der Geschichte* (Freiburg 1985), 221.

35. On the act of taking possession of unknown territory as viewed by international law in early modern time, cf. Urs Bitterli, "Amerikanische Entdeckungsreisen im Wandel," in André Stoll, ed., *Sypharden, Morisken, Indianerinnen und ihresgleiche: Die andere Seite der hispanischen Kultur* (Bielefeld 1995), 161–176, esp. 168.

36. I am leaving aside the chronological inaccuracy that there were no Vikings when Stonehenge was erected.

37. I am using the sense-category's meaning of understandability. Odo Marquard distinguishes three meanings, ability to remember and enjoy *(Merk- und Genußfähigkeit),* understandability *(Verständlichkeit),* and the emphasis on what is rewarding *(die Emphase dessen, was sich lohnt).* Leaving aside his criticism of the excessiveness of the modern craving for sense, and in view of

our topic, the "sense of history," I would like to combine Marquard's second and third meanings because only this combination reflects the ordinary meaning of this text. The first meaning, too, is linked to history as "historical sense" and refers to the ability to perceive differences between times and interpret them historically. Odo Marquard, "Zur Diätetik der Sinnerwartung: Philosophische Bemerkungen," in Günter Eifler et al., eds., *Sinn im Wissenschaftshorizont (Mainzer Universitätsgespräche*, SS 1983) (Mainz 1984), 35–52.

38. Epression of the chronological objections to Hägar's culture critique would be apropos at this juncture.

39. On this, cf. Klaus E. Müller, "Identität und Geschichte: Widerspruch oder Komplementarität? Ein ethnologischer Beitrag," *Paideuma* 38 (1992): 17–29, esp. 23.

40. On this, see Jörn Rüsen, "Historische Sinnbildung durch Erzählen: Eine Argumentationsskizze zum narrativistischen Paradigma der Geschichtswissenschaft und der Geschichtsdidaktik im Blick auf nicht-narrative Faktoren," *Internationale Schulbuchforschung* 18 (1996): 501–543.

41. I would like to refer this question to Jan Assmann's concept of *Sinngeschichte* where sense is characterized as a category of fictionality. To Assmann, sense is a "fiction of coherence" *(Kohärenzfiktion),* a mere projection and a "fiction" close to a lie (p. 19). Accordingly, historiography, having to rely on sense *(Sinnangewiesenheit),* is characterized by "fictiveness" *(Fiktivität)* (p. 20). What does this mean? Surely no more than that a given infused with sense has a different ontological status than a given that is real. But in simple terms, fictionality means one thing above all else: not given or confirmed by experience, something beyond experience, even counterfactual (cf. I. Bandau, "Fiktion," in Joachim Ritter, ed., *Historisches Wörterbuch der Philosophie,* vol. 2 (Basel 1972), cols. 951–954).

This can hardly be said of the subject matter of historiography, especially not when it is about "sense." Assmann is quite clear when he says about the empirical status of sense: "Even experiences themselves are ... structured in a semantically organized way" (p. 20). But then, what is fictionality? Apparently it is a counterconcept of another mode of thought—that, I assume, of a positivistically conceived empirism. The use of the category of fictionality makes sense only if something other than the real, bodily-sensuous human world, which—as Assman has convincingly demonstrated—is imbued with, and constituted by, sense, is assumed to be real and constituted by experience. "The coherence endowing our life with structure and identity is partly imposed on us from outside, or develops eventually to implicate us" (p. 23). "The light in which we see things is always derived from the memory of experience" (p. 24). Likewise, the moral duty of a historiographic treatment of the cultural sense-production of the past could hardly be shown to be plausible, if it were not for the reality of sense and the weight of experience such a duty carries in an individual world that is made accessible through historical experience.

On the other hand, the term fictionality may simply point to the fact that sense is always precarious, ambivalent, refracted, one might even say objectively despairing, so that, as an orienting element, it can never fully merge with, or become integrated into, any true cultural creations. Put differently: it will forever make reality seem refracted, endangered, threatening, so that human individuals can never cease reflectively to be aware of the sense-dimensions of their worlds. At any rate, the category of fictionality tends more to prevent insight into the organization of historical experience than it does to provide enlightenment on the semantic procedures of the human mind. Robbed of the epistemological veil of fictionality, sense acquires the very ambivalence, and with it the empirical status, that inspires humanities-based thinking as a continuation of the impact of sense on the human life-world by other means.

42. On this, cf. the remark by Herta Nagl-Docekal that "das Verhältnis des Geschichtsdenkens zur Vergangenheit nicht demjenigen des Konstrukteurs zu seinen beliebig kombinierbaren Bausteinen entspricht" (the relation of historical thought to the past does not correspond to that of the constructor to his or her building blocks that can be freely arranged) ("Ist Geschichtsphilosophie heute noch möglich?," in Nagl-Docekal, ed., *Der Sinn des Historischen: Geschichtsphilosophische Debatten* [Frankfurt/ M. 1996], 7–63, quote on 25).

43. On this, cf. David Carr, "The Reality of History," chap. 7 of this vol.; idem, "Narrative and the Real World: An Argument for Continuity," *History and Theory* 25 (1986): 117–131; idem,

"Phenomenology and historical knowledge," in Ernst Wolfgang Orth and Chan-Fai Cheung, eds., *Phenomenology of interculturality and life-world* (Phänomenologische Forschungen, Sonderband) (Freiburg 1998), 112–130; Paul Ricoeur, "Geschichte und Rhetorik," in *Der Sinn des Historischen*, 107–125.

44. I believe it would be exaggerating, even intellectually dishonest, to lump the theorists of history whose subject is historical sense and who reflect on the latter as a condition of scientific knowledge, together with those professors—already castigated by Max Weber—who want to be prophets and, by calling them "C-4 shamans," have exposed them to intellectual derision.

45. Ludwig Ammann has presented a much more differentiated interpretation of Muhammad: *Die Geburt des Islam: Historische Innovation durch Offenbarung* (Essener kulturwissenschaftliche Vorträge, vol. 12) (Göttingen 2001).

46. On this, see Jörn Rüsen, "Was ist Geschichtskultur? Überlegungen zu einer neuen Art, über Geschichte nachzudenken," in idem, *Historische Orientierung: Über die Arbeit des Geschichtsbewußtseins, sich in der Zeit zurechtzufinden* (Cologne 1994), 211–234.

47. Generally on the subject of reason: Wolfgang Welsch, *Vernunft: Die zeitgenössische Vernunftkritik und das Konzept der transversalen Vernunft* (Frankfurt/ M. 1996).

48. On this, see Jörn Rüsen, "Vom Umgang mit den Anderen—zum Stand der Menschenrechte heute," *Internationale Schulbuchforschung* 15 (1993): 167–178; Charles Taylor, *Multikulturalismus und die Politik der Anerkennung* (Frankfurt/ M. 1993).

49. In my *Grundzüge einer Historik* I have tried to present a systematic outline focusing mostly on the cognitive side of historical sense-making: Vol. 1: *Historische Vernunft: Die Grundlagen der Geschichtswissenschaft* (Göttingen 1983); Vol. 2: *Rekonstruktion der Vergangenheit: Die Prinzipien der historischen Forschung* (Göttingen 1986); Vol. 3: *Lebendige Geschichte: Formen und Funktionen des historischen Wissens* (Göttingen 1989). Cf. the critiques by Volker Steenblock of the concept of reason developed here, "Historische Vernunft—Geschichte als Wissenschaft und als orientierende Sinnbildung. Zum Abschluß von Jörn Rüsens dreibändiger 'Historik,'" *Dilthey-Jahrbuch für Philosophie und Geschichte der Geisteswissenschaften* 8 (1992/93): 367–380, and by Allan Megill, "Jörn Rüsens's Theory between Modernism und Rhetoric of Inquiry," *History and Theory* 33 (1994): 39–60.

50. Horst Dieter Rauh gives expression to this by presenting the history of the sense-category by means of the labyrinth metaphor, insisting that the labyrinth is not a "mere metaphor of history," but its "real symbol" *(Realsymbol)*. Horst Dieter Rauh, *Im Labyrinth der Geschichte: Die Sinnfrage von der Aufklärung zu Nietzsche* (Munich 1990), here p. 10.

CHAPTER 4

"The Meaning of History"
A Modern Construction and Notion?

JÖRN STÜCKRATH

A Historicolinguistic Exploration

It is remarkable that the expression "meaning *(Sinn)* of history," which rapidly came into fashion in the twentieth century, can barely be traced back in the German language further than the mid nineteenth century. The search for the origin of the expression—starting from Joseph Bernhart to Karl Heussi, Nikolaus Berdjajew, Heinrich Rickert, Max Nordau, Georg Simmel, Wilhelm Dilthey, and Ernst Bernheim—so far only goes back to Hermann Lotze.[1] In the third volume (1864) of his *Mikrokosmos: Ideen zur Naturgeschichte und Geschichte der Menschheit—Versuch einer Anthropologie,* which was informed by Herder's *Ideen zur Philosophie der Geschichte der Menschheit,* Lotze deals with the subject of "history." The volume is divided into five chapters, the second of which is entitled "The Meaning *(Sinn)* of History." In other words, the expression "meaning *(Sinn)* of history," still rather unusual in the middle of the nineteenth century, was given a prominent place as a chapter heading in the *Mikrokosmos.*[2] This chapter is demonstrably the source from which Bernheim, Dilthey, Simmel, and Nordau draw the expression. Any attempt to trace the expression back beyond Lotze, either in the history of the philosophy of history or in the German language, fails. Ludwig Feuerbach in his *Wesen des Christentums* (1841) does use the expression "meaning *(Sinn)* of history"[3]; unlike Lotze, however, he does not use the new expression repeatedly or as a fundamental concept of the philosophy of history.

When Hegel, in the *Vorlesungen über die Philosophie der Geschichte,* explains: "The only thought philosophy introduces is the simple thought of Reason, the

---

Notes for this section begin on page 85.

thought that Reason rules the world, that therefore world history was rational. This conviction and insight is a presupposition with regard to history as such …" one would think that he is also talking about the "meaning *(Sinn)* of (in) history." This is not the case, however. Hegel's central concepts in the philosophy of history are—in keeping with the tradition of the philosophy of the Enlightenment—"design" and "purpose" or "pure last purpose of history."[4] The philosophical mind, as Schiller puts it in his academic inaugural speech (1789), takes "this harmony out of itself and uproots it into the order of things, i.e. it puts a rational purpose into the course of the world and a teleological principle into world history"; the thought sounds modern and reminds one of "*Sinn*-interpretation" and "*Sinn*-creation," but Schiller does not know the expression "meaning *(Sinn)* of history" either.[5] And when Kant, who Schiller draws on, skeptically reasons about people in his essay *"Idee zu einer allgemeinen Geschichte in weltbürgerlicher Absicht"* (1784), the phrase *"Sinn oder Widersinn der Geschichte"* seems to be within one's grasp: "One cannot help but feel a certain indignation when one sees their activities set up on the big world stage; when, apart from the occasional wisdom in individual cases, one largely finds foolishness, childish vanity, often childish malice and destructive frenzy…. There is no other clarification for the philosopher, given that he cannot presuppose in man and his activities on the whole a rational intention, except in the attempt to locate an intention of nature in this absurd course of humanity; beings without a plan of their own may thereby nevertheless have a history according to a particular plan of nature." The common expressions "meaning *(Sinn)* of history" or "meaning *(Sinn)* of life/existence/the world," however, cannot be found in Kant's works. Kant, like Hegel some time later, talks about "nature's hidden plan" and its "purpose."[6]

The expression "meaning *(Sinn)* of history" does not appear in the vocabulary of Lessing, Herder, or Humboldt; and even Schopenhauer, Marx, Droysen, and Burckhardt do not use it.[7] Even after Lotze's *Mikrokosmos* it takes another few decades for the expression "meaning *(Sinn)* of history" to become established. Even the comprehensive article on the word *"Sinn"* in the *Grimmsches Wörterbuch* (vol. 16; 1905) does not mention the expression "meaning *(Sinn)* of history," which, like "meaning *(Sinn)* of life," rapidly became a vogue-word during and after the two world wars.[8] The German phrase "meaning *(Sinn)* of history," then, originates in the linguistic usage and—as remains to be shown—the conceptual world of the second half of the nineteenth century. Neither the phrase, nor its equivalents in other languages—"sensus," "le sens," "meaning" (in connection with "history/life etc.," otherwise "sense")—are common in earlier European historical thought.[9] *"Sinn"* as word and idea has not come into history via Greek or Roman classical antiquity,[10] nor via the Christian middle ages or the Enlightenment. "Meaning *(Sinn)* of history" is linguistically and notionally a modern coinage.

The "Sinn"-Legend

The suggestion that the expression "meaning *(Sinn)* of history" is less than 150 years old is particularly surprising if one consults more recent studies on the history of European history of philosophy. Historians of philosophy from the most diverse backgrounds use the expression "meaning *(Sinn)* of history" to portray European historical thought from Augustine to Burckhardt without mentioning that the expression (and its equivalents in other languages) originates from their own description of it.

Karl Löwith, for example, asks: "Who would nowadays still dare to prove the meaning *(Sinn)* of history through the fulfillment of prophecies 'precisely to the hour'? For Bossuet as well as for Augustine, this was the most convincing of all possible proofs...." Clearly, Löwith realized that the term *"Sinn"* cannot straightforwardly be applied to the history of the philosophy of history, as on various occasions he puts it in quotation marks. The same is true for Rickert. Löwith, however, does not comment on his use of quote marks, nor does he apply them consistently. Of Burckhardt, who himself never talked about the "meaning *(Sinn)* of history," Löwith remarks: "Burckhardt finally rejected the theological, philosophical and socialist interpretations of history and thereby reduced the meaning of history to a mere continuity—without beginning, progress or end. He had to over-emphasise this mere continuity, as it was the meagre remainder of a fuller endowment of meaning. But nevertheless, for him, as well as for Dilthey, Troeltsch and Croce, the belief in history was the 'last religion.'"[11]

Golo Mann creates the impression that the term *"Sinn"* was a category that Schiller, Kant, Hegel, and Burckhardt employed to think about the aim and purpose of history. According to Mann, Hegel, Schiller, and Kant were "searching" for the "meaning *(Sinn)* of history." This can be viewed as the start of the modernistic conception of the history of philosophy as the search for meaning. These extracts, from a contribution by Golo Mann on the subject of "meaning *(Sinn)* of history," read in context: "Yet another one, a real historian, a philosophical observer only incidentally, Jacob Burckhardt, despaired at the meaning of history, just like Hegel, Schiller and Kant sought for it, and returned to the view of antiquity: The doings of mankind will always be as they were previously, they move up and down, but do not bring anything fundamentally new, nor do they contain an inherent salvation."[12] Mann's outline of the history of the philosophy of history from Plato to Hegel culminates in a criticism of the Marxist totalitarian demand for recognition.

The philosophers of history in East Germany were, of course, of a different opinion; however they also, use the term *"Sinn"* and, like Löwith and Golo Mann, do not always distinguish between its use in the meta- and object language. Manfred Buhr, in the *Philosophisches Wörterbuch,* writes: "To enquire after the meaning of history means to investigate whether there is a goal in historical development and in the change of society. The theorists of the different classes answer the question in different ways, depending on historical position and task and the historical conditions of their class. The bourgeoisie, in the period of its ascendancy, advocates the idea of progress as a synthesis of correct insight into the elements of the developing society and optimistic speculation.... For Herder, meaning and goal of history is the realisation of humanity, for Lessing, the education of mankind for the realisation of world reason, for Kant, the spread of the rule of moral freedom and for Hegel, the evolution of the Spirit to the awareness of freedom...."[13]

More recent enquiries have increasingly tended to describing the history of literature and philosophy using the term *"Sinn."* From this point of view, the philosophy of history of the Enlightenment, which itself did not know the term, is said to have oscillated between *"Sinn-*crisis" and *"Sinn-*creation." It seems almost unthinkable nowadays to describe the history of the philosophy of history other than by means of the term *"Sinn."* Although Horst Dieter Rau in his book *Sinnfrage von der Aufklärung zu Nietzsche* emphasizes the historicity of the term *"Sinn,"* his use of the word does not distinguish between object and meta-language: "Because the traditional theological system of interpretation loses its persuasiveness, the rational researcher will have to compensate with his own explanatory model; for this very reason he will have to become encyclopaedic, keep an eye on the 'whole'. The demands of reason point to a will for *Sinn-*creation: out of it arises genuine philosophy of history ... in the progress of mankind Condorcet saw an objectifiable *Sinn* confirmation, a measurable indicator of happiness.... The arising *Sinn* crisis in the eighteenth century reveals history as being in need of interpretation—as a labyrinth created by the daedal human being. The question for *"Sinn"* has its historical origin and place in the age of reason: It compensates for the crisis by engaging in the philosophy of history."[14]

The *"Sinn"* legend has a charming punch line. The conceptual critic Reinhart Koselleck, who identified the word "history" as a modern collective singular originating from the last third of the eighteenth century, writes of its emergence: "The epic unity, determined by beginning and end, was increasingly demanded of the story teller.... And so the demands of history and poetry cross, one influencing the other, in order to bring to light the immanent meaning *(Sinn)* of 'history.'"[15] The historicophilosophical collective singular *"Sinn,"* which has its origin in the second half of the nineteenth century, would have, in the context of the eighteenth century—in connection with "history"—merited the critical inverted commas even more than its older sister, "history."

The conceptual obliviousness of philosophy and the science of history with respect to the phrase "meaning *(Sinn)* of history" is astonishing. The contributors to the *Historisches Wörterbuch der Philosophie* do not explicitly address the problem of *Sinn* in the articles "History" *(Geschichte)* and "Philosophy of History" *(Geschichtsphilosophie);* nor do the editors give this central notion in the philosophy of history, "meaning *(Sinn)* of history," a separate entry.[16] Ever since Lotze, philosophers of history have often said that we cannot understand the "meaning *(Sinn)* of history." Interestingly, we do not even understand what it is possible to understand, namely, the historicity of the expression and notion "meaning *(Sinn)* of history." Many authors evidently take it for granted that the familiar term *"Sinn"* in the philosophy of history should have an equivalent within the history of the philosophy of history, so that the question of its origin never even arises. Some have even deliberately pushed the question to one side since talking about the "meaning *(Sinn)* of history" became common practice in textbooks on the philosophy of history, like the one by Georg Mehlis. In a speech given in 1930, Karl Heussi asks and answers the following question: "What does one mean when one talks about the 'meaning *(Sinn)* of history'? ... A few examples will demonstrate it right away. It will be irrelevant for the question in point whether these thinkers actually *used* the expression *"Sinn"* or any equivalent." Following this maxim, Heussi interprets Kant's, Herder's, Hegel's, and Marx's philosophy and theory of history as an answer to the search for the "meaning *(Sinn)* of history."[17]

The Ambiguity of the Term "Sinn"

As we have seen, the neologism "meaning *(Sinn)* of history" replaces the older historicometaphysical expressions from the traditions of the Enlightenment and Idealism, namely "plan" and "purpose." "Meaning *(Sinn)* of history," however, does not integrate very well with this meaning *(Bedeutung)*. The Marxist Manfred Buhr, for example, avoids the theological and teleological connotations of "plan" and "purpose" by equating the question of the "meaning *(Sinn)* of history" with the question of the "goal" of its development. Buhr must have felt, however, that *"Sinn"* does not just mean "goal," for he also talks about the "meaning *(Sinn) and* goal of history." The direction to take in search of further meanings of *"Sinn"* is indicated in Löwith. The question of the "meaning *(Sinn)* of history" is also aimed at the problem of whether and how the costs of history—devastation and destruction, misfortune and suffering—can be justified theologically or philosophically. The meaning of the expression "meaning *(Sinn)* of history," however, is not exhausted in the "plan," "purpose," "goal," "cost/benefit ratio" spectrum.

The philosopher and conceptual historian Alwin Diemer ends his résumé on the philosophy of history with the sentence: "All these enquiries culminate in the question for the meaning *(Sinn)* of history." He goes on to say: "There are not many concepts that are as ambiguous as the term *"Sinn,"* which results in the emergence of the most diverse views."[18] Diemer refers to Rudolf Lauth, who worked out sixteen different meanings of *"Sinn"* using evidence from comparative linguistics:[19]

A. Awareness or object awareness: "It never came into my *Sinn*."*
B. Intentional awareness: "I did not have my *Sinn* directed toward that."
C. Receptiveness, understanding (instinct, affection): "I have no *Sinn* for music." Engl. *moral sense,* older Fr. *sens* (= ability to make moral judgements).
D. Ability to see or make connections: "My poor *Sinn* is broken up" (Goethe, Faust I).
E. Specific sensory perception: "The ear is a *Sinn* organ." Fr. *le sens,* Lat. *sensus.*
F. Ability to grasp inner states and events: "The inner *Sinn*." Fr. *le sens intérieur,* Lat. *sensus internus,* Engl. *inner sense.*
G. Ability to combine the specific outer sensory perceptions: "Collective *Sinn*."
H. Meaning *(Bedeutung)*: "The *Sinn* of this word. The *Sinn* of this sign." Fr. *signification, acceptation.*
I. Intention, the intended: "He has something in his *Sinn* that I would like to find out about." Fr. *intention.*
J. Opinion, conviction: "I am of a different *Sinn* in these matters." Fr. *sentiment.*
K. Purpose, value, constituent direction towards a goal: "What *Sinn* do your actions have here? What *Sinn* does this arrangement have here? What happens here is *Sinn*-less." Fr. *dessin.*
L. Direction (side): "In the *Sinn* of the clock-hand." Fr. *sens.*
M. Prudence (memory): "He is off his *Sinn*. He is not entirely with *Sinn*."
N. Disposition, imagination: "My distraught *Sinn* burrows back and forth between doubts" (Mörike).
O. Uncontradicting (order, integration): "This sentence is *Sinn*-less. It is a *Sinn*-less notion. What you are saying is *Sinn*-less."
P. Harmony.

* Translator's note: The example sentences have been translated as literally as possible in order to convey the various senses of the German word *"Sinn."*

It would be natural to assume that the expression "meaning *(Sinn)* of history" delimits the spectrum of the meaning of *"Sinn."* This is only true to a certain degree, however. It is therefore to be expected that the word *"Sinn"* in the discourse of the philosophy of history variously assumes all the listed meanings. Odo Marquard attempted to reduce the diversity of the meaning of *"Sinn"* to three basic concepts: (a) *"Sinn"* relating to perception: "he who can notice," has *"Sinn,"* (b) *"Sinn"* relating to understanding: that which is understandable" has *"Sinn"* and (c) *"Sinn"* relating to the emphatic: "that which is worthwhile" has *"Sinn"* (is important, fulfils you, makes you content and happy, lets you not despair, emphatically—as its value and purpose—related to the human life, history, the world), if necessary absolutely."[20] The division into three parts is helpful; it reduces, however, the range of subconcepts that make sense with respect to history. In order to define the spectrum of meaning of "meaning *(Sinn)* of history" historicogenetically more precisely and make it more systematic, I would like to set up a division, for heuristic purposes, that partly summarizes, partly specifies, and partly expands Lauth's classification:

I. Psychological *Sinn*
(*Sinn* = subjective ability; A, B, C, D, E, F, G, M, N)

II. Intentional *Sinn*
(*Sinn* = Intention, the intended; I)

III. Hermeneutic-rhetorical *Sinn*
(*Sinn* = meaning of a text. Note the three dimensions: meaning put into the text by the author; meaning contained within the text; meaning as understood by the reader; H)

IV. Structural *Sinn*
(*Sinn* = order; wholeness/completeness; harmony; O, P)

V. Teleological *Sinn*
(*Sinn* = the qualities a rational subject or object possesses; purpose, value, constituent direction towards a goal, direction, side; K, L)

Closely related to the teleological term *Sinn* are two components that Lauth does not mention:

VI. Economical-energetic *Sinn*
(*Sinn* = purposefulness, "economy"; expenditure/result ratio)

VII. Ethical meaning *Sinn*
(*Sinn* = "immanent justice," the principle that the reward for one's own labor benefits oneself)

The teleological *Sinn* has one further component:

VIII. Functional *Sinn*
(*Sinn* = qualities that some thing has for human beings; purpose, value; K)

"*Sinn*" in all these general senses can be combined with "history." Whether and how the different subconcepts can be connected remains unclear. Alwin Diemer comes up with the following pessimistic conclusion: "All the problems mentioned however, have one fundamental difficulty in common: a clarification of what is meant by *"Sinn."* It could be said that *"Sinn"* can neither be characterized nor defined; for such attempts presuppose *it* as well as its notion."[21] Whether such pessimism regarding the word *"Sinn"* is justified remains to be seen.

The Historicolinguistic Problem:
The Origin of the Modern Term "Sinn"

The idea that the expression "meaning *(Sinn)* of history" did not emerge before the nineteenth century becomes even more plausible if one considers etymology. Until the middle of the nineteenth century *"Sinn"* had two main senses, neither of which naturally links up with "history."[22]

One of the main meanings is the psychological. As Lauth has shown, it has a number of different sub-meanings: "meaning" *(Sinn)* is awareness, receptivity, etc. The expression "historical sense *(Sinn)*" also belongs to the psychological concept of "meaning" *(Sinn)* (analogous to "aesthetic sense *(Sinn)*" or "sense *(Sinn)* of beauty") that Wilhelm von Humboldt demands of the historian and Nietzsche critically evaluates in his work "Vom Nutzen und Nachteil der Historie für das Leben."[23] From the "historical sense *(Sinn)*" as a perceptual faculty, as a faculty of receptivity, interest, and understanding, there is no bridge to the modern expression "meaning *(Sinn)* of history" (in the sense of "purpose," "goal," "value" of history).

If the expression "meaning *(Sinn)* of history" had been derived from the psychological aspect then that would presuppose the idea that history has an immanent mental faculty (intentional consciousness, spirit, reason, the ability to create coherence). This idea is implicit in Idealism and in the theology and philosophy of history of the Enlightenment, i.e., God the Creator is present, in history or the world spirit, as realizing himself in history. But still, the idea that a subject equipped with a psychological faculty is at work in history did not lead to the emergence of the expression "meaning *(Sinn)* of history" in Goethe's times.

The other basic meaning of *"Sinn"* is the hermeneutic one (*Sinn* is the meaning of a word, a sentence, a speech; multiple senses of a text). The supposition that the expression "meaning *(Sinn)* of history" developed from the hermeneutic aspect requires that the genitival attribute "history" be understood linguistically. And indeed, the idea that the world is a book, a text, or a sign system is very old.[24] Kant, in his work *Über das Mißlingen aller philosophischen Versuche in der Theodicee,* talked about practical reason, through which God "gives meaning *(Sinn)* to the letter of his creation."[25] This metaphor was evidently not strong enough, however, to coin and establish the expression "meaning *(Sinn)* of history." And although the hermeneutic sense of *"Sinn"* does allow connections to be drawn to "goal," "purpose," and "value," it does not give rise to them necessarily.

Today, "meaning *(Sinn)* of history" also refers to a third basic sense of *"Sinn"* (that of purpose, goal, value, purposefulness), which emerges much later in philosophical usage. *"Sinn"* then refers to objects outside language: "meaning *(Sinn)* of existence," "meaning *(Sinn)* of life," "meaning *(Sinn)* of the world." Wilhelm Traugott Krug, an authority on the Enlightenment and Idealism, in his book *Allgemeines Handwörterbuch der philosophischen Wissenschaften*[26] quotes under *"Sinn"* only the psychological and hermeneutic senses: *"Sinn"* is the ability to imagine something given as a consequence of a stimulus (affection of the soul).... For *"Sinn"* of a word, a speech, a text, see *"Bedeutung"* (meaning)." The words "purpose" and "value," which are related in today's usage, Krug treats accordingly, namely without reference to *"Sinn."*

When, where, and why did the expression "meaning *(Sinn)* of history" emerge? Several hypotheses suggest themselves.

One would think that "meaning *(Sinn)* of history" simply activates the original etymology of *"Sinn,"* namely "direction." Hans Urs von Balthasar refers to this meaning when he writes: "Only in the shape of biblical salvation-history did human history obtain a direction and a chronologically comprehensible *'Sinn'* (Sinn: OHG sinnan: travel, walk; Lat. sentire: to follow a track; 'clockwise' [Im Sinn des Uhrzeigers] French 'sens' as direction). That is how it was and remained not only until Otto von Freising, but also until Bossuet...." Furthermore, "The historical direction of the Christian salvation" expanded during the Enlightenment "as if automatically, to a general natural direction of history as 'education of mankind' or simply as secular belief in progress."[27] The question remains, through: Why does the philosophy of history, in the eighteenth century and to some degree also in the nineteenth century, not talk about the "meaning *(Sinn)* of history" despite the many metaphors for progress?

"Meaning *(Sinn)* of history," one could suppose, is made possible through the predominant idea of the Enlightenment of God as the creator of history. Equating history with a divine novel (Leibnitz) or theater could have engendered the term *"Sinn"* and rendered its use possible in connection with history. Alexander Demandt has shown how widespread the idea of a divine theater was: "Each in their own way, Kant, Schelling and Hegel tried to illustrate the meaning *(Sinn)* of history with the help of the idea of a world theatre. For this purpose they divided human beings into three functions, the acting politician as actor, the designing God as author of the play and the philosophical spectator who, from his seat in the box, sees through the coherence of the great drama. For the players, but not for the real actors, this coherence remains concealed."[28] But this metaphor, through frequently used, did not give rise to the expression "meaning *(Sinn)* of history," let alone lead to its establishment.

The phrase "meaning *(Sinn)* of history" could have originated in the evolutionary-teleological idea that God or a wise nature created the history of mankind, which strives for a goal; in it, a higher value gets realized. Indeed, Hegel uses the term *"Sinn"*—in a prominent place at that, namely the chapter on the course of world history—in the context of the theory of history.[29] There, Hegel connects the perfectibility principle with the ideas "purpose and goal" via the concept of development: "The principle of development further implies that there is an underlying inner purpose, an implicit presupposition that brings itself into existence. This formal purpose is essentially Spirit, which has world history as its setting, property and field of realization.... What the Spirit wants is to attain the concept of itself; but it conceals it from itself, it is proud and full of joy in this self-estrangement."

The passage where Hegel uses the term *"Sinn"* follows: "The process of development is thus not the harmless and peaceful mere emergence, as it is with the development of organic life, but rather hard and reluctant labor against itself; and furthermore, it is not merely the formal self-development in general, but the fulfillment of an aim with a specific content. We have stated this aim at the outset; it is Spirit, in conformity with its essence—the concept of freedom. This is the fundamental object and thus the guiding principle of development; it is this principle that gives the historical development its sense and meaning (just as Rome was the object in Roman history and thus the guiding principle in the considerations of events). And vice versa, the events emerge from the object and only make sense in relation to it, as their content is in it."

This section is significant, as Hegel seems to anticipate the modern ambiguous term *"Sinn."* The problem is that he does not later take the term up again, in particular not in connection with "history" or "historical development," so that the phrase "meaning (*Sinn*) of history" falls on a barren ground. In his lectures on the philosophy of history Hegel talks about "purpose" and "final purpose" when he means the goal, the purpose and the value of history; perhaps it is therefore no coincidence that amongst Hegelians on the left and right alike, no reference can be found to the expression "meaning *(Sinn)* of history."[30]

One could conclude that the expression "meaning *(Sinn)* of history" is derived from the melancholy-pessimistic awareness and experience that history, as Kant put it, follows an "absurd path" and that people, according to Schopenhauer, are driven along by a "senseless mania." But even *ex negativo* the term *"Sinn"* does not develop. Schopenhauer holds on to the term "purpose" and talks about the "value" of life, when we, ever since Nietzsche, are used to talking about *"Sinn."*[31] When considering the human race, Schopenhauer writes: "But the final purpose of Everything, what is it? To keep alive, for a short while, ephemeral and tormented individuals, in the best case in tolerable poverty and comparative painlessness, which is immediately followed by boredom; and furthermore, the reproduction of the race and its activities. Given this evident discrepancy between effort and reward the will to live seems to us, from this point of view, taken objectively, as foolishness, or subjectively, as a delusion, which is seized by every living being in order to work towards something, with supreme effort, that has no value."[32]

Even around Georg Büchner's historic-pessimistic fatalism the expression "meaning *(Sinn)* of history" does not evolve; and Jacob Burckhardt, who talks about "happiness and unhappiness in world history," the "rather illusory purpose of world history," and the power of "evil" over the "good," does not elaborate the meaning of world history.[33]

Certain, as yet not mentioned, traditions of thought and a specific interest were therefore required in order to tie together the terms *"Sinn"* and "history."

Lotze's Idea of "Sinn" and "Meaning (Sinn) of History"

There are many reasons, in my opinion, for assuming, as postulated at the outset, that it was Herman Lotze who introduced the expression "meaning *(Sinn)* of history" into the philosophical discourse. The question of whether this is the true origin of the expression can be bypassed for now. For the purposes of the course of the investigation it will be enough to establish that Lotze was one of the first to use the new expression, and that such diverse thinkers as Bernheim, Dilthey, Simmel, Rickert, and Nordau depend on Lotze when they write about the "meaning *(Sinn)* of history."

Lotze does not use the neologism "meaning *(Sinn)* of history" exclusively to refer to its psychological aspect, but rather connects it with the historicometaphysical concepts of the Enlightenment and Idealism, "plan" and "purpose." Lotze then bridges the gap to the modern term *"Sinn"* and its meaning components "goal," "purpose," and "value." In addition, Lotze's understanding of *"Sinn"* also implies the economic-energetic and ethical meaning components. Even this early mention of "meaning *(Sinn)* of history" refers to a usage that is replete with the manifoldness of meaning of today's word *"Sinn."*

In the introduction to the chapter "Meaning *(Sinn)* of History," Lotze asks a question that can serve as the first definition of the *"Sinn"* question in the philosophy of history: "And this inner spiritual history of the human race, what is its meaning? What are the laws of its course, or the plan that ties together the colorful richness of its appearances to form a rational unity?"[34]

In order to understand this question one needs to know that Lotze distinguishes between two different views of history: a (naturalistic) view that rejects the quest for meaning because, in this view, history is nothing but an "event of nature ... one has to yield to, an event that does not allow for the question of right and purpose;" and a teleological view that "believes in providence, which will lead this tangle of destinies to a higher good."

Lotze's inquiries into history unite almost all of the above senses of "Sinn":

I. the psychological *"Sinn"*: "inner, spiritual history";
II. the intentional: "plan," "providence" (reminiscent of a divine creator);
III. the hermeneutic: "meaning *(Bedeutung)*" of the "inner spiritual history"; the deciphering of the plan that ties together the richness of its appearances into a "rational unity";
IV. the structural: "rational unity"; nomological "law";

V. the teleological: to enquire after the "purpose" of the course of events; "higher good"; the German expression "laws of its course of events" further contains "direction";

VII. the ethical: to enquire after the "right" of the events;

VIII. the functional: it is man who enquires after the events' "right and purpose."

Is there an idea that allows this spectrum of meaning to be thought of as *one* and that explains its diversity from one point? Following Hegel, Lotze expresses his view of the "appearances" (the "events" and "creatures") and their knowledge in the chapter on *"Sinn,"* which hints at a solution to our problem: "With respect to all appearances we feel we have two tasks, one of explicating little by little the possibility and form of its emergence, and the other of deciphering the rational meaning *(Bedeutung)* that justifies its Being with all its fundamental underlying presuppositions. The world view that had produced the aforementioned view of history does not hide the conviction that the *"Sinn"* or idea that each event or creature is destined to realize forms its true essence and that the search for this innermost point of life is the highest task of all investigation, including the historical" (32).

In summary: From a very early point in Lotze's writings, *"Sinn"* means something like "rational meaning," which justifies "the existence of an appearance" (of a being, for example). As a Leibnitzian, Lotze was convinced early on that each appearance "has a rational meaning content."[35] How does one recognize that an appearance has a "rational meaning content"? Several qualities are conceivable, all of which indicate that an appearance has to be seen as rational and as having meaning *(Bedeutung)*. The appearance has a consciousness, intentionality; it can understand and create contexts; it is the work of a designing creator; it forms a whole; it is orderly and without contradiction; it has a law; it is aimed towards a goal; it pursues a purpose; it realizes values; it displays rationality concerning the cost and result ratio; it is internally consistent; it appears meaningful to the observer. In a word, all the components of *"Sinn"* listed above refer to qualities that a "rational appearance" can exhibit if it *has* a "rational meaning-content." The traits that Lauth explicated as subconcepts of *"Sinn"* are recognizable as components of the idea of the "rational meaning-content" of an appearance. *"Sinn"* unites all these qualities; in it all these qualities are integrated.

Depending on the specific form of the appearance—nature, living being, human being, work of man, world—certain components integral to the term *"Sinn"* can stand out. In this way *"Sinn"* can stand for a certain "quality." Most commonly, however, *"Sinn"* will point beyond a single quality, as is evident from the many different combined expressions already found in Lotze, like *"Sinn"* and "purpose," *"Sinn"* and "meaning" *(Bedeutung)*, *"Sinn"* and "value." *"Sinn"* therefore, with respect to appearances, potentially always refers to all qualities, in particular also the economic-energetic, the ethical, and the functional. Previously, other integrational concepts had been used for all these qualities: divine wisdom and loving-kindness, God's plan, spirit, reason. There is an inner and an outer explanation as to why Lotze instead talks of *"Sinn."* Early on, Lotze was accustomed to talking about the *"Sinn"* of appearances (of "existence," the "world").[36] Because of Hegel's attempt to demonstrate that there is divine plan and reigning rationality in the historic appearances and in particular in universal history, it was natural for Lotze to use the familiar concept *"Sinn."*

Why it is that Lotze uses the term *"Sinn"* so early on, and why he prefers it, can at this point only be hinted at. Leibnitz played an important role in Lotze's thought, in particular Leibnitz's notion of appearances as monads, each of which has a "soul" with different grades of consciousness and behaves like the *"Mikrokosmos"* to the divine *"Makrokosmos."* Both "soul" and *"Sinn"* exist in the world, and are meaningfully perceived by man, who himself is soul and has *"Sinn,"* as *"Sinn."* Early on, Lotze associates the term *"Sinn"* with further components that are important for his thought: *"Sinn"* is a concealed rational content that one cannot decipher but that one meanwhile believes in. As a metaphysician, Lotze is more skeptical than Hegel. *"Sinn"* is also meaning that has an appearance for man; an appearance can have *"Sinn"* only if man perceives and experiences it. Lotze thinks of the world of appearances as relative to the individual subject. *"Sinn"* is then also "value," which people enjoy in perceiving the world and which they take pleasure from.[37] Above all, the term *"Sinn"* expresses something that is important for Lotze's ethically based metaphysics and that distinguishes him from Hegel: If the world is not senseless or meaningless, then, according to Lotze, all its creatures' endeavors will not, in the end, have been futile or in vain.

In summary, *"Sinn"* is a transcendental idea that unites all conceivable qualities that an appearance with "rational meaning-content" could have. The expression "meaning *(Sinn)* of history," then, is employed if the question arises whether a "mental meaning-content" in history is conceivable.

Lotze's Idea of the "Meaning *(Sinn)* of History"

In his chapter "The Meaning *(Sinn)* of history" Lotze reflects upon several very different positions in the philosophy of history, which he, by means of the chapter heading, for the first time interprets as answers to the question of the "meaning *(Sinn)* of history." If one reconstructs these positions from Lotze's perspective five viewpoints of the "meaning *(Sinn)* of history" can be distinguished, which he assesses differently:[38]

1. The unhistorical-religious *Sinn* position, which Lotze rejects. This position is shaped by the thought that historical development does not possess an inher-

ent *Sinn*. God alone is *Sinn*. Human life does not "in its earthly entirety" move towards "a here attainable or even advanced goal of imperfectness." Everything is futile. "Only the ever immediate return of the individual heart to God is progress, all earthly life is a continuous circle of old imperfectnesses." History here is thought of from the vertical relation of man to God and from the end, the Last Judgement. Later on Berdjajew advocated this position and resolutely rejected the idea of progress: "History has positive *Sinn* just in case it comes to an end.... If history was an infinite process, infinite in essence, then history would not have a *Sinn*."[39] Keyword: "unhistorical-religious *Sinn*-giving of the world."

2. The historical-religious *Sinn* position, which Lotze supports. History has an inherent absolute *Sinn,* knowledge of which, however, eludes man.[40] If historical development is not to "appear as incomprehensible and futile noise" one has to assume that all effort will find its reward and everything endures. Keyword: "religiously motivated absolute *Sinn*-giving of the world."

3. The historical-metaphysical *Sinn* position of the Enlightenment and Idealism, which Lotze criticizes. In this view, history contains a wise plan and a higher purpose. History is seen as the "education of the human race" (Lessing), or the "development of the idea of mankind" (Kant, Hegel). History, then, serves God, wise nature, or the world spirit, to the realization of a higher good. History is seen as analogous to a human life in that it forms a whole, has a beginning and an end, and advances towards a goal. Lotze attributes the philosophical term *Sinn* to this position. Keyword: "attributed historical-metaphysical *Sinn*-giving of the world."

4. The "historical" *Sinn* position, which Lotze explicitly advocates.[41] The attribute "historical" summarizes three characteristics:

    (a) The concrete life of each individual human being has a specific *Sinn*. Lotze talks of the "meaningful purpose of the true warm-hearted life." Keyword: "Existentialist *Sinn*."

    (b) Historical work has a *Sinn*. Despite all retrograde steps and failures, individual human beings work on the improvement of their circumstances and the humanization of their environment. Keyword: "cultural-philosophical *Sinn*."

    (c) The observation of the historical drama has instructive-aesthetic *Sinn* for the observer. He enjoys: "the colorful embers and passion of human life," "the impenetrable idiosyncrasies of the individual goods," "fate's deeply distressing complications."[42] Keyword: "meaningful study of history."

5. The naturalistic position, which Lotze rejects as tendentious. Here, history is nothing more than "examples of a general law of happenings," "each caused by the forces behind it, nothing caused by a purpose in front."[43] This is the position of the causal-mechanical examination of history, which is informed by the natural sciences. This position excludes belief in the reli-

gious and absolute *Sinn*-giving as well as the "historical" *Sinn* position. (Lotze himself, however, advocates the "historical" position. The individual life is meaningful *[sinnvoll]*, and so are man's intellectual and artistic work and the examination of history.)

The philosopher of history Lotze, who may have introduced the concept "meaning *(Sinn)* of history," particularly criticizes the supposed historical-metaphysical "*Sinn*-giving" of history and thereby puts himself in direct opposition to Lessing, Kant, and Hegel. The "meaning *(Sinn)* of history," understood as a metaphysical plan or purpose of history, is not verifiable: "… the true demonstration of the plan that history pursues makes neither itself nor empirical knowledge (of it) possible. The latter because we know of the limitations of our knowledge in comparison to the multiplicity of life our planet has seen and how little these fragments allow us to decipher the course that earthly history is going to take.… And so history still appears to us as it always did, as a path from an unknown beginning to an unknown end, and the general views that we think we must take on about its direction cannot serve to understand history's course and cause in detail."[44]

The expression "meaning *(Sinn)* of history" then enters the philosophical discourse within the critique of knowledge. Perhaps it is no coincidence that the only sentence in the text itself where Lotze uses the expression "meaning *(Sinn)* of history" as it occurs in the chapter title is in the skeptical remark that "God alone understands the meaning *(Sinn)* of history."[45] The whole quote reads: "For if God alone understands the meaning *(Sinn)* of history, what view would not join into this modest confession?" The emergence of the metaphysical term *Sinn,* then, is not motivated by the religious or metaphysical doubt about the meaningfulness of the world in principle, but rather by the critique of a philosophy of history that attempts to determine it metaphysically with the aid of the idea of progress.

It would have been conceivable that Lotze viewed the attempts by the philosophers of history of the Enlightenment to find a common thread in the "absurd path" of history with admiration, or that he mourned their vain efforts to find a metaphysical "*Sinn*-giving of history." That is not the case, however. Lotze criticizes and contests the supposed historical-metaphysical "*Sinn*-offers," from Lessing to Hegel, because they do not measure up to his "requirements" for an absolute meaning *(Sinn)* in history.

Lotze weighs the wisdom and reason that Lessing, Kant, and Hegel demonstrate in history against his absolute *Sinn,* and in particular against the idea of historical justice. If the path of history has been demonstrated to be rational, then this reason is indivisible. For example, history must not be unjust: "no education of mankind is conceivable without the final result also being of benefit to those who stayed behind during the earthly course of events."[46] Here, Lotze obviously does not consider that Lessing was aware of this problem himself. In an attempt to solve the problem, Lessing brings into play the idea of reincarnation. Lotze, however, is less concerned with an examination of Lessing than with a critique of the basic idea of progress, insofar it carelessly sacrifices the happiness of former generations in favor of a better, more dignified and humane life for future generations. This idea stood in opposition to his religious and metaphysical desire that the world "appeared as a rational and dignified whole": "Not for the sake of our happiness do we demand our happiness; but rather because the *Sinn* of the world would turn into nonsense if we rejected the thought that the work of all generations gone by only ever benefits those that follow and is lost for those generations themselves."[47]

Lotze does not entirely reject the notion of progress in his ethical considerations. There is something that warns us "to give up that, which we do not understand, and that calls upon us to honor a true good in the earthly progress of history." But, this voice does not argue with the historical metaphysics that sacrifices the past and present to the future; rather, it is based on a historical-psychological understanding (which Walter Benjamin would later on take up in his theses on the philosophy of history[48]): "It is one of the remarkable peculiarities of human nature ... that there is much egotism in particular cases and a general lack of envy of each present for its future. And it is not only that we do not begrudge this future a greater happiness that we can only gather by looking ahead; rather this thread of self-sacrificing work for the creation of something better that we cannot enjoy ourselves moves through all times, sometimes in a grand form, sometimes habitually ... This wonderful appearance might instill in us the belief that there is a higher connection where the past is not simply *not* but rather where everything that the chronological course of things separates is together and side by side, where the goods that this course of events created are not lost to those who helped produce them without enjoying them."[49]

Lotze's critique of the plain idea of progress takes a stand for human beings, for the generations that have been utilized by the philosophers of history for the sake of the path of history. This historical model also influences Lotze's critique of Hegel and the Hegelians. Lotze rejects as false the theory that history serves an absolute final purpose, whose realization is independent of the happiness of individuals and peoples, that has hitherto been concealed from mankind. Lotze does not address in detail the issue that Hegel does not view history as simply a development of an abstract notion but rather also sees this "Spirit" "as freedom." Lotze's main concern was to contest a historicometaphysical idea of a goal that takes no account of the life of people and their concrete history.

In a passage in the chapter on *"Sinn,"* Lotze's "historical" motives in his struggle against the historical metaphysics of the Hegelians finds expression particularly succinctly:

"... not a means to an end but rather the final *Sinn* and purpose of historical development, not a theme that strings together life's actual goods but rather the best of those goods is what they feel to have found in this concealed self-realizing of the idea. ... For as long as we breathe we want to fight against this sober and yet so terrifying superstition, which, absorbed in the worship of facts and forms, does not recognize the rational purpose of the true warm-hearted life and fails to notice it with unfathomable levity, in order to search for the deepest *Sinn* of the world in the observation of a secret chain of development.... And when in history the colorful embers of human life open up before them, the impenetrable idiosyncrasy of the individual temperament, fate's deeply distressing complications that are often similar in their outline but remarkably dissimilar in detail: when this big picture opens up before them, then they ask whether there is a means by which the great can be traced back to the small; for we move back, not forwards, if we are made to believe that the final *Sinn* and purpose of the world is the tedious boredom of a necessary development.... And they will keep on professing to find *Sinn* in that the appearances merely happen and are not seen, that symbols merely occur even if no-one understands them, that ideas are merely expressed by matters of fact even if there is no-one to make an impression on."[50]

The concept "meaning *(Sinn)* of history," then, evolved in a specific context: the critique of universal historicometaphysical "*Sinn*-giving." In this context it takes on a function that, from today's point of view, one would not have expected, for it serves to discredit the demands for recognition of historical metaphysics. Lotze, after all, does not criticize the *"Sinn"*-emptiness but rather the supposed demand for *"Sinn"* in the universal-historical speculative historical metaphysics. He can no longer appreciate the final models of progress of the Enlightenment and Idealism. To put it in modern terms: The great stories much discussed by the postmodernists make no sense for Lotze any more; instead, following Meineckian historicism, he wants the life of the individual and the concrete historical life to be perceived and recognized in all their happiness and misfortune.

He introduces the term *"Sinn"* as a ferment into an intellectual movement that gained acceptance in various areas in the nineteenth century and is undiminished to this day: a rejection of an abstract metaphysical picture of the world and history and a turn to the lived life and empirical history. Lotze does not ask, as is fashionable today, whether the life of the individual, empirical history or the study of history has *Sinn;* as a Leibnizian he is already convinced that that is the case. Unlike the *Sinn*-scientists, -prophets, and -politicians, he does not criticize people for leading a meaningless life simply in order to offer them some kind of *Sinn*-orientation in the end.[51] It is his aim to fend off the, as he sees it, abstract and inhuman Hegelian historical metaphysics as "*Sinn*-giving" of life and of history. In doing so he attempts not to speak out in favor of a physics of life and history, like the naturalists, but rather (to put it in modern terms), to know that a rational self-will *(Eigensinn)* of the individual life and history is acknowledged and recognized. His world of ideas and his use of the term *"Sinn"* refer to a crisis of Hegelian metaphysics, but not to the modern *"Sinn"* crisis. Lotze qua philosopher of history is not one of the *"Sinn"*-givers Max Weber warns against in his speech *"Wissenschaft als Beruf,"*[52] who have appropriated the term *"Sinn"* in the twentieth century, in particular after the experience of the two world wars and the Holocaust.

"Meaning of *(Sinn)* History" in a Polemical Context

Like Löwith, Golo Mann, and Buhr, Lotze analyzes the theology and philosophy of history of the Enlightenment using the modern term *"Sinn."* He does this without making clear that the term was never part of Lessing's, Kant's, or Hegel's language or conception of the world. This step is very important, for Lotze assumes that Lessing, Kant, and Hegel claimed to have identified the "final *Sinn* and purpose" of history and then goes on to criticize this alleged claim.

This yields a new question: Does the term *"Sinn"* receive a specific function within a polemical argumentation that is directed against the theology and philosophy of history? When Lotze assumes that Lessing and Hegel saw the "meaning *(Sinn)* of history" in the "education of mankind" or in the "development of the idea of mankind," then such an aim, measured by his absolute conception of *"Sinn,"* always has to be insufficient, insignificant, and incomplete. How could the historical context, the entirety, the meaning *(Bedeutung),* the value of history be contained in one concept that only refers to one specific final goal? Does history not need several goods to realize, instead of a goal; can its intrinsic value be sacrificed to one goal; is it *just* to leave the tribulations of past generations unrewarded; can an abstract idea grasp the meaning *(Bedeutung)* of historical life?

The term *"Sinn,"* then, gains its standing also within the framework of a polemical rhetoric along the following lines: In order to be able to criticize your opponents, you must exaggerate their claim for knowledge and then demonstrate that they did not do it any justice.[53] With the term *"Sinn"* Lotze suggests a claim for knowledge within the history of philosophy, which, as far as I know, was not raised by Lessing, Kant, or even Hegel in an attempt to uncover the "plan" or "purpose" of history. Lotze exaggerates Lessing's, Kant's, and Hegel's teleological claim for knowledge by putting it in terms of a claim for *"Sinn."* He develops two standards by which he measures and fails the traditional historicometaphysical goal: the idea of an absolute divine justice on the one hand, and the empirical knowledge of the individual lived life and concrete history on the other. To summarize: The term *"Sinn"* was introduced into the philosophy of history in order to drive out a supposed historicometaphysical term *"Sinn"* from the study of history and to put in its place a "rational purpose of the real warm-hearted life" and the "big picture" of human history.

Preview

The constellation in which Lotze takes up the term *"Sinn"* is also of importance for Dilthey's *Einleitung in die Geisteswissenschaften* (1883). Dilthey even widens it by averting not only the old theology and philosophy of history but also Comte's generalizing theory of history. In this constellation Dilthey not only takes over Lotze's use of the term *"Sinn"* but also its strategic function. While Lotze polemicizes that Hegel "forces upon us the tedious boredom of a necessary development as the final *Sinn* and purpose of the world," Dilthey argues: "Those theories of sociology and the philosophy of history that see in the depiction of the singular mere raw material for their abstractions are wrong. This superstition subjects the works of the historians to a secretive process in order to take their singular material and alchemistically turn it into the pure gold of abstraction and to force history to reveal its deepest secret. This is precisely as adventurous as was the dream of the natural philosopher who sought to elicit the big word from nature. There is no such final and straightforward word in history that might expresses its true *Sinn,* just as nature cannot reveal anything similar."[54]

Insofar as Dilthey utilizes the term *"Sinn"* to reject metaphysical and generalizing concepts of history and in this context identifies them with the supposed metaphysical term *"Sinn"* (final meaning *(Sinn)* and purpose of the world), the usage of the historicaometaphysical term *"Sinn"* is tied to the conflict between Hegelianism and historicism, generalizing and individualizing notions of history. And indeed, outside this context, the expression "meaning *(Sinn)* of history" plays no particular role in Dilthey's work.

There are, however, various impulses that keep alive the term *"Sinn"* within the philosophy of history and give it particular momentum. Lotze opposed certain values to the historicometaphysical term *"Sinn"* that exploit the history of mankind for a goal. I have summarized these values as "historical" (following Friedrich Meinecke): the individual life; the historical work of human beings, which is objectified in institutions and developments; and finally, the sight of historical life, which is instructive and enjoyable. All three values are laden, partly by Dilthey himself, with the term *"Sinn."* The individual human being, society, and historiography emerge as producers of *"Sinn,"* creating a great diversity of values that in turn become the object of scientific and philosophical investigation. Dilthey asks: What *Sinn* do individuals like Augustine, Rousseau, and Goethe give their life in practice and in their autobiographies?[55] What are those values that "constitute the *Sinn* of historical reality?"[56]

The exploration of personal identity and of objective cultural constructs is still current and has led to the development of the personal term *"Sinn"* (Spranger) and its use in the humanities (Rickert), both of which have spread widely.[57] What history means for mankind remains an open question.[58]

Within the narrower context of the philosophy of history another thought has contributed to the spread of the term *"Sinn."* Lotze himself attributes the various historicometaphysical ideas of goal and purpose to the "yearnings" of their authors,[59] Dilthey follows the thought through: "Within the historical course of the world we naturally find again its value and *Sinn* which, in the system of our energies, is felt to be a value and is introduced to our will as a rule; any formula we use to express the meaning *(Sinn)* of history is merely a reflection of our own lively inner being."[60] This view suggests an interpretation of the concepts of the theology and philosophy of history as expressions of a value attitude that is conditional on the author's life history. Georg Mehlis, following his teacher Rickert, took up this approach for his systematic account of the philosophy of history:

"A meaning *(Sinngebung)* of history presupposes a theory of value. As a rule, these values will be connected with a system, which causes one of the values to be a leading or final value, which is the starting-point of all *Sinn*-interpretation and which, as the final purpose of history, sheds light on the whole development.... Corresponding to those values, 4 basic forms of speculation within the philosophy of history arise as pure forms of universal history: 1. religious universal history: the meaning *(Sinn)* of history is redemption, or: its meaning is the revelation of God's secrets; 2. speculative universal history: the meaning of history is absolute or relative knowledge; 3. ethical universal history: the meaning of history is the awareness of freedom; 4. aesthetic universal history: history is the revelation of God's beauty."[61]

This paved the way for "meaning *(Sinn)* of history," detached from the critical-polemical context of Dilthey's *Einleitung,* to become a central category of the historicosystematic reconstruction of the history of the philosophy of history.

However, another factor is the precondition for the ascent of the phrase "meaning *(Sinn)* of history" to the status of vogue word. The meaningfulness *(Sinnhaftigkeit)* of the individual life, the objectivizations of society, and the study of history, which Lotze and Dilthey intuitively affirm, were caught in a crisis in the twentieth century in the wake of two world wars and the Holocaust. It was Nietzsche who first succinctly articulated this awareness of crisis in all three areas, including the philosophy of history.

In the second edition of his *Fröhliche Wissenschaft* Nietzsche reformulates Schopenhauer's pessimistically answered question of the "value of being" as a modern question for *Sinn:* "Does existence have a *Sinn?*" Nietzsche judges the use and disadvantage of history for life, in contrast to Lotze and Dilthey. While the latter draw instruction and enjoyment from the study of history, Nietzsche analyzes the problem of an inundated and ossified historical culture. In particular, Nietzsche radically calls into question the relation between the cognizing subject and the values of history. Dilthey also considers the possibility that the cognizing subject projects its concepts of values into history.[62] Nietzsche follows the thought through: The subject does not find *"Sinn"* in history, but rather puts it in; it is not driven by honorable longings, but by a will to power. "Our 'new world': we have to recognize to what degree we are the *creators* of our values—whether we *can* put meaning into history."[63]

The tension between Dilthey, Nietzsche, and the experiences of the twentieth century outlines a constellation that elevates the term *"Sinn"* (and the question of *Sinn*) within the philosophy of history to a central leitmotiv of the twentieth century: on the one hand, the increased expectation of *Sinn* for the individual life and the historically created world, and on the other hand, the experience of historical catastrophes. Finally, this configuration is shadowed by the suspicion, first formulated by Nietzsche and then put into concrete terms by Theodor Lessing after the First World War, that *Sinn* is not the finding of *Sinn* but rather *Sinn*-projection and will to power.[64]

Notes

1. Joseph Bernhart, *Sinn der Geschichte* (Freiburg im Breisgau 1931); Karl Heussi, *Vom Sinn der Geschichte: Augustinus und die Moderne* (Jena 1930); Nikolaus Berdjajew, *Der Sinn der Geschichte: Versuch einer Philosophie des Menschengeschicks,* with an introduction by Graf Hermann Keyserling, translated from the Russian by Otto Freiherr v. Taube (Darmstadt 1925); Heinrich Rickert, *Die Probleme der Geschichtsphilosophie: Eine Einführung,* 3rd rev. ed. 1924 (cf. the section "Der Sinn der Geschichte," 109ff); cf. idem, *Die Grenzen der naturwissenschaftlichen Begriffsbildung: Eine logische Einleitung in die historischen Wissenschaften* (Freiburg 1902), 612, fn.1 (I owe this reference to Uwe Barrelmeyer); Max Nordau, *Der Sinn der Geschichte* (Berlin 1909); Georg Simmel, *Die Probleme der Geschichtsphilosophie* (1892), in idem, *Gesamtausgabe,* vol. 2 (Frankfurt/ M. 1998) (see chap. 3 "Vom Sinn der Geschichte," 380ff.); Wilhelm Dilthey, *Einleitung in die Geisteswissenschaften: Versuch einer Grundlegung für das Studium der Gesellschaft und Geschichte* (1883), 5th ed. (Stuttgart and Göttingen 1959), 86ff. Odo Marquard refers to Dilthey as the possible originator of the "emphatic term meaning *[Sinn],*" "Zur Diätetik der Sinnerwartung: Philosophische Bemerkungen," in Günther Eifler et al., eds., *Sinn im Wissenschaftshorizont* (*Mainzer Universitätsgespräche,* SS 1983) (Mainz 1984), 35–52, here 38f. Ernst Bernheim, *Geschichtsforschung und Geschichtsphilosophie* (Göttingen 1880), 9, 16, and 85; Herman Lotze, *Mikrokosmos, Ideen zur Naturgeschichte und Geschichte der Menschheit: Versuch einer Anthropologie,* 3 vols. (1856–64), vol. 3 (1864), 6th ed. (Leipzig 1923), 20ff.

2. Bernheim was a private lecturer *(Privatdozent)* in Göttingen, where Lotze taught from 1844 till 1880. In his work *Geschichtsforschung und Geschichtsphilosophie,* as well as in his *Lehrbuch der Historischen Methode und der Geschichtsphilosophie* (3rd/4th completely revised and expanded edition, Leipzig 1903), he acknowledges Lotze. Dilthey, Lotze's successor at the chair in Berlin, frequently cites the *Mikrokosmos* in his "Einleitung;" fn. 2, p. 103 suggests that Dilthey was familiar with the chapter on *"Sinn"* in particular.

3. Cf. the article "Sinn des Lebens" by Volker Gerhardt in Joachim Ritter, ed., *Historisches Wörterbuch der Philosophie,* vol. 9 (Darmstadt 1995), columns 815–824.

4. Georg Wilhelm Friedrich Hegel, *Vorlesungen über die Philosophie der Geschichte* (= *Werke,* vol. 12), ed. Eva Moldenhauer and Karl Markus Michel (Frankfurt/ M. 1970), 20 and 40.

5. Friedrich Schiller, "Was heißt und zu welchem Ende studiert man Universalgeschichte?" (1789), in Kurt Rossmann, ed., *Deutsche Geschichtsphilosopie: Ausgewählte Texte von Lessing bis Jaspers* (Munich 1969), 144–161, here p.158.

6. Immanuel Kant, "Idee zu einer allgemeinen Geschichte in weltbürgerlicher Absicht" (1784), in idem, *Werke in sechs Bänden,* ed. Wilhelm Weischedel, vol. 6 (Darmstadt 1975), 33–50,

here 34 and 45. Although a selection of Kant's work is entitled *Deines Lebens Sinn* (ed. Wolfgang Kraus, Zürich 1987), the title does not correspond to *Kant's* usage. Cf. also Hans Reiner, *Der Sinn unseres Daseins,* 2nd ed. (Tübingen 1964), 63, fn. 1: "Kant came relatively close to our question by asking after the 'final purpose of creation'. This led to a further question, which is almost identical to our own, namely what it is that gives the existence of human beings 'alone an absolute value'. (Kritik der Urteilskraft, § 86)."

7. This hypothesis is based on my investigation of the most important historical-philosophical works of these authors and, as far as possible, on the use of indexes and some secondary literature. Whenever there is talk about "meaning *(Sinn)* of history" or similar expressions with regard to the above authors, no reference to any such expression can be found in the *primary* texts.

8. The crisis situation during the First World War may have contributed to the establishment of the phrase "meaning *(Sinn)* of history." A memory related by Werner Kraft substantiates this hypothesis: "He (Walter Benjamin; J. St.) appears in front of me on that evening in the Charlottenburger Siedlungsheim in 1915, when a small number of young people discussed the meaning *(Sinn)* of history and the war. Kurt Hiller had been talking about the meaning *(Sinn)* of history the week before." In Siegfried Unseld, ed., *Zur Aktualität Walter Benjamins* (Frankfurt/ M. 1972), 59 (I owe this reference to René Schilling). Rudolf Eucken's book *Der Sinn und Wert des Lebens* (Leipzig 1907), very popular during the First World War, may also have acted as a catalyst.

9. Comte talks about the "sens général de l'évolution humaine," a turn of phrase Dilthey translates as "allgemeiner Sinn der menschlichen Entwicklung (general meaning *(Sinn)* of human development)." While for Comte the expression meant the "direction" and "goal" of a development, the term *"Sinn"* becomes critical for Dilthey. See Dilthey, *Einleitung,* 107; Gerhardt, "Sinn des Lebens," col. 817.

10. Alexander Demandt, *Metaphern für Geschichte: Sprachbilder und Gleichnisse im historisch-politischen Denken* (Munich 1978), 423: "The expression 'meaning *(Sinn)* of history' can be translated neither into Latin nor into Greek, its heritage within the history of ideas is of considerable importance."

11. Karl Löwith, *Weltgeschichte und Heilsgeschehen. Die theologischen Voraussetzungen der Geschichtsphilosophie* (1953), 6th ed. (Stuttgart 1973), 132 and 176.

12. Golo Mann, "Die Grundprobleme der Geschichtsphilosophie von Plato bis Hegel," in Leonhard Reinisch, ed., *Der Sinn der Geschichte: 7 Essays von Golo Mann, Karl Löwith, Rudolf Bultmann, Theodor Litt, Arnold J. Toynbee, Karl R. Popper, Hans Urs von Balthasar,* 4th ed. (Munich 1970), 11–30, quote on 28.

13. Georg Klaus and Manfred Buhr, eds., *Philosophisches Wörterbuch,* 2nd ed. (Leipzig 1965), 506f. Igor S. Kon consistently puts the word "meaning" *(Sinn)* in inverted commas: *Die Geschichtsphilosophie des 20. Jahrhunderts. Kritischer Abriß,* vol. 1: *Die Geschichtsphilosophie der Epoche des Imperialismus,* translated into German by v. W. Hoepp, 2nd ed. (Berlin 1966).

14. Horst Dieter Rau, *Im Labyrinth der Geschichte: Die Sinnfrage von der Aufklärung zu Nietzsche* (Munich 1990), 18f. Cf. the approach of attributing a *"Sinn"* paradigm to the Enlightenment: Thomas Immelmann, *Der unheimlichste aller Gäste: Nihilismus und Sinndebatte in der Literatur von der Aufklärung bis zur Moderne* (Bielefeld 1992), 44ff.

15. Reinhart Koselleck, *Vergangene Zukunft: Zur Semantik geschichtlicher Zeiten,* (Frankfurt/ M. 1979), 51 and 52f.

16. I would like to take this opportunity to thank Claus von Bormann, Maja and Paul Christ-Gmelin, Ulrich Dierse, the co-author of the article "Geschichtsphilosophie" in the third volume of the *Historisches Wörterbuch der Philosophie,* and in particular Jörn Rüsen, for their advice and encouragement.

17. Heussi, *Vom Sinn der Geschichte,* 2; Georg Mehlis, *Lehrbuch der Geschichtsphilosophie* (Berlin 1915), 330.

18. Alwin Diemer, *Grundriß der Philosophie,* 2 vols. (Meisenheim am Glan 1962), vol. 2, 171f., and vol. 1, 114.

19. Cf. Rudolf Lauth, *Die Frage nach dem Sinn des Daseins* (Munich 1953), 28ff.

20. See Marquard, "Zur Diätetik der Sinnerwartung," 35

21. Diemer, *Grundriß,* vol. 1, 114.
22. Cf. also Johannes Erich Heyde, "Vom Sinn des Wortes Sinn: Prolegomena zu einer Philosophie des Sinnes," in Richard Wisser, ed., *Sinn und Sein: Ein Philosophisches Symposium* (Tübingen 1960), 69–94; Donatus Thürnau, "Sinn," in Hans Jörg Sandkühler, ed., *Europäische Enzyklopädie zu Philosophie und Wissenschaften,* vol. 4 (Hamburg 1990), 283–289.
23. Wilhelm von Humboldt, "Über die Aufgabe des Geschichtsschreibers" (1821), in idem, *Werke in fünf Bänden,* ed. Andreas Flitner and Klaus Giel, vol.1 (Darmstadt 1960), 585–606, 595: the "examination carried out with real historical sense." An article in *Kindlers Literaturlexikon,* vol. 8 (Munich 1988), 194f, gives the impression that Humboldt was talking about the "meaning of history." That is not the case, however. Friedrich Nietzsche, "Unzeitgemäße Betrachtungen. Zweites Stück: Vom Nutzen und Nachteil der Historie für das Leben" (1874), in *Sämtliche Werke: Kritische Studienausgabe,* ed. Giorgio Colli and Mazzino Montinari, 15 vol. (Munich 1988), vol. 1, 243–334.
24. Numerous references in Demandt, *Metaphern für Geschichte,* and also in Hans Blumenberg, *Die Lesbarkeit der Welt,* 3rd ed. (Frankfurt/ M.1993).
25. Blumenberg, *Die Lesbarkeit,* 191, cited according to Imanuel Kant, *Gesammelte Werke,* ed. Königlich Preußische Akademie der Wissenschaften, vol. VIII (Berlin 1968), 264.
26. Wilhelm Traugott Krug, *Allgemeines Handwörterbuch der philosophischen Wissenschaften,* 2nd ed., vol. 3 (Leipzig 1833).
27. Hans Urs von Balthasar, *Das Ganze im Fragment* (Einsiedeln 1963) 135. Cf. also Wilm Pelters, *Lessings Standort: Sinndeutung der Geschichte als Kern seines Denkens* (Heidelberg 1972), 26, who, following von Balthasar, interprets Augustine using the term *"Sinn":* "God is the master of history, it is orientated towards him; the meaning *(Sinn)* of history lies in the preparation for the kingdom of God" (17).
28. Demandt, *Metaphern für Geschichte,* 353.
29. Hegel, *Philosophie der Geschichte,* 74ff.
30. Cf. discussion of the Hegel pupils and groups in Jürgen Gebhardt, *Politik und Eschatologie. Studien zur Geschichte der Hegelschen Schule in den Jahren 1830–1840* (Munich 1963).
31. Friedrich Nietzsche, *Die Fröhliche Wissenschaft* (2nd ed. 1887), in idem, *Werke in drei Bänden,* ed. Karl Schlechta, vol. 3 (Munich 1994), 407.
32. Arthur Schopenhauer, *Die Welt als Wille und Vorstellung,* ed. Arthur Hübscher, 2nd ed. (Wiesbaden 1949), vol. 2, 407.
33. Jacob Burckhardt, *Weltgeschichtliche Betrachtungen. Über geschichtliches Studium* (Darmstadt 1970), 190f (published in 1905 posthumously).
34. Lotze, *Mikrokosmos,* 20f. The following page references will refer to this edition.
35. The term *"Sinn"* appears in Lotze's *Metaphysik* of 1841and also in the first two volumes of the *Mikrokosmos.*
36. Max Wentscher, *Herman Lotze,* vol. 1: *Lotzes Leben und Werk* (Heidelberg 1913), 34ff.; see also Ernst Wolfgang Ort, "R. H. Lotze: Das Ganze unseres Welt- und Selbstverständnisses," in Josef Speck, ed., *Grundprobleme der großen Philosophen (Philosophie der Neuzeit IV)* (Göttingen 1995), 9–50.
37. Amidst one of Lotze's many proposals is the philosophical definition of the term "value." See also Rüdiger Bubner, *Geschichtsprozesse und Handlungsnormen. Untersuchungen zur praktischen Philosophie* (Frankfurt/ M. 1984), 138.
38. Lotze, *Mikrokosmos,* 20, 47f.
39. Berdjajew, *Der Sinn der Geschichte,* 280; see also Paul Althaus, *Vom Sinn und Ziel der Geschichte* (Bonn 1947), 10: "It is from Jesus Christ alone that we derive the *Sinn*-giving of history."
40. Lotze, *Mikrokosmos,* 40.
41. Friedrich Meinecke, *Von geschichtlichen Sinn und vom Sinn der Geschichte,* 5th unrevised ed. (Stuttgart 1951).
42. Lotze, *Mikrokosmos,* 44.
43. Ibid., 52.
44. Ibid., 54.

45. Ibid., 40.
46. Ibid., 53.
47. Ibid., 51.
48. Walter Benjamin, "Über den Begriff der Geschichte" in idem, *Gesammelte Schriften,* ed. Rolf Tiedemann and Hermann Schweppenhäuser, vol. I. 2 (Frankfurt/ M. 1991), 691–704, here p. 693; On the Benjamin/Lotze relationship, see Heinz Dieter Kittsteiner, "Walter Benjamins Historismus," in ed. Norbert Bolz and Bernd Witte, *Passagen: Walter Benjamins Urgeschichte des neunzehnten Jahrhunderts* (Munich 1984), 155ff.
49. Lotze, *Mikrokosmos,* 51.
50. Ibid., 44f.
51. See also Marquard, "Zur Diätetik der Sinnerwartung," also Klaus Berger, *Wissenschaft als Beruf: Zur Kritik literaturwissenschaftlicher und verwandter Sinnproduktion* (Frankfurt and Bern 1983).
52. Max Weber, "Wissenschaft als Beruf" (1917), in idem, *Gesammelte Aufsätze zur Wissenschaftslehre,* ed. Johannes Winckelmann, 3rd ed. (Tübingen 1968), 582–613.
53. Marquard, "Zur Diätetik der Sinnerwartung," 38, characterizes the term *"Sinn"* in Dilthey's *Einleitung* aptly as a "defence word within the theology and philosophy of history."
54. Dilthey, *Einleitung,* 91f.
55. Wilhelm Dilthey, *Der Aufbau der geschichtlichen Welt in den Geisteswissenschaften* (= *Gesammelte Schriften,* vol. 7), ed. Bernhard Groethuysen (Leipzig and Berlin 1927), 196ff.
56. Dilthey, *Einleitung,* 97.
57. Eduard Spranger, *Lebensformen. Geisteswissenschaftliche Psychologie und Ethik der Persönlichkeit,* 8th ed. (Tübingen 1950). The first edition contains the draft (in Heinrich Scholz, ed., *Festschrift für Alois Riehl,* Halle 1914, 413–522); the later editions go back to the second edition of 1921. For more about the term *"Sinn"* within the humanities, see Rickert's work and also Hans Freyer, *Theorie des objektiven Geistes: Einleitung in die Kulturphilosophie* (Berlin 1928).
58. Cf. Friedrich Jaeger, *Bürgerliche Modernisierungskrise und historische Sinnbildung. Kulturgeschichte bei Droysen, Burckhardt und Max Weber* (Göttingen 1994). Droysen and Burckhardt themselves however do not use the term *"Sinn."*
59. Lotze, *Mikrokosmos,* 51.
60. Dilthey, *Einleitung,* 97.
61. Mehlis, *Lehrbuch der Geschichtsphilosophie,* 330; cf. Rickert, *Die Probleme der Geschichtsphilosophie,* 109f.
62. Dilthey, *Einleitung,* 97.
63. Friedrich Nietzsche, "Aus dem Nachlass der Achziger Jahre," in idem, *Werke,* vol. 3 415–925, here 503, 918, and 487.
64. Theodor Lessing, *Geschichte als Sinngebung des Sinnlosen* (1919) (Munich 1983).

CHAPTER 5

The Meanings of History
Enacting the Sociocultural Code

JOHAN GALTUNG

Let us imagine that not we, but animals, plants and micro-organisms were attending a meeting. And let us imagine that they had all accepted the invitation to come and discuss the meaning of history, all sitting in a wonderful room—the lion, the wolf and the lamb, the scorpion, some amoebae, some choice roses, some rather ugly weeds, and so on. All well prepared.

And the chair animal puts this question to all of them: *What is the meaning of your historicity?* An introductory talk follows from a lion, Léon-Coeur, and he explicitly states, "the meaning of my life is to be a lion, realizing fully my lionhood. That is my *projet*, and when I have archieved that, there is still one more task: To see to it that lions will never perish from the earth—lionhood forever."

All the other participants say exactly the same for themselves: Our task is to realize the biogenetic code implanted in us, and the survival, ontogenetically and phylogenetically. The chair then has an additional question: *How about the aesthetics of your historicities?* And the participants all answer: It is not a question of aesthetics—what has to be done simply must be done. It is a question of living and giving life, and by living enacting the code. Of course, there is a beauty to the Curve of Life: Birth-Growth-Maturity-Decay-Death-New Birth. And to the Curve of the Species: Creation-Growth-Maturity-Decay-Extinction-Birth of a New Species. If this is aesthetics, so be it. If not, then not. And that´s it. We are our own meaning; our existence is our justification.

But, they add, on one point we agree: none of us believes that our task is to ensure that all other animals and plants in this world become lions, scorpions, amoebae or whatever. Each species has its own code, and each code car-

---

Notes for this section begin on page 106.

ries one meaning, *Sinn,* biogenetically transmitted. None of us possesses an exclusive supercode to be imposed on all others. None of us wants to perish from the world; none of us wants to be alone in the world. Sometimes we serve each other up in rather indecent ways. there is a food chain, and to eat and/or be eaten is in our biogenetic code, in our historicity. We eat down-chain and are eaten up-chain, except for two species: at the top, so-called humans, and the bottom. Like humans we kill before eat. Unlike humans we usually do not kill more than we can eat.

But, as stated earlier, there is one thing we never wanted to do, and that is to implant in all other animals the code of any one species. In other words, we believe in diversity and symbiosis. And one reason why we believe in diversity may sometimes seem rather sinister and should not be uttered too openly: Our fate is together to constitute the food chain.

Given the diversity of species we have to talk about meanings in the plural. We note in passing that the German word *Sinn* does not work well in the plural, because it connotes one universalist meaning rather than particularist meanings of meaning. Our understanding of meaning, or *Sinn*—as the German animals say—is to realize our code, and to provide space for that code in a suitable niche so that the code can be carried forward, enacted. To identify and protect that niche is of the essence.

So my short answer to the question "What is the meaning of historicity?," only eight words long, is that *meaning of human history is to realize codes,* whether historians see it that way or not. Humans, like other forms of life, have biogenetic codes, some very similar to those of some animals. But in addition, people have sociocultural codes transmitted not by procreation, but by a process of sociation and culturation—socioculturation.

Let us assume, with biologists, that among animals, human beings possess a particularly poor code when it comes to biologically transferred instincts, and we get:

Assumption no. 1: The human biogenetic code does not generate a sufficient program, for the "meaning (or meanings) of history," and for a theory of human action in general.
Assumption no. 2: We cannot, as a precondition for every act, engage in a Habermasian dialogue. Doing so would only lead to our early demise, for the simple reason that the dialogue would occupy all our time.

In other words, we must to some extent be (programmed) influenced beyond the biogenetic, by a sociocultural code that sets the course for some action, or at least defines the space of action. Moreover, that code has to satisfy two conditions: on the one hand it has to be *subconscious,* and on the other it has to be *collective.*

Assumption no. 3: The sociocultural code has to be *subconscious* because were it conscious, then that consciousness would drive us into an endless, recursive discussion before we could act.

Assumption no. 4: The code has to be *collective*, with a high level of sharing, so that when I act my neighbor will see my action as normal and natural, because his or her concept of what is normal and natural is the same as mine. If not, we would be on collision courses most of the time. No "collective soul" is implied.

So, by a collectively shared subconscious code I mean the shared understanding of what is normal and natural. But among whom should there be shared understanding? Do I mean among all humans, searching for a universal sociocultural code for *homo sapiens*?

Possibly, but the unit of discourse here is a civilization; the sociocultural code defines, oversimplifying, that civilization. And then there is room for sub- and sub-subcivilizations down to the code for one person, called the personality of that person. On the next page there is an attempt to describe the codes of six civilizations in seven "spaces." Personally, I am impatient with people who talk about codes in general without ever specifying any single element of a particular code, as a hypothesis. Only when one tries to specify the code, and to formulate that specification, does it become interesting. That is also the moment one becomes vulnerable to people in the civilization to which the code applies, who with all good reason can say: I do not recognize that as our code. Yet that is exactly the risk we have to take, so I willingly and knowingly try to enter into such a dialogue.

Assumption no. 5: Humans with basically the same sociocultural code constitute a *nation*. Nations with basically the same code constitute a *civilization* (supernation, with a supercode). Parallels to biological species are interesting but should not be carried too far (Social Darwinism is around the corner.)

Realizing the sociocultural code is here understood to be the meaning of human history. But we immediately encounter an important implication. Since there are several civilizations on earth, and since the deep culture, or "cosmology" (as I prefer to call it), or simply the code, is seen as something that applies to each unit called a civilization, then there will be several meanings, or pluralities of history. To talk about *the* meaning of history, in the *singular*, is in itself an indicator of Western universalism, to which Germans seem to be particularly vulnerable (Kant, Weber).

One minor point, which may not be quite so minor: I can say "meanings" in English with no difficulty. But I cannot say *die Sinne* in plural in German, only *der Sinn*. There is a linguistic boundary engraved on our mind that probably conditions, not determines, German thinking in this field, and in the direction of universalism.

The Codes of Six Civilizations Expressed in Seven Spaces

Let me now comment on this chart with code-formulations for six civilizations, expressed in seven spaces[1]. As a summary it is brutally inadequate, but it will stand as a useful guidepost for the purposes of this chapter. The logic of the chart is, roughly speaking, as follows.

Six civilizations have been selected. Some of them have been given Toynbee-esque names in order not to confuse them with geographical regions. The *Occident* is defined as the space covered by the religions of the *kitab*: *Judaism, Christianity,* and *Islam*. And the *Orient* is defined as the space touched by the teachings of the Buddha: the *Buddhic,* the *Sinic,* and the *Nipponic* (and some more that are not included). The Sinic and the Nipponic are eclectic civilizations. In the Sinic civilization, Buddhism is amalgamated with Daoism and Confucianism. In the Nipponic civilization, Buddhism is amalgamated with Shintoism and Confucianism. But there is also a purer Buddhic civilization, with its Southern Hinayana, its Eastern Mahayana, and its Northern tantric/lamaist Tibetan-Mongolian branches.

The Occident has been divided into Occident I and Occident II. Occident I is perceived as a wolf culture and Occident II as a lamb culture, together representing the wolf side and the lamb side of the Occident. Occident I, is expansionist, imperialist, and historically identifiable with the Greeks, with the Roman period up to the Antonines—let us say from 750 B.C.E. to 250 C.E.—and with the modern period to the present. Occident II in the Christian part of the Occident can be identified with the so-called Middle Ages, let us say 250–1250 C.E. There is a speculation that, the present Occident I period may come to an end, and that a less expansionist, softer Occident II will show up again as the "New Middle Ages." A similar periodization for the Islamic, and Judaeic pasts should be possible.

Finally, there is the *Indic* civilization. Neither Orient nor Occident, but *sui generis,* a cradle, or a crossroads for the other two, like them a mega- or meta-civilization, but reducible to neither one nor the other.

The Occident I covers Judaism, Christianity, and Islam. There exists a hypothesis of the countercyclicity of Christianity and Islam: as Christianity goes up, Islam goes down, and vice versa. Being very similar but mutually exclusive religions, operating by and large in close geographical proximity, the hypothesis should be a plausible basis for a crude image of Occidental macro-history.

Indonesia—mainly Muslim—and the Philippines—mainly Catholic—belong to the Occident according to this type of cultural geography, while Occident II comes close to being an oriental time-pocket in occidental history.

	Occident I	Occident II	Indic	Buddhic	Sinic	Nipponic
NATURE	Humans over nature *Herrschaft* Meatism	Humans over nature *Herrschaft* Meatism	Humans and sentient life over non-life Vegetism	Sentient life over non-life *Partnerschaft* Vegetism	Humans over nature Mixed Mixed	Humans over nature Mixed Mixed
SELF	Weak super-ego Strong ego Strong id	Strong super-ego Weak ego Mixed id	Mixed super-ego Mixed ego Mixed id	Strong super-ego Weak ego Weak id	Mixed super-ego Mixed ego Mixed id	Strong super-ego Weak ego Mixed id
SOCIETY	Vertical class and gender individual Knots	Vertical caste and gender collective Knot sets	Vertical caste and gender mixed Knot+net	Horizontal *sangha*, but gender collective Nets	Vertical mixed but gender mixed Knot+net	Vertical mixed but gender collective Nets+sets
WORLD	Three parts: *Center Periphery Evil* Unbounded	Many parts: *each part a Center* Bounded	One part: *unity-of-humans* Bounded	Many parts: *each part a Center* Bounded	Five parts: *Zhong guo N, S, E, W Barbaria* Unbounded	Three parts: *Nippon dai-tō-ā Resourcia* Unbounded
TIME Self	Bounded	Bounded	Unbounded	Unbounded	Unbounded	Unbounded
Society	Bounded	Bounded	Bounded	Unbounded	Unbounded	Unbounded
TRANSPERSON	Transcendental One God Chosen people(s) One Satan One soul Eternal heaven or hell Sing./univ.	Transc. & immanent One God Chosen people(s) One Satan One soul Eternal heaven or hell Sing./univ.	Transc. & immanent More gods No Satan One soul *Moksha* Reincarnation Plur./univ.	Immanent No God No Satan No soul *Moksha* Rebirth Plur./part	Transc. & immanent No God No Satan No soul? Rest Mixed Plur./part	Transc. & immanent One/no God Chosen people No Satan No soul? Rest Mixed Plur./part
EPISTEME	Atomistic Deductive No contradiction	Holistic Deductive No contradiction	Eclectic Eclectic Eclectic	Holistic Dialectic Contradiction	Eclectic Eclectic Contradiction	Eclectic Eclectic Contradiction

Graphic scheme by Johan Galtung, *Peace by Peaceful Means* (London 1996), 213

Let me now turn to the spaces and dimensions used to characterize the civilizations. There are numerous ways of unraveling the DNA of the civilization, the civilizational code, and what follows is only one way. Methodologically it is a construction similar to the psychological construction of a personality. A psychologist makes systematic observations and tries to construct someone's personality, his or her code, in order to fathom the inner logic of the person's physical and verbal action, nonverbal thought, dreams, non-action. As a construction it offers an axiomatic base for a theory of the synchronic and diachronic, physical and symbolic, behavior of that civilization.

The chart was originally developed to explore the fifteen synchronic relations among the six civilizations for their peace/violence potential, but it can also be used for macrohistorical, diachronic purposes.

As a construction, the chart's validity can only be tested along its margins in the way W. O. Quine describes the scientific process.[2] In other words, one tries to derive some hypotheses from the nucleus and then to confront them with empirical data. The level of credibility generally rises with the amount of qualitatively different confirmation (or, perhaps better, compatibility) between theory and data, and falls with incompatibilities, or a narrow range (e.g., only synchronic relations) of compatibility.

In the chart, the six civilizations are all seen as macrocultures. There is no evaluation involved, nor any notion of any civilization being high or low, in terms of culture.[3] These six civilizations have been selected because they cover the bulk of humanity, and also because the author believes he has understood something of them, but does certainly not believe he has understood the kind of cultures anthropologists are usually concerned with: Amero-Indian, Pacific, African, and a variety of other Asian cultures. But it should be possible to say something meaningful about 95% of humanity today on the basis of that chart alone.

But why have these spaces and dimensions been selected? Others could certainly have been included. But even if insufficient, efforts to identify the basic positions of these civilizations with regard to nature, self, society, the world and time—both as the historicity of self and the historicity of society—the transpersonal and the underlying epistemology, are at least necessary, indeed indispensable. The reason these dimensions have been selected is, simply, that if we fail to comprehend how a civilization encodes these categories, then we have no basis for any understanding of that civilization. The scheme is minimal, callously simplified, but not empty. It has to be crude, to enter the collective subconscious in a fairly shared manner of human beings of vast numbers.

Thus, the episteme of Occident I is seen as generalizing, atomistic, deductive, and filled with the conviction that any contradiction is erroneous, abnormal, and unnatural. This should then be contrasted with the Sinic and the Nipponic *eclectic* episteme, and the Buddhic dialectic, *contradictory,* episteme (also the case for the Daoist component of the Sinic amalgam). The contradiction of Daoism, including the *yin/yang,* is a form of understanding in the Orient, like the Aristotelian/Cartesian—particularly Cartesian—atomism and deductivism in the Occident, the trickle of dialectic in Heraklitos, Hegel, and Marx notwithstanding (relative to full-scale Daoist dialectics).

One way in which *yin/yang* operates in the Occident is through the dialectic between Occident I and Occident II. There is another way, but it is not visible on this chart. There is no assumption to the effect that the collective subconscious is symmetrically built into everybody who inhabits a civilization. For Occident I, the assumption would be that the code is more embedded in men than women, more valid for middle-aged than for young and old people, more applicable to people in the urban (secondary and tertiary) sectors of the economy than in the primary sectors closer to nature, and more prevalent in central areas than in of the periphery of a country. In other words, there would be diversities, as well as a sociocultural dialectic. But generally, to paraphrase Marx: *die herrschende Kosmologie ist die Kosmologie der herrschenden Klasse.* For anyone with Occident I as the manifest coding, there would be a latent Occident II as a reserve cosmology; and vice versa: This doubleness is a major strength of the West.

To say something much more concrete, let me begin with Occident I. I would like to point out four important differences between Occident I and the five other macro-cultures. The *first difference* is the combination of singularism and universalism in occidental religion and ideology, meaning in manifest, conscious cosmology. There is a strong insistence that when Occident I has produced some religion or ideology, then that same religion/ideology expresses the *only* truth. That in itself is not problematic for the other five macro-cultures. Problematic is the second idea: that single truth is universal and applies to the whole world at all times, for Christianity and Islam, liberalism and Marxism, capitalism and socialism alike. But the universal pretension only holds for the hard, Occident I, versions of these occidentalisms. There is also the soft (Occident II) Christianity of a Francis of Assisi, very different from the hardline (Occident I) Christianity of Tomás de Torquemada. There is the soft Islam of the Sufis, very different from the Islam of a Khomeini. There is the soft Judaism of Spinoza and Buber, very different from the Judaism of aggressive Zionism.

One place where I am unable to find a meaningful soft version is Nazism, and one place where I am unable to find a meaningful hard version is Buddhism. But I can find ritualized, weakened versions of both of them. I say this to mollify my own concepts, in an attempt to make them somewhat less occidental, to "yin/yangize" them, so to speak. In sum, the Occident comprises both the hard and the soft, but with one being dominant and the other recessive, depending on the historical phase.

The *second difference* is a consequence of singularism and universalism: namely missionarism and evangelization. If the meaning of Occident I history is to realize whatever truth it has produced, and to realize that truth not only in the occidental heartland but throughout the world, then Matthew 28: 18–20 is the logical conclusion: "[18] Then Jesus came to them and said, 'All authority in heaven and on earth has been given to me. [19] Therefore go and make disciples of all nations, baptizing them in the name of the Father and of the Son and of the Holy Spirit, [20] and teaching them to obey everything I have commanded you. And surely I am with you always, to the very end of the age.'" This sets the tone for a clash of civilizations; Occident I against the rest of the world. No single word covers this idea so well as the French word *projet*. Occident I produces many *projets,* and then there is the meta-*projet* of bringing these *projets* to the whole world. No true, well-encoded *homo occidentalis I* can rest satisfied and content until whatever gospel or message that has been produced has been brought to the very last corner of the world, and been gratefully accepted as a light unto the nations.

The *third difference* is the very strong feeling in the Occident that historical time is finite. Time is limited, not only in the sense of a Beginning, a Creation (with the American idea of a New Beginning, the new creation through America), but in the sense that there is an *Endzustand, l' état final, lo stato finale,* the final state of everything. The code having been realized, everything can come to rest. This does not mean no further existence, only that the basic shape of that continued existence has now been found. There is an end to history, suggestive of a book written by a person more Francis than Fukuyama, an exemplar embodying the major characteristics of Occident I, almost an occident museum exhibit.

Now for the *fourth difference*. A civilization that enters this world with a (rather immodest) universally valid, final-state *projet* for the whole world will run into difficulties. The other civilizations may simply disagree with the *projet*. The scorpion, the roses, and the vegetables may admire the lion, but when offered the lion's seed as their own code, they may decline. Here the weakness of Occident I—and particularly its Western/Christian part—is revealed: fundamentalism, fanaticism. Having found universal, final truth, all that stands in the way must be eliminated. More importantly, the Occident, seeing itself as the lone possessor of the truth, will blame all others for its own vice of being fundamentalist, like the West blames Islam. Occident I regards itself as right/valid, not as fundamentalist; fundamentalism is by definition a faith that stands in the way of Occident I. But in fact Occident I *is* fundamentalist, and the history of Occident I is "one damn fundamentalism after the other," to build on the quip that "history is one damn fact after the other."

The strength of the Occident is that it maintains a reserve cosmology, where Occident I becomes latent and Occident II is then manifest: soft, modest, introverted. Instead of one, two, or three polities in the medieval European space, there are suddenly five hundred in uneasy coexistence with weak (Carolingian, ecclesiastic) superstructures. Today they are heading for one, two, or three polities again. This duality, the Janus aspect combining hard and soft, is the strength of the Occident rather than Occident I or Occident II alone, per se. Such elements are observable in other civilizations, but not so pronounced.

If the meaning of history is interpreted as the meaning of occidental history, and if occidental history is seen as universal history, as pioneering history on behalf of all the others, then—and only then—does it make sense to use the word *meaning,* and the word *Sinn,* in the singular. It does not matter here how Occident I ends, or whether the world ends as Christian or Muslim, or as Marxist or liberal. From the point of view of the general *projet* these are just different articulations, variations on the same theme. What matters is universalization of Occident I.

Of course there will be more articulations. From Occident I as the general sociocultural code, more religions and more ideologies will be produced, all having singularism cum universalism as the common element (meaning that *this* combination is the deep message of the Occident). As a consequence, an endless struggle within and without is preprogrammed in Occident I (but not in Occident II).

Let us now turn towards the other five macrocultures. They do not have the characteristics discussed so far. They have other features. What would be the meaning of their histories? One basic meaning would be to continue as they are, in their own niche in the world cultural space, not to alter others by imposing on them, or offering them, their codes. They may go half the way, with some cases, of some regional neighbors being prevailed upon, and even included as "inner Periphery" or "outer Center." Japan has tried to do with colonialism and conquest in the period 1895–1945.

In the Christian Occident I division of world space, as I have tried to characterize it, the world has three parts: the occidental Center, the Periphery waiting to be occidentalized, and beyond that, Evil. Evil rejects the Occident (that is the definition of being "evil"), and for that reason has to be conquered and crushed. Pope Urban II's Clermont speech of 27 November 1095, nine centuries ago, when he spoke of Muslims as a "wicked race" and launched the Crusades, may serve as example. Pagans are waiting to be converted; heretics are simply evil having seen the light and rejected it. A *de facto* declaration of war, with no declaration of peace, the state of war has so far lasted more than 900 years.

In other words, the *projet* of Occident I is precisely to deprive the other five civilizations (and alternative articulations of Occident I) of their historicity, of their *projet*. Islam has done the same, but less so than the other two alternative articulations of Occident I. The imperialisms of so many European countries have provided a setting for the propagation of sacred and secular occidentalisms, such as the cause of human rights, that impose the Western historical dialectic—its historicity—on other civilizations, be it as a thin veneer on the top, a solid conquering crust, or an ethnic purge that leaves the territory weeded for Occidental cultural seeds more easily to take root.

This paper based on a lecture for a conference taked place in Germany, with Hitlerism as a recent articulation embraced at the time. *Homo hitlerensis* can be seen as *homo teutonicus in extremis,* and *homo teutonicus* as *homo occidentalis in extremis.* They are carriers of the same themes, with varying degrees of extremism, but with a softer Occident II working under the surface. When the Nazis wanted to deprive the Jews not only of life but also of their historicity—or perhaps mainly of the latter—they were standing on solid Occident I ground. They differed from other colonial powers in modern times, only in that the latter had focused on the overseas for such exercises. The same goes for *homo stalinensis* as *homo russicus/sovieticus in extremis,* and *homo americanus fundamentalis* as *homo americanus in extremis.* There is in each case high readiness to kill whenever something stands in the way, dialogue and coexistence being ruled out by singularism *cum* universalism. Whether the killing is decided by a committee (on national security, foreign affairs), within a democratic institution (a national assembly elected by popular and secret ballot), or by a gang of thugs, is a moot distinction for the victims. Of far greater importance is how many people are killed, the genocide aspect; how much culture is eliminated, the culturocide aspect; how much history is curtailed; the historicide aspect.

Leaving the Occident aside for now, it should be noted as we turn to the Orient that the Indic and the Buddhic are somewhat different from the Sinic and the Nipponic civilizations: the latter two draw borders in geographical world space.

The *Sinic code* divides the world into five parts. These five parts are *Zhong Guo,* China, the Kingdom in the Middle, and the four others: the North Barbarians, the East Barbarians, the South Barbarians and the West Barbarians. The North Barbarians seem to have been considered the most dangerous, judging by the fact that the Great Wall is built to the north.

Whoever inhabits the territory north of that wall is by definition dangerous. The wall may have been built not so much to keep the barbarians out as to keep the Chinese in. The warning to the Chinese is that if you walk outside this wall then you do so, as it is so beautifully expressed in German, *auf eigene Gefahr,* at your own risk. But what this means is that there is no *projet* for making the whole world subject to the Chinese sociocultural code. The basic meaning of Chinese history, their *projet,* is for China to remain China, keeping the barbarians out. By all means learn from the barbarians, but keep them out. To try to teach them is meaningless. The Sinic code is exclusive (including, however, Tibetans, Muslims, and others who may not like to be included); the occidental code is inclusive.

If the rest of the world disappeared it would be a relatively minor problem for the Sinic code—though a pity for the four types of barbarians, less. There is a sense of being chosen, but not by God. There is no God. Moreover, to be chosen by God would mean that there is something above China. Only one other country seems to labor under this code: France, *un peuple élu, mais par lui-*

même, as Napoleon might have thought when, as incarnation of France, he took the crown from the Pope in 1804 and placed it on his own head.

The point here is not what Napoleon did, but the fact that he got away with it. The French agreed, deep down, and that is what matters. He was supported by, and contributed to, the collective, subconscious, the idea of a chosen people above others, as by Law, or by Nature, or both. Chosen as a verbal form without a subject.

Permit me an anecdote. I was once on an OECD mission with a leading French politician, Edgar Faure, who told me what happened when he met Zhou Enlai in 1954, as their two countries were about to establish diplomatic relations. There in the same room are the two representatives of perhaps the two most chosen countries in the world. No other countries are actually necessary, except to radiate admiration, sound the applause, and imitate. As in Eckermann's description of Goethe's meeting with Napoleon, the parties are both, so taken with each other and by what they represent, so overawed by the occasion, that there is silence. But then they start talking about food: absolutely nothing in this world can compare with Chinese and French food. Chosen food for chosen people. They readily agree that Chinese food is the French food of the Orient, and French food the Chinese food of the Occident. The world needs no other cuisines. Mutual diplomatic recognition flowed from the mutual cuisine recognition as a foregone conclusion. Edgar Faure had a rich sense of humor; not speaking with a stiff upper lip. Both statesmen acted their codes beautifully.

We can generally assume that the leader of a country, particularly when the country is in a crisis, can only be a person who never pronounces himself against the deep culture of that country. This stringently limits both, the people's choice of leader and current and aspiring leaders' freedom of speech. When the country is in a crisis, even the selection process will favor those who are explicitly in line with the code. When there is less of a crisis, leaders may relax, permit some humor to emerge; yet still they must do their jobs of enacting codes.

What would be the *Nipponic code?* Japan divides the world into three parts, with *Nichi-hon,* the *Origin of the Sun, Nippon,* in the center. Around that center is the outer center or inner periphery, the *dai-t-kyoeiken,* the Great East Asian coprosperity sphere, which consists of countries similar to Japan, meaning China, Korea, and Viêtnam (the Mahayana Buddhist—Confucian countries.) When the Japanese say "Asia," they refer mainly to that part, perhaps with some elements of South East Asia too. To them, India is as different from Japan as are Botswana, Paraguay, and Norway. These four countries—the inner core of Japan and the outer core of China, Korea, and Viêtnam—have the rest of the world as outer periphery—as a resource.

If Occident I has Evil outside its periphery, China the Barbarians, and Japan the Resources, then what is the *projet?* For Occident I to pacify or even conquer Evil and convert the periphery is obviously a long-term project, especially since the concrete content of the code changes once in a while. After centuries of evangelizing to convert heathendom to Christianity, the Occident embarked on something called Enlightenment, *Aufklärung,* and started propagating "rationality" and "modernization" in the same crusading spirit, with Napoleon setting the tone. Rationality also comes at the tip of the sword, as "opening up for trade" and *economism* (famous recently for its impact, through a Harvard professor, on the Bolivian and Russian economies). This should be more than enough to keep Occident I busy till the next basic change of paradigm.

The Nipponic *projet* is to create an East Asian coprosperity sphere. This is much closer to fruition than the media are able to report. An East Asian Common Market of those four countries, with the massive economic potential of its 1,500 million citizens, capable of producing goods of Japanese quality for Chinese prices, will have considerable impact on the rest of us. This does not mean that the Japanese have never shown any military aggression inside and outside the core; indeed, they may do so again. Japan is self-assertive and penetrating. But there is no desire to convert anybody outside the inner periphery to the Nipponic sociocultural code. As a matter of fact, the opposite is the case. The Japanese become extremely uneasy when somebody begins to understand Japan, "creeping under their skin."

The *Sinic code* is more defensive: China must survive, China being geopolitically defined as the region between the steppe, the desert, the mountain range, and the sea. In that territory today we find parts of Russia, Mongolia, Kazakhstan, unlucky Tibet, and the border regions of Viêtnam and Korea. There are grave problems involving these countries. But further abroad, the Chinese are essentially engaged in drycleaning and Chinese restaurants, maybe also as a measure of how much significance they attribute to the rest of the world. They are the kind of people you send to Barbaria. Unless there is a secret scheme to the effect that in year 2050, for instance, when all chemical cleaners and all restaurants have become Chinese, they will take over the world. In that case it would correspond to the end of the Yuan empire. But apart from that bit of social science fiction, the sociocultural code defines China as highly defensive, but threatening to nobody except some border regions (Xinjiang, Tibet). More recently securing resources flow and markets has been added, by economic means.

The *Indic* and the *Buddhic* codes are distinguished by their unique relations to concepts of time and space. The meaning of Indic history is to go down, to regress, not to progress, and then to be reincarnated, starting the regression again. I got a shock some thirty years ago while talking in India about the world's geopolitical, economical, environmental problems, and the like. The more desperate the problems I came up with, the more loaded with catastrophe, the happier the audience was. *Yes! That's exactly what we say—it's getting worse and worse!* I had difficulty understanding this elation, so contrary to—for example—the soft Teutonic sense of progress that Norwegians have. This sense of regression in history is deeply ingrained in India. It is welcome because at the nadir of a *kalpe* cycle, there is a reawakening: the *avatar* comes, initiating a new cycle. This represents a very different time conceptualization: certainly not progress, not regress only, not linear, not pendular—simply Hindu.

The Indic space concept is also different, because the conglomerate conveniently wrapped up as "Hinduism" carries a strongly developed idea that Hinduism is the richest of all religious idioms, and all other religions are really Hinduism badly understood. There is a Hindu in everybody, even if somewhat misconceived. *The world is one family* is one of the most famous sayings in the Sanskrit tradition: *vasudaiva kuttumbakam*. That world's center of understanding may reside in India, but its economic-military-political center does not.

The *Buddhic code* has much of the same, but the realization comes in small units, and consequently with more diversity. The meaning of history is to realize oneself in the *sangha,* the small village and monastery, with the temple and the tanka at the center. This is by far the most peaceful space image among the six codes. The Buddhic time cosmology locates dynamic progress in the spirit, as a nonmaterial; it is soft on the material world by favoring material stability, with people neither too rich nor too poor.

What is happening today is fairly obvious. Occident I is at work realizing its *projet* by conquering intellectual, warrior-bureaucratic, and merchant elites everywhere, and markets. The giant sociocultural transplantation taking place makes colonialism pale in comparison. The Occident I sociocultural code reaches elites through, to fabricate a typical example, somebody who has studied at Princeton University, taken a Ph.D. at Harvard, and returned to his birthplace. He has two diplomas stating that he has not only understood but also received the Western code. During his stay as a student he has received surface knowledge. But he has also lived an occidental life, replete with codes implemented everywhere for Nature, Self, Society, World, Time, the Transpersonal and Episteme (the latter being all over the pages he has been reading). Upon return he brandishes the diplomas, and gets a job.

What happens next will be one of four things.

First, he may have terrible problems with himself. As the meeting-place of two codes, like Goethe's two souls in one body, he himself will be the battleground for something more problematic than the struggle between superego and id, namely the struggle between two superegos. The second possibility is that he is a successful sociocultural transplant, and precisely for that reason gets into problems not with himself but with his colleagues. The third possibility is that he and all his colleagues as well have been effectively transplanted, but have problems with the rest of the population. Sooner or later they may be purged, as is happening in Algeria right now and can happen anywhere in the non-Western world—except in the case of the fourth possibility, that the indigenous carriers of alternative codes are no longer there. A holocaust solved that problem.

What is the solution from the Occident I point of view? An atom bomb, a gas chamber, a concentration camp is one solution, extermination in Hiroshima, Auschwitz, or the Gulag another. Get rid of those who resist, get rid of the "fundamentalists" standing in the way. The Crusaders, sent out 900 years ago, were such a solution. So was the Inquisition. The Occident, or more particularly the West, is perfectly capable of executing such thoughts, and of defining those about to be exterminated as nonhuman.

Indeed, one way the Occident I defines *human* is through the unconditional acceptance of the sociocultural code of the Occident. To the extent that this is the case, we are dealing with a highly energetic predator civilization that bodes no good for the future of nonpredators. The question is not whether another people is well served by being transformed by the occidental code, but whether they accept or resist. Accept: they are human; reject: they are Evil.

As we are not talking about biogenetic codes—nobody is born Occident I or Buddhic—it is evident that a sociocultural code must be transmitted: this takes place through a combination of symbolic and material carriers such as religion, language, history and geography—the elements we use to define nations. The stability of a macronation like the European Union relies on skillful development of these carries. War inside the European Union is not unthinkable; that depends on who does the thinking. The supercode will tend to wash out the national code, so in the former European Community, less tight, a war would have been highly unlikely. But the European Union now taking shape is very tight. And the war the European Union wages on other parts of Europe, like Yugoslavia, is already there: most of the arms used by the Croats were of German, Austrian, and Swiss-German origin, and most of the arms used by the Serbs are of Russian or CIS origin, while the Muslim arms come from Iran and Saudi Arabia. The branches of Occident I are enacting their codes, but prefer to do so via the peoples of Yugoslavia.

A dozen belligerent national codes cannot produce a pacifist supercode for a supernation. However, there are also material carriers of the sociocultural code to consider. A prime example is the isomorphism between the Air France network with France at the center, the French road network emanating from Paris, and the boulevards radiating from the Place d'Étoile. And of course the name of the airport is the same as the latest official name of Place d'Étoile: *Charles de Gaulle*. In other words, France displays a very heavy isomorphism of very similar center-periphery structures, the kind of thing that will be imprinted on young people as they grow up. Center-periphery structures are likely to shape their perception of the world forever, tending to make the French see themselves either as the center within its periphery, or as in a "splendid isolation" high above others, where the problem of a lost periphery does not arise. But France is never seen by itself as anybody's periphery.

Let us now look at a much more fascinating carrier of time cosmology: the way sexuality is carried out in different cultures. Male western sexuality follows the occidental time curve, building up tension to a climax, with a bifurcation into the possibility of apocalypse called impotence, and the possibility of salvation called orgasm. It so happens that Chinese intercourse does not necessarily take place the same way, but is to a large extent drawn out in a more curvilinear fashion. I will not go into details—something has to be left to the imagination and to weekend exercises for those who do not believe what I say. Tantric Hindu *coitus* consists of inserting the penis into the vagina and staying there for an hour, or even for a day. It involves a high level of mutual awareness, but at the same time a relatively high level of constancy of the time rhythm, with very low frequencies. Similar rhythms can be found in food, for instance in a good occidental meal, the kind of thing that would merit three stars in the *Guide Michelin*. A Western meal has the same pattern as male intercourse, leading up to a point of climax via the lighter white to the heavy red wines, which coincide with delicious but heavy meat. It all ends on the tray of *profiteroles,* with the most wonderful coffee you can get. The conversation in a good French restaurant should of course have its climax when the wine is at its heaviest, and then the contradictions should gradually be dissolved as sleepiness descends; the better the coffee, the less the chance of rolling over on one's side and snoring.

The carriers of the codes are many, and not confined to such categories as religion and history. They constitute a dense network of patterns inviting pattern recognition and pattern internalization, which is exactly what sociocultural codes are about.

How does this end, how do civilizations, seen as implementations or realizations of sociocultural codes, come to an end? Here are four points on exactly that problem, flowing from the concepts discussed earlier.

Point one: A civilization comes to an end when the final state has been realized. What does Occident I do after the whole world has embraced democracy and a globalized free market? Once the task has been done, the earth has been fulfilled. There remains but one possibility for continuing the *projet:* there are other planets where sociocultural seeds might be sown. Evil people could be brought there so that there is somebody to conquer, just as colonies were conquered. But let us imagine this is not achieved. My prognosis is that Occident I will start dying upon having realized the *projet* because it is the process that sustains the civilization, not the final state. For that reason it may be much better for a civilization not to have a final stage. The Occident I idea of final state has a smell, a taste, of Death.

Point two: A civilization comes to an end if it cannot be realized. At the beginning of the 1970s, the Soviet Union as an Occident I articulation was a perfect case of inner demoralization. The people's goal was unclear; nobody seemed able to define the goal of Marxism/socialism-communism in terms sufficiently distinguishing it from the other great occidental *projet,* liberalism/capitalism. How to attain the unclear goal was even more unclear. Moreover, the prophecy that the other *projet* would fail—that the Evil of the Soviet cosmology, meaning the liberal/capitalist world, would disintegrate—had also failed. If an ideology fails on three points so basic as goals, strategy, and prophecy at the same time, then the rest (the arms race, no goods on the shelves) are small details. Eroded morale, cynicism, and loss of faith follow. People become spectators of social processes rather than their subjects or objects. In the USSR, collapse came shortly afterward.

Point three: A civilization survives by implanting its seeds somewhere else. The *projet* might be abandoned, in the space where it originated, but the sociocultural code can be transported elsewhere. Much of what is Roman comes directly from the Greeks; much of what is Christian, from the Jews. The occident went through a "medieval" period of latency, followed by the Renaissance as an enormous period of replanting the sociocultural code of the Greek or Roman period in new soil, or the same soil.

Point four: A time may come when a civilization with a reserve code must show its alternative side—a more modest side, like the case of Occident II for the Occident. In Germany this realization came—roughly speaking—thirty years after 1945, dressed up in green clothes, the Greens being for some time the carriers of Germany II. If Occident I-II-I-II is the general pendular superrhythm of the Occident, then a hypothesis could be that Germany swings with a quicker rhythm, *das Erste Reich* up and down, *das Zweite Reich* up and down, *das Dritte Reich* up and down, *das Vierte Reich* now picking up. The periods in between are perhaps the best periods in German history—say, from the Rhine Confederacy to Bismarck, 1806–1870; the Weimar period, so disparaged in its inability to realize greatness and bigness geopolitically, but a fantastic period culturally; and the post-1945 period, now possibly coming to an end, with the economic, social, and cultural blossoming of Germany. So, the big question: where can the Germans find more meaning, more *Sinn?* In Germany I? In Germany II? Or in the oscillation between the two?

The Germans realize the general occidental rhythm more quickly than other occidentals, and hence may often be out of synchrony with the rest. The expansionist code of Germany I can cause the population to accept advances eastward and southeastward with no debate; they just *happen,* something normal, natural. Life is a law of nature. So maybe one day, when the Fourth Reich is headed for catastrophe and the whole Teutonic enterprise is once again in danger, some of the softer Germany II sociocultural code may have survived in Princeton, carried by refugee scholars to the Institute for Advanced Studies, whence they may one day return to the *Teutoburger Wald* and replant the culture in another Institute for Advanced Studies in Bielefeld.

In conclusion, let us address, very briefly, two basic problems in cosmology analysis and consequently in historical analysis: where do the codes come from, and where do they go, that is: How do they change? As to their destination, two answers have already been mentioned: a code can be fully enacted, in other words its meaning can be realized, with the final state depriving society of more historicity, ushering in the famous "end of history"; or it can become a *cul de sac*, unrealizable. In either case there will be desperate calls for alternative sociocultural codes. A social order cannot exist without them.

As to where the cosmologies come from, I know no clear and unfalsifiable answers. No doubt the religions are one answer in the sense of being vast depositories of the basic assumptions of a civilization, but this only begs the question: where do religions come from? Why are occidental and oriental religions so different? Why are the former monotheistic (with some reservations for Christianity), and the latter poly- and even atheistic, yet profoundly religious? Why is one based on a longing for eternal life and the other on a longing to be released from the cycles of rebirth and reincarnation, the *samsara*? Of course, some basic traumas, or their absence, may have influenced the time cosmology; geography may have shaped the space cosmology. But I know of no generally valid answers. Maybe the question is wrong.

As for the process whereby cosmologies change: again, I know no clear and unfalsifiable answers, except for the two given. But why should they change? If a cosmology provides meaning not only to something abstract called "history," but also to the people living within the cultural space (not always contiguous) covered by that code; if it provides work, something meaningful to do, for everybody from birth to death, for new generations; if furthermore it does not run on a collision course with others, but instead defines a live-and-let-live attitude to them, neither trying to subdue nor to be subdued, then why should it be changed? Such a code works; it defines one type of human life out of an unbounded set of potential types. Even within the discourse defined by the chart at the beginning of this chapter, a high number of potential civilizations can be determined; yet humankind has so far realized only a few. Just as any number of species can be imagined, so can any number of civilizations, for future history.

But what if the civilization is, in fact, on a collision course with others? Two such civilizations are described above: Occident I and the Nipponic civilizations. The dangerous gene in the codes is the idea of Periphery-Evil in the occidental space code and of Resource in the Nipponic space code. If Japan were to be seen as Evil by Occident I, and the West as a Resource by Japan, then the collision course would be obvious.

One implication of cosmology analysis is that efforts to realize the code by the leaders will meet with acceptance or acquiescence by the followers; whatever is compatible with the code will meet with tacit approval, including collisions. Intercivilization relations can be predicted from the chart, and the conclusion may be that changes in Occident I and the Nipponic are called for. But the question of how is outside the scope of this chapter: that would be an exercise in peace studies, not in studies of meaning.

Let us end with an educated guess. If the key to the "animal kingdom" is diversity *cum* symbiosis, then maybe this is also the case for the human kingdom. Maybe the level of a civilization should not be measured by the height and length of its durable monuments (pyramids, walls, towers, columns, skyscrapers), but its ability to coexist with other civilizations.

Looking back at the six civilizations and the meaning of their historicities, it seems that Occident I wants to impose its meaning on others. This is fulfilled by being alone, by being the only one. Occident II had similar ambitions (the Crusades, again) but in the meantime accomodated enormous diversity and symbiosis within itself, and had to recast itself as Occident I to really launch that *projet* of singularism *cum* universalism. Some five centuries of imperialism later, occidental codes have been implanted with more or less successfully everywhere, and Westerners have learnt, practically speaking, nothing from the peoples they exterminated or dominated, not the languages, nor the religions, nor the arts; only some spices, and some exotica for their museums.

There is more promise in the Hindu, Buddhic, and Sinic codes, though some of the Occident I megalomania can be discerned in the Sinic code. That the Hindu civilization conceives of itself as universal is no problem, as long as that universalism is not imposed on others. Buddhic civilization seems able to coexist with almost anything. Sinic civilization solves problems by minimizing contact; Nipponic civilization, by being regionalist rather than universalist. Only the Occident has a final state, because only the Occident has a *projet* with an end to it. The others are all *sin fin*. For that reason, they may all be around after Occident I in its present incarnation has expired, and transformed itself into a new, more modest, less universalist Occident II.[4]

Notes

1. Some terms in need of clarification: "meatism": the tendency to eat meat, much and frequently; "sangha": a small Buddhist community, like a monastery or retreat; "Zhong-guo": Chinese for China, the Middle Kingdom; "Nihon": Japanese for Japan, the Origin of the Sun; "dai-to-a": Japanese for Greater East Asia; "moksha": spiritual liberation; "resourcia": the outside as resource, raw materials, and markets. The time curves for self and society reflect the images of what is normal and natural in terms of ups and downs, in personal life, and for the society as a whole.

2. See W. O. Quine, *From a Logical Point of View,* 2nd rev. ed. (New York 1963).

3. More particularly, the Spenglerian sense of civilization as degenerate culture is not implied.

4. For an effort to conceive of Western history as an oscillation between Occident and Occident II logic, see Johan Galtung, Tore Heiestad, and Erik Rudeng, "On the Last 2,500 Years in Western History. And Some Remarks on the Coming 500," in Peter Burke, ed., *New Cambridge Modern History,* vol. 13 (Cambridge, Mass. 1979), 318–361.

CHAPTER 6

The Three Levels of *"Sinnbildung"* in Historical Writing

FRANK R. ANKERSMIT

Introduction

Twentieth-century philosophy is predominantly a philosophy of language and of how language relates to the world. Until some twenty to thirty years ago, in what I shall refer to as the modernist phase of contemporary philosophy of language, one focused on the singular true statement and on the kind of statements of reality that are found in the sciences. Modernist philosophers of language, convinced that the true statement and the scientific theory provided the philosopher of language with paradigmatic models for how language and reality are related, therefore concluded that the statement and the scientific theory held the key to all problems pertaining to the relationship between language and reality.

Postmodernism can be defined in many different ways—the term has different meanings for the architect, the literary theorist, and the artist. But insofar as postmodernism has manifested itself in the field of philosophy—here one may think of such philosophers as Derrida, Lyotard, or Rorty—one may observe a unanimous rejection of the statement and the scientific theory as the exclusive model for the relationship between language and reality. It was argued that the text—the story, the novel, the historian's narrative—occasioned different problems in that relationship, and that therefore a new and different approach would be required to deal adequately with this new set of problems. In a word, instead of the modernist inquiry into the relationship between the true statement and reality, postmodernists turned to an investigation of the nature of the *representation* of reality in and by the text.

Notes for this section begin on page 122.

However, a high price had to be paid for this liberation of philosophy of language from the fetters of modernism. Not only have postmodernist philosophers of language been unsuccessful in devising a workable strategy for dealing with their newly discovered set of philosophical problems, but it might also be argued that they have never even seriously tried to develop such a strategy. The consequences are in proportion. Though interesting new and valuable results have been obtained with regard to the relationships between texts themselves, the really crucial question of the relationship between the representation and the reality represented was never really addressed. This lack of balance effected an exclusive interest in the text, while the represented reality itself completely vanished from sight, as may be clear from Derrida's notorious and ill-famed "il n'y a pas dehors texte."

This has resulted, again, in the postmodernist so-called "representationcrisis." In order to overcome this crisis, we shall have to ask ourselves what category is systematically marginalized by postmodernism, without, however, abandoning ourselves to the fetters of modernism anew. I hope to show in this essay that the notion of experience satisfies this requirement and therefore may help us out of the impasses of the present representationcrisis.

This periodization of twentieth-century philosophy of language will also enable us to discern the major phases in contemporary philosophy of history. One might say that the philosophy of history from the 50s to the 70s corresponded to modernism as defined above. Both the debate about the covering-law model and Anglo-Saxon hermeneutics were mainly concerned with the problem of the justification of individual statements (either descriptive or explanatory) about the past. More specifically, as Gadamer made clear in his critique of traditional hermeneutics as culminating in Dilthey, the antipositivism of traditional hermeneutics should never tempt us to ignore the extent to which it shared with positivism the typically modernist ideal of the true statement about the past.

Along with so-called narrativism and with the narrativist's interest in the kind of problems occasioned by the historical narrative when taken as a whole, historical theory has entered its postmodernist phase. Historical representation has now become the major topic of investigation in historical theory. And, as might be expected, the fate of postmodernism closely parallels that of narrativist historical theory. If the main weakness of postmodernism is its inability to give a satisfactory answer to the question of the relationship between the represented and its representation, narrativist historical theory has likewise sidestepped this question. One might even argue that most narrativists tend to regard this question as suggestive of a naive and outdated kind of "positivism." Obviously, historical theory has been marginalized in the eyes of most practicing historians, whose professional problems always originate in their sincere wish to do, in some way or other, "justice to the past." One should not allow oneself to be so blinded by theory as to condemn the question as meaningless only because (postmodernist or narrativist) theory seems to successfully thwart every effort to raise it. For this theory allows for an indeterminacy in the relationship between the represented past and its representation that is hopelessly at odds with the facts of historical practice.

Postmodernism and narrativism thus must be emended in such a way that the historian's intuitive ability to represent a past reality in and by his narrative is respected. Moreover, the narrativist's critique of modernism is sufficiently convincing to prevent us from expecting modernism to provide clues for how to explain and justify the historian's intuition. We should avoid interpreting the shortcomings of postmodernism as an invitation to return to modernism—instead, we now must transcend the debate between modernism and postmodernism. Hence, our problem will be how to define anew the relationship between past reality and historical narrative while avoiding traditional empiricist and positivist simplifications. I hope to show here that the notion of (historical) experience can help us answer this question.

But in order to do the job properly, the notion of experience will have to be freed of its current empiricist and positivist connotations. The Aristotelian concept of experience and the notion of aesthetic experience are our best point of departure. I end this introduction with a comment on how this transition from modernist truth, via postmodernist (narrativist) interpretation, to post-postmodernist (or premodernist) experience should be interpreted.

I believe that all three positions contain part of the truth about historical writing. There is in all historical writing a dimension where the historian attempts (often successfully) to tell the truth about the past. This is where the modernist model of the true statement undoubtedly is the appropriate one. This is the first level of *Sinnbildung* in historical writing. But the historian does more than make true statements about past reality: the whole of the narrative is expected to offer us a representation of part of the past. And this brings us to a second level, that of *historische Sinnbildung*. Yet both these first two levels remain embedded in a third level of *historische Sinnbildung:* the one that has its origins in historical experience. That is to say, each phase in the history of historical writing (and, though quite rarely, individual works of history) presupposes a certain form of "historical experience" that is seldom recognized as such because the subject of this experience is the community of historians rather than the individual historian. But—and this is essential—each of the three levels of *historische Sinnbildung* has its proper domain and function. Never should we be tempted to exclude one level from the list because of an exaggerated love for one or two of the others. Historical writing always comprises each of the three levels of *Sinnbildung*.

Statement, Representation and Narrative

Let us first investigate the claim that the transition from modernist truth to postmodernist representation confronts us with a new set of philosophical problems, for we cannot reject outright the possibility that representation can be analyzed in terms of truth and of the true statement. The crucial difference between the statement and the (textual) representation of reality is that the former can be analyzed epistemologically, whereas this does not hold for representation. Epistemology investigates the logical ties between notions such as reality, meaning, reference, and truth and in this way presents us with the matrix within which the relationship between the true statement and reality can be defined. Representation can never be reduced to this matrix since representation permits an indeterminacy in the relationship between the representation and the represented that would be utterly unthinkable within the matrix of epistemology. A circle may represent a city on a map, the sun, the earth, or a human face, and is, as such, dependent on tradition, stipulation, and simple convention. It is clear that epistemology could never permit this almost unlimited autonomy of the representation with regard to the represented.

And indeed, success has eluded all attempts in the last few decades to achieve an epistemological reduction of the representation of reality to the kind of problems occasioned by the true statement. This failure can be explained with the help of more general argumentation and an argument derived from the nature of historical narrative. In the more general argumentation, it is pointed out that epistemology is necessarily blind to the problems specific to representation: if we examine a represented on the one hand and its representation on the other, both the represented and the representation will give rise to exactly the same epistemological problems. For example, the categories of the understanding of Kantian epistemology do not, and cannot, distinguish between a representation and what is represented by it. Epistemology does not enable us to philosophically articulate what differentiates the represented from its representation, just as, for example, the purely physical properties of two books are useless if we want to articulate their difference in content. In other words, by its very nature epistemology is indifferent to the problems of representation, and therefore it is of no help in our attempt to solve the problems of representation.

Next, taking historical writing as our point of departure, we must recognize that the historian's narrative—undoubtedly the paradigmatic example of representation—defines a (metaphorical) point of view from which the historian proposes that we see the past. Put differently, representation and historical narrative are essentially proposals for ways to organize knowledge (as expressed by the true statement) without being knowledge themselves. And since the organization of knowledge presents us with a set of philosophical problems different from those occasioned by the true statement, we can never expect epistemology to be of assistance in our quest for the best or most convincing representation or narrative. We may conclude that the problem of the representation of reality cannot be answered by epistemological insights into the nature of the true statement. This is where postmodernism has correctly demonstrated the shortcomings of modernism and where narrativism, thanks to its interest in the problems of (historical) representation, has been an indispensable supplement to the modernist account of the true historical statement (either descriptive or explanatory).

The Representation and the Represented

Apart from modernism's shortcomings there is another conclusion following from these considerations: namely, that when considering the problems of representation, historical narrative is best suited to deal with them. Since the historian's narrative typically consists of true statements (which cannot be said, for example, of pictorial representation), historical narrative best exemplifies where and why representation (in general) goes beyond epistemology and all that we have learned to associate with it. This is also why historical theory might rightly claim far more interest than philosophers of language are generally prepared to grant to it. The writing of history is the most appropriate background for a discussion of the merits of modernism, postmodernism, and (aesthetic) experience. All the more reason, then, to regret the historical theorist's perennial habit of applying to historical writing results that have already been achieved in other disciplines[1] instead of recognizing historical writing as a unique and independent source of challenging intellectual problems.

If, then, the true statement cannot be the right model for assessing the nature of the relationship between the representation and what it represents, our primary task will have to be a closer investigation of this relationship. To that end, the nature of both—representation and represented—must first clarified further.

So let us start with representation and focus on historical representation. Where and how can we discover the representation that is being proposed in a historical narrative? Decisive here is the following. Although an introduction and summary, or certain statements uttered by the historian himself, may help the reader to ascertain which chapters, paragraphs, or sets of statements in the historian's narrative determine what picture of the past is presented in it, this will rarely be sufficient. To be more precise, we can never tell whether a specific statement really contributes to that picture or that merely serves the historian's purpose to present his readers with true information about the past. The historian's task is essentially twofold: to state the truth about the past, and to select and organize statements that do so in such a way that a certain picture of the past arises out of the text. But the text itself offers insufficient clues to properly distinguish between these two levels of meaning in the text.

This already suggests what clue the reader has at his disposal: whereas a narrative itself does not unambiguously define the nature of how it represents part of the past, the contrast with other narratives on the same topic will contribute to such a definition. (Hence the postmodernist's interest in the Saussurian theory of the sign, where we find much the same argument.) For example, if we discover in Foucault's narrative on the Enlightenment many statements about the social and political regimentation of the modern individual while such statements are absent from more traditional narratives on the Enlightenment, we may be sure that these statements are part of Foucault's representation of the Enlightenment, while the statements that one can also discover in these more traditional narratives are not. In short, we can recognize representations only in contrast with other, competing representations.

Three postmodernist theses can be derived from this line of reasoning. With regard to representation, "negativity" is of greater significance than "positivity." Representations owe their contours to conflict and denial, not to confirmation. Confirmation only stimulates indeterminacy and formlessness. Here we may discern the "dialectical" character of representation: just as Hegel's dialectics can only unfold thanks to negativity and denial, all understanding of the past is essentially a denial of previous understandings.

A second implication is the postmodernist thesis of the so-called "intertextuality" of historical representation. If a representation is at heart a denial of other representations, these denied representations can be said to be the "subtexts" of the historian's text. In that sense, we may say that a representation is what it is not and that historical meaning is the result of a process of "dissemination" of representative meaning.

But within the present context a third thesis is of more importance. Hegel believed that dialectics would bring us ever closer to the truth, but such optimism is not easy to justify with regard to representation. For whereas the statement can be tested by what reality shows to be the case, the peculiar dependency of textual representations on the availability of other representations leaves us without objective and independent data for assessing their plausibility. We must conclude that the plausibility of historical representations will largely be determined by the interplay between representations themselves, rather than by their relationship to what is represented by them.

At this stage we should recognize the extent to which representation has ushered us into a philosophical world entirely different from that of the true statement. This will become clear as we now turn our attention to the nature of the represented. We are naturally inclined to model the represented on what the true statement is true of: that is, on an objective "given" having an inexorable priority to whatever we might wish to say about it. But this is not true of the represented. Just as a certain territory on our globe becomes a country like Germany or the Netherlands only after people start using that name for that territory, so the represented comes into being thanks alone to its representation. This is no form of idealism: we could not say that simply using the name Germany is sufficient to create a certain part of our globe's surface, and the same holds true for the represented and its representation. Yet we may say that representation gives us access to something that in a certain sense was not there before the representation was proposed. This is why there exists such a thing as representation at all: without representation we would have no represented (at least, not in the way that we can have states of affairs even without the statements describing them), which would have disastrous implications for our grasp of reality. To find our way about in (historical, social, or political) reality, we need the kinds of *organization* of knowledge that only representation can give us. Without representation we would be just as helpless as the toddler who is still unable to use words like "here," "there," "me," or "you"—words that have no meaning in themselves yet are indispensable for bringing order and coherence in the world in which we live.

Hence, and this is most important, we should not regret the priority of the representation over the represented as an imperfection of representation or lamentable failure to live up to the pure and demanding standards of the true statement (which is the customary source of all modernist opposition to the notion of representation): that representation does not satisfy these standards is precisely the reason we have it. That it cannot be "true" is not a shortcoming of representation (as modernists tend to believe), but the reason we so need representation in addition to truth. A "true representation" would be as useless as a *facsimile* of a text being handed to us in response to our question how to interpret it. Representation has always been condemned by the modernist, who is fixated on truth and is unable to recognize that truth simply is not enough to orient us in reality.

Needless to say, all this is not an attack on truth, but merely a thesis about the limitations of truth as our compass in reality and about our possession of instruments for orienting ourselves in reality that are more intellectual than truth or scientific validity. Put differently, reality has two faces: what the true statement is true of, and what is represented by a representation. If the former is called first reality "as such" and the latter "phenomenal" reality, we can even discern here a postmodernist variant of Kantianism.

The Representationcrisis and Historical Experience

It is precisely these just-mentioned features of representation that occasioned the "representationcrisis" to which I referred in my introduction. It was the autonomy and the logical priority of the representation over the represented that stimulated postmodernist hermeneuticists and deconstructivists to focus exclusively on the representation while suggesting that nothing of interest could be said about the relationship between the representation and the represented. Thus Gadamer argued that each representation is part of a *"Wirkungsgeschichte"* (history of reception) in which the representation moves away from, rather than closer to, the represented, and deconstructivists even completely eliminated the represented by declaring the text to be its own context, thus reducing the represented to sheer irrelevance. But the historian cannot be satisfied with this repression of the represented in favor of the representation. To put in the naive and, admittedly, misleading language that I used at the end of the preceding section, the historian does aim at such a "true representation"; he may be well aware that saying true things about reality is infinitely easier than to achieve such a "true representation"—nevertheless, he will not be prepared to abandon that notion even if it lingers only in the guise of a disciplinary goal or ideal that can never actually be realized.

Precisely because representation always is at the mercy of Gadamerian *"Wirkungsgeschichte,"* precisely because representation possesses this rhetorical autonomy that the deconstructivist attributes to it, precisely because such relatively weak forces as tradition and the text's own rhetoric prove to be a determinant so much more powerful than the nature of the represented itself, the historian feels continually challenged to escape from the powers of tradition, context, and rhetoric as well as he can.

How, then, to escape from "the prisonhouse of language" to use Jameson's memorable metaphor? Where may we observe the resistance of the represented against tradition and rhetoric, and how can we articulate this resistance without returning to the naive empiricism of the "myth of the innocent eye" that Ruskin already attacked? When trying to answer this crucial question we are well advised to consider so-called "historical sensation" or "historical experience." Many historians and poets since Herder and Goethe have described how they experienced a direct contact with the past in a moment of supreme intellectual grace.

The most important features of "historical experience" have been summed up by Huizinga.[2] According to Huizinga, historical experience is typically effected by relatively trivial objects, such as an antique print, an old song, or, the foyer of a building that has not changed for centuries. The explanation is that, for example, a painting by Titian or Rafael is to us so much the exponent of the development of the history of art, that we become unable to still see it as the expression of a certain historical reality. Secondly, historical experience is "an intoxication of the moment," as Huizinga put it: something that the historian undergoes that cannot be deliberately provoked or repeated. And, thirdly, historical experience is founded in the historian's conviction that direct and completely authentic contact has been made with the past. It is telling, in this connection, that Huizinga relates historical experience to the sense of touch rather than to the eye or the ear. The eye and the ear are our most "educated" senses in that what they present to the mind always is part of a history of seeing and hearing, and part of our being the product of such a history of seeing, and is therefore in need of decodation. The sense of touch, meanwhile, adapts itself to the actual forms that we have in our fingers or hands. The eye has history, but the sense of touch is without a past. It is really the sense of touch, therefore, that gives us the most direct and immediate contact with reality. It is the un- or ahistorical that truly confronts us with history, while the historical *sui generis* never can objectify history as such. Similarly, the social, is only truly experienced as such in its contrast to the private and the individual.

Having arrived at this stage, three questions have to be answered. First, can the claim be justified that historical experience really transcends a representation-tradition? Second, if so, how can the content of historical experience find its way to a representation of the past? And, third, what place must we assign to historical experience in historical practice? I have dealt with the second question elsewhere,[3] while the third question will only be answered toward the end of this chapter.

Starting with the first question, we should observe that almost all of 20th-century philosophy opposes this idea of the possibility of the direct and immediate contact with reality that is suggested by historical experience. We have all become Kantians in one way or another: we dismiss out of hand a contact with reality that is not mediated by language, narrative, scientific theories, Kantian categories of understanding, or what have you.

It is not my intention to join issue with this near-universal consensus. Indeed, all experience, even historical experience, is irrevocably contextual. Surely, when a Van Eyck exhibition in the summer of 1902 prompted Huizinga's historical experience of the late Middle Ages—from which his *The Waning of the Middle Ages* originated—he could only have had this susceptibility to these paintings thanks to what he already knew of the period. A caveat—we should observe is that this also might seem to require us to embrace the contemporary dogma of the context-bound character of the content of experience. Nevertheless, my thesis is that the undeniable fact that the occurrence of a historical experience is context-bound need have no implications as to the content of that experience.

A metaphor may clarify my intentions. Suppose we are looking down from an airplane to the ground beneath. Often clouds will prevent us from seeing the ground, but when there is an opening in the clouds we will have an unobstructed view. So it is with historical experience. Most often "the clouds of tradition and context" will prevent us from seeing the past itself, but that does not exclude the possibility of a "glimpse" of the past itself in the case of a momentary absence of these contextualist clouds. We can justifiably in argue that it is the *clouds* that determine whether this may happen or not, and in that sense historical experience is indeed context-bound. However—and this is crucial—though the fact that we see the ground (or the past) may be determined by the clouds, they cannot determine what we will actually see under these circumstances. This unwarranted shift from the "that" to the "what" is the *non sequitur* that we may discern in much contemporary argumentation in favor of the context-bound character of all experience.

The metaphor of the airplane suggests a further determination of the conditions of the possibility of historical experience. We can see the ground from the airplane only when the airplane (and we ourselves) are located above an opening in the clouds. Similarly, the past can be experienced only when a certain "harmony" prevails between the relevant part of the past itself and the subject of experience. Consequently, the exclusive preoccupation with these contextualist and traditionalist clouds (as we may find this in Gadamer or Derrida) is inevitably at odds with the desire to escape from the representationcrisis. More specifically, we may expect that such a preoccupation will necessarily lead to an attack on experience. Both Derrida and Gadamer were well aware of this: the former's "il n'y a pas dehors texte" eliminates experience together with its potential object. Gadamer is even more explicit: *"wir wissen, was für die Bewältigung jeder Erfahrung ihre sprachliche Erfassung leistet. Es ist, als ob ihre drohende und erschlagende Unmittelbarkeit in die Ferne gerückt, in Proportionen gebracht, mitteilbar und damit gebannt würde."*[4] Language as the embodiment of context and tradition—as *"das Haus des Seins das verstanden werden kann"*—destroys, as Gadamer himself recognizes, the structure of experience and places itself between us and the world, just as the Kantian had already done two hundred years ago for the first time.

The "harmony" between the subject and the object of experience in direct experience that I mentioned a moment ago can be further clarified with the help of Dewey's analysis of aesthetic experience. Three considerations require our attention here. In the first place, it can be demonstrated that historical experience as defined above is a variant of aesthetic experience. Not only is historical experience most often provoked by works of art; more importantly, the submission of our perceptual apparatus to the object of experience is the common feature of both historical and aesthetic experience.[5] Second—and following on from the previous consideration—Dewey makes clear that this harmony can come into being only when the subject and the object of experience meet on equal terms. Similarly, as interhuman contact is richest amongst those who are socially each other's equals, so experience loses content when there is a master-slave relationship between the subject and the object of experience and it thereby ceases to be an experience of (historical) reality in the sense meant here.

And this leads to a third consideration: This last condition can only be met when the content of experience has a certain structural *complexity*. If not, if the content of experience is, so to speak, an experiential *atom;* alone it will be unable to resist the constraint of the structures of context and tradition. This may also explain why, in the history of Western epistemology, we may observe transcendentalist patterns of argument, according to which theory, language narrative, and other are the condition for the possibility of all experience, and a concomitant tendency to focus exclusively on the most elementary, simple sort of experience. Indeed, as soon as our point of departure becomes not simple, but complex experience, both transcendentalism and the foundationalist fascination with so-called sense-data, *"Protokollsätze"* (protocol sentences) immediately lose their plausibility.

Capping these three considerations is the paradox that a direct and immediate experience of reality is possible only in the case of a complex experience. Complexity does not tie us to the present and the subject—as we might initially have expected—but is the condition that makes the subject susceptible to reality "as such."

Statement and Representation

Let us return for a moment to the statement and the representation. I want to argue that from the point of view of the foregoing, the true statement, that traditional paradigm of knowledge in the tradition of Western philosophy, does not deserve its prestigious status because it is essentially "incomplete," or "unsatiated" and still in need of perfection. The lawlike statement perfects the true statement because by expressing a relationship between predicates it eliminates the indeterminacy in the relationship between the subject-term and the predicate-term in the true statement, (for we may make many different true statements about what the subject-term refers to). The representation, in its turn, perfects the true statement because, as I have shown elsewhere,[6] it ties all the statements contained in the representation to itself by a relationship of analyze. In this way the representation eliminates the randomness in the relationship between the subject- and the predicate-term characteristic of the true statement. Future epistemological analyses of the true statement should bear in mind that we should not argue from the true statement to the lawlike statement and the representation, but the other way round.

That, paradoxically, the true statement is logically more complex than the representation and dependent on it can be argued as follows. If a certain narrative representation of, for example, the Enlightenment or the Cold War were to be accepted by all people, one might say that an "essentially contested concept" (to use Gallie's terminology) has turned into the concept of a "thing," i.e., the historical "thing" that these words refer to. Speaking more generally, it is in this way that our notions of things come into being. Hence we may conclude that, contrary to our intuitions, representation does not presuppose a certain ontology, a certain inventory of what things reality contains; but that such an inventory is the result of a tacit agreement with regard to representation. Representation precedes our knowledge of things and their properties as expressed by true statements. As Hegel saw, the true statement is a highly complex and abstract linguistic artifact, even more so than the representation. So we should not think that there is an everyday reality that is unproblematically given to us, in which we may observe certain regularities that are expressed by lawlike statements and certain vague patterns that we define with the help of representations. The scientist's reality—is an abstraction of that reality; it is utterly "unreal" to us, though it consists of *phenomena bene fundata* (to use Leibniz's most appropriate terminology); everyday reality is, indeed, so much more "real" to us than the scientist's reality—but it is, in fact, a codification, determined by context and tradition, of our representations. In this way the misleading concreteness of everyday reality is unveiled together with empiricist and positivist illusions about the true statement.

All this has its counterpart on the level of experience, as may become clear from a short excursus in the field of intellectual history. Since Dilthey, Lukasiewicz, and Mates it has often been pointed out that Western epistemology and metaphysics since Descartes can best be seen as a reprise of the Stoic tradition. We must primarily think here of the Stoic speculation about the *"logoi spermatikoi"* that were believed to inhere both in reality itself and in our rational thought about the nature of reality—thus guaranteeing that reliable knowledge of reality would indeed be possible. It might be argued that ever since seventeenth-century rationalism most of Western philosophy, has been a series of attempts to develop an epistemological and metaphysical definition of these Stoic *"logoi spermatikoi."* Or, put differently, one was always looking for the *tertia comparationis,* that would enable us to argue from reality to our knowledge, or vice versa. Needless to say, this search made sense only given the assumption that there are such things as these "logoi spermatikoi" or *tertia comparationis.*

We can now understand why the kind of experience that is discussed in this essay can only play a subordinate role in Western philosophy: these *tertia comparationis* tended to take the place of experience—as the intermediate between the subject and the object—and that therefore the success of Stoicism and its modern(ist) variants can be measured precisely to the extent that they were able to get rid of experience. Empiricist systems tend to see reality as the strong partner in the "transmissionline" from reality to knowledge, whereas rationalist systems tended to see the subject as the stronger partner. But both systems require the *tertia comparationis* in order to argue from the one to the other.

Furthermore, it is here that postmodernism continues in modernist patterns of thought rather than breaking with them. It is true that we may discern in postmodernism a sovereign disdain for reality, and in this sense the *tertia* now tend to become a useless wheel in the machine, or, rather, a wheel that, as soon as it started to turn, invariably produced twentieth-century textualist variants of nineteenth-century idealism. A break with both modernism and postmodernism can be achieved only if we are prepared to radically abandon the notion of the *tertia.* This is where postmodernism, for all its alleged interest in aesthetics, has most conspicuously failed, for it is art and aesthetics that pose the most serious challenge to the *tertia* and it need not surprise us that Stoicism never attempted to develop even a rudimentary aesthetics. Indeed, what interests us in a work of art, and where we may discover its never-ending "newness," is that it constantly disappoints each content that we might wish to give to the relevant *tertia*. It is precisely the absence of the *tertia* and, more specifically, our continuous awareness of their absence, that prevents the domination of the subject over the object (or vice versa). By eliminating the *tertia* we have also broken down the bridge that the subject and the object might use to dominate each other. In a word, the foregoing argument with regard to the *tertia* will have made clear what aesthetic experience and historical experience have in common, where the former may contribute to a better understanding of the latter, and why in both cases the complexity of the content of experience will guarantee the directness and immediacy that Huizinga associated with historical experience.

I now return to the three questions asked earlier: (1) Can experience transcend a history of representation? (2) How can historical experience be put into words? (I have dealt with this issue elsewhere), and (3) What is the function of historical experience in historical practice? Turning now to the third question, it should be noted, above all, that the creation of a discipline and of a disciplinary "discourse" can best be understood as the creation of (a set of) *tertia* in the sense meant above. As soon as a domain of intellectual pursuit becomes a discipline, conceptual and disciplinary instruments are developed in order to integrate knowledge and the results of disciplinary experience. Put differently, these instruments aim at making all knowledge within the discipline commensurable and compatible. Hence, there is an intrinsic relationship between the Stoic *tertia* and the disciplinary discourse that is in use within a discipline.

This enables us to respond to the paradoxical place of historical experience within *historische Sinnbildung*. Since historical experience transcends the disciplinary Stoic *tertia* it cannot function as an argument in disciplinary discourse. No historian can appeal to historical experience in order to convince his colleagues. Rather, historical experience may motivate a historian to agree or to disagree with his colleagues. An even more appropriate assessment of historical experience would be the following. Just as the sense of touch adapts itself to the forms of reality itself, so the historian's mind is formed *(ausgebildet)* by the past in historical experience, a process transcending tradition and context. This "formation" or *"Bildung"* of the historian's mind will determine the kinds of things he will prefer to say about the past without ever being itself subject to the processes of argumentation and justification that characterize the discipline. Historical experience belongs to what Collingwood referred to as the domain of "absolute presuppositions" rather than to what can be said on the basis of these presuppositions. In this way historical experience is both part of the discipline and outside it.

Objections will be raised that historical experience is a rare phenomenon, and that most historians will even deny having any familiarity with the experience. There would be no point in disagreeing with this objection: history, as a discipline, is predominantly carried along by the weight of its own history, discourse, and traditions unhampered by direct experiential contact (as defined here) with the past reality that it investigates. Historical experience is not required for being an excellent historian. Nevertheless, there have been some individual historians, such as Herder, Michelet, Burckhardt, and Huizinga, whose most important and influential historical work was born from a historical experience. And that is not all, nor even the most important conclusion. For we may say that each phase in the history of historical writing originates from a vaguely intuited historical experience whose subject is not the, or an, individual historian, but the collective subject of the discipline as a whole. Each phase in the history of historical writing articulates a specific relationship to the past that cannot be justified by acquired insights into the past but that provokes these insights. Historical experience may confirm, challenge, or condemn an existing historical discourse without ever being itself subject to confirmation, challenge, or rejection. It determines the flow of *historische Sinnbildung,* which we can accept only as long as we have no perspective from which to effectively and meaningfully question it.

Conclusion

Modernists believe that the true statement is the key that will open the door to the most important philosophical secrets. Postmodernism, with its interest in the text and the representation of reality presented in and by the text, demonstrates what was wrong with this intuition, which had come to underlie much of twentieth-century philosophy of language. Postmodernism is not so much a supplement to the text of what modernism says about the true statement, but rather a correction of modernism in that it makes clear that we can understand the true statement only on the basis of an adequate insight into the nature of representation. In this way postmodernism has displaced modernism.

Nevertheless, we must not forget that postmodernism has failed on two counts. It never developed a well-considered theory of representation. And, more importantly, it uncritically accepted one of the major tenets of modernism, namely, the idea that our theories, our narratives, our language—in short, all the variants of the Kantian categories of understanding that have been invented in the resourceful past century—determines our knowledge and experience of the world. It is here that hermeneuticists, deconstructivists, and other theorists of context and tradition are even more radical than their modernist predecessors.

A post-postmodernist stage is therefore reached only if we consistently and relentlessly de-transcendentalize both modernism and postmodernism. This task can be achieved by taking aesthetics as the point of departure in reflections on how we relate to the world, by eliminating the *tertia* from our conceptual inventory, and by recognizing that the notion of experience is best suited for carrying out these new tasks of philosophy. In sum, we should move away from modernist truth, via postmodernist representation, to post-postmodernist experience.

All the while, though, we must remember that each of these three phases in the recent history of contemporary philosophy corresponds to one of the three stations on our itinerary to *historische Sinnbildung*. Historical writing has its modernist, postmodernist, and post-postmodernist (or pre-modernist) dimensions, each of which corresponds to something that is essential to our understanding of the nature of the writing of history. Each attempt to reduce any of these three levels of *historische Sinnbildung* to one or more of the others will inevitably result in distortion and incomprehension. Thus, in order to understand historical writing we shall have to take together the recent developments in the philosophy of language and experience, instead of extolling one at the expense of the others—as we are always inclined to do. In this way the philosophical shortcomings of modernism, postmodernism, and post-postmodernism are overcome in the practice of history and of *historische Sinnbildung*.

Notes

1. Historist historical theory as developed since Ranke, the only exceptions to this rule being Humboldt and Droysen.

2. See J. Huizinga, *Verzamelde werken*, 9 vol. (Haarlem 1950), vol. 2, 564ff; id., *Verzamelde werken* (Haarlem 1950), vol.7, 71ff. For a "phenomenology" of historical experience, see the last chapter of my *History and Tropology* (Berkeley 1994), my "Can we experience the past?" published in R. Torstendahl and I. Veit-Brause, eds., *History-making: The intellectual and social formation of a discipline* (Stockholm 1996), 44–77; my "Historism: an attempt at synthesis", published in *History and Theory* 34.1 (1995): 143–162; my *De historische ervaring* (Groningen 1993); my "Van taal naar ervaring" in S. Alexandrescu, ed., *Richard Rorty* (Kampen 1995); my "Language and historical experience," in this volume; my "Die postmoderne Privatisierung der Vergangenheit," in H. Nagl-Docekal, ed., *Geschichtstheorie nach der grossen Erzählung* (Frankfurt/ M. 1995) and my "Representatie, waarheid en ervaring," in J. Klukhuhn, ed., *Postmodernism Revisited* (Utrecht 1995) and my *Sublime Historical Experience* (Stanford 2005).

3. This question, which I shall not discuss here is dealt within my "Language and historical experience."

4. H. G. Gadamer, *Wahrheit und Methode* (Tübingen 1960), 429. (Translation: H. G. Gadamer, *Truth and Method,* translation edited by Garrett Barden and John Cumming [London 1975]).

5. J. Dewey, *Art As Experience* (Carbondale 1987), 287ff. The structural similarities between historical and aesthetic experience are demonstrated in my essay "Can we experience the past."

6. I argued this thesis in my *Narrative Logic* (The Hague 1983).

CHAPTER 7

The Reality of History

David Carr

History as a branch of knowledge begins with a distinct handicap. While there may be serious disputes about whether theology, for example, has any object, there is a broad consensus that the object of history does not exist at all. In view of this fact it is perhaps no wonder that skepticism about history's claims to knowledge has always been widespread.

Reasons for this skepticism are not hard to come by. The events of the past cannot be seen, heard, or felt, and any assertions we make about them must be grounded by the most indirect means. Testimony to their existence is often such that we cannot be sure even of its meaning, much less its truth. What is worse, historians may be even less trustworthy than the evidence they examine. The personal, political, religious, or other prejudices of the investigator seem more likely to affect the study of past human events than they affect the study of animals, plants, or inanimate nature.

In our own day skepticism abounds regarding the objectivity and truthfulness of even the physical sciences. Many feel that the "scientific" pretensions of the so-called "human sciences," history in particular, need even more obviously to be deflated. One form of skepticism about history has arisen from reflections on the narrative form in which historical knowledge is often presented. If historians are essentially telling stories about the past, their activity seems more literary than scientific. The standards of story-telling are different from those of truth-telling: the point is to produce a coherent tale with beginning, middle, and end, and perhaps a moral lesson to convey. The proper place for narrative is fiction, which is by definition unconcerned with the reality of the events it portrays. Story-telling about real events thus runs the risk of being inadvertently fictional, more concerned with aesthetic than with scientific crite-

---

Notes for this section begin on page 135.

ria. In this view, history seems condemned, by the very form in which it is written, to distort or misrepresent the events about which it claims to know.

Against this skeptical view, it can be argued that the very reality of history—*res gestae*, which are human acts and experiences, plans and projects—already has the narrative form in which historical writing is largely cast. Far from being merely the literary form of either fictional or historical writing, narrative is found at the level of human events themselves. Story-telling is, to use Rüsen's expression, the manner in which natural time is transformed into human time.[1] For Paul Ricoeur, similarly, "time becomes human to the extent that it is articulated through a narrative mode."[2] Agreeing with Rüsen, Ricoeur, and other theorists on this point, I have argued elsewhere at length for the narrative character of ordinary human experience and action, both individual and social. I have claimed that this form is found even below the level of explicit story-telling and is characteristic of the way time is humanly experienced and structured.[3] If this theory is true, it undercuts the skeptical challenge to historical and other narratives. It cannot then be said that they impose an alien structure on the realities they deal with, systematically distorting them in the process. Far from differing in structure from historical reality, historical narrative shares the form of its object, and can be seen as an extension and refinement by other means of the very reality it is about. This theory thus affirms a continuity, rather than a disparity, between historical reality and historical narrative.

I am convinced that this "continuity theory" (as I shall call it) is substantially correct. But there are some serious challenges to this theory that have not yet been met by its defenders, myself included. The theory seems to me to be particularly vulnerable at two points, and in what follows I would like to focus on these weak points, examine the corresponding challenges as I see them, and defend the theory against them.

The two points I refer to are located at the two ends of the continuum the theory affirms. The first concerns the narrative character of ordinary experience and action. Against the claim that narrative structures are found at the root of our temporal and practical experience, it can be argued that there are other ways time can be experienced and organized, and that the continuity theory in fact invokes a parochial conception of time—one that is specifically Western and perhaps even modern—in its analysis of human experience.

If the continuity theory can respond to this challenge, it faces another one at the other end of its continuum. It may be that historical narrative is simply a sophisticated and specialized form of the same story-telling that takes place in the world of ordinary experience, and is thus continuous with it. But one also has to account for how it differs from that "ordinary" world, and this turns out to be very complicated. It could be argued that the motives, principles, and intentions of historical narrative are so different from those of nonhistorical narrative that their similarities seem insignificant by comparison. Most important, one must take account of the fact that historical narratives are not just stories that differ in various ways from the stories that characterize ordinary actions and experiences; they are also about those stories. That is, they are second-order narratives whose purpose is to tell about the ordinary (and extraordinary) actions and events of individual and especially social life. What is more, they seek to evaluate these first-order stories in a disinterested or objective way. This seems to impart to historical narrative a character that so sets it apart from the "first-order" level of narrative structures that the idea of continuity is seriously challenged. It is these two challenges, then, that I propose to take up in turn.

Narrative and the Everyday Experience of Time

It is easy enough to question the narrative analysis of everyday life on grounds that are derived from a simple reflection on one's own experience. Stories bring coherence to the flow of events, shaping them into wholes with beginnings, middles, and ends, grouping them around characters with persisting identities and personalities, introducing problems, crises, and turning points only to lead them toward satisfying solutions and conclusions. How different our lives really are! Incoherence, if not downright confusion, seems more typical than coherence: rather than actually beginning, things just gradually emerge; plans are interrupted, things go wrong, loose ends are left hanging, nothing is ever settled, few problems are ever really solved or resolved. Nothing ever ends: each apparent ending is just the beginning of something else.

It is no doubt this sort of consideration that has led theorists like Louis Mink and Hayden White to affirm the artificiality of narrative. "Stories are not lived but told," says Mink. "Life has no beginnings, middles and ends.... Narrative qualities are transferred from art to life."[4] According to White, "no given set or sequence of real events" has intrinsically narrative features; they acquire these features "only by the imposition of the structure of a given story type on the events."[5] But it seems obvious to me that these theorists are operating with distinctions—life vs. art, real vs. "imposed"—that are not very clearly thought out. The "real" events of "life," after all, are not a meaningless sequence of unrelated nows but rather the actions and sufferings of persons and groups of people. To be sure, sometimes these are chaotic and confused. But this is only because we judge them—indeed, experience them—by standards of coherence that function as the rule in our daily lives. By the term "rule" here I do not mean merely that our lives are more often organized than disorganized, our plans and projects more often successfully carried out than not. This differs from individual to individual and from time to time. Rather, I refer to the temporal values that are part of the sense of events as we experience and live through them.

The point is that human events and actions derive their sense from their relation to past and future, i.e., from their place in a temporal configuration in which they follow from something and lead up to something else. The idea of coherence in human affairs derives from the very way we experience and exist in time, not from the imposition on it of alien or artificial categories. Only because of this can we experience and lament the contrasting incoherence and confusion that so often plague us.

Thus the deepest and most significant structures we find in narrative—beginning/middle/end, problem (or crisis)/solution, suspension/resolution, reversal of fortune, and so on—are structures that characterize our very existence as human beings. This is not just the way we tell about our lives after the fact; this is how we live them from the start. In this case it turns out to be true that art—at least in its narrative form—indeed imitates life. Before it is a literary genre, or indeed a form of historical writing, narrative is the practical and "existential" form of human time. It is through the implicit construction (and constant revision) of a life story that the individual achieves or acquires an identity.[6]

Moreover, it is not merely as individuals that we exist in this way. Groups of persons too—those we refer to as communities—can be said to constitute themselves around and through narratives. Just as the individual exists through the implicit life-story, so the community exists through a "story" that draws together the shared memory and expectation or projection. Here too, the social present derives its sense from past and future.

Such then, briefly, is the response of the "continuity" theory to the above objection. Narrative structure is not "imposed" on anything. It constitutes the principle of organization for our action and experience, even though it may fail as often as it succeeds. It is not merely the structure of a certain kind of writing or even a certain kind of knowledge; it is the structure of our very being. As such it is the very "reality" of history. This is the sense in which the term "historicity" has been used in the philosophical tradition, and some version of this view was held by earlier philosophers of history, even though they did not speak directly of narrative. Vico's notion that we can understand history because we are the makers of history suggests the analogy of form between historical existence and historical knowledge. The same is true of Dilthey's statement that "we are historical beings first, before we are observers of history, and only because we are the former do we become the latter."[7] Hegel believed it was no accident that the German term *Geschichte* (history) denotes both the *res gestae* and the *historia rerum gestarum*: "we must suppose historical narrations to have appeared contemporaneously with historical deeds and events. It is an internal principle common to both that produces them synchronously."[8]

This quote from Hegel's lectures on the philosophy of history already, perhaps inadvertently, points in the direction of a deeper and much more serious challenge to the theory of continuity. Historical narrations have not always existed: they are not found in nonliterate and so-called traditional societies, and Hermann Kulke informs us that even a highly sophisticated and literate culture, like that of classical and medieval India, can be without any demonstrable sense of, or interest in, history.⁹ Does this have any significance for the continuity theory? Not necessarily, for this theory claims that historical narration derives from the narrative structure of human existence, but not that this narrative structure always gives rise to historical accounts.

Nevertheless, this new consideration brings out something about this theory that introduces a suspicion. Narrativity is being affirmed as a universal human characteristic. Claims are being made about the temporal structure of human experience, indeed human existence, as such. Yet some of the most important and by now "classical" work in anthropology and comparative religions—I am thinking of Claude Levi-Strauss and Mircea Eliade respectively—has suggested that "peoples without history" have a completely different way of experiencing time itself.¹⁰ I find this conclusion being reaffirmed, if I understand him correctly, by Klaus E. Müller in his paper *"Prähistorisches Geschichtsbewußtsein."*¹¹

Is it possible that we have put forward as a universal human trait what is in fact only one way of experiencing time? In order to answer this question it may be necessary to engage in more empirical research into the mentality of other peoples. But prior to that we can ask ourselves if we can imagine experiencing time in any other way. According to what was said above, time is experienced in such a way that the present derives its significance from the past and the future. But what if the true significance of the present derived instead from its relation to what is divine and out of time altogether? It is important to note that we are talking about sense and significance, not just chronological order. Thus, while the present may differ from the past chronologically, this difference may not be experienced as important. Sameness, rather than difference, may be the most significant relation of present to past, and indeed to future as well. Such are the elements of a nonhistorical conception of human time, one based on repetition, ritual, and commemoration. Everyone recognizes that there are cyclical elements in our everyday experience of time—the pattern of bodily functions, the rhythm of day and night, the changing of the seasons. Nor is it the case that the cyclical is confined to the "natural" as opposed to the cultural: the weekly calendar, the pattern of work and rest, the alternation of social and personal, public and private lives also follow a plan of repetition whose chief value is stability rather than change.

If we can recognize in our own everyday existence elements of an experience of time that is very different from the "narrative" pattern described earlier, we may be inclined to look at the latter in a very different way. The tendency to tell stories about our actions and experiences, the linear-teleological conception of time, and the interest in the past that leads us to preserve and write history about it, may all be different aspects of an approach to time that is specifically Western. Reinhart Kosellek has written about the shift in European thought from prophesy to prognosis, in which the envisaged future came under human control and management.¹² Both sides of this transition belong to the same general conception of time as consisting of qualitative change moving toward the future. But the advent of Western modernity intensifies the narrative conception of time and diminishes the influence of cyclical features that persist in the largely religious ideology of the premodern period.

From this point of view the narrative interpretation of time would be seen not as the way human beings per se exist in and experience time, but as the way modern, Western human beings exist in and experience time. To affirm this as a universal trait would be to consign nonhistorical peoples to a status that is not—or perhaps not yet—fully human.[13] After contrasting the modern with the premodern experience of time in this way, the next step is to envisage a postmodern experience of time, in which the values of narrative coherence would be supplanted. And indeed, this is suggested by many theorists of the postmodern. We are invited to consider the possibility that the diverse events we live through, as individuals and as groups, do not and should not add up to a coherent story at all, and that the belief that they do is at best wishful thinking, at worst a form of violence we do to each other and even to ourselves. The rejection of narrative goes hand in hand with the rejection of "instrumental" reason and technology. Ultimately it leads to the rejection of history itself and of the concept of the subject, especially that of the subject of history—"man" as hero and central character of his own story. Terms like "collage," "pastiche," and "bricolage" express values held in higher esteem than coherence and unity.

Can the continuity theory respond to this challenge? I want to propose a response on two levels. First, even if narrativity is not a universal character of human experience, it is still possible to affirm the continuity that is at the heart of the theory, and to deny the discrepancy or discontinuity alleged to exist between historical narrative and human reality. What I mean is this: even if the historical consciousness that leads to historical writing is largely Western and even modern, it is still reflective of, and thus continuous with, the reality of modern Western existence. It is still true to say that narrative structure pervades the way "we" live our lives, rather than being imposed upon it from without. It is just that the "we" is no longer the universal "we" of humanity, but admittedly and openly the "we" of modern Western life, however far that designation may reach. If "historicity" and "narrativity" are features of Western, or even Western modern thought, rather than of all humanity's, they are still features that are found at all levels of life, from everyday experience and action to the manifestations of literary culture, including historical research and writing.

But perhaps it is not necessary to concede that narrativity is not a universal feature of the human experience of time. Here I come to the second level of my response. Above I proposed, in lieu of an empirical investigation, that we reflect on a possible nonnarrative experience of time. Recall that "we" found it quite easy to articulate what such an experience might be, and "we" were able to discover elements of it in "our" own experience. But if "we" (Westerners? Moderns?) can find these in our experience, perhaps non-Westerners, nonmoderns, and even postmoderns can find elements of the narrative conception of time in their experience. Perhaps there are two (or even more) different ways or aspects of existing in time, one of which is linear, teleological, narrative, and historical, while another is cyclical, repetitive, and stable. Perhaps we could say that both aspects are equally universal or equally human, but that each has been brought to the fore and manifested in cultural forms by different societies at different times. This would allow for a full vindication of even the universal claims of the continuity theory, meanwhile opening the door to an even richer and more elaborate account of the basic human experience of time.

To some extent the foregoing consists of speculations about forms of human experience that can best be filled in by concrete empirical research. Yet the risks and dangers of the empirical investigation of "mentalities" are well known, and it is hard to imagine what "observation" would be like when dealing with the human experience of time. Any such investigation stands in need of flexible conceptual guidelines; perhaps these reflections can serve in that capacity.

Historical Reality and Historical Narrative

We now turn to the second major challenge to the continuity theory. The claim of this theory is that historical narrative—the research and writing that express historical knowledge of the past—is on a continuum with historical reality, ultimately sharing the same form and constituting a "higher-level" expression of the same features we find in everyday life. But the theory must still account for what happens in the transition from one end of the continuum to the other. The problem is: Can we account for this transition in a way that does justice to the distinctness of historical knowledge while still maintaining that the continuum exists?

One way to deal with the transition in question is to focus attention on the relation between the individual and the social. When we speak of the narrative character of ordinary life as the way (or one way) in which human beings organize their experience of time, it is natural to reflect on one's own individual life, and to think of the temporal structure of one's own actions and experiences. My analysis of this structure has been largely inspired by the phenomenological accounts of temporality found in such philosophers as Husserl and Heidegger. These thinkers devote their attention primarily to the conscious life and existence of the individual, often to the neglect, according to some of their critics, of the social dimensions of human existence.

History, of course, is about social reality, and is concerned with the lives of individuals only to the extent that they figure in social life. If historians devote their attention to individuals, it is typically to important political figures or, at the opposite end of the spectrum, "ordinary" individuals regarded as representative of some broad social or political phenomenon. If our theory is going to account for the connection between history and ordinary life, it must somehow relate the individual and social aspects of time. But as we have seen, it can be shown that the narrative organization of time is a pervasive structure of social as well as individual life. Where the first-person plural becomes as important as the first-person singular in social discourse, we can think of the cohesive community as a kind of large-scale individual that is the "subject" of certain kinds of experiences and actions. Within such a community, persons are related to each other not merely as individuals facing other individuals, but as members of the same group. For individuals who stand in this relation of membership, experiences, actions, opinions, and even feelings are not "mine" but "ours." Where the communal "we" is operative, whether at the family, ethnic, political, religious, or even the universal-human level (as in, "we" landed on the moon in 1969), social time can be said to be structured along the same narrative lines as individual time.

This is the sort of consideration that leads to the familiar notion that history is "society's memory." As memory is to the individual, so history is to the community. As the individual implicitly or explicitly composes a life story that constitutes his or her identity, so the community composes its own biography in the history it writes for itself.

The problem with this familiar notion is that it does not really do justice to the specificity of historical inquiry as we think of it today. The idea of history as a *"Wissenschaft"* (science) appealing to critical standards of objectivity may be a fairly recent one, but it does exist, and the philosophy of history needs to take it seriously—though of course not uncritically. If the continuity theory is to do its job, it must at least find a place for historical knowledge in this modern sense.

It seems to me that the notion of history as society's memory, while extremely important, is really in a different place on our continuum. Here it is not only the narrative structure of individual experience that is replicated at the social level, but also the underlying motives that go with it. By that I mean that the community holds on to its past for the practical purpose of organizing and orienting itself in time, and of maintaining its identity in the face of the threat of fragmentation—a threat that is faced to a greater or lesser degree by any community. It is here that the past is kept alive in traditions, legends, monuments, public buildings, and folk music and art. No doubt popular history belongs here, too, and even the officially chosen history books of the public schools. But the underlying motivation here is practical: it is values such as group cohesion, and good citizenship, that guide the maintenance of the public memory.

What goes along with this, it seems to me, is that the primary orientation of this social organization of time is, like that of the individual, toward the future. In the broadest sense, as noted already, it is concerned with sustaining the community against the threats of an uncertain future. But it is also connected with action, with "getting things done." This is why it would be a mistake to think of the "social memory" as something static. On the contrary, it is always being appealed to and subtly manipulated, especially in the context of political rhetoric. A community may owe its coherence to a generally accepted social narrative, but that does not prevent its dividing into factions, which often differ—as do, for example, the progressives from the conservatives—by virtue of attitudes toward the past. The past is important in this context because of how it affects the future. Is it a golden age from which we have fallen away? Then we must return to the values of our fathers. Is it merely the first steps toward a goal as yet unrealized? The we must continue to move toward the future. In the political arena, the struggle is often for control of the past. But the past is prized because of its significance for the future.

In one of my earlier writings on this topic I had occasion to cite as an example of political rhetoric, in the best sense of the word, Abraham Lincoln's Gettysburg Address. This famous speech, known to every American schoolchild, has been brilliantly analyzed by the classicist and historian Gary Wills.[14] Wills's detailed treatment confirms my view that Lincoln's speech is paradigmatic in a discussion of the role of narrative in the political context. A few references will show how this is so.

The President's brief remarks, delivered on 19 November 1863, were part of the ceremonies dedicating a military cemetery at the site of a fierce and crucial Civil War battle that had occurred just four months earlier. Lincoln spoke for only about three minutes, but his words were telegraphed across the country and almost immediately achieved the iconic status they still have today. According to Wills, all those who heard Lincoln's message, admiring its eloquent simplicity and directness, accepted along with it, almost without knowing it, a major reorientation of American history.

Wills locates the speech, composed in the tradition of military-funeral oratory extending back to Pericles and Gorgias, in the context of the Greek revival of nineteenth-century America. Lincoln's words, he says, have "the chaste and graven quality of an Attic frieze" (p. 55). He notes that, like Thucydides' version of Pericles, Lincoln assumes the communal "we" (p. 53): "Four score and seven years ago our fathers brought forth on this continent a new nation ..." he says. "Now we are engaged in a great civil war, testing whether that nation ... can long endure." What struck me, though it is not emphasized by Wills, is the narrative character of the address: The occasion, an event in the life of the nation, is part of a story, the story of the American republic itself. It derives its sense from an origin or foundation in the past, and from an envisaged future placed in jeopardy by the present crisis.

On the surface the hortatory purpose of Lincoln's oration is obvious: "It is for us the living ... to be dedicated here to the unfinished work." The war must be won so that the great experiment, begun eighty-seven years before, shall not fail, so that "government of the people, by the people, for the people, shall not perish from the earth." Wills's analysis shows that Lincoln's rhetoric is expressive of a deeper and more radical purpose: a recasting of the nation's past. It is not the Constitution of 1787, which emphasizes confederation and states' rights, but the Declaration of Independence of 1776 that is the founding document of the United States. This document, "dedicated to the proposition that all men are created equal," permits Lincoln an oblique reference to the slavery question. But even more important, according to Wills, Lincoln believed that in the Declaration "Americans had constituted themselves a single people long before the Constitution was drafted or ratified" (p. 129). Thus it was not the states that created the union; the people as a whole came first. This gives a completely different sense to the Constitution. Wills says that Lincoln "altered [the Constitution] from within, by appeal from its letter to the spirit" (p. 38).

To be sure, Lincoln did not invent the idea of the primacy of the union over states' rights, much less present it for the first time in the Gettysburg Address. Along with slavery itself, it had been the central issue in the debates leading up to the Civil War, and the founding role of the Declaration had been championed eloquently by Daniel Webster in the 1830s (p. 130). But at Gettysburg Lincoln compressed these ideas into a few words, and the success of his speech etched them for good into the national consciousness of Americans.

Thus Lincoln's speech is important here not because of the originality of its ideas, but as a prime example of social or communal narrative with a practical purpose. As Wills shows, this purpose lies far beyond rallying the people to continue to fight and win the war. It is about the future, but its intent is far more serious, and so it must engage the past as well. As Wills puts it, "the crowd [at Gettysburg that day] departed with a new thing in its ideological luggage, that new constitution Lincoln had substituted for the one they brought there with them. They walked off... into a different America. Lincoln had revolutionized the Revolution, giving people a new past to live with that would change their future indefinitely" (p. 38).

I have examined Lincoln's speech as an illustration par excellence of the way the past functions as "society's memory" in the context of a social narrative. Here the past is anything but static; it is changeable, a vital and important dimension of the life of any community. Above all it is a serious matter, something to be struggled over. As we have seen, the basic motive of the social narrative at this level is practical, and its primary orientation, despite its preoccupation with the past, is really the future.

It is against this background that we must now assess the character of historical narrative proper, the sort we associate with our historical discipline today. In contrast to the future-orientation of social narrative, historical narrative seems explicitly occupied with the past for its own sake. Its underlying motive could be characterized as strictly cognitive, not practical. Moreover, the cognitive interest is largely equivalent to the critical interest. The historian often examines with a critical eye precisely those versions of the social past that exist in the collective memory. These are now regarded as myths and legends, in the pejorative sense of those terms, and the practical—or partisan—character of their origin is what comes under critical scrutiny. By contrast, the historical narrative is meant to be unbiased, objective, purely "scientific." Whether it can ever achieve this goal is not at issue here; we are speaking of its underlying values and intentions. It is important to note that the value of objectivity extends beyond securing "facts" by attending to sources. As Rüsen has shown, the critical use of sources, already enshrined as a value in Enlightenment historiography, was not enough for the historicists of the nineteenth-century: the interpretation of facts and their incorporation into narratives were likewise supposed to live up to rigorous methodical standards.[15]

Thus historical narrative differs from social narrative not only in its past-orientation and its aim of objectivity; it also lies beyond the social narrative, not so much by being a different story as by reflecting back on social narratives with an eye to critical evaluation and, if necessary, revision. This formulation gives a first approximation to an account of how historical narrative relates to the first-order practical narratives of historical "reality," whether they be individual or communal. We begin to see specifically what it means to assert a "continuity" between historical narrative and what it is about.

These considerations permit us to answer at least one critical assessment of the continuity theory.[16] If historical narrative is not imposed on historical reality as an alien and distorting medium, but rather shares with it the narrative form, then perhaps this means that the only task of the historian is to report or even repeat the content of those implicit and explicit narrative self-descriptions of historical agents. This would place the continuity theory very close to Collingwood's idealist theory of reenactment and the classic concept of *Verstehen*.[17] The task of the historian would be to grasp the thoughts or reasons behind the actions of historical agents, to understand events as they understood them. In narrative terms, this would mean to retell the story such agents told themselves and others, implicitly or explicitly, in order to act as they did.

But there are well-known difficulties associated with Collingwood's idealism, and they would be found in this narrative version of it as well. It would give us a simplistic caricature of what historians actually do. It would ignore the critical and revisionist motive behind historical narrative. The historian needs to go beyond any single description of an action or event by comparing it with other descriptions of the same event, thus having to deal with problems of identification across multiple descriptions. (Compare, for instance, Luther's description—or "story"—of what he did in 1517 with the Pope's description of the same events.) More important, this notion ignores what many theorists, from Dilthey to Danto, have seen as history's unique cognitive advantage, that of hindsight. The retrospective glance of the historian permits the self-descriptions and practical narratives behind historical actions to be viewed in light of their actual outcomes. The ironic disparity between the envisioned or intended result and the actual consequences of an action is very important for the historian.

It is true that the "reenactment" or revival of agents' own narratives is a vital part of this retrospective comparison, a point often forgotten by those who, like Danto, stress the retrospective point of view.[18] The historian can, and usually cannot but, view past events in light of their actual consequences. The interest and value in historical accounts often lies precisely in retrieving a perspective on events that has been lost to us because of our hindsightful wisdom. Luther did not plan, envision, or desire the Protestant Reformation that was unleashed by his actions. Seeing such a person's action just as he saw it, deliberately blocking out all that we know of what came later, must surely be one of the most difficult feats of the historical imagination. It should be pointed out in passing that this problem is not confined to narrative history, nor is it only a problem of "empathizing" with a remote historical individual. A history of mentalities or concepts, of the sort inspired by Foucault, similarly seeks to block out the vision of hindsight by refusing to see past events (including theories or writings) merely as precursors of what came later. Thus, for example, Newton's theories must be viewed in light of the religious cosmology of his time, not merely as precursors of the physical theories of our own day.

There is another sense in which this operation of reenactment is important. Many historians, especially today, see their activity as one of redressing certain imbalances, of rediscovering or retrieving what has been lost, forgotten, or covered over. The lives of those excluded from the stories of the past or relegated to their margins, such as women and minorities—those selected out of the standard narratives of both historical agents and later historians—are to be reinstated in our historical consciousness. The first task is to give them back their own voice if possible, to let them tell their own stories just as they are articulated in diaries, speeches, sermons, court testimony, folk art, or other expressions. Here too the historian must in a sense block out hindsight and efface himself before the voice of the past.

Important and necessary as these operations of retrieval are, one should not conclude from them that they make up the whole work of historical narrative. Any account that would restrict its role to repeating the narratives of historical agents would overlook the most important thing: history has its own story to tell; its purpose is to generate a narrative that differs from and goes beyond any of the narratives it may incorporate. Even in retelling stories, the historian makes a contribution, in choosing which stories to retell. And these stories are typically integrated into the larger context provided by the broader view, and of course the retrospective view, of the historian. This in turn introduces the critical perspective from which the individual and social narratives are evaluated in objective and unbiased terms. To put it crudely, the historian is interested in events as they were lived and described by participants, but with a view to contrasting those descriptions with events as they "really were," that is, as the historian sees them and integrates them into new historical narrative.

Thus the relation of narrative history to the narrative "material" with which it works is a complex one. Its link to the continuum of individual and social narratives is threefold: First, it reflects back on them in order to retrieve them as they are, to revive or reenact them so as to come as close as possible to how they were experienced by participants. Second, it reflects critically on them by comparing them with each other and with their real, as opposed to their intended, consequences. Third, these narratives are incorporated into a new story, that who is working with them of the historian. Once this last point is recognized, the claim of the continuity theory is borne out, namely that in an important sense history does the same thing as individual and social narrative, even though it may do it at a different level and by different means.

It also does it for different reasons. It was suggested earlier that historical and social narrative differ in motivation and in temporal orientation. Social narrative is practical, we said, and is oriented toward the future, while historical narrative is purely cognitive and is occupied only with the past. Do these differences constitute an irreconcilable disparity that undermines the point of the continuity theory? Can we really compare the activity of telling a "likely story" that will contribute to getting things done, with that of recounting the past "wie es eigentlich gewesen" (as it really was)? Is there not all the difference in the world, indeed, between telling a useful story and seeking the truth?

In fact I think this is probably a false dichotomy and at most a matter of emphasis. Story-telling at all levels of practical life, provided it is not admittedly fictional, is always constrained by truth. Falsehood may in some circumstances, and in the short run, be more useful than the truth, but ultimately the truth is more practical. Our story-telling must come to terms with the world as it is, not as we wish it were. "Making sense" cannot be separated from "being true." "Getting the story straight" is a value at all levels of individual and social existence, not just at the level of science or scientific history. Methods of evaluating sources, notions of objectivity, injunctions of impartiality, are ways of trying to do better what we often do poorly in ordinary life. Thus the historian's concern with the truth about the past is ultimately practical, too. And to say that it is practical is to say that it has value for the future.

With this account we can thus conclude our response to the second of the two challenges to the continuity theory. This theory can do justice to the specificity of historical narrative while still relating it closely in structure and motivation to the practical narratives of individual and social life.

Notes

1. Jörn Rüsen, *Historische Vernunft* (Göttingen 1983), 52.
2. Paul Ricoeur, *Temps et Recit,* 3 vol. (Paris 1983), vol. 1, 85.

3. See David Carr, *Time, Narrative and History* (Bloomington 1986), chap. 2 and passim.

4. Louis Mink, "History and Fiction as Modes of Comprehension," in Brian Fay, Eugene O. Golob and Richard T. Vann, eds., *Historical Understanding* (Ithaca 1987), 60.

5. Hayden White, "The Question of Narrative in Contemporary Historical Theory," in idem, *The Content of the Form* (Baltimore 1987), 44.

6. See Paul Ricoeur, *Oneself as Another*, trans. K. Blamey (Chicago 1992), esp. fifth and sixth studies, 113–168.

7. Wilhelm Dilthey, *Gesammelte Schriften,* ed. Bernhard Groethuysen, vol. 7, 5th ed. (Stuttgart 1968), 277–278.

8. G. W. F. Hegel, *Vorlesungen über die Philosophie der Geschichte* (1833) (Frankfurt/ M. 1976), 83.

9. See Hermann Kulke, "Geschichtsschreibung als Heilung eines Traditionsbruches?" *Report Nr. 2/94 der Forschungsgruppe Historische Sinnbildung* (Bielefeld 1994/95.)

10. See Claude Levi-Strauss, *The Savage Mind* (Chicago 1966), 234–35; Mircea Eliade, *Cosmos and History* (New York 1956), chaps. 3 and 4.

11. Klaus E. Müller, "Prähistorisches Geschichtsbewußtsein," in Jörn Rüsen, Michael Gottlob and Achim Mittag, eds., *Die Vielfalt der Kulturen* (Frankfurt/ M. 1998).

12. See Reinhart Koselleck, "'Historia Magistra Vitae' Über die Auflösung des Topos im Horizont neuzeitlich bewegter Geschichte," in Hermann Braun, ed., *Natur und Geschichte. Karl Löwith zum 70. Geburtstag* (Stuttgart 1967), 196–219; and other essays in his *Vergangene Zukunft: Zur Semantik geschichtlicher Zeiten* (Frankfurt/ M. 1979).

13. See Levi-Strauss, "Attack on Sartre," in idem, *The Savage Mind*, 248–249.

14. Gary Wills, *Lincoln at Gettysburg: The Words That Remade America* (New York 1992).

15. Jörn Rüsen, *Konfigurationen des Historismus: Studien zur deutschen Wissenschaftskultur* (Frankfurt/ M. 1993), 61f.

16. See Andrew P. Norman, "Telling It Like It Was: Historical Narratives on Their Own Terms," *History and Theory* 30.1 (1991): 124.

17. See Robin G. Collingwood, *The Idea of History* (London 1969), 282ff.

18. See Arthur Danto, *Analytical Philosophy of History* (Cambridge 1965).

CHAPTER 8

Language and Historical Experience

FRANK R. ANKERSMIT

Introduction

In the autobiographies and letters of several historians since Herder we may find testimonies of their having undergone what I shall call a "historical experience." As becomes clear from their accounts, historical experience gave them a sudden revelation of "what the was past actually like." This unexpected revelation of the past—often experienced by them as a sudden falling away of all temporal distance—is always accompanied by a conviction of complete "authenticity"; that is, by the conviction that this experience of the past can not be a delusion, but is as real and reliable as what is given to us in immediate sensory experience. At such moments it is historical writing that appears as a mere "dream of historical reason," an abstraction far removed from actual historical reality.

On several other occasions I have expounded the nature of historical experience;[1] I shall therefore restrict myself in this introduction to what is of importance for the present argument. Here I am primarily concerned with the decontextualization that always takes place in historical experience; that is to say, the quality of historical experience that effects the isolation of the experienced past, both from other aspects of the past and from all the pregiven knowledge that the subject of historical experience may have of the relevant part(s) of the past. Historical experience is, so to speak, a "hole" or "break" in the continuity of both our experience and knowledge of reality alike. It can be argued that historical experience is, in the end, a variety of aesthetic experi-

---

Notes for this section begin on page 150.

ence.[2] And it has been demonstrated by theorists of aesthetic experience, especially in the pragmatist tradition, that aesthetic experience has, amongst other features, above all the propensity to isolate itself from other experiences. Both aesthetic and historical experience resist contextualization: as soon as they are conceived as part of a larger context, or are influenced by an encompassing context, however defined, they lose their specificity and thereby cease to exist at all.

As has been emphasized repeatedly by philosophers representing the whole spectrum of twentieth-century philosophical thought, a large part of the context of all experience is language. Our experience of the world, the way we experience reality and discuss our experience, and our susceptibility to experience are all permeated through and through by language. This is essentially the argument that was put forward by Gadamer in his magisterial *Wahrheit und Methode* (Truth and Method). For Gadamer the world, experience, and language are so intertwined that it is impossible to say where one begins and the other ends. If, then, aesthetic and historical experience are the sole exceptions to this contextualist web of world, language, and experience, we must conclude that there is in their case a distance between experience and language that we do not encounter in other areas of our experiencing the world. And indeed, who does not recall the peculiar difficulty of finding the right words to describe the experience one has when standing before a painting that really "strikes us," as we like to put it? In most other cases, the language we need for expressing experience comes to us so naturally, and so easily suggests itself, that experience seems to adapt itself to language rather than the other way round.

Hence, aesthetic and historical experience confront us with both the philosophical heresy of de-contextualized, immediate experience, a contact with reality that is not predetermined by the nature of language—and, consequently, the problem of how this "distance," this radical incommensurability of art or the past on the one hand and language on the other, is to be bridged in art and history when we wish to express in words our experience of history or of a work of art. An examination of these problems may also suggest in what way this "philosophical heresy" of an unmediated and direct contact with reality, for which contemporary philosophy has left no room at all, may be seen as a correction of the linguistic idealism that is so all-pervasive in contemporary philosophy of language.

These considerations may also make clear this essay's contribution to the theme of *"historische Sinnbildung";* for the question that will be discussed below—that is, the question "How can historical experience be put into words?"—concerns the question of how the transition from the past "as it was" and "as it has been experienced by the historian in historical experience" to the verbalization of that reality and that experience can take place in historical writing. This undoubtedly is at stake when we ask ourselves how "to make sense of the past," and how to conceive of *"historische Sinnbildung":* there remain a historical reality and a historical experience that are still mute and unarticulated, whereas the past that has effectively been put into words gives us historical meaning and *"Sinn."* Meaning and *"Sinn"* emerge in the trajectory that will be explored below. It also follows that the significance of the problem of *"historische Sinnbildung,"* as conceived here, should not be restricted to what is of interest for the historical theorist only; on the contrary, *"historische Sinnbildung"* as the expression of the content of historical experience requires us to reconsider several assumptions underlying contemporary philosophy of language and current conceptions of the relation of language to the world.

Sensitivism and Historical Experience

I shall discuss in this essay two attempts[3]—one by a historian,(Johan Huizinga) and one by a historical theorist (Hayden White)—to bridge the gap between the past itself and how it is experienced, on the one hand, and the historian's language on the other. Indeed, when we pose the question of *"historische Sinnbildung"* as defined just now, we are well advised to turn to Huizinga, whose writings contain a more complete account of the nature of historical experience than those of any other historian or theorist. We should note, then, that Huizinga does not speak of "historical experience" but of "historical sensation"—and this will provide us with the beginning of an answer to the question of how to bridge the distance between experience and language in the case of historical experience.

When Huizinga prefers to speak of "historical sensation," he demonstrates his indebtedness to the Dutch literary movement of the 1880s, the so-called "Tachtigers" (i.e., "those of the eighties"), that deeply influenced his style and thought. Huizinga's conception of historical sensation was undoubtedly inspired by the notion of "sensation" that had been proposed by Lodewijk van Deijssel, the best and most influential theoretician of this literary movement. Van Deijssel distinguished between "observation," "impression," and "sensation" and used the last term to refer to the most intimate contact that we can have with reality.[4] For a correct appreciation of van Deijssel's intention, it must be observed, above all that his "sensitivism" was an intensification or radicalization of literary realism. Literature should not merely give us a believable and "realistic" account of what our social world actually is like, but aim to impart to the reader of a novel what one might call "the feel of reality," with all the connotations of sensory perception held by that notion.

This is where van Deijssel's sensitivism crucially differs from the symbolism in late nineteenth-century literature that succeeded realism. In all cases there is an awareness of the gap between language and reality that literary realism had vainly attempted to bridge, but whereas symbolists tended to fall back on an hermetic idealism in order to penetrate the secrets of reality that realism remained blind to, the sensitivist movement radicalized realism by focusing on our most direct and immediate sensory experience of reality. In opposition to Mallarmé's well-known "*le monde est fait pour aboutir à un beau livre* (The world was made to end in a beautiful book),"[5] the sensitivist's experience is that when looking, for example, at the colors of the evening sky, one feels affected by the silence of its clouds and subconsciously recognizes oneself to have become himself these clouds and their majestic silence.[6] Symbolism represents a movement toward the abstract; sensitivism, on the contrary, is a movement toward the concrete or even an attempt at identification or unification with reality.

Kemperink gives a succinct synopsis of the characteristics that van Deijssel attributed to sensation in the rampant volumes of his collected literary critiques. Sensation is momentary and has little or no duration; it is abrupt and cannot be predicted. It is accompanied by a sense of anxiety and of alienation: the direct experience or sensation of reality provokes a loss of the naturalness of even the most trivial objects. This explains why sensation is so enigmatic and why the right words seem to fail us for describing its content: experience here precedes language and the whole complex web of associations that are embedded in language. There is, furthermore, a feeling as if space has suddenly acquired extra dimensions, a different awareness of colors, and an attendant propensity for synaesthesis, in which the fullness of sensory experience causes an overflowing of the senses into each other. The result of all these elements of sensation is that the customary demarcations between self and external reality momentarily disappear: This identification with reality is not, however, a triumph of the self over reality but rather a "pathos,"[7] a passive submission and complete receptivity to it. But what is perhaps most striking in van Deijssel's account of sensation is the disruption of temporal continuity, of the normal sequence of before, now, and afterwards. Sensation therefore produces in us the conviction that its content is a repetition of something that has already happened in precisely this same way, maybe centuries ago. Sensation effects a fissure in the temporal order so that the past and the present are momentarily united in a way that is familiar to us all in the experience of "déjà vu."[8]

Most of these elements ascribed by van Deijssel to sensation return in Huizinga's observations on "historical sensation."[9] More specifically, like van Deijssel, Huizinga associates historical sensation with the sense of touch rather than with sight and thus deliberately frees historical sensation from all the visual and optical metaphors that have determined traditional epistemological accounts of knowledge and experience or of historical thought. The eye dominates and domesticates what is seen by adapting it to the knowledge we already have of what reality is like—it is the most imperialistic of the five senses. It need not surprise us, therefore, that epistemology, in its attempt to justify the knowledge we acquire for adapting reality to our aims and purposes, takes the eye as its favorite model.[10]

Putting Historical Experience into Words: Huizinga

The problem of translating the data of sensory experience into language belongs to one of Huizinga's oldest and most persistent preoccupations. When discussing Huizinga's historical theory, one should never forget that Huizinga was trained as a linguist, not as a historian, that he began his scholarly career as a Sanskritist, and that his doctoral dissertation was devoted to the role of Vidusaka in Indian comedy. Young Huizinga's interest in linguistics can be directly related to van Deijssel's sensitivism.

What most deserves our attention here is Huizinga's initial plan for a doctoral dissertation. Huizinga makes a short comment on this abortive project in his autobiography, where he writes that it had been his aim to investigate the expressions employed for the sensory perception of light and noise in the Indo-Germanic languages.[11] Huizinga's recent biographer Krul informs us that Huizinga wanted to demonstrate in his thesis that the words we use to express sensory perception come about through by a "direct lyrical formation" or "by the lyrical metaphor of an already existing word for expressing feeling or sensation."[12] Such words originally express a mood or an atmosphere, not a well-defined concept. Huizinga clarified his ideas with example of the synaesthetic metaphor of "the red sound of a trumpet." This metaphor, he argued, has a peculiar plausibility that we can explain only by assuming that one word that can express what we associate with both seeing something red and hearing the sound of a trumpet. For Huizinga this is the word "fierce" (*fel* in Dutch).

It follows that we can say of the word "fierce" that it expresses something that seeing and hearing have in common. That common quality, in this case, is apparently not yet differentiated, or torn apart, to correspond to the nature of these two senses; therefore, it necessarily refers us to a level in our contact with reality that is prior to, or deeper than, both seeing and hearing. Hence the word "fierce" has a more intimate and direct relationship with sensory experience than do words that give us literal descriptions of what we either see or hear. "Fierce" therefore belongs to the category of words that express the most intimate and direct experience we can have of reality. Here we really have reached the closest possible contact between language, experience, and reality. This closest contact is not achieved, as in Gadamer's case, by intertwining of reality, experience, and language together, but by contact between the three where the individual nature of each of them is carefully respected in spite of the intimate relationship that has been effected between them. It will be obvious that Huizinga's effort—as shown in this example—to bring language into maximally close contact with reality is in complete agreement with van Deijssel's speculations about sensation, or can even be regarded as the most radical operationalization that one could possibly give to them. Huizinga himself admitted in his autobiography that this project for a dissertation was the result of literary influences that he had undergone rather than of some research program already existing in the linguistics of his time.

It has been observed that Huizinga's best known book, *The Waning of the Middle Ages,* is stylistically quite different from anything that he wrote before or after it,[13] and that the difference consists in its close adherence to the style of van Deijssel, Gorter, and other prominent authors of the movement of the 1880s. It is a plausible hypothesis that Huizinga adopted this style in order to give expression to a historical sensation or experience, a sensation that he apparently did not feel, or felt with less intensity, when writing his other major works. The relatively few remarks that Huizinga devotes in his autobiography and elsewhere to the inception of *The Waning of the Middle Ages* suggest that the Middle Ages had for him a meaning quite different from that of all the other topics he studied in the course of his career as a historian. If, then, we read Huizinga's own declarations about how he had been deeply impressed by Huysman's *La bàs* and even more so by the Van Eyck exposition in Brugge in the summer of 1902,[14] it seems a plausible hypothesis that we will find here the historical experience that inspired *The Waning of the Middle Ages.*

It was the Van Eyck exposition, as Huizinga he himself stated, that satisfied his yearning for direct contact with past reality, a direct contact that the visual arts, more than anything else, can bring about. In an essay Huizinga wrote in 1916 on Van Eyck's art which preludes the ideas to be developed in *The Waning of the Middle Ages* of three years later, he adds that in our relationship to the past, *reading,* which traditionally gave us access to the past, will have to yield its privileged position to *seeing.* "We want," thus Huizinga writes, "half dreamt, unclearly delineated images, leaving free play to our imagination, and this need is better satisfied by a visual than by an intellectual appercention of the past" (my translation).[15]

We should note, furthermore, that there is a persistent tendency in *The Waning of the Middle Ages* to contrast the present and the medieval past again and again, and to present the Middle Ages to the readers in terms of only that difference—one need only think here of the well-known first sentence of the book: "When the world was five centuries younger, all events had much sharper external forms than now." The whole of history lying between the Middle Ages and our own present seems to have been forgotten or obliterated momentarily: in this, the directness of historical experience is suggested by the text itself. This directness effects the decontextualization of the past that I referred to in the introduction to this essay. Even more so, the fact that Huizinga does not tell us a story in *The Waning of the Middle Ages* but instead presents us with a synchronic section perpendicular to the movement of time, permits us to ascribe this propensity to decontextualize to the book's form no less than to its content. Both the content and the form of Huizinga's study exemplify its resistance to subsumption within either the context of the past itself or within the context of historical writing.

This naturally brings me to the question of how Huizinga sought to translate historical experience into language. The authors of the movement of the

1880s developed an idiom that they believed capable of realizing sensitivist aspirations. It could best be characterized as a deintellectualization or materialization of language. Neologisms were coined to produce a language that was permeated by all that we associate with sensory experience, feeling, and emotions. The possibilities of synaesthetics were greedily explored in the attempt to absorb language in the concrete realities of sensory experience. It was as if language had become a sense organ like the eye—or, rather, like the sense of touch—and as if reality was now discovered and explored anew with the help of this extra and most refined sense organ.

We will find all this in the dense and amazingly rich prose of *The Waning of the Middle Ages*. We need only read how Huizinga writes in the preface to perceive the mood he had written it in: "when writing this book it was as if my gaze was directed into the depths of an evening sky—but a sky full of a bloody red and angry with a threatening lead-grey, full of a false copper shine."[16] Thus did Huizinga express, in one single, profoundly impressionistic sentence, how he had experienced, in the most literal sense of that word, the "atmosphere" of the late, Burgundian Middle Ages. The reader who cannot read such a passage without feeling a shiver down the spine will realize the power of Huizinga's language to evoke this atmosphere, in which the life of late medieval man is to be situated, and to put his historical experience of that world into words. Form and content once again mutually reinforce each other here. For when Huizinga writes about medieval man that "all experience had yet to the minds of men the directness and absoluteness of the pleasure and pain of child-life," he attributes to medieval man a contact with reality that is both the subject of his book and the way he himself attempts to account for that subject. Huizinga attributes to medieval man a contact with reality that is structurally similar to his own experience of the medieval past investigated by him. There is a deep and meaningful resemblance between medieval man as depicted by Huizinga and the sensitivism of the movement of the 1880s.

Next, we shall not be surprised to find that the Huizinga of *The Waning of the Middle Ages* had recourse to the stylistic instruments of the movement of the 1880s for this book. Indeed, as was pointed out by Jansonius, the synaesthetic and metaphorical uses of the words for colors, most often red and black, proved to be so effective for Huizinga in producing the illusion of a sensory perception of past reality, that numerous parallels can be found in the writings of van Deijssel, Gorter, and other exponents of that movement of the "Tachtigers." No less frequent is the use of words like "high," "heavy," and especially "sharp," which enable Huizinga to mobilize the associations we have with the most elementary sensory perceptions in order to resuscitate the past.[17] The title of the first chapter, "The Fierceness of Life,"[18] almost suggesting the transformation of the abstraction *life* into a material object, is an example in point. What is abstract, and what might move us away from the blunt directness that life in the Middle Ages shared with how Huizinga chose to present it to his audience, is rendered on the level of language in the most concrete terms. The perennial propensity of language for abstraction is continuously and systematically resisted by Huizinga, who ties language deliberately and consistently as closely and firmly to reality as possible. Historical truth is sought not by "saying true things about the past," where the very correspondence of statement and state of affairs emphasizes their belonging to different realms, but by obstinately denying language any opportunity to move away from reality and the way it has been experienced by the historian.

Huizinga created many neologisms were by transforming a substantive into a verb or vice versa. The effect is the suggestion either of movement or of checking movement and, in both ways, sometimes abstract terms like "seriousness," "romantic," or "time" descend from the sphere of the idea to that of what our eyes can see and our fingers can touch. This is not merely a matter of presentation. It was no less inspired by Huizinga's conviction that the deepest truths can be found by exploiting the association with concreteness that the words and concepts we use may have. There is in each word or concept a key to the secrets of reality that the historian should always be eager to discover. Here a striking parallel can be discerned between Huizinga's own intuitions about language and relevant conceptions of the late-medieval mentality that was so much the subject of his book. Kamerbeek has drawn our attention to a passage in which Huizinga concurred with the medieval realist when holding that beauty, tenderness, and whiteness, in the end, have the same origin. Beauty is what whiteness is. Truth is in reality, not in what we say about it; it is to be found in the movement toward reality and not in that toward abstraction that is the perennial seduction of language. Surely, this is a quite different kind of truth than the one the philosopher is customarily interested in. It is a truth that arises from a quasimystic union with the world[19] and no longer allows itself to be enchanted by the abstractions that we all so unproblematically use. It is a mysticism that does not move us away from reality but brings us to its heart.

Putting Historical Experience into Words: White

I shall now turn to another proposal on how to verbalize historical experience, which can be found in the most recent writings of Hayden White. In order to avoid misunderstandings: I am not suggesting here that White attempted to deal with the problem of historical experience in the publications that I shall discuss; rather, here he gives a twist to his previous writings that brings him closer to the views that are proposed here.

As is well known, White postulated the existence of a number of linguistic codes that determine the structure of each narrative the historian tells about the past. Surely, we could not possibly conceive of a more radical antithesis to the views of Huizinga that were discussed in the previous section. For where Huizinga wishes to deny to language even the slightest freedom of movement with regard to the past, White seems prepared to grant to language an almost unlimited autonomy with regard to the nature of the past itself. This position elicits the obvious objection that there are parts of the past, like the Holocaust, that evidently do not permit of an ironic or satirical reading. The Holocaust both cognitively and morally conforms to a certain tropological encodation while inexorably excluding others. This seems to be at odds with White's claim, as put forward in *Metahistory* and elsewhere, that the past itself cannot determine its linguistic encodation in the historian's language. In two recent essays White has proposed an initially amazing rejoinder to his critics by attempting to mobilize the possibilities of Greek grammar for his defense—though it might be more accurate to say that White's appeal to the possibilities that are promised by that language's middle voice, have resulted in an altogether new theoretical position that differs fundamentally from the one that is ordinarily associated with his name. The idea behind White's appeal to Greek grammar is that the Greek verb allows us to reduce the distance between language and historical reality. To the extent that this distance is reduced, the past itself gets, so to speak, a firmer grasp on how it has to be represented in the historian's language. In this way, clearly unacceptable tropological encodations of parts of the past like the Holocaust can be effectively be ruled out.

The point of departure in White's redefinition of his position is the Greek middle voice, a grammatical form in Greek that indicates an aspect of action in between the active and the passive voice. In the aorist and in the futurum Greek has specific forms for each of the voices; in the aorist one may think of *elousa* (I washed—the active voice), *elousamèn* (I washed myself—the middle voice) and *elouthèn* (I was washed—the passive voice). White's attention to these peculiarities of the middle voice was provoked by an essay by Roland Barthes,[20] to which his attention had been drawn by Berel Lang.[21] Barthes suggests in this essay that we can think of using the verb *write* in the middle voice so that it becomes an intransitive verb. In that case there is no longer an "I" that writes "a text"; rather, the "I writes itself," so to speak: the "I" can articulate itself only in and by writing. One only becomes oneself by writing, a process for which neither the active, nor the passive, but only the middle voice is the appropriate form.

White clarifies these ideas by appealing to an essay in which Benveniste hazards the amazing thesis that in a remote past of the Indo-Germanic languages, in the second millennium before Christ or even earlier, the crucial grammatical distinction was whether the agent was presented as "interior to the action"—as in Barthes's intransitive writing—in which case the middle voice was used, or whether the agent was "exterior to the action" and describes the action in question, even if it is his own action, from a perspective outside the self, whereupon the active or the passive voice of a later time was to be used.

Gradually, the distinction between being either interior or exterior to the action lost its significance and had to surrender its prominent position to the other, later distinction between the active and the passive voice that we so naturally think to be of primary, if not, of exclusive importance. From then onward the middle voice became the modest form between the active and the middle voice that we know from classical Greek, and when in the course of time it died off, it was no longer an important loss to the expressiveness of language. "The middle voice," runs White's summary of this evolution, "expressed a relationship that later became sublimated into the reflexive and deponent forms, while the passive voice became progressively differentiated from the active, not in terms of interiority-exteriority, but in terms of whether the subject of the verb was presumed to be the patient [object] or the agent [subject] of the action."[22] Anyhow, what is of interest in the context of my discussion is that we may discern in the original use of the middle voice a use of language (and a culture preferring that use) where language is not yet placed into opposition to, or outside of, reality: only after "interiority" lost its former predominance to "exteriority" did language and reality become different spheres.

White gives concrete form to his insight into the peculiarities of the middle voice by relating them to the modernist novel as written by Joyce, Proust, or Woolf, and as characterized in Auerbach's *Mimesis*. In this way White attempts to answer our question of what narrative style is best suited for rendering what we have learned to associate with the middle voice. It is White's thesis that the modernist novel presents us with the kind of text that respects our "interiority" to our action, which was the original meaning of the middle voice. The "medial" character of the modernist novel manifests itself in its rejection of an objectivist presentation of the facts as we know from the realist or the naturalist novel, where what is represented (corresponding to the passive voice) and representation (corresponding to the active voice of the novelist or the historian) are always neatly separated. This stylistic feature of the modernist novel is seen, for example, in the use of the interior monologue, in which the novel's protagonist "tells him or herself" instead of "being told" by the author of the novel.

Other features that the modernist novel shares with the middle voice are the blurring of the distinction of what is "external" or "internal" to the novel's protagonist, the disappearance of the author as the alleged "narrator of objective facts" and of "any viewpoint outside the novel from which the people and events are observed," "the tone of doubt and questioning" that replaces the objectivism of naturalism, and lastly, the use of a number of new techniques such as abandoning the distinction between "internal" and "external" time, i.e., discarding the notion of an objective, chronological time scale on which all events mentioned in the novel can be organized.[23]

Two arguments can be given to demonstrate that the middle voice is a linguistic form well suited for the verbal expression of (historical) experience. First, if White is correct in assuming the modernist novel to be the textualist analogue to the middle voice as originally used in Indo-Germanic languages, we will observe that this textual analogue follows the flow of experience—the experience of both our internal and external reality—rather than that experience is forced into the matrix of narrative representation. The crucial datum here is the intrinsic opposition between experience and narrative. We will be aware of this opposition as soon as we recognize that the flow of narrative often forces us to privilege aspects of our own life or of history that are less, or perhaps not at all relevant from the perspective of experience.

Considering one's own life may be illuminating. If one is asked to tell the history of one's life, for example, for a curriculum vitae, this narrative by its nature often excludes events in our life that were vividly experienced and are still remembered as such: a certain atmosphere in our parental home, a certain moment during a vacation, how we were enraptured by a certain work of art or piece of music. From the point of view of narrative such experiences are irrelevant, and a curriculum vitae mentioning them would rightly be considered impracticable and too idiosyncratic to satisfy the requirements of narrative. The "history of our experience" does not have the coherence of narrative, is without a plot or intrigue, and completely disregards the criteria for the important and the unimportant that narrative always hopes to satisfy. If we were to write "the history of our experience," this history would inevitably either be incoherent or fail to do justice to the nature of our experiences. Narrative is centripetal, experience is centrifugal. Narrative and experience even mutually exclude each other: if we opt for narrative the realm of experience is relegated to the background; if we opt for experience the constraints of narrative must be disobeyed. If, then, we consider the account of the modernist novel by Auerbach as given above, we shall agree that each of the defining characteristics of the modernist novel testifies to its preference for experience and its rejection of narrative.

But there is a second argument for relating the language of the middle voice to experience and to see the former as appropriate for expressing the latter. Let us recall that White's interest in the middle voice was occasioned by the question of the representation of the Holocaust. This is not difficult to explain; one cannot doubt that the historian of the Holocaust more than any other is forced into "probing the limits of representation." The highest demands, both cognitive and moral, are made upon the historian of this greatest crime committed against humanity in the whole of the history of mankind: never is the historian's failure less forgivable than when he addresses the unspeakable horrors of the Holocaust, never is the historian morally more responsible for a deficiency in historical accuracy and tact than when he attempts to translate the undescribable of the Holocaust into writing. In that sense the task of the historian of the Holocaust is an impossible one since only perfection, and nothing less than that, can save him from a tacit complicity with the Holocaust. And for similar reasons I am most reluctant to make use of the

Holocaust as an argument in a theoretical debate like the present one. Perhaps this is a part of history that one should not write or theorize about and leave only to the victims and the perpetrators of the crime.

Yet precisely this is already, I believe, an important part of the answer to the question raised by White. The issue of the representation of the Holocaust is an issue that can be considered only from the point of view of the victims of the Nazis. It is, therefore, not primarily a question of what satisfies the historian and his discipline, but instead a question of what their memories of the Holocaust must mean for the victims themselves. Representation of the Holocaust, therefore, can only have the form of testimony. For it is exclusively in testimony that the victims of the concentration camps can find the answer to the question how life can still be lived with the traumas that were inflicted in the concentration camps. Many, or rather, most of the survivors of the concentration camps have tried their best to live with their memories and the trauma of the concentration camps. Some succumbed to a past that could never be forgotten and assimilated. But for some of them, like Celan of *Todesfuge,* the anonymous author of *Sunrise over Hell* or the camp survivors in Felman's and Laub's *Testimony*,[24] it was only possible to live with their terrible memories by speaking and writing about them—and in the case of Celan or Primo Levi life could not be recovered, even by the expression of the trauma. Their speaking and writing about the Holocaust was not primarily meant to be an indictment of what the Nazi regime had done to the Jews (as when we testify against somebody in litigation); rather, it was of vital importance for their own mental and physical survival. Only by this speaking and writing could the personality's integrity be saved; silence would have meant a permanent suffocation by the horrors of the past.

The traumatic experience is such that it cannot be assimilated at the very moment when the unspeakable happens. The trauma effects, therefore, a kind of suspension of the experience in question; the past as such is borne along by the subject of the traumatic experience in an unassimilated, "fossilized" form.[25] In this way the past itself, the past "as it actually was," is carried along by the subject of the traumatic experience and remains, in a sense, contemporary with him or her. Yet, by trying and by trying again and again to verbalize the traumatic experience, the fossilized traumatic past can slowly and gradually be reactivated in the present and reexperienced in such a way that it can finally be integrated in one's personality. Insofar as this takes the form of a poem, or novel (or of what is said to the psychoanalyst), this reexperiencing is identical with the intransitive kind of writing, that writing in the middle voice that Barthes referred to in which the author, so to speak, "writes himself" or "becomes himself" by writing and speaking. Hence the experience of a traumatic past, an experience as intense as experience can ever be, can only be expressed by the middle voice, and when representation is confronted with the ultimate challenge of the Holocaust, experience and the intransitivity of the middle voice require one another.

Conclusion

History is an empirical discipline in two respects. First, in the more trivial sense history is an empirical discipline in that it deals with the data the past has left us that can empirically be verified or falsified. But history is also an empirical discipline in the sense that it can be seen as a continuous experiment with language; an experiment in relating language to the world. This experiment is not peculiar to history: the sciences have developed artificial languages in order to meet that challenge. The option of the sciences is not open to history. If historians cease to speak ordinary language, a language accessible to all our civilized fellow-citizens, they betray their cultural duty and responsibility. But that does not mean that only one style is available to the historian. As far as his cultural responsibility is concerned, the historian is in a position not unlike that of the novelist—and we know that the novel has had a complex and variegated history. Likewise, the history of historical writing can also be seen as a series of experiments with language. I have briefly discussed two such experiments in this paper and emphasize that no a priori restriction can be made on the number of such experiments with language. The philosopher is always tempted to come up with such restrictions and, by doing so, to lay down the law for historical writing.

This is the transcendentalist seduction that has dominated philosophy of language up to the present day, however much philosophers like Rorty or Derrida may protest that they reject a philosophy of language where language is merely the latest variant of the Kantian categories that are the conditions for the possibility of all experience and knowledge. Language is not such a latter-day variant of the Kantian categories, and there are no a priori schemes for relating language to experience and knowledge. Nor should language be seen as a Wittgensteinian tool used for "coping with reality," in the way that the painter uses his brushes for painting a picture. To pursue the latter metaphor, language should be seen on a par not with the painter's brushes, but with the paint that is not so much used as spent by the painter. That is to say, in contrast to the former metaphor, language has no existence outside the infinity of concrete instances of its use: whereas we can always distinguish between the brush itself and the way it is used, this distinction is no longer possible with the picture's paint. If we consider this difference between the way the brush and the paint are used by the painter, it will become clear why the Wittgensteinian proposal of language as a tool gave Kantianism and transcendentalist philosophy of language a fresh impetus. The brush is a metaphor of the transcendental self that always accompanies representation but is never itself part of it. And just like the picture's paint, language, so to speak, "spends" or "loses" itself in its use.

Again, like the paint used by the painter, language is used to express or to materialize the (aesthetic) experience of the historian. The historian's use of language to this end may or may not satisfy the historian and the individuals among the audience. In fact, it will rarely meet all the requirements of both the historian and his audience and will most often have the character of an experiment that can possibly be improved upon by later experiments. But there is nothing philosophically "deep" or "interesting" about these partial successes and failures in the sense that there exist a priori "given" criteria that may explain success and failure in individual cases. Looking for "depth" here would inevitably entail a return to "the metaphor of the brush" and thus to transcendentalism.

Hence, the relationship between history and philosophy is rather the reverse. The philosopher should consider the history of historical writing as a series of experiments with language and reflect on its successes and failures, not in order to explain them but rather to guess what follows from them and what they may mean for the relation between language and reality. Philosophy, that is, philosophy of language should be an aposteriorist rather than an apriorist discipline, taking its points of departure in what actually takes place in disciplines like history. Philosophy should not have the pretension to offer the foundations of knowledge and look instead in the opposite direction, concentrating on the results of scientific or historical research. The philosopher who wishes to formulate transcendentalist laws for the proper use of historical language, as is still the aim of in much contemporary historical theory, will be blinded to much of the "beauty" of the history of historical writing. I use here deliberately the word "beauty" since the question of how to properly relate language to reality, how to put into words the way reality has been experienced by us, is essentially an "aesthetic" question. The history of historical writing is, in the final analysis, a chapter in the book of the history of aesthetics.

Notes

1. See F. R. Ankersmit, *De historische ervaring* (Groningen 1993); idem, *History and Tropology* (Berkeley 1994), especially chapter 7; idem, "Historism: An attempt at synthesis," *History and Theory* 34.2 (1995): 143–162; idem, "Van taal naar ervaring," in S. Alexandrescu, ed., *Richard Rorty* (Kampen 1995); idem, "Antwoord aan Nauta," *Theoretische Geschiedenis* 20 (1993): 523–534; idem, "Can we experience the past?," in R. Torstendahl and I. Veit-Brause, eds., *Historymaking: The intellectual and social formation of a discipline* (Stockholm 1996), 44–77; idem, "Ervaring, waarheid en representatie," in I. Bulhof, ed., *De representatiekrisis* (Kampen 1995); idem, "The Postmodernist "Privatization" of the Past," in H. Nagl-Docekal, ed., *Geschichtsphilosophie nach der grossen Erzählung* (Frankfurt/ M. 1995).

2. This is the argument in Ankersmit, "Antwoord aan Nauta."

3. As I deliberately suggest with the word "attempt," the possibilities for solving the problem of how to translate experience into language may be as numerous as are the varieties of historical writing. Other possibilities (which will not be discussed here) include be Ginzburg's proposal to use ekphrastic poetry as a model for the historian's language. See C. Ginzburg, "Ekphrasis and quotation," *Tijdschrift voor filosofie* 50 (1988): 3–19. Elsewhere I have used Tocqueville's political and historical writings to demonstrate how the trope of paradox can effect a direct contact with past reality. See my "Tocqueville and the sublimity of democracy. Part 1," *The Tocqueville Review* 14 (1993): 173–201 and idem, "Tocqueville and the sublimity of democracy. Part 2," *The Tocqueville Review* 15 (1994): 193–218.

4. M. G. Kemperink, *Van observatie tot extase* (Utrecht 1988), 87.

5. It is possible to see much of contemporary French literary criticism and philosophy, as exemplified by *Tel quel* or Derrida, as an elaboration of the philosophical intuitions underlying Mallarmé's "pure poetry". Mallarmé would have agreed with Derrida's "il n'y a pas dehors texte"; the extravagancies of poststructuralist French philosophy and its peculiar disregard for the real is, to a large extent, a repetition of nineteenth-century symbolism's reaction to literary realism and naturalism. This is where sensitivism and symbolism are diametrically opposed to each other.

6. See E. Endt, *Herman Gorter: Documentatie 1864–1897* (Amsterdam 1986), 179. I am referring with this example to a passage in Gorter's rejected doctoral dissertation of 1888. Gorter's *Verzen,* published two years later, are probably the best and purest expression of sensitivism in Dutch literature.

7. Kemperink, *Van observatie,* 85–88.

8. Lodewijk van Deijssel, *Verzamelde opstellen: Tweede bundel* (Amsterdam 1897), 185, 298f.

9. For a more elaborate discussion of Huizinga's conception of historical sensation or experience, and for the difference between this notion and that of *"Erlebnis"* in German hermeneutics, see my *De historische ervaring.* References are also given there to what other historians have written on the subject of historical experience.

10. Ankersmit, *History and Tropology,* chap. 7.

11. J. Huizinga, "Mijn weg tot de historie," in idem, *Verzamelde werken* (Haarlem 1948), vol. 1, 23.

12. W. E. Krul, *Historicus tegen de tijd: Opstellen over leven en werk van Johan Huizinga* (Groningen 1990), 132.

13. F. Jansonius, "De stijl van Huizinga," *Bijdragen en mededelingen betreffende de geschiedenis der Nederlanden* 88 (1973): 195–215, here 196.

14. Huizinga, "Mijn weg," 32.

15. J. Huizinga, "De kunst der Van Eyck's in het leven van hun tijd," in *Verzamelde werken* (Haarlem 1948), vol. 1, 436.

16. This is from the preface to the Dutch edition (the preface to the English edition is not a translation of the original Dutch preface). It must be observed that almost all of the features of Huizinga's style that are discussed here are absent from the English translation (which is, moreover, a much abbreviated version of the Dutch version). Though it may readily be conceded that it would be well-nigh impossible to preserve Huizinga's exceedingly idiosyncratic use of the Dutch language in the English translation, it should never be forgotten that the English translation is a mere shadow of the book that Huizinga originally wrote and that it sadly fails to do justice to what are precisely its most interesting properties. For an exposition of the literary antecedents of the sentence from the preface that is quoted in my test, see W. E. Krul, "In de schaduwen van morgen," in R.T. Segers, ed., *Visies op cultuur en literatuur* (Amsterdam 1991).

17. Jansonius, "De stijl van Huizinga," 198ff.

18. Though "the fierceness of life" surely is not an entirely satisfactory translation of the far more dramatic Dutch "s levens felheid" because semantically "fel" is somewhere between "sharp" and "fierce," this translation is nevertheless preferable to the peculiarly inept and impotent "violent tenor of life" of the English translation.

19. J. Kamerbeek, jr., "Huizinga en de beweging van tachtig," *Tijdschrift voor geschiedenis* 67 (1954): 150.

20. The essay in question is Roland Barthes, "To write: An intransitive verb," in R. Macksey and E. Donato, eds., *The Languages of Criticism and the Sciences of Man* (Baltimore 1970). White also relates Barthes's views to comparable suggestions made by Freud and Derrida.

21. B. Lang, *Act and Idea in the Nazi Genocide* (Chicago 1990), 147.

22. Hayden White, "Writing in the middle voice," *Stanford Literature Review* 9 (1992): 185. Benveniste's thesis about the origins of the middle voice is well-known amongst classical philologists, but no final proof of the correctness of the thesis has ever been given, and in view of the available evidence it is not likely that it will ever be possible to prove or to disprove it conclusively.

23. Hayden White, "Historical emplotment and the problem of truth," in S. Friedlander, ed., *Probing the Limits of Representation* (Cambridge, Mass. 1992), 50f.

24. S. Felman and D. Laub, eds., *Testimony: Crises of witnessing in literature, psychoanalysis and history* (New York 1992).

25. See D. Laub, "Bearing witness, or the vicissitudes of listening," in S. Felman and D. Laub, eds., *Testimony*.

Part II
REPRESENTATION

CHAPTER 9

Flights from History
Reinventing Tradition between the 18th and 20th Centuries

ALEIDA ASSMANN

History is a nightmare from which I'm trying to awake.
(James Joyce, Ulysses)

Introduction: What is tradition?

"Tradition does not consist of relics, but of certificates and legacies."[1] Hans Blumenberg's statement draws attention to the originally legal character of the concept of tradition. Tradition does not consist of relics. This means, first of all: tradition does not generate itself, it does not arise naturally. Geological structures, for instance, can develop by themselves, one stratum overlaying another. Over a period of several thousand years, this growth results in a profile that makes the depth of time legible. In Blumenberg's view, tradition has nothing to do with such organic patterns in nature. Yet this is not to say that there are no overlapping "time layers" (to use Koselleck's coinage) in the realm of culture as well. For as soon as they are engraved in relatively enduring material media, cultural signs gain a resistance to time that exceeds their current utility-value in a specific culture or epoch. The "cultural detritus" of past times piles up and is preserved in archives and museums, where it exists in separation from the concerns and values of the changing present.

Such a state of preservation which carries the connotations of (out-) datedness and alienation. It can be regarded as a strategic defense against time's ongoing tendency toward decay, loss, rupture, and forgetting. It is forgetting

---

Notes for this section begin on page 167.

that comes naturally, not tradition. Tradition depends on specific precautions and efforts to establish and maintain continuity, a process that is unlikely to succeed without human and cultural efforts.[2]

Unlike remnants or "relics," "certificates and legacies" are documents from which legal claims are derived. As long as the past is considered as a "repository of documents upon which the rights of governments and nations depend," it cannot be called "past."[3] In order to identify more clearly the legal substrate in the concept of tradition, we must consider that the term *traditio* originated in Roman inheritance law, where it referred to the transfer of movable property from one hand to another. Tradition, therefore, is originally conceived as a legal transaction between a giver and a receiver. Thereby, the transfer of rights and obligations, authority and power, property and possessions is arranged in such a way as to bridge the gap of death that profoundly threatens the continuation of communal life. The testament is the nucleus of tradition. In the contract of inheritance, a paradigmatic bond is sealed between father and son, and more generally between the dead and the living, guaranteeing continuity across the succession of generations.[4] In a diminished form the legal connotation of tradition can still be discerned in such terms as "cultural heritage" or "patrimony." In such terms, the original legal meaning of "tradition" has become increasingly abstract and neutralized. A more concrete notion of legal obligation and responsibility has only recently been introduced into the word "heritage" in the UNESCO context of world cultural politics.

Another legal term that is rooted in the semantic field of tradition is *depositum*. In Roman law, this refers to the practice of taking movable property into custody or safekeeping. In this situation, nothing is permanently transferred, but only temporarily entrusted and then reclaimed; the rightful owner does not change. But the person entrusted with something is held responsible for it. The object must not be damaged, reduced, altered, consumed, or exchanged; it is to be preserved entire and, when the moment arrives, to be passed on or returned. In Catholic doctrine, the *depositum fidei* is the stock of revealed articles of faith entrusted to the Church for safekeeping. But the institution of depositum is much older than Roman law and the Roman Catholic Church. It appears as a motif in fairy tales, in which the damaging of an entrusted object through falsification, reduction, squandering, and so on often produces dire consequences in the narrative.

Tradition versus Fashion: Swift's *A Tale of a Tub* (1704)

Jonathan Swift wrote a story describing the nature of tradition and deploring the forms of its decay. In *A Tale of the Tub,* the Anglican clergyman encoded a satirical allegory of the schism between denominations.[5] The text, he intertwines the legal aspects of *traditio* and *depositum*. It tells the story of a father who feels his end is nearing. He summons his three sons to instruct them about the inheritance they are to expect. Instead of money and goods, he has something special to bequeath to them: three coats with most extraordinary qualities; unlike ordinary clothes, if they are used well, they will never wear out, and on top of that they have the ability to grow at the same rate as the body and will therefore always fit properly. Along with the coats, the man leaves a testament containing specific instructions on how to treat the unusual clothes. Before he dies, the father advises his sons to follow his instructions to the letter and dismisses them with the warning that otherwise something terrible would lie in store for them.

Before long, the problems with these simple instructions arise. The father's testament soon comes up against another authority, the dictates of fashion, which the sons, as urban careerists, also feel obliged to follow. So a conflict arises between the norms of the past and those of the present. The father's testament, as the mouthpiece of tradition, commands that the clothes remain unchanged, but each season makes new demands for decoration. The sons' problem is how to reconcile, one after the other, shoulder straps, gold braid, flame-colored lining, and silver fringe with their father's rigid and unambiguous text. The testament not only fails to provide for these types of ornamentation, in part it even explicitly forbids them; so a new means must be found to deal with this dilemma. The magic solution is *hermeneutics*.

Hermeneutics is understood as an art of reading that makes the word of canonized texts compatible with contemporary interest. But even this procedure, flexible as it may be, eventually becomes a burden. The business of interpretative acrobatics requires increasing exertions and stands in the way of the unbridled display of the will to fashion or power. So finally the wretched testament is locked up in a heavy chest and discreetly disposed of.

Swift's tale is a transparent allegory of the history of the Christian religion, which leads from a common experience of salvation through the arbitrariness of priests to tyranny, schism, and civil war. At the same time, Swift delineates a pessimistic genealogy of modern times, the various stages of which he sees as marked by the changing relationship to tradition. The first phase is characterized by the *natural state of tradition*. According to Swift, traditions are originally timeless and, like the wonderful coats, tailored to fit mankind and its needs. They are not a rigid armor, but fairly flexible and adaptable attire that becomes larger and wider as growth requires. Nor are they old rags bearing the mark of the day before yesterday, but rather timeless shells, able to adapt smoothly to the moving present.

Against the foil of this ideal condition, Swift offers the following variations of the decline of tradition, which he sees as determining the continuation of human history. The first petrifaction occurs when *tradition becomes explicit,* in the form of the last will and testament. Being set down in the medium of writing renders tradition fixed, objective, reflexive. The norms lose their character of unconscious orientation and take on the form of binding instructions. Swift characterizes the next step as the *violation of tradition* through the medium of interpretation. This is a route leading from the present to the past and rigorously subordinating the past to the imperatives of current interests. Then follows the *removal of tradition from the living world* by dismissing it as taboo. This method removes tradition from the field of current political interests. It is canonized and made sacred, whereby it loses its orienting potential for the living world. The logical final stage of this development is the unconditional rule of man over man, who, no longer constrained by any ties of loyalty or obligation, ends in fraud, violence, and civil war.

Swift does not describe modernity nostalgically as a calamitous process of man's separation from tradition; rather, he sees the calamitous dynamics as a potential based in tradition itself. For him, modernization is not simply a turning away from tradition, but a change in how we deal with tradition. Here, he also refers to the erosion and exhaustion of tradition in the milieu of the modern city. The significance of mutual observation and display and the quick and fleeting accent of glaring signals constitute the new social phenomenon of fashion, which drew Swift's attention two hundred years before the prophetic awareness of the sociologist Georg Simmel. Traditions do not disappear, but only change their form with the beginning of modern times; they shift from adaptable forms of life to rigid monuments, they are removed from custom, and appropriated by the few, in whose hands they degenerate into instruments of power.

Reinventing Tradition under the Name of Nature: Pope's "Essay on Criticism" (1711)

Swift's contemporary Alexander Pope also thought about tradition under the conditions of modern times. Here, "modernism" means three things: democratization, market rationality, and the acceleration of social and technological change. Specifically, this implies that more and more people can write and read as they wish; the question of quality is decided by the paying public; values are no longer stable, but dictated by a rapidly changing taste, called fashion. Pope responds to this syndrome of modernity with an all-encompassing counter-concept that combines authority, value, and duration. The concept that Pope chooses, under the conditions of the modernization of society, to replace the lost "tradition" is "nature." In his *Essay on Man* he writes:

> First follow Nature, and your judgment frame
> By her just standard, which is still the same:
> Unerring Nature, still divinely bright,
> One clear, unchang'd and universal light,
> Life, force, and beauty, must all impart,
> At once the source, and end, and test of Art.[6]

The surrogate that Pope discovers is far more comprehensive than the lost tradition. While traditions were always diverse and particular, the concept of nature is holistic and anthropological, matching the new universal concept of mankind. From now on, nature stands for a norm that transcends cultural particularity; it becomes synonymous with stability and reliability and is used by Pope to back up the notion of a canon of classical literature.

"Classics" and "nature" stabilize each other mutually. To give his broad and unspecific concept of nature the form of tradition, Pope fills it with the works of Greek and Latin literature that are considered exemplary. Homer, Virgil, and Horace supply him with a canon that defines the exemplary norms for literary writing. In order to transfer this universal and timeless authority to the authors, they must first be removed from history and "naturalized." As Pope stresses, they are not subject to historically contingent norms, because they themselves have chosen nature as their source of inspiration and can thus be regarded as part of nature themselves.

> But when t'examine ev'ry part he came
> Nature and Homer were, he found, the same ...
> Learn hence for ancient rules a just esteem;
> To copy nature is to copy them. (vv.134f., 138–140)[7]

Pope's "naturalization of tradition" can be interpreted as an attempt to reinvent tradition under the conditions of its loss. The traditions that existed had not withstood the pressures of social change; a new form of tradition had therefore to be reinvented that would be inherently resistant to change and subversion and that would furthermore counteract modern culture's new categorical imperative, "innovation." Pope and other classically oriented authors call this enduring, innovation-resistant tradition "nature." Unlike later minds, for whom nature connotes a lack of rules, for Pope and these authors it implies rule-giving: not uniqueness (originality), but generality; not the awesome appeal of the sublime, but the reliable solidity of truth.[8]

Pope makes it explicit that the loss of tradition is very closely related to the accelerated pace of change within the world of everyday experience. He no longer sees any transgenerational nexus securing the enduring validity of knowledge and values:

> We think our fathers fools, so wise we grow,
> Our wiser sons, no doubt, will think us so. (vv. 438f.)

Today, as Andy Warhol remarked, fame lasts barely ten minutes; at the beginning of the eighteenth-century, Pope was already thinking about the ever-quickening expiration dates for fame:

> No longer now the golden age appears,
> When Patriarch-wits surviv'd a thousand years:

> Now length of Fame (our second life) is lost,
> And bare threescore is all ev'n that can boast:
> Our sons their fathers' failing language see,
> And such as Chaucer is, shall Dryden be. (vv. 478–483)

As Chaucer is in the present, so Dryden will be in the foreseeable future: as his language will no longer be understandable, his work is doomed to become obsolete. Unlike the poets before him, Pope no longer believes in the inherent immortality of literature; he no longer expects material texts to provide a guarantee for art's perpetual duration. Nor does he, touched by the spirit of a new historicism, believe in the revitalizing power of later eras to rekindle the sparks of times past. So he has to find a new force to maintain the continuity of major works beyond the grasp of time. "Nature" is Pope's name for this tradition, which he reinvented under the conditions of the accelerated time and historization. It is designed as a force that can provide an effective antidote to the erosive forces of time, innovation, fashion, and history.

Throughout the eighteenth-century, the concept of nature underwent various changes. Toward the end of the century, it was taken up by Schiller, who also used it as a substitute for tradition. In a letter addressed to two ladies in the year of the French Revolution, Schiller describes nature as something that is wholly passive and receptive, thus opposing it implicitly to the revolutionary forces. Nature can not act on its own but is dependent on man, who projects himself into it. It cannot do "anything for itself, but receives everything from the human soul. Only through that which we have invested in her does nature charm and delight us." There is a clear separation of roles: Man gives, nature takes and preserves. And not only does Nature take, it also gives back. The next passage in the letter focuses on this aspect: "And again how benevolent is this identity, this uniform persistence of nature. When passion, inner and outer tumult, has thrown us about long enough, when we have lost ourselves, we always find her as her same self again and *ourselves in her.* During our flight through life, we place every enjoyed pleasure, every image of our changing existence into her faithful hands, and she returns the entrusted goods to us safe and sound when we come and ask for them."[9]

Here we return to the previously mentioned concept of tradition as a "trustee" administering a depositum. There is an unbreakable bond of trust that what is placed in the care of the trustee will not be embezzled, squandered, or lost. Man, who is becoming ever more mobile, changeable, and change-producing, assigns nature the role of a reliable, steadfast partner. Under the conditions of loss of tradition in a dynamic culture that has elevated free thought and the invigorating soul to its driving force, nature appears on the one hand as a negative foil to man, characterized by "eternal sameness of appearance," "eternal self-imitation," and "deadly calm," and on the other hand as a positive complement to man, identical to itself through time and a guarantor of human identity. Schiller assigns to nature the task that was once associated with tradition. In a world of revolutionary change, nature rather than tradition becomes the guarantor not only of the endurance of literary works, but also of the poet's self: "How unhappy we would be, we, who find it so necessary to thriftily make the joys of the past our own property, if we could not bring these fleeting treasures into our friend's safekeeping. We owe our whole personality to her, because if tomorrow she were to stand before us changed, we would search in vain for our self of yesterday." (Ibid.)

Exorcising the Demon of Chronology: The Modern Concept of Tradition

These examples from the beginning and end of the eighteenth-century underline the dynamics of tradition: the concept of tradition is eroded by an intensified experience of temporality and mutability in culture. While some discard tradition and replace it with innovation, thereby endorsing the energy of historical change, others invest nature with an intransient dimension unaffected by time. Tradition, history, and nature thus stand in a relationship of dialectical determination. We have seen that the notion of tradition did not disappear under the conditions of modernity, but was transformed, or rather reinvented, under the name of nature.

Plunging out of Time: Kierkegaard, Overbeck, and the Concept of "Existence"

The all-encompassing brace of continuity that Hegel placed around history and Christianity, around God and the world—his magic word *Geist* (spirit or mind)—was broken up by a number of radical religious thinkers who seriously pondered the problems of time and eternity in the nineteenth-century. These thinkers criticized Hegel's vision of continuity and stressed rupture, incompatibility, contradiction, and paradox instead. Their point was the irreconcilability of being and time, of spirit and history. A generation before Nietzsche wrote his famous essay on the elementary opposition between "history" and "life," in which he argued for the vital energy of forgetting, Kierkegaard had already built up similar oppositions.[10] He distinguished sharply between the essence of Christianity on the one hand and its temporal history as a worldly institution on the other. Since the Reformation, Christianity had become "modernity-compatible"; it was in a position to keep abreast of the progressive course of world history. Its ability to compromise and complicity with worldly institutions was boundless: it was able to reconcile itself equally with the spirit of capitalism and historicism. Under the influence of liberal Protestantism, a theology developed that was marked by historical-critical thought. Such developments toward reconciliation between belief and knowledge were more often than not massively thwarted.

Kierkegaard formulated the dilemma of modern Christianity as caught in the radical dichotomy between "time and eternity." He saw Hegel's secularization of Christianity, with its immanence and its synonymity with humanity and progress, as a distorted, updated, and pagan form of Christianity. In Kierkegaard's view, real Christianity lay hidden under the debris of history. He identified the hallmark of Christianity as its alienating power, and the endless adaptability that secured its duration in history with its as its false mask. To the false objectivity of history, Kierkegaard opposed the radical interiority of subjectivity, the act of existentially private appropriation. According to Karl Löwith, Kierkegaard's "existential experiment" consists in his "wish to dissolve the historical distance in the inner 'simultaneity' and to restore original Christianity, at the end of its decline, to each individual existence" (451). As a historical reality, Christianity is an obstacle to itself; what is required is to become at least inwardly simultaneous and, in accordance with Kierkegaard's categorical imperative, "to wipe out the 1800 years as if they never existed" (ibid.).

The dilemma of the Christian truth that had come to be identified with the past was a concept also addressed by Nietzsche's friend, the theologian Franz Overbeck, who noted at the end of the century, "that the oldest history of Christianity ... has become the past."[11] After two thousand years, Christianity had grown old. Just as there is hardly any likeness discernible between older people and their youthful appearance, there is no similarity remains between an originally world-renouncing Christianity awaiting *parousia* and the institution of the Church with its worldly expansion and greed for power. For Overbeck, original Christianity is in every way the opposite of what it has become in the course of history. It entered the world as a contradiction of history and an affirmation of helplessness, as a wisdom of death and not as wisdom of life. "Christianity, that has lived for so long, can no longer stand in the world as it did in the beginning, after all the experiences that once lay ahead of it and are now part of it!" (268f.)

Because "a centuries-old and extremely complicated experience has inserted itself between Christianity and all of us," (12) it is no longer possible to "simply identify with it" (11). Overbeck's guiding principle assumes that those who believe they can simply adhere to a Christianity that has undergone accommodation with history have not really understood true Christianity: "Christianity's own will can never allow for history and Christianity to come together" (9). Overbeck even goes so far as to dismiss the Christian calendar as a delusion. The expectation of the imminent end of time has degenerated to the permanence of the calendar; Christianity's thoughtless duration is its untruth.

The influential distinction between "historical origin" and "historicity of decay" derives from Overbeck. This model of thought blasted Hegel's evolutionary optimism, with its insistence on unity and completeness. The confident view of historical development yielded to the pessimistic understanding of history as a process of decay, forgetting, and falsification. Overbeck bracketed off the history of Christianity; following in his footsteps, Heidegger later did the same to the entire history of Western philosophy and returned to the pure origin, to the dark fragments of the pre-Socratics.

The same is true for Overbeck's exodus from history. For him, history is not simply gradual and inexorable decay, but the product of an intentional cultural project, a systematic falsification. What separates us from the beginning is much less sheer time than "tradition that has solidified in canon and exegesis," which spreads "a veil of amnesia over the beginnings" (10). It is thus necessary to veer away from historically petrified tradition, if anything of the timeless content of Christianity is to be rescued. Only an ascetic way of life can maintain the "soul" of Christianity, "namely the negation of the world." Christianity itself offers the most remarkable example of an exodus from history, which Overbeck describes as a "stepping into the air." He was firmly convinced "that we humans can progress it, from time to time we are able to step out into the air." (77)

Kierkegaard's tragic existentialism, which used passion and despair as explosives against reason and history, affected artists and thinkers, especially those who harbored leanings toward heroic loneliness and the verbal power of the prophet. One of these was Miguel de Unamuno, to whom Ernst Robert Curtius dedicated a portrait on the occasion of his seventieth birthday, in which he wrote: "The tragicism of Unamuno (which is also redolent of Kierkegaard and Nietzsche) is more compatible with our situation today than it was with prewar Europe, because it assumes the concrete existence of the individual who knows the threat of transience, need, fate. But on the other hand, it is the thousand-year-old genius of Spain that can twist the metaphysical plight of existence into a glowing urge toward eternity. The last word is not nihilism … but eternism, the plunge into timelessness. The mankind of Unamuno consumes itself in a burning thirst for immortality."[12]

In such lines, the weariness with history and reason acquires a titanic force. A new heroism is needed to overcome the dimension of historicity and with it the major achievements of the nineteenth-century: science and humanism. The retreat from time resulted in a "plunge"; the "new certainty" was born "on the brink of despair." These images, blown into catastrophic proportions, no longer refer to "refuges of security, spaces of evasion," but rather to the potential for violence that can be used to besiege the fortress of history. Unamuno does not flee the present or imagine himself a contemporary of other times; he is a prophet who sees himself as the "stimulant of the national forces of Spain" and who "testifies to the wish for a new future." This vision lies neither outside, nor beside history, but makes a point of exploding it altogether.

From Inventory to System: T. S. Eliot's Concept of Tradition

The exodus from European history that took shape around 1900 also affected the arts. Literary critics became weary of literary history and searched for an essential quality of literary works that lay buried underneath thick layers of dates and circumstances. Interest was awakened in a new immediateness, a desire to reconnect directly with works of earlier epochs in a new proximity, unbroken in spite of a growing temporal distance, and unburdened by the mass of scholarly erudition.

This was roughly the mood in which the English novelist E. M. Forster gave his famous lecture series entitled *Aspects of the Novel* at Trinity College (Cambridge) in the spring of 1927. The word "aspect" was intentionally chosen as a term without any reference to time. In the introductory lecture, Forster warned his listeners that he would not discuss "influences," "periods," "trends," and "directions." What's more, he promised to banish the demon of chronology from the field of aesthetics: "Time, all the way through, is to be our enemy. We are to visualize the English novelists ... as seated together in a room, a circular room, a sort of British Museum reading-room—all writing their novels simultaneously.... They come from different ages and ranks, they have different temperaments and aims, but they all hold pens in hands, and are in the process of creation. Let us look over their shoulders for a moment and see what they are writing. It may exorcise that demon of chronology."[13]

With his motto *History develops, Art stands still,* Forster stands against the historicism of literary history and the burden of knowledge collected in the institution of literary criticism, which he believes has no use except to keep academics off the streets. He calls for a new naiveté that would meet the texts with the freshness of personal curiosity and place them within immediate reach.

A year before Forster, T. S. Eliot had given the Clark lectures at Trinity College. More than any other before him, he gave voice to a mood we would now call *posthistoire:* the feeling of living late, of standing on a spot from which everything can be viewed at a glance, the impression that the end of history has been reached. This context, clearly visible in retrospect, Eliot called tradition. In his view, history is temporal and thus contingent, arbitrary, fragmentary, while tradition is timeless and thus meaningful, orderly, and whole. The decisive word is "whole," which returns in Eliot's text with the insistence of a religious invocation. Completeness is possible through simultaneity; Eliot moves from a fragmenting and distancing temporality to a relational and ordered one. The synchronistic glance that encompasses the simultaneity of the temporally separate ("the sense of everything happening at once") Eliot somewhat ambiguously calls the "historical sense": "The historical sense involves a perception, not only of the pastness of the past but of its presence; the historical compels a man to write not merely with his own generation in his bones, but with a feeling that the whole of the literature of Europe from Homer and within it the whole literature of his own country has simultaneous existence and composes a simultaneous order."[14]

Eliot's reinvention of tradition is based on the experience of transience, fragmentation, and forgetting, against which he constructs a new concept combining simultaneity and "wholeness." The term wholeness here involves the *wholeness of the canon,* comprising the sum of "eminent texts" (Gadamer), as well as the *wholeness of the organism.* On the one hand, wholeness suggests a secure inventory and normativity of models in the past, and on the other, a productive "mechanism" of renewal for the future.

The traditional form of conceiving unity is the organism. De Quincey, for example, understood an "organic science" (such as economics) as one researching the dialectical relationship between parts and whole: "no part, that is to say, but what acts on the whole, as the whole again reacts on each part."[15] Today, we would view Eliot's concept of the whole as the whole of the system. His concept of tradition is systemic. Without naming it as such, he describes tradition as a system that reorganizes its economy with each change and renewal. Historical categories such as "development" and "cause" are replaced with aesthetic categories of tradition like "whole" and "unity." It is a whole in which old and new are in the constant process of adjusting to each other: "What happens when a new work of art is created is something that happens simultaneously to all the works of art which preceded it. The existing monuments form an ideal order among themselves, which is modified by the introduction of the new (the really new) work of art among them. The existing order is complete before the new work arrives; for the order to persist after the supervention of the novelty, the whole existing order must be, if ever so slightly, altered; and so the relations, proportions, values of each work of art toward the whole are readjusted; and this is conformity between old and new."[16]

One of Nietzsche's aphorisms had already established the basic features of this type of systemic thought: "Given that the world has a quantum of force, then it is obvious that any shift of power anywhere will affect the whole system—therefore, along with causality *in sequence to* each other, dependency beside and *with* each other must also be taken into account."[17] This reference makes clear what Eliot gains from his systemic concept of tradition: he can allow for movement and change, independent of causal and chronological models. Like Forster, Eliot deconstructs the framework of chronology that was the backbone of historicism. But he does not do this by simply abstracting time and arresting his object in synchronous space. Unlike Pope, he does not create a strong canonical norm, and unlike Kierkegaard and Overbeck, he does not create the idea of an a-temporal essence. Instead, he stresses the internal dynamics of a system built on the coevolution of old and new.

It is not altogether surprising that Eliot develops systemic thinking when reflecting on tradition. In many ways, Eliot's concept of tradition as a process of permanent inner restructuring resembles the model of memory as theorized at the beginning of the twentieth-century. In 1925, six years after Eliot's essay on tradition, Maurice Halbwachs presented the laws of memory in similarly systemic terms, using the idea of the "framework." Halbwachs wrote in *Les cadre sociaux de la mémoire*: "Every time we integrate our impressions into the framework of our current ideas, the framework changes our impression, but the impression also modifies the framework.... This results in a constant work of adjustment that, with every event, requires us to return to all of the concepts we have worked out on the occasion of prior events. If it were a matter of simply moving from a prior to a later fact, we could remain constantly in the current moment, and in it alone. But in reality, we must incessantly change from one framework to the next, which doubtlessly differs very little from the first, but in any case differs."[18]

The last sentence sounds almost like a translation of Eliot's "the whole existing order must be, if ever so slightly, altered."[19] Eliot's tradition is detemporalized, but not rendered motionless; he invokes no apocatastasis, no "all in all," no "total recall." It is completely quotable, but with the important limitation that it will be quoted ("if ever so slightly") *newly* and *differently* in each "present time."

Here it is appropriate to mention another theorist who developed a dynamic concept of the literary process and who published it in the 1920s under the term "system." Jurij Tynjanow's essay *On Literary Evolution* (1927) defines "system" as a whole, the unity of which is determined by the interrelationships of the individual components. Such a system is anything but a harmonious and indifferent order. "A system does not mean the coexistence of components on the basis of equality; rather, it presupposes the pre-eminence of one group of elements and the resulting deformation of others."[20]

In this view, the history of literature is not a neutral continuum, but, like memory itself, a process of rewritings and deformations, as they arise from the conditions of perception and the dynamics of dominance at each present moment. The word "deformation" here has no negative connotations, because there is no standard of a binding norm that transcends history. What does exist is continuous appropriation, perspectivization, and rewriting from respective historical standpoints. As a literary critic, Eliot was interested in this potential of creative deformation; it was his endeavor to free himself from the dictates of conventional judgements that had become sterile, and to make paralyzed literary history productive again by aligning it congenially with his own innovative impulses. In light of his concept of system, Eliot was able to make the ends of "tradition" and "innovation" meet.

In the famous quote from James Joyce's "Ulysses" that I have chosen as a motto for this essay, Stephen Dedalus captures the spirit of his age when he says: "History is a nightmare from which I'm trying to awake."[21] For Joyce, writing after the First World War, history was a self-supporting continuum of violence and prejudice. But even before the war itself, historical thinking was seen as a corollary of modernity with an inbuilt tendency towards deprivation by abolishing tradition and cultural values. This dilemma has created a discourse in which the "traditional" concept of tradition has become self-reflexive and is translated into various models. The problems of historicity are especially acute in the context of religion and art, which, even in modern society, cannot exist without some notion of the normative as stemming from tradition and canonization.

While in the eighteenth-century "nature" could still be trustingly invoked as an unchanging and enduring resource against the acceleration of history, antiliberal Protestant theologians of the nineteenth-century pressed conceived of existence as a site that could transcend history into a realm removed from the flow of time. T. S. Eliot, at the beginning of the twentieth-century, was particularly concerned with the problematic effects of fragmentation and alienation in historic experience. This is why his remarks on the concept of various flights from history that we have examined thus lead into different directions, but we should add that all of these flights occurred *in* history as well.

Notes

1. Hans Blumenberg, *Die Lesbarkeit der Welt* (Frankfurt/ M. 1981), 375.

2. There are two possible concepts of tradition, a strong and a weak one. The weak concept of tradition is descriptive and retrospective. It is used where a continuity of motifs, ideas, topoi, etc., is retrospectively discovered. The strong concept of tradition is a normative one and refers to the production of continuity with the intent to counter the erosion of time, decay, and forgetting. In this context, we will be dealing exclusively with the strong concept.

3. David Macaulay views the French Revolution as a caesura that, at one stroke, relieved history of its normative function as a foundation of values and rights.

4. I would like to thank Walter Magaß for this information.

5. Jonathan Swift, *A Tale of a Tub: Written for the Universal Improvement of Mankind*, (1704), ed. Lewis Mellville (London 1968).

6. Alexander Pope, "An Essay on Criticism (1711)," in D. J. Enright and Ernest de Chickera, eds., *English Critical Texts* (London 1968): 111–130, vv. 68–73. Further page numbers of quotations are given in the text.

7. This equating of antiquity and nature that Winkelmann stressed in 1755 can be traced back to the Renaissance; cf. Erwin Panofsky, "Renaissance—Selbstbezeichnung oder Selbsttäuschung?" in idem, *Die Renaissance der Europäischen Kunst* (Frankfurt/ M. 1979), 15–54.

8. Another example of this concept of nature is found in Samuel Johnson, who, a generation after Pope, made "nature" the epitome of what triumphs over historical time. The canonization of Shakespeare, his entry into a binding tradition, is marked by the phrase "Shakespeare as the poet of nature." Johnson writes of Shakespeare's characters: "they are natural, and therefore durable; the adventitious particularities of personal habits are only superficial dyes, bright and pleasing for a little while, yet soon fading to a dim tinct, without any remains of former lustre.... The sand heaped by one flood is scattered by another, but the rock always continues in its place." Samuel Johnson, "Preface to Shakespeare" (1765), in Enright/Chickera, eds., *English Critical Texts,* 139.

9. Friedrich Schiller to Caroline von Beulwith and Charlotte von Lengefeld, Jena, 12. Sept. 1789, in Eberhard Haufe, ed., *Schillers Werke. Nationalausgabe,* vol. 25 (Weimar 1979), 291f.

10. Karl Löwith gave his pioneering work *Von Hegel zu Nietzsche* [From Hegel to Nietzsche], first published in 1941, the subtitle *Der revolutionäre Bruch im Denken des 19. Jahrhunderts* [The Revolutionary Break in 19th Century Thought] in its second printing in 1950.

11. Franz Overbeck, *Christentum und Kultur, from the literary bequest* (1919), ed. C. A. Bernoulli (Darmstadt 1963), 11.

12. Ernst Robert Curtius, "Alkaloid Spaniens: Zu Miguel de Unamunos 70. Geburtstag am 29. September" *Berliner Tageblatt* 30. Sept. 1934. I am grateful to Hans-Ulrich Gumbrecht for drawing my attention to this source.

13. E. M. Forster, *Aspects of the Novel* (1927) (London 1964), 16, 21. A relevant subtlety should be pointed out here: Forster eliminates the time dimension for critics, but not for novelists: "It is never possible for a novelist to deny time inside the fabric of his novel: he must cling, however lightly, to the thread of his story ... otherwise he becomes unintelligible" (37). He adduces the example of Gertrude Stein, who broke and pulverised the clock in her novels "to flee from the tyranny of time." The innovation-shy Forster characterizes this as an "instructive failure" (48).

14. T. S. Eliot, *Selected Prose*, ed. John Hayward (Harmondsworth 1953), 23. Eliot demands a sense of history from critics as well. In his view, one of their tasks is "to see literature steadily and to see it whole; and this is eminently to see it not as consecrated by time, but to see it beyond time; to see the best work of our time and the best work of twenty-five hundred years ago with the same eyes" (idem, *The Sacred Wood* (London 1960), xvf.)

15. Thomas de Quincey, *Confessions of an Opium-Eater* (Harmondsworth 1971), 99.

16. Eliot, *Selected Prose*, 28f.

17. Friedrich Nietzsche, *Werke in drei Bänden*, ed. Karl Schlechta (Munich 1962), vol. 3, 490.

18. Maurice Halbwachs, *Das Gedächtnis und seine sozialen Bedingungen* (Frankfurt/ M. 1985 [1st printing in French 1925]), 189. I quote Halbwachs at such length because this view of memory as a framework or immanent network of relations seems to me to anticipate the outline of the new, systemic theory of memory. Cf. Gerhard Rusch, *Erkenntnis, Wissenschaft, Geschichte: Von einem konstruktivistischen Standpunkt* (Frankfurt/ M. 1987); and Siegfried J. Schmidt, "Gedächtnis—Erzählen—Identität," in Aleida Assmann and Dietrich Harth, eds., *Mnemosyne. Formen und Funktionen der kulturellen Erinnerung* (Frankfurt/ M. 1991), 378–397.

19. Eliot, *Selected Prose*, 28f.

20. Victor Erlich, *Russian Formalism: History - Doctrine*. 2nd, rev. ed. (The Hague 1965), 199.

21. James Joyce, *Ulysses* (1922) (Harmondsworth 1969), 40.

CHAPTER 10

Memory and Identity
How Memory Is Reconstructed after Catastrophic Events

ALESSANDRO CAVALLI

Preliminary Remarks

In this paper I will present the theoretical framework of a long-term research project I have been engaged in since 1985. This project entails extensive empirical field work, but I will not go into the details of the empirical findings; I will use the results of the empirical work only to illustrate the main theoretical guiding concepts.

The first piece of empirical material I am referring to is a study conducted in the early 1980s on orientations and representations of time by young people. One aspect of this research focused on what German scholars call the "problem of historical consciousness" *(das Problem des geschichtlichen Bewusstseins)*. What we tried to analyze and to measure was the extension of temporal horizons in the dimensions of both memory and life projects.[1] I was struck not only by the lack of historical knowledge but by the fact that most young people I interviewed showed not even the slightest curiosity about things that happened before their birth; they lived, as we called it later, in a "presentified dimension of time" where future and past played a very minimal role. Fascism, to give only one example, was for them located in some remote historical time, unconnected with life in the present. Later on I shall add a few comments on the problem of the collective memory of fascism.[2]

The second body of empirical work I am referring to is a series of "community studies" I did between 1985 and 1994 in various parts of Italy on the process of reconstruction of communities destroyed by "natural" calamities. All but one of these communities were destroyed by the three major earthquakes

---

Notes for this section begin on page 181.

that have hit Italy 1968, Belice Valley in West Sicily; 1978, Friuli in the Northeast; 1981, Irpinia Northeast of Naples. The only non-earthquake community, Longarone, in the mountain region of Veneto, was wiped out in 1963 by a huge wave of water unleashed by a tremendous landslide from an artificial lake located some 600 meters above this small town. These communities represent "natural laboratories" for the study of processes of social discontinuity[3] and collective memory.

The Conceptual Framework

Before telling the story of memory's reconstruction within these communities, I shall illustrate the main traits of the conceptual framework that guided my thinking about memory.

The starting point is the concept of the "crucial event." During the life of every individual, group, community, or even large society, events occur that mark turning points in its life course. These events structure the flow of time by dividing it into "what was before" and "what came after." We grasp this processes intuitively at the level of the single individual. When people are asked to produce a narrative of their life (what we call a "biography"), the structure of this narrative is organized around such turning points.[4] The reasons for this way of proceeding are very simple; in fact, these very events make up our identity. Since "what came after" differs from "what was before," this distinction means that we have undergone a process of change, that these events have changed our life and therefore jeopardized our own identity. They mark a discontinuity and the consequent reconstruction of a sense of continuity. After a turning point we are no longer the same as before; however, we are still the same person.

This paradox, that continuity is established as a response to discontinuity, has been widely discussed by philosophers and psychologists concerned with the problem of identity.[5] Personal identity in fact depends upon the capacity of the subject to recognize himself or herself as the same person, even if major changes affecting the physical and/or psychological structure have occurred. The construction of identity requires that we keep track of the chain of major events that made us what we think we are. In doing this, we select only a limited number out of the almost infinite number of experiences we have had up to the present and apply criteria of relevance in order to make the selection. Memory is the product of the operation of these selective criteria; without oblivion there is also no memory.

Michelangelo is rumored to have said that in order to give shape to a statue, the sculptor has to eliminate, to carve away, all the insubstantial material. The same happens with memory. Humans must be able to forget, if they want to remember. These selective criteria, however, are not stable. They change at every turning point according to the problems people are facing in the present and the tasks and goals that confront them in light of the future. The definition of personal identity is therefore an ongoing process. Successive experiences modify the memory of past events, not because of the growing temporal distance from these events (we may recall events remote in time more accurately than recent ones), but because we modify the criteria by which we select, elaborate, and interpret them. Individuals continually rewrite their own biographies.

I do not argue that groups and societies are like individuals. However, even without supporting an organic and anthropomorphic view of society, it is possible to think of groups, societies, and human collectivities in general as having identities, minds, and memories. I do not want to discuss here social theory's highly controversial question about holism versus reductionism, or the debate about the so called "methodological individualism." Let me assume, without discussing the matter further, that if individuals have social identities and share social memories, it is legitimate to speak of societies as also having identities and memories. In fact, every society develops institutions and practices dealing with collective memory. In preliterate societies, for example in ancient Greece, we find the *mnemones,* "rememberers" officially charged with the tasks of recalling past sentences in case of judicial decisions, keeping track of important witnesses of public acts, and organizing the calendar of social events. Later we find the annalists who year after year annotated public events that they judged worthy of remembering. Still later, and up to our time, come the professional archivists, librarians, historians, and all those who are entrusted with or assume the task of perpetuating the memory of the past. In the spring of 1995 solemn ceremonies took place in London, Paris, Berlin, and Moscow to celebrate the fiftieth anniversary of the end of the Second World War. This is one example of the kinds of rituals and practices that deal with social memory.[6]

Other practices deal more directly with the link between memory and identity. National holidays perform the function of evoking the event that gave birth to the nation-state, and the celebration ceremonies held on those days reaffirm the social bond of collective identity. Monuments are erected to perform the same function. In almost every town and village of Europe there are monuments to remember the soldiers who fell during the First World War. The monument to the "unknown soldier" is a "sacred" place of every capital city.[7]

Before getting into an illustration of what I have called "patterns of collective memory," let me first clarify the way in which I am using the concept of an "event." An event is a mental construct, that enables us to designate a plurality of micro-events combined together in a conceptual synthesis with a single word. As stated before, events structure time in "before" and "after." In personal life many such events concern the individual's private sphere: we remember as turning points the day we finished school, the important stages of our career, when we fell in love with partners we feel are, or were, important to us, when we got married, the births of our children, the death of somebody we were strongly attached to. All these are by all means "social events": they are shaped by the laws and customs of the society we live in but concern us as private persons, and we may share their memory with a few others within our private circle.

Such largely "private" events, however, are not the only category of events that structures our biographies. Public events can perform the same function. Events that shape the history of the collectivities we belong to, such as wars, revolutions, changes of political regime, economic crises (or, as we shall see later, emergencies affecting our community), all may interfere deeply with our personal life and everyday activities. The experience of these historical events enters the life of a multitude of individuals and contributes to structuring their biographies, but each individual or group elaborates these common experiences according to his or her own subjectivity.

We can also enlarge the notion of event to encompass even prolonged periods of time. Fascism, for example, in the case of Italians aged over 65, can be rightly understood as an event (one that lasted over 20 years in Italy), since people refer to it as a unique phenomenon and construct an unitary representation of it.

Even events easily localized in time and space, like the earthquakes I shall consider later, or a battle during a war, are composed of thousands and thousands of personal cases that all differ from one another, and each participant or witness has his or her own story to tell, even if each is fully aware of referring to the same event.

Three Patterns of Collective Memory

I assume that, in constructing collective identities, human societies follow typical patterns of dealing with memory. I propose to concentrate on three such patterns. I shall call the first the "zero point" pattern. In this case, the "crucial event" is taken as a new starting point in the life of the group or society concerned: the discontinuity with the past is maximized, a new foundation is required, and the crucial event performs the symbolic function of closing past accounts and opening a new era. The event itself is often monumentalized and thereafter celebrated as rebirth. The "monumentalization" is both material and ideological in nature. Real monuments are erected to remind the members of the collectivity of the turning point marking its history, but ideal monuments also dominate the ideological landscape, as every society has its own foundation myths. In the "zero point" pattern, the ingredients of collective identity are mainly taken from the repertoire of images of the future:[8] what matters is not what "we" have been, but what "we" want to become. The past, or at least the past most recently preceding the crucial event, is considered at least to be discharged, since it must not hinder the path toward the actualization of the images of the future. In heading toward the future, society must not feel constrained or limited by its own past.

Sometimes, though not necessarily, continuity is reestablished with a more remote past, and the idea of rebirth is connected with a remote origin that becomes revitalized. This process comes close to what in psychoanalysis is called "removal" or "displacement" (in German, *Verdrängung*, in French, *refoulement*). We "remove" or "displace" what we do not want to remember, because to remember would hurt our own identity. In the psychic dimension, this work is performed by the unconscious; in social life it is the unintended outcome of the decisions of a plurality of actors (policy makers, journalists, schoolteachers, and other opinion makers). In some cases, it can be the outcome of a deliberate or semideliberate attempt to overcome disturbing memories of the recent past.

A variant of this first type of pattern is what I will call "museification." Memories of the past in this case are carefully preserved, but somehow insulated or segregated in specific locations apart from everyday life. They are made available to a selected public, and access to them requires a positive act of will. Archives, libraries, and museums are—if I may use this expression—"ambiguous" places, where information no longer used in "real" life is stored as objects to be preserved. These represent a kind of "frozen" memory that needs to be warmed up by an act of fruition.

The second pattern runs in the opposite direction. I propose to call it the pattern of reestablishment or reconstruction of continuity. The "crucial event" is thought of as something to be neglected or even canceled. Life must continue as if nothing had happened. People need only to regain the interrupted path, to find themselves once more. In individual life this pattern comes close to the experience of the "adventure." According to Georg Simmel,[9] an adventure (whatever its nature: a trip to an exotic country, an erotic experience, or a "trip" with the aid of drugs, to name but a few) has a beginning and an end, and does not belong to the temporal dimension of "real" life. When the adventure comes to its conclusion, people resume their usual routines; the past where identity is rooted takes over management of the present.

Sometimes, in collective life, the "crucial event" takes the shape of a traumatic experience. We have many accounts, for example, of soldiers returning from the battlefields of the First World War. What they had seen and experienced went so far beyond anything possibly imagined that they were unable to relate it to their friends and relatives.[10] Normal mental and linguistic tools were unable to give expression to their experiences. What cannot be told cannot be remembered either. All these veterans wanted to do was to forget. When the texture of social life is lacerated by traumatic events, the tear has to be mended and the threads leading to the past restored (in dealing such phenomena the use of metaphorical language is almost inevitable).

In both of the two patterns discussed so far, we have to deal with processes of removal/displacement. In the first case, conspicuous segments of the past are removed/displaced; in the second case, what is removed/displaced is the crucial event itself. One might question the legitimacy of using the psychoanalytic concept of removal/displacement in dealing with collective memory. But I can find no better word to designate a process by which societies express a willingness or a desire to forget. What gets removed/displaced is not canceled; rather, the removed/displaced experiences are kept in a layer of memory that we deny ourselves access to. In collective life, this process has to do with the content of "public discourse" that presupposes speakers and listeners, and with what is considered legitimate or nonlegitimate content of public communication and discussion. A removed/displaced experience is one that people don't want to talk about or listen to; they tend to feel embarrassed and "reticent" when it is touched upon. The embarrassment of speakers and/or listeners is evidence of something being removed/displaced.

Following this digression on the concept of removal/displacement, I come now to the third pattern, which I shall call the "elaboration of memory." Here, again, I borrow a word (and a concept) from psychoanalytic theory, the Freudian notion of *Trauerarbeit* or "elaboration of mourning." Retaining from this concept only its meaning as a process concerned with the redefinition of identity after a major turning point in the life of the subject, I ask: Is it possible for societies to develop a "critical" attitude toward their collective memory? This is of course a rhetorical question: to ask it is to have already given it a positive answer. Assuming a critical attitude toward "collective memory" implies full awareness of the fact that collective memory is part of collective identity and that collective fears as well as collective enthusiasms can (and in fact do) disturb the process of memory formation. The "elaboration of memory" expresses the will not to "remove/displace" what may be experienced as disturbing. Removed/displaced experiences survive underground, in the depths of the collective unconscious, and manifest themselves in the compulsion to repeat. The past should not be disregarded as either nonexistent or insignificant; it must be interpreted. True, remembering and forgetting are one and the same process; but, just as mature persons can decide what has to be remembered or forgotten and how, groups and societies can also become mature enough to deal in a responsible way with their own memory.

Excursus. A case of "historical removal": the memory of Fascism in Italy

The memory of "fascism" in Italy offers a good example not of "elaboration of memory," but of the lack of it. The three main ideological-political streams of postwar Italy (political Catholicism, liberalism, and Marxism) all had "good reasons" for preventing a critical elaboration of the historical memory of fascism. Catholics had to conceal the Vatican's ambiguous attitude toward both fascism and national-socialism (the treaty signed between the Vatican and the Italian state as early as 1929, called *il concordato,* was an important factor in the consolidation of the regime, and the attitude of the Church toward anti-Semitism was far from unambiguous). Liberal democrats had to conceal the fact that "fascism" was, after all, the outcome of the crisis of liberal democracy that followed the First World War and cannot be understood without taking into account the incapacity of the democratic forces to provide a stable government; for them "fascism" was an "obscure parenthesis" in the country's history that could be canceled merely by reestablishing the interrupted continuity with prefascist Italy. Marxists had to conceal the fact that "fascism" was also a reaction of the middle classes threatened by the prospect of a Bolshevik-type proletarian revolution. Everyone had to conceal the fact that "fascism" had enjoyed a large consensus among Italians and was by all means *not* an unpopular regime.

All these factors, taken together, explain why the fascist regime's "elaboration of memory" in postwar Italy has been very incomplete. The resistance movement, which, along with the Allied armies, contributed to the liberation of the country, has been erected as a historical-ideological monument (a good example of the process of "monumentalization" I referred to above), with all the concomitant shortcomings of taking a civil war as the new republic's foundation myth.[11] "Fascism" has therefore been displaced from collective memory, either as the obscure parenthesis I mentioned before, or as a "puppet regime" supported by its mighty German ally. At the end, no one was assigned historical responsibility for its rise, but all could claim to have contributed to its fall. Both forms of "displacement" illustrated above have been made use of in this case. Certainly it is no wonder that Italians born after 1945 (more than three quarters of the present Italian population) lack any understanding of the meaning of fascism in the history of the country. Until very recently, the teaching of history in schools very often stopped at the end of the First World War or skipped Fascism altogether since many teachers were hesitant to approach the subject and did not know how to deal with it.

Since, these patterns are ideal-types (in the Weberian sense), no real development fits the models perfectly. Real cases can approach one or another, or turn out to be combinations of the three. When complex societies face problems of historical memory, each of the patterns can be supported by competing groups. There is never only "one" memory, and there is most often a plurality of competing memories. In other words, memory reflects the structure of society's dominant groups, which try to impose their memory—or, better, their version/interpretation of collective memory—on the rest of society. After a successful struggle, the winners are always in a position to influence the process of memory's construction and, as they usually do so with vigor, the memory of the losers survives, if at all, only at a subterranean level.

Collective Memory and Catastrophic Events

The described patterns, and their combinations, also apply when a community faces the problem of dealing with its own memory within the process of reconstruction after a catastrophic event. Let me very briefly make some statements about "natural" catastrophic events:

1. There are no "pure" natural calamities: natural events are but one causal factor in producing a catastrophe. For example, it is possible to predict very accurately the amount of damage (and also the number of victims) that an earthquake will produce taking into account a set of three factors: the magnitude of the seismic shock (this is the "natural" component), the average age of the buildings in the region, and the amount of resources spent during the previous, say, twenty-five years to implement preventive measures. These last two factors are "social" and not "natural." This explains why seismic shocks of the same magnitude can produce a disaster in Turkey or in Italy, but only minor damages in Tokyo or Los Angeles. An important effect of this circumstance is that people can always blame some human actor for the effects of a natural disaster. According to where responsibilities are located (at the local or national level), elites can be more or less legitimized. The question is, who is entitled to decide upon reconstruction? Sometimes elites do acquire legitimation by voicing claims and successfully shifting responsibilities to outside actors.
2. Disasters "globally" affect the life of a community: the structure of everyday life is broken, and people are confronted with the need to meet basic survival needs (clothing, food, and shelter) in a nonroutine manner. Disasters therefore represent extreme examples of discontinuity.
3. During the first phase of emergency, a disaster represents a threat to the very identity of the community: Abrupt changes distort the spatial reference points of everyday activities and the elements by which people recognize themselves as localized entities in time and space. Many people seek relief from relatives and leave the place, believing there are no longer good reasons to stay, everything (house, property, jobs) having been lost. In all the communities I have studied there was a long tradition of emigration. People were accustomed to the idea that to escape misery one had to abandon the native place. The expectation and fear of extinction is frequently a widespread sentiment.
4. During an emergency the old elite confirms its legitimacy or new leaders emerge. Legitimacy is established through capacity, first to provide and coordinate immediate aid to meet basic needs, and second, to respond to the identity threat. Elites are such if they are able to endow the people with new confidence and trust in the possibility of recovery and reconstruction, to capitalize upon the spontaneous solidarity that always emerges in emer-

gency situations. In short, they must both interpret collective feelings and respond to collective anxieties with a call for mobilization. The structure and culture of the elites become the crucial variables in explaining the development of social processes after a catastrophe. The tensions produced by the consequences of catastrophic events do not always strain the cohesiveness among elites and their legitimacy. The society's ruling echelons can be both strengthened and weakened.

5. It is during the delicate period of emergency and recovery that the first ideas and plans about reconstruction take shape. The elaboration of reconstruction plans gives people the message that the community is willing to survive. The basic lines of planning must be already formulated and made public before the ruins are removed; otherwise, people who are unable to imagine their future environment are likely to resist the demolition of damaged and dangerous buildings. It is precisely at this point that the elites have to deal with memory. Everything being destroyed, memory itself becomes an object of conscious planning. In normal times, city planning has to do with selective elements or portions of the physical environment. But the reconstruction of a destroyed community requires an act of global planning. City planners cannot avoid confrontation with the local elite, nor the local elite with the opinions and sentiments of the population. What is at stake is not only the distributions of functions in space, but the very identity of the community. What has to be reconstructed and how?

The ways this problem was faced in the communities I studied can be summarized in three models. The first model can be called "relocation." The community is not reconstructed where it was, but relocated in a more or less distant territory. The planning criteria tend to be very modern in this case. A "new town" (which in principle could be located anywhere in the world) takes shape. Almost nothing resembles the old habitat, the culture of its inhabitants, or their traditional ways of using space. The "new town" is likely to be the product of the culture of outsider experts (architects and city planners) who refer to models alien to the local culture. The future should not look like the past. The roads are wide and cross regularly at ninety-degree angles; the houses are modern, provided with garages and modern appliances. Here people have to forget their traditional way of life. They are expected to migrate to a new environment, as if they were migrating to a foreign land. This is likely to happen when local elites have been educated away from the community and are oriented toward cultural models rooted in a different environment. The outcome can be very innovative. The reconstruction after the "crucial event" is taken as an opportunity to abandon tradition and to plunge into "modernity."

It is interesting to remark, however, that this pattern can be found also in premodern times, when the task of reconstruction was usually assumed by the distant authority of an autocratic government. The reconstruction of Noto

(Sicily), which was destroyed by an earthquake in the seventeenth-century, is an example of the work of an absolutistic government. Visitors to Noto even nowadays are struck by the magnificent homogeneity of the baroque architectural style in which the town was rebuilt, following the dominant culture of the then cosmopolitan aristocracy.

Sometimes (as in the case of Noto or, in modern times, that of Salaparuta in the Belice Valley) the ruins of the old village lie abandoned, eroded by natural elements and neglected as a relict. The inhabitants of modern Salaparuta, built just a few miles away from the old site, can gaze from the windows of their new homes at the ruins of the village where they once lived. The locale of the past differs from that of the present (and the future), and the past itself is nothing but a set of remains in a state of decay and dilapidation.

Monuments are often erected to remember the disaster; in some cases the ruins themselves are transformed into a monument. In the case of Gibellina (Belice Valley), for example, the new town is located far away from the old site, on the other side of a small chain of mountains that render the two locations "out-of-sight" from one another. Following the design of Burri, one of the most famous visual artists of modern Italy, the slopes where the old village stood have been covered by a huge stretch of white cement, creating a kind of landscape-monument visible from a distance. The people of the new Gibellina often cross the mountains to reach the original site and visit the old cemetery, where the victims of the earthquake were buried. The "town of the dead" stands apart from the "town of the living."

In other cases the ruins are turned into an open-air museum. Conza di Campagna (in the Irpinia region) was built, as were many villages in Central and Southern Italy, on a hill above a river-plain that in former times was quite marshy. Such villages all show the "natural" tendency to slide gradually downhill, where access to the communication network becomes more comfortable. After the earthquake the obvious decision was taken to relocate the community on the plain; less obvious, however, was the decision to turn the ruins of the old village into an archeological exhibit where people can admire, from a lofty vantage, the landscape of the valley where the new town now stands. The contrasting element is quite visible, since the new environment is an example of modern urban planning, has no historical roots in local architectural traditions, and might just as well have been built in New Zealand or Australia.

In all these cases, the disaster itself tends to become a trait of collective identity. Having lost (or removed) the memory of the previous community, people feel and define themselves mostly as "victims" of the earthquake and construct on this identity their image of the future. Since they live in an alien, if comfortable, new world, they expect to be treated as "victims" and claim support from the outside world for a long time to come.

Longarone represents a variant of this first model. In this case no relocation took place and the community was reconstructed on the same spot. In fact, no ruins were left, since the tremendous impact of the huge wave flattened all man-made artifacts and killed almost all the inhabitants (more than 3,000). The survivors, who comprised the inhabitants of the few spared houses plus those who were absent at the moment of the impact or had migrated abroad, are now only a tiny minority of the population of the new town, since it was not only the physical setting of the community that had to be reconstructed, but also its demographic base. Some of the, at that time, best architects and city planners of the country were asked to participate in the planning of the new town (as probably had been the case in Noto three centuries earlier). If the water wiped out the community, the architects wiped out its memory. Nothing in the new town is reminiscent of the old, except a monumental church erected to celebrate the victims and the event.

The second model is the opposite of the first one and can be called "philological reconstruction." According to this model, everything has to be rebuilt as it was before the event. Even stones from old buildings that can be reutilized are carefully numbered, to be put later in their proper place. Where it was, it will be ("dov'era, com'era") is the guiding principle. The effects of the disaster have to be canceled as if it never happened. The new should be a trustful copy of the old. The case that comes closer to this model is that of Venzone (in the Friuli region at the Northeast corner of the country, close to the Austrian and Slovenian border), but other examples can be found in Southern Italy. The contrast here consists in the fact that city centers that were built over the course of centuries now look "brand new" and artificial, like villages reconstructed in a film studio. They inhabit a timeless dimension, like a modern copy of an old painting. Many decades will pass before these new-old villages resemble their former selves. The intention, however, is to cancel the catastrophic event and reestablish the past. Not one monument is erected to remember the event, not even to celebrate the sacrifice of the victims. To identify those who died in the disaster, one must read the inscriptions on the burial stones in the cemetery.

The third pattern can be called "selective reconstruction of symbolic elements of the past." In this case, a conscious attempt is undertaken to reconstruct, "where they were and as they were," only the symbolic elements in which people recognize the identity of the community. In most cases these elements are the main church (dome or cathedral), the city hall and the theater, but sometimes also the facades of the buildings of the main streets, the shape of the network of roads, and the volumetric relationships of the built-on space. In the case of Gemona, a small town at the epicenter of the Friuli earthquake, the town's historic center had been partly abandoned even before the disaster as a consequence of emigration and also because in previous decades the built-up area had gradually drifted toward the plain. In Gemona almost all the houses of the city center were reconstructed, even if they no longer had inhabitants, since a partial reconstruction would not have fulfilled the symbolic function of a historic center. A few modern-style buildings were included in the reconstruction plan (a theater, a multistory parking garage, town hall offices, the headquarters of the savings bank, a student hostel). "We did not operate," said the major ten years after the earthquake, "with the intention of reproducing the past (it would have been a historical fake), but with the objective of not distorting the memory of the past." One of the most difficult problems the local administration had to face when the reconstruction was completed was convincing the inhabitants to move back to the rebuilt center. Almost two decades after the earthquake, we can say that the reconstruction plan was a success.

The combination of historical memory and modernity is a singular feature of present-day Gemona. Almost all historic centers in European cities grew in time without being planned in the current sense of the term. Every generation has left on them its mark, sometimes canceling those of previous generations, very often adding something new to the old. Present-day Gemona is not the unintended outcome of historical processes, but the product of a project on "historical memory" and the juxtaposition of memory and modernity, not in the result of the workings of time, but in a plan drawn up at a precise moment, under pressure from a threat to the cultural identity of the community. Without the catastrophic event of the earthquake, the community would in time have evolved gradually: the drifting toward the plain would probably have continued; the historic center would probably have become increasingly inhabited only by the elderly. The process of loss of identity, symbolized by the historic center, had begun before the earthquake. The earthquake provided the opportunity to rediscover an identity that was fading, and the plan to reconstruct the historic center with a residential capacity twice that of the original, was the response to the threatened loss of collective identity. Moreover, Gemona today has, as do almost all communities in earthquake areas, a complete archive of its cultural and artistic heritage that nobody would have ever have dreamed of drawing up before. It was as if the destroyed community rediscovered the memory of its past precisely at the time when the catastrophe forced it to think of its future in terms of planning.

Concluding Remarks

From time to time the life of societies is shaken by both "victories" and "defeats." Following Durkheim, we can assume that societies go through experiences of collective enthusiasm and of collective despair. Exalting or traumatic as these experiences may be, they have to be dealt with or removed displaced if social life is to regain a minimum degree of stability and continuity. We have seen how different communities react to the traumatic experience of a catastrophic event. Some remove the past and celebrate the event, some remove the event; and reconstruct the past; some adopt a selective attitude, trying to elaborate memory while balancing tradition and modernity. Since all three patterns can be found in each of the culturally different regions of the country where the study was conducted, it is not the traits of the surrounding culture but the culture of each singular community's elite and its interpretation of tradition and collective identity that are the crucial variables in explaining which alternative will be chosen. Two neighboring communities can in fact take opposite decisions. As I argued before, communities destroyed by catastrophic events are natural laboratories for the study of processes of collective memory. Their example can be generalized.

We might ask under what conditions are societies more likely to proceed toward the "elaboration of memory." "Elaboration," as I said, is a process that unfolds from public discourse. It requires the existence of a public arena where public opinion is formed by competing views and differing interpretations. It requires freedom of inquiry and freedom of expression. In short, it requires a truly pluralistic society in which nobody can pretend to have a monopoly on, or to be the depository of, truth, and where elites operate according to this principle.

Historians are fully aware that it is impossible to reconstruct the past "wie es eigentlich gewesen" (as it really was) as Ranke pretended, History and memory are both selective reconstruction, but they do not tell the same story; their selective criteria are different. History (if it pretends to have something in common with scientific knowledge) should in principle be oriented toward "truth." Memory is oriented toward "identity." Between history and memory there is, and should be, a tension-filled relationship. The claims of identity will inevitably tend to overwhelm the claims of truth, and historians will tend to become the ideological arm of the ruling elite(s). Only in pluralistic democratic societies will the claims of identity and the claims of truth be able to converge, though they will never coincide.

Notes

1. Alessandro Cavalli, "Zeiterfahrungen von Jugendlichen," in Rainer Zoll, ed., *Zerstörung und Wiederaneignung von Zeit* (Frankfurt/ M. 1988), 387–404. This article is a brief summary of the main results of that study, which were published extensively in idem, *Il tempo dei giovani* (Bologna 1985).

2. Alessandro Cavalli, "I giovani e la memoria del Fascismo e della Resistenza," *Il Mulino* 65 (1996): 51–57.

3. The concept of social discontinuity has been recently reintroduced in sociological reasoning by R. Mayntz, *Soziale Diskontinuitäten, in Soziale Dynamik und politische Steuerung* (Frankfurt/ M. 1997), 115–140.

4. For studies of "turning points" in individual biographies see: Ian H. Gotlib and Blair Wheaton, eds., *Stress and Adversity over the Life Course: Trajectories and Turning Points* (Cambridge 1997).

5. See Derek Parfit, *Reasons and Persons* (Oxford 1984), chaps. 10–15.

6. A rich account of these practices is provided by G. Namer, *La Commémoration en France: de 1945 à nos jours* (Paris 1987).

7. See P. Nora, *Les lieux de memoire,* vol. 1 (Paris 1984).

8. The concept of "image of the future" was used by W. Bell in his studies of nation-building in the West Indies. See W. Bell, ed., *The Democratic Revolution in the West Indies* (Cambridge, Mass. 1967). See also his *Foundations of Futures Studies* (New Brunswick 1997), where the concept is further developed.

9. Georg Simmel, "Das Abenteuer" (1910), in idem, *Philosophische Kultur: Über das Abenteuer, die Geschlechter und die Krise der Moderne: Gesammelte Essays* (Berlin 1983), 13–26.

10. See, for example, Eric J. Leed, *No Man's Land: Combat and Identity in World War I* (Cambridge 1979).

11. See G. E. Rusconi, *Resistenza e postfascismo* (Bologna 1995).

CHAPTER 11

The Material Presence of the Past
Reflections on the Visibility of History

Detlef Hoffmann

The focus of this chapter is on how past events are currently present, how they are existing and visible in present times. This is not the place to discuss whether past events can jump unproblematically into history. However, the title suggests not only the heightening of a difficulty, but also that it is settled between two poles: The material presence of history (the past) aims at the pleasure of the knowledgeable collector, that is, it is a heuristic intention, whereas the question of the visibility of history tends to fundamental nature. To collect positive material is possible; act of the collection hides in itself the intention, a plan, a principle. With each access of old, real facts, a collector of material past picks out, as a central theme, its presence to the past. The collection itself might consist of very old, initial pieces, younger artifacts of yesterday, and today's relics. Uncle Scrooge's money silo, in fact a live-historical collection, holds the beloved *Thaler* his wealth was started with. Certain picture sequences of the Duck Tales show that Uncle Scrooge possesses a submarine to reach the deepest levels of this repository. All these *Thaler*-realities are symbolizations of events; they hide stories—which are told then. I do not want to get lost in my examples, but the Beagle Boys—unlike the banker—are not aware of the *Thaler's* symbolical power; they only see the thing itself, a gold coin.

Behind the collection of artifacts of the past there exists a historical plan. Thus this text will unavoidably approach the meaning of the term "history." The "visibility of history" will be the central problem of my considerations, particularly because my aim is not to elaborate how A changes to A' and how, in this alteration of forms, a process singles out a central theme—for example, of a social kind—and arrives at an opinion. The differences between A and A'

Notes for this section begin on page 205.

describe a change that can easily take over a narrative form. This is the everyday life of a reflective art history.

But here I would like to try something different, in asking whether the visual (and also tactile) qualities of objects serve more or even different narratives than does language. I assume that language—even if it is highly differentiated—has at its disposal only a few abstracts for a large variety of appearances. The picture, even the real object, always takes one of many possible appearances. The appearance that in its manifest singularity allows the presence of different latent appearances will here be called symbolism.

In an attempt to arrange the abundance of phenomena relating to how the past is embodied in objects, I have created three categories: (1.) imprint, or more commonly, trace, (2.) form, and (3.) symbolism.

Imprint, trace

It is only consequent to start our formulation of the question of the material past with a material that has been handed down without text, without recorded language. Such a narrative originates in time we call early history, and prehistory, because no source is a text. Here scientist and criminologist become one. In our specialized world this merging is not merely metaphorical. For instance, the scientist of the downfall of the Franklin expedition, Owen Beattie,[1] is a forensic anthropologist; he works over long phases using exactly the same research methods as a forensic laboratory. The "trace" seems to consist of the simplest visual and tactile information.[2]

The traces the detective discovers are seldom written: they are scratches or fingerprints, things that are conspicuous in their area. It can also be footprints or tire tracks that the detective must evaluate. But not only traces must be found, they must also be preserved and often they must be transmitted, too, without loosing their evidential value. The forensic people have limited knowledge of whom they are looking for: someone who committed a crime. In the view envisioned by the searcher, the scene of crime, its physical existence, forms a hollow space into which a positive fits. The one who combines vision and reality into a congruent whole is a good detective.

While from time to time the detective is lucky enough to compare his imagined scenario to a suspect's confession, the historian never will be so fortunate. Here the imagination competes with the mere evidence of physical traces, a puny rival. Each narrative brings a kind of conclusiveness to the traces as long as the positive, the perpetrator, is found. The traces, with their visual and tactile character, bear their history in themselves, chemical and physical information.

Yet, a narrative can still disturb after traces are secured: to reliance on a early reading might lead to misinterpretations. In his story "The Murders in the Rue Morgue," Edgar Allen Poe not only shows that the securing of evidence demands a keen talent for observation and a vivid intellect; he also shows that if traces point to something inconceivable, something that has not yet been told, this possibility must not be excluded. As the detective August Dupin remarks, "In investigations such as we are now pursuing, it should not be so much asked 'what has occurred', as 'what has occurred that has never occurred before'."[3]

Lovely examples of traces and their visual interpretation are provided by the history of the earth. Mountains, valleys, grottos and caves, rocks and original rock formations loom from the past over the always-new present times that surround the wordless but present, suggestive objects. That is how the shapes of the earth's surface transformed into memorials of prehistoric events.[4] But if the stories are fantastic, they cannot be maintained against the sources' right of veto. We cannot avoid an equally banal and effective fact: the caves and rocks date from a time long ago that is still present in our time. Often they are provided with information that past civilizations interpreted in their accounts, and which we are able to interpret anew. Our texts must be every bit as plausible as old narrations are, acknowledging meanwhile that visual material of the past is not only interpreted through texts, but is also revived to life through pictures.

One such depiction of the farthest past in pictures was the brainchild of a professor named Paul Hoffmann, who opened his traveling exhibit in 1858. In the theater of Josefstadt he delivered his "first big geological performance." Projecting the hand-painted glass slides on a three- by four meter screen. The playbill pointed to what he was going to show to the audience: "The formation of the earth's surface from the beginning to the appearance of the species of mankind." And he did not forget to add: With careful consideration of the latest sciences on the field of geology."[5] The dramaturgy of his talk consists of development and passing, the genesis of new scenery and its volcanic and Neptunian destruction in an apocalyptic catastrophe such as that depicted in "Nothosaurus giganteus on a coral-reef" (Ill. 11.1, 2). Silvery moonlight shines on the waves that wash around the last rock in a water desert. Here, the doomed Nothosaurus sits, howling to the moon like a wolf. The scenery of the time of "Muschelkalk," the middle phase of the geological Triassic Period, which began 215 million years ago, is not an invention of Professor Paul Hoffmann but dates back to a 1851 publication of the paleontologist Franz Unger.[6] This work is equipped with fourteen scenic tableaus by the painter Joseph Kuwasseg. Having lithographed his native German views. He transferred the experience acquired in front of cities and mountains of the Steiermark to prehistoric time. He must have been so successful that he transfers the sceneries of the prehistoric time to large watercolor paintings.[7]

Paul Hoffmann, with his magic lantern pictures, is one of many who made use of these influential landscape paintings. In 1851 and 1852 a detailed report was published in the *Illustrierte Zeitung* by Professor Bernhard Cotta, Freiburg.

Fig. 11.1 "Nothosaurus giganteus on a coral-reef," painted lantern picture, from the property of Paul Hoffmann (before 1858), Historisches Museum, Frankfurt am Main.

Titled "Geologische Bilder"[8] it describes the history of the earth as depicted in the woodcut transferred pictures by Unger-Kuwasseg.[9] 1855 appears—again with the in woodcut-transferred landscape paintings reappear in 1855 in the book *Geologie,* edited by Otto Spamer.[10] It is after these illustrations that Paul Hoffmann's magic lantern pictures were painted. The suggestive power of these images reaches so far that Franz Unger describes the lithography and not his research results; the text explains the pictures. "The lower country, which time wrested away and elevated to a place of diverse developments again, has

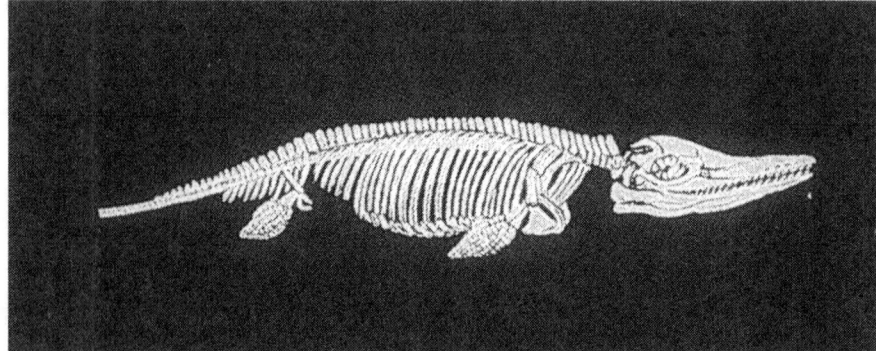

Fig. 11.2 "Reconstructed bone find of a Nothosaurus," painted lantern picture, from the property of Paul Hoffmann (before 1858), Historisches Museum, Frankfurt am Main.

fallen prey to the all swallowing up water.... On the bottom of the sea, which is as well a construction as a habitation for corals and other marine fauna, ... we see the variety of animal life in the depths of the ocean ... spreading. With greedy looks she watches as a welcome prey, a strange, crocodile-like monster ... it is the Nothosaurus gigantheus.... The infinite melancholy spreading out over the region, ... is tremendously enhanced by the night's veil."[11]

Some elements of the picture, like the shells, can be derived from found traces, petrifactions. But neither the "Nothosaurus on the coral-reef" nor the other pictures exhaust in reconstruction: They describe natural atmospheres, working in a few relics of dramatic or arched motifs and thus creating a surplus of meaning, which—removed from the relics—integrate the picture into a symbolical order. The pictures in our example endured more than half a century.[12] Even if the presence completely exhausts its monopoly of interpretation, the relics jut into present time. And like data carriers, they must be made compatible with a new symbolical order.

The story of the Swiss buildings on stilts is another fascinating example. During the very dry winter of 1853/54, when the lake in Zurich had the lowest water level in living memory, remains of posts became visible at the lake's shore in Obermeilen. Ferdinand Keller, president of the antiquarian society in Zurich, recognized the find as the remains of a pile village. He published the interpretation of his finding in the *Züricher Freitagszeitung* of 17, March 1854. The report was a sensation, and from then on buildings on stilts were found everywhere.[13] Within a short time these settlements were integrated into the vision of Swiss prehistory and early history. Carl W. Neumann writes in his book 1932 *Das Werden des Menschen und der Kultur:* The copious finds of the Swiss pile village *(Pfahlbaustationen)* allow excellent impressions in the culture of the neolithic period and anyway since their discovery are one of the most important sources of prehistoric science. The buildings on stilts stood above water level...."[14]

Neumann continues describing how the relics that are the basis for science, have preserved: "All of everyday life's garbage, all the damaged household equipment, often the product of long and arduous work, sank in the depths of the lake and was tightly surrounded with mud so that nothing disappeared, not even its former shape. No wonder that the discoverers of this lost world brought in a rich harvest, or that during the following decades, when more and more new villages surfaced from the lake's bottom, the treasures obviously piled up."[15]

Ferdinand Keller had already drawn a pile settlement; other scientists followed. To painters, this world above water has been again and again an incentive for invention—of people's everyday occurrences: In the morning men go to work; in the evening they return home. At late hours of the evening young people sit on platforms, where relaxing conversations spark a good many delicate romances. Women mind their often-quarrelling children, bring over

Fig. 11.3 Karl Jauslin, Pfahlbausiedlung (Pile Village), watercolor painting (1891), Basel, Birkhäuser Verlag.

food, or mend fishing nets (Ill. 11.3). These pictures bed down the historical peculiarity in general human life. Not only is the pleasure to narrate satisfied, but at the same time meaning is constituted.

Switzerland needed the buildings on stilts urgently. The confederates had been fiercely at war with one another as recently as 1846. This big threat to the unity of the alpine republic had ended on 30 November 1847 with the occupation of Valais under General Dufour. With the new constitution of 12 September 1848, the confederation of states became a federal state. Now the vision of a first Swiss nation with one culture and the same habits had a relieving effect. No evidence of segregated religions, segregated languages, or segregated everyday life emerged from the bottom of the lake.

The yearning for a unity brought about by history set all doubts aside. The "building-on-stilts mania" spread to other countries, which unlike Switzerland had not had to overcome a civil war. Today we read in the *Meyers Konversationslexikon* (Meyers Encyclopedia) from 1877 about "Pfahlbauten": "One brought up the question, why the Swiss natives built their lodgings in lakes. Obviously we can assume that the Swiss buildings on stilt should serve as a safe refuge against wild animals and human beings as well as the same settlements of the above mentioned still nowadays living people should. As presumed, in Switzerland possibly Gallic tribes (Celts) built these house. No historiographer reports on them, and when Caesar penetrated Helvetia, he did not find, as it looks like, any hints of farmers living in buildings on stilt."[16]

Of course the finds, the traces, can be read in a different way, and indeed this has happened. Since the end of the 1930s the theory of buildings on stilt has lost validity; nowadays no one considers the possibility of pile villages any longer. Climatic science and geology, even dendrochronology, as well as diving archaeology and aerial photographs, support the different interpretation the relics are explained by today. The finds bear information in themselves that do not allow arbitrary pictures. Yet, the pressure to constitute a certain meaning through relics can be enormously high. Before Ferdinand Keller favored the idea of buildings on stilts, different considerations had existed to interpret the traces, which have been noticed since the sixteenth-century.

In 1981 an expedition led by the anthropologist Owen Beattie exhumed the dead of the Franklin expedition. Their bodies gave information about the circumstances of their death. "Especially important to Beattie's research was the analysis of hair. They took hair samples 10 cm long from the nape of the neck. This hair was long enough to give information about the level of lead ingestion during the first eight months of the Franklin expedition."[17] The Franklin expedition was defeated more by progress than by nature: the seamen were poisoned by the lead content of their canned food. Thus it should be noted that subtly differentiated things need not appear monocausal.

A dead person unearthed from the glacial ice of Ötztal was a much more exciting find than the dead of the Franklin expedition. The meticulous examination revealed information about the habits of the man from the third millennium before Christ. Interesting in my context is the fact that the pieces of information about clothes, weapons, hunting habits, tattoos did not draw peoples attention as long as a narrative could be reconstructed from their traces.[18] The man was thought to have taken flight. "Tormented by painful fractured ribs 'Ötzi' had been caught in a sudden drop in atmospheric temperature high above the Southern Tirol Tisental shortly before his death."[19] On 19 August 1993 the magazine *Stern* published a photo showing how the man drops to his knees, illuminated by the last sunbeams. This did not seem to be dramatic enough for the front page (Ill. 11.4), where the man fights his way through the snow as if he was going at Stalingrad with the German 6th

Fig. 11.4 Wislaw Smetek, "Die letzten Tage des Ötzi" (Ötzi's Last Days), title page of *Stern*, 19 August 1993.

army into Russian captivity. The story would not be complete if the whole thing was not revealed to be a fabrication. Michael Heim and Werner Nosko[20] have written a book against Konrad Spindler,[21] who published the find. Like the interpreter of the traces, the critics have a role in the same media story. Typical of all argumentation chains is that the imagination needs the evidence of the traces. In 1996, a contribution to the magazine *Geo* proves that with almost the same stock of traces the man from the Hauslabjoch looked absolutely different.[22] Whereas Wislaw Smetek in *Stern* had drawn the man from Ötztal putting on his clothes—like a doll and facing his death, *Geo* reconstructed the man like a sculpture (Ill. 11.5).

The whole article uses visually a technique that, applied to texts, Johann Gustav Droysen would describe as "*untersuchende Darstellung*" (examining depiction). According to this systematology the *Stern* report is "erzählende Geschichtsdarstellung" (narrative depiction of history).[23] The symbolical order in Smetek's depiction refers to the world of fighting and war, whereas the soft *Geo*-man belongs to an ecological utopia. To ecological oriented beholders the hunters and gatherers of the Neolithic time pick out as a central theme the dream of simple a life. The read traces are integrated in both picture worlds of different generations—though often only with technical help. Their information stored, they loom into presence, a "*Gedächtnis der Dinge*" (memory of things).[24]

A final example of how past is currently present is Kaspar Hauser's bloodstained trousers. Hauser, who was murdered in 1833, was assumed to be an expelled hereditary prince of the house of Baden. Blood samples from two still living women of this aristocratic family were tested to clarify whether this assumption was right. Since each single genetic molecule serves as a "biological identity card," forensic doctors subjected the blood to a DNA-examination; they managed also to process the blood from the trousers Kaspar Hauser had worn when he was killed. "The search for genes in blood more than one hundred years

Fig. 11.5 "Reconstruction of Ötzi," from *Geo*, October 1996. © Patrick Landmann. Every effort has been made to trace the copyright holder and to obtain his permission for the use of this image.

old is, even for the experts of the Munich Institute of Forensic Medicine, new ground in science. For after 163 years the DNA has become a faded, eroded and worn out document. It was split by enzymes, digested by microorganisms, oxidized by oxygen. From the often meters-long molecule cords only tiny fragments remained."[25] Result: His genetic card did not match the ones of the Baden royal house. The assumption that Hauser was a distant prince proves wrong.

This examination has reduced speculation on the secrets of this young man only slightly: in our context it becomes obvious that durable objects themselves let information from the past be currently present. Whether these pieces of information appear as curves on screens or are reconstructed like the man from Ötztal, they have to be integrated into the current symbolical order. In this process a surplus of meaning is caused that goes beyond the explanation, the making of the visibility of information. Always it concerns "traces," bringing historian and detective closer together in the drive to decipher them. Occasionally they indicate actions, events and incidents, like the mountain hiker's fractured ribs; now and then they point at the condition of clothes or cultivable spores in his shoes. The oldest kind of trace is the imprint that preserves in a negative form what once was, for example, the lower part of a dog's paw. Because in our experience an imprint emerges only where something has been, we want to look at the cause of the trace. In Loccum (Lower Saxony, Germany) one can have a look at traces of dinosaurs that are approximately 135 million years of age. Well before the fame of Jurassic Park, the municipality of Rehburg-Loccum advertised itself with images of friendly dinosaurs (Ill. 11.6).

Now, it would be totally wrong to call the Ötztal man, as depicted in the emotiveness formula of the 6th army or the Napoleonic retreat from Russia, and

Fig. 11.6 "Traces of a Saurian, 135 million years before Christ," brochure of the City Rehburg-Loccum (about 1982).

Fig. 11.7 Windsor MacCay, "Gertie der Dinosaurier" (Gertie the Dinosaur), cartoon from 1909.

the dinosaur that is the reincarnation of a cartoon dinosaur called Gertie's drawn by Windsor MacCay (Ill. 11.7), "non-historic." The reconstructions use existing constructions, "Pathosformeln" (emotiveness formulas as Aby Warburg calls them) that are waiting. Waiting means the formulas are loaded with experiences of the past that can provide meaning to the given results. I will deal with this aspect more precisely in the third section of this chapter, on symbolism.

Along the road from Tel Aviv to Jerusalem in Bab el Wad or Sha'ar Hagajai, one can see burned-out vehicles, traces of combat, war equipment rendered useless by explosions and fires (Ill. 11.8). It is not for want of ecological consciousness that we still can see this scrap metal today; rather, it is kept up, always newly painted. In general it signals the warlike beginnings of the state of Israel and in particular the battles in this valley. Although narratives exist about the defense of the access to Jerusalem these preserved and probably

Fig. 11.8 Burnt-out chariot from the 1948 War of Independence in Bab el Wad or Sha'ar Hagajai, photo by Naomi Salmon (1994).

arranged symbolical traces give that place, that road, that way from and to Jerusalem, a meaning different from that of an ordinary thoroughfare.

Traces take a different shape at Yad Mordechai,[26] a kibbutz whose defenders fought against an Egyptian superior strength. In this settlement we find a reconstructed scale model: the old weapons and the tank riddled with bullets date from 1948; the Egyptian soldiers are dummies standing in the battlefield; over loudspeakers one can hear the story in a choice of languages. The traces are reconstructed. The life-size diorama in situ (Ill. 11.9) is meant to preserve the evidence as interpreted traces in memory. The trace gives authority to the production, it shows how it really was: the trace, the imprint, impressed the happenings on the surface of the earth.

One time-honored tradition of keeping up traces is represented by memorial stones. On the place Johann Hus was burned on 6 July 1415 a simple stone was erected shortly after the event took place. The hill on which the German Emperor William stood during the battle in Gravelotte is marked with a stone inscribed: "From this place King William led the battle of 18 August, 1870."[27] The Napoleon stone in Leipzig, a cube, marks the place from which the Emperor watched the *Völkerschlacht* (Battle of the Nations) on 13 October, 1813.

Imprints of a special type remain of Visuvius' victims in Pompeii. Over time, the body of anyone who died in a rain of ashes, i.e. the dog (Ill. 11.10) became a negative space. Filled with plaster, the last figure of, for example the dog appears as a positive. The photograph of it passes on the negative-positive appear-

Fig. 11.9 Lifesize reconstruction of the battlefield of 1948, Yad Mordechai (photo taken in 1993).

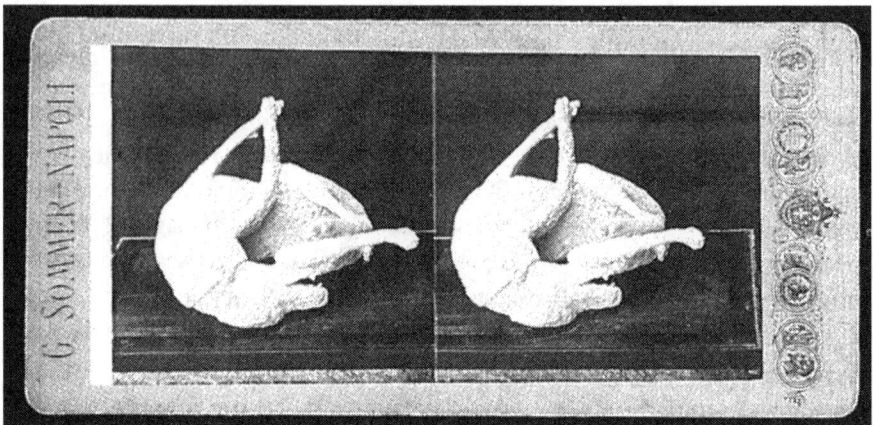

Fig. 11.10 The Pompeian dog, stereoscopic picture by G. Sommer, Naples (1880–1890).

ance once again. The chain can get longer and longer. I illustrate a stereoscope-picture of the 1880s that in the contemplation gadget shows the dog in a three dimensional picture.

Finally, photography has to be listed under the heading "imprint, trace." Granted, a photo is not left over like a remnant; it is intentionally produced. But the course of its making is symptomatic. By opening the lid of the camera I allow light to fall on the photosensitive plate, leaving a trace of the objects it was reflected from. Yet the photo might depict more than the photographer intends. Daguerre's daguerreotype *Boulevard du Temple,* dated spring 1838, is a good example.[28] Several photographs he took in his residential building (rue des Marais 15) still exist. Because the place is known, the position of the sun, indicated by the shadows, reveals the time. Michelangelo Antonionis' movie *Blow up* (1966) revolves around the central theme of the photo's trace character. Daguerre knew of this character, he loved to photograph fossils and plaster casts and in so doing he followed the tradition of conservation and redoubling of manifestations.

That is how picture chains with the same, the same looking, links loom out of the past into present times, thereby making specific former times relevant to present times.

Form

I try to unite the second grouping of incarnations of the past under the venerable term "form," which I will use in the simplest sense of the Latin *forma* (from *ferre*—to do). Form means a specific outline, a specific shape of an object: in other words, the distinctive, caused appearance of an artifact to the visual and emotional senses.

Whereas imprints are coincidental, passive (except for intentional casts of nature[29] made by, say, Renaissance sculptures or photography), forms (in my use of the term) result from a human production process. I expressly want this term to be understood separately from the antithesis of matter and form. The intended appearance of an object (or in the modern age, intended unintentional appearance that is accepted) shall be called form, because it is able to bridge the gap between human handiwork and to things that are not artificial but result from the process of nature. Here the cast of nature and the imprint of nature lie very close together.[30]

In *Vita activa oder Vom tätigen Leben* (1960), Hannah Arendt distinguishes between working and manufacturing. The differences are obvious in the produced things, work produces consumer goods; manufacture produces articles for everyday use (bread, table). In contrast to these creative acts, speaking and thinking have in common that they are "schlechterdings unproduktiv" (absolutely unproductive).

> "In order to become worldly things, that is, deeds and facts and events and patterns of thoughts or ideas, they must first be seen, heard, and remembered and the transformed, reified as it were, into things—into sayings of poetry, the written page or the printed book, into paintings or sculpture, into all sorts of records, documents, and monuments. The whole factual world of human affairs depends for its reality and its continued existence, first, upon the presence of others who have seen and heard and will remember, and second, on the transformation of the intagible into the tangiblitiy of things. Without remembrance and without the reification which remembrance needs for its own fulfillment and which makes it, indeed, as the Greeks held, the mother of all arts, the living activities of action, speech, and thought would lose their reality at the end of each process and disappear as though they never had been. The materialization they have to undergo in order to remain in the world at all is paid for in that always the 'dead letter' replaces something which grew our of and for a flecting moment indeed existed as 'living spirit'."[31]

In the form that each "thing becoming object" *(Vergegenständlichung)* takes, the process of *"Vergegenständlichung"* itself leaves its mark; it is not a killing of—as Arendt puts it—*"lebendigen Geistes"* (living spirit) so much as a taming, dealings with the living.

Aby Warburg was aware of that into the process of "things becoming object" *(Vergegenständlichung),* the creation of forms is a specific kind of working on affects, *"Affekt-Bearbeitung"* as Aby Warburg calls it. "The reality and realiability of the human world rest primarily on the fact that we are surrounded by things more permanent than the activity by which they were produced, and potentially even more permanent than the lives of their authors."[32] But objects that have survived their original context have to be asked about their constitution. Warburg wants to show how to look at things, and especially at works of art, that are resonant with imaginations that have fallen into oblivion. Edgar Wind describes this as follows: "This can only be achieved with an indirect method. With the study of all sorts of documents which with a historical critical method can be connected with that picture one has to lead a circumstantial evidence for the fact that a single complex of imagination which can be revealed played a part in the arrangement of the picture."[33] To the scientist, seeing develops "into a conceptual governed course of memory through which he gets access to the entrance in the line of those who keep the 'experience' of the past vivid."[34] The important sentence follows: "Warburg was convinced that he in his own work, i. e. in the reflecting act of the picture analysis, did perform a function which the picture memory of people under the pressure of the urge of expression carries out in a spontaneous act of picture synthesis: their memory of already existing shaped forms...."[35]

It is a fascinating thought that one unconsciously falls back upon older forms. That is how the chain stays in latency, manifesting itself in every specific manner, carrying the signature of its time as well as of former times. Fritz Saxl points out that the origin of a type (a pathos formula) is as much a selection process as an experiment where things are selected. He describes the specific of what Hannah Arendt called *"Vergegenständlichung"* (things becoming objects) as follows: "One must know right from the beginning that each pictorial depiction of an action tends to interpret this action as gesture: because the pictorial depiction only is able to show one single moment out of the process. Furthermore our examples show that during the stage of 'searching' originated depiction shows the action, compared with the type-created depiction which excellently shows the gestures of expression."[36]

Saxl describes this "searching's" as a selection process: "Art chooses from these transitory gestures that happen in the fullness of space and time special gestures to depict an expression.... The expression formula of artistic sign language is in relation to sign language of the vivid which already is "a way of expression," only (or better: even) at the same time ways of expression in the second ability."[37] Saxl writes that the form of expression would have such power that it would stay alive for centuries, even for thousands of years. It would be able to *"die verschiedensten Inhalte aufnehmen"* (take in many different contents).[38]

The melancholy gesture is a good example of such a form. It surely is one of the most famous pathos formulas; Walter von der Vogelweide was not the first who had *"in hant gesmogen daz kinne und ein min Wange,"* which means that the poet tells that he sat on a stone, his elbow on his knee, his chin resting in his hand. By comparing of Dürer's depiction of the silent sufferer Job (Ill. 11.11) and Hilmar Pabel's photo of a German soldier[39] (Ill. 11.12), I want to point out that a lot of people make this gesture daily. We see that within our culture group this gesture is comprehensible on a level besides that of visual reception.

A more detailed examination of the melancholy gesture would have to show what the comparison of Dürer's oil painting with Pabel's photo yields, and whether the results differ from, for instance, the comparison of a depict-

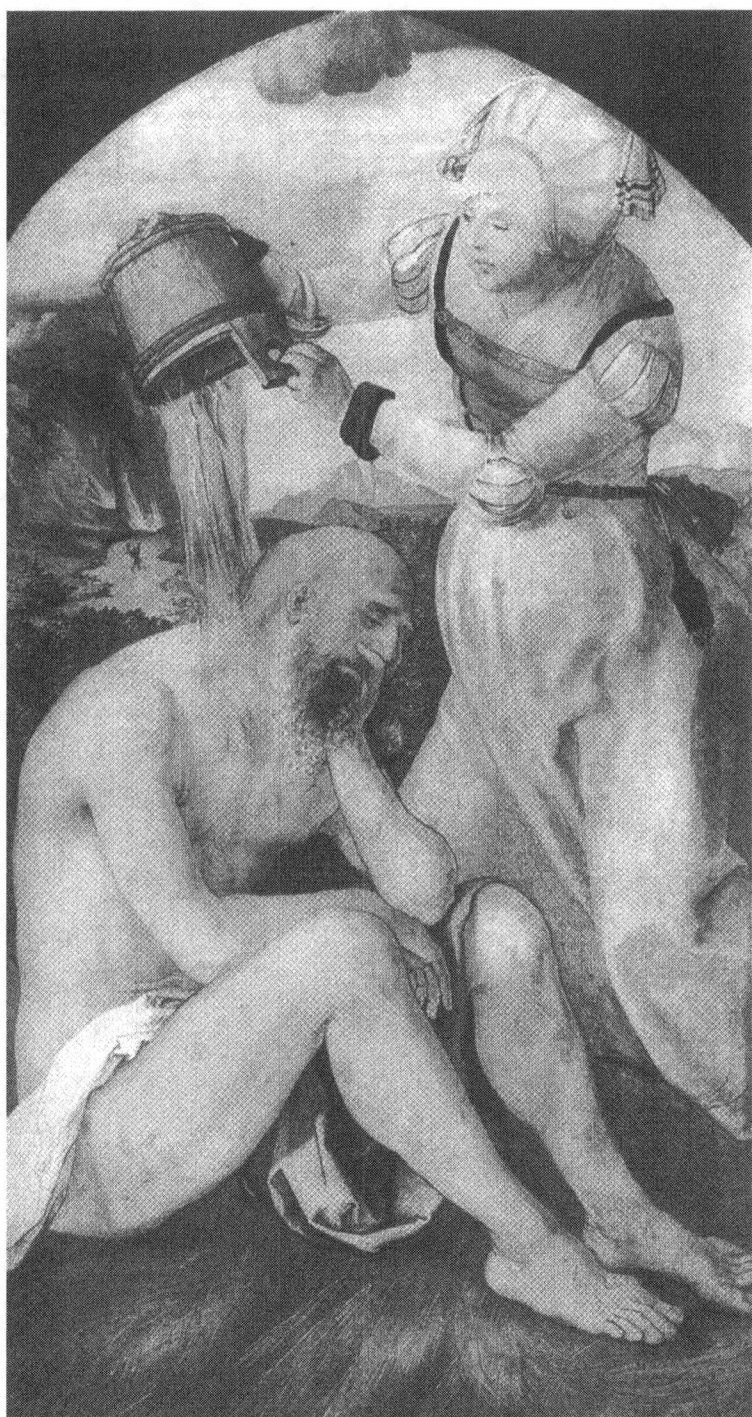

Fig. 11.11 Albrecht Dürer, *Hiob wird von seinem Weib verspottet* (Job scoffed by his wife, 1500–1505), oil on limewood, Frankfurt am Main, Städelsches Kunstinstitut.

Fig. 11.12 Hilmar Pabel, *Soldat* (Soldier, 1944).

ing the housing in an attic in Theresienstadt drawn by Bedrich Fritta (Ill. 11.13) who was murdered in Auschwitz.[40]

In his *Kriegsfibel* (war fibula) Brecht reinterprets the gesture, still using an objective description.[41] The German postwar era saw a marked upswing in depictions of melancholy gestures. In his book *Denk ich an Deutschland* (Thinking of Germany, Ill. 11.14), published in 1959, Michael Mansfeld illustrates,

Fig. 11.13 Bedrich Fritta, *Theresienstadt* (between 1942 and July 1944), quill, wash drawing, Prague, Jewish Museum.

apart from Hilmar Pabel's photo of 1944, a new type of *"skeptische Generation"* (skeptical generation).[42] It now appears more often. This image of "The Thoughtful" had a determining influence on public communication in West Germany up to the seventies. Whereas in West Germany the melancholy gesture is provable on photos and election posters, East Germany falls back upon this pattern in painting and graphic arts. Yet, the gesture is equally responsive to the captivity of German soldiers thinking about the collapse and to the cap-

Fig. 11.14 Bookcover *Denk ich an Deutschland* (Thinking of Germany) by Michael Mansfeld (1959).

tivity of victims of persecution (Ill. 11.15), even if Strempel uses a bigger interpretation of history stressing God's saving grace. Up to the 1980s this gesture is maintained in the always imitation (Mimesis) obliged painting of GDR.

The melancholy gesture has been handed down in the western culture group for more than two and a half thousand years. Yet its use, as regards content, is possible in many different kinds of contexts. Like the Pompeian dog the same form, the same physical posture, gains acceptance. In the dainty way young Möllemann[43] rests his head on his hand (Ill. 11.16) in a press photo from the 1970s, Dürer's silent sufferer is latently present, as the past is in present time. This I would defend even if it could be proved that a head, becoming heavy with brooding, needs the support of the hand,

Fig. 11.15 Horst Strempel, *Gefangen* (Caught, 1946), Berlin, National Gallery. ©VG Bild-Kunst, Bonn 2006

Fig. 11.16 Melancholic gestures from *Vorwärts*, 30 April 1981, p. 7).

because whenever the head sinks into the hand, it sinks because of a unique reason in an irretrievable moment—and every time the gesture gains a new facet.

Symbolism

When gestures and physical expressions (and though here I stay with this group of motifs, this holds good for land formations, signs, and other motifs) are provable through time in all sorts of content contexts, do they not have something in common? Does not in their use the content coins a specific form and that this form cannot be seen without a latent knowledge of the content? If so I call it symbolism. According to Fritz Saxl, it is not arbitrary which gesture turns into a form of expression, into a pathos formula. Such forms always have the capacitiy to take in many contents—often of contrasting kind—because they already have adopted many contents. Yet, they do not become arbitrary; they have their own specific material consistency (this holds true for dance gestures and also for objects and buildings).

Symbols have a relative clearness. A host in the context of the Catholic Sacrifice of the Mass signals that it **is** the Body of Jesus; in the context of a Protestant service the bread **means** Body of Christ. Two hands, inside one another, for example at the facade of a little temple in an English landscape garden, describe friendship; in the later nineteenth-century the same hands can symbolize the uniting of two German workers' parties. After the Second World War the same hands describe the merging of the KPD and SPD to the SED; here they can no longer be described as a symbol, for they are also a sign, a party badge.

In an article on symbols that Aby Warburg later drew on, Friedrich Theodor Vischer defines symbol as a "bloß äußerliche Verknüpfung von Bild und Inhalt durch einen Vergleichspunkt,"[44] in contrast to the Age of Romanticism a conceivable pragmatic way of tackling the problem: When symbols are introduced, pictures and contents are unambiguously tied together. Symbolism cannot be awarded this clearness. I assume that pictures correspond to interlocked contents. This interlocking takes place along an axis we would—according to Friedrich Theodor Vischer—call comparative point and which I treat as equivalent to my description of form.

Symbolism operates with a signal system and notation that each society, each culture understands. Momentary occurrences—physical expression, facial expression, gesture—here lie side by side with objects of longer duration, from advertising posters to decorations of apartments, from depictions in newspapers to national emblems. They are all connotations of interpretations, some with meanings. Some of these signs and signals are exhausted in their pragmatism, like the signs for women's and men's toilets; others claim to constitute meaning for the whole society, like the Federal German Eagle. Some sign systems function—if their context is settled—in various motifs, like male and female toilet. Over the one- and two legged figures up to queen of hearts and jack of hearts functions each picture, which clearly shows the difference between the sexes. In Poland some have problems interpreting the signs O (circle) and D (triangle) that mark the doors, but for the most part people come to the right decision. In the case of the Federal German Eagle this freedom to interpret of form does not exist. The image must correspond to that on the five-mark—a coin (to quote a currency gone with the Euro), as the one-mark version appears archaic and the NS version is, even without the swastika-tail, no longer acceptable. In addition it has to be set off in form against the US-Eagle (to name but one competitor). But each eagle between the one-mark and the five-mark coin claims to differentiate the national emblem of German society formally as well as to differentiate the way the society sees itself. These signs assume a society whose members communicate with each other and so set themselves against other societies that also communicate with each other.

In this field symbolism functions surrounded by a larger field of meanings that can even mean the opposite, though there is a common core. On the one hand they can be interlocked in the visible field as pictures; on the other they also can be interlocked in the area of meaning. After all, they are able to enter each recipient's private specific picture sequence as well as that of each receiving groups. That there always remains a common axis allows us to speak of symbolism.

Take for example an etching by Herbert Sandberg—"Die Überlebenden" (The Survivors)—dated 1963 (Ill. 11.17). Sandberg's topic in this print is the liberation of the Buchenwald concentration camp. At the center of the picture

Fig. 11.17 Herbert Sandberg, "Die Überlebenden" (The Survivors, 1963), etching from the cycle *Der Weg* (The Way, 1962–1964). © VG Bild-Kunst, Bonn 2006

is a gate with infinite wide-open wings. The prisoners are dancing with joy, embracing each other. Of course Sandberg's graphic is no account of what happened. He tries to make understandable the happiness at the end of imprisonment. The most important element is the gate. Because of its functional connection it is excellently suited as a central theme for the liberation—even though fence, on the contrary, symbolizes imprisonment. Fences—in the experience of many people—divide areas, separate an inside from an outside. Usually fences cannot be stridden through. The only place where this is possible is a gate, which signals permeability. Put into a picture, many people associate this quality with a gate that is open in its generality and in its fundamental nature, symbolizing intention. This is what enables the gate of Auschwitz-Birkenau to acquire much more meaning than its function ever had. Correspondingly, photographers and painters tend to use it in images of liberation (Fig. 11.18).

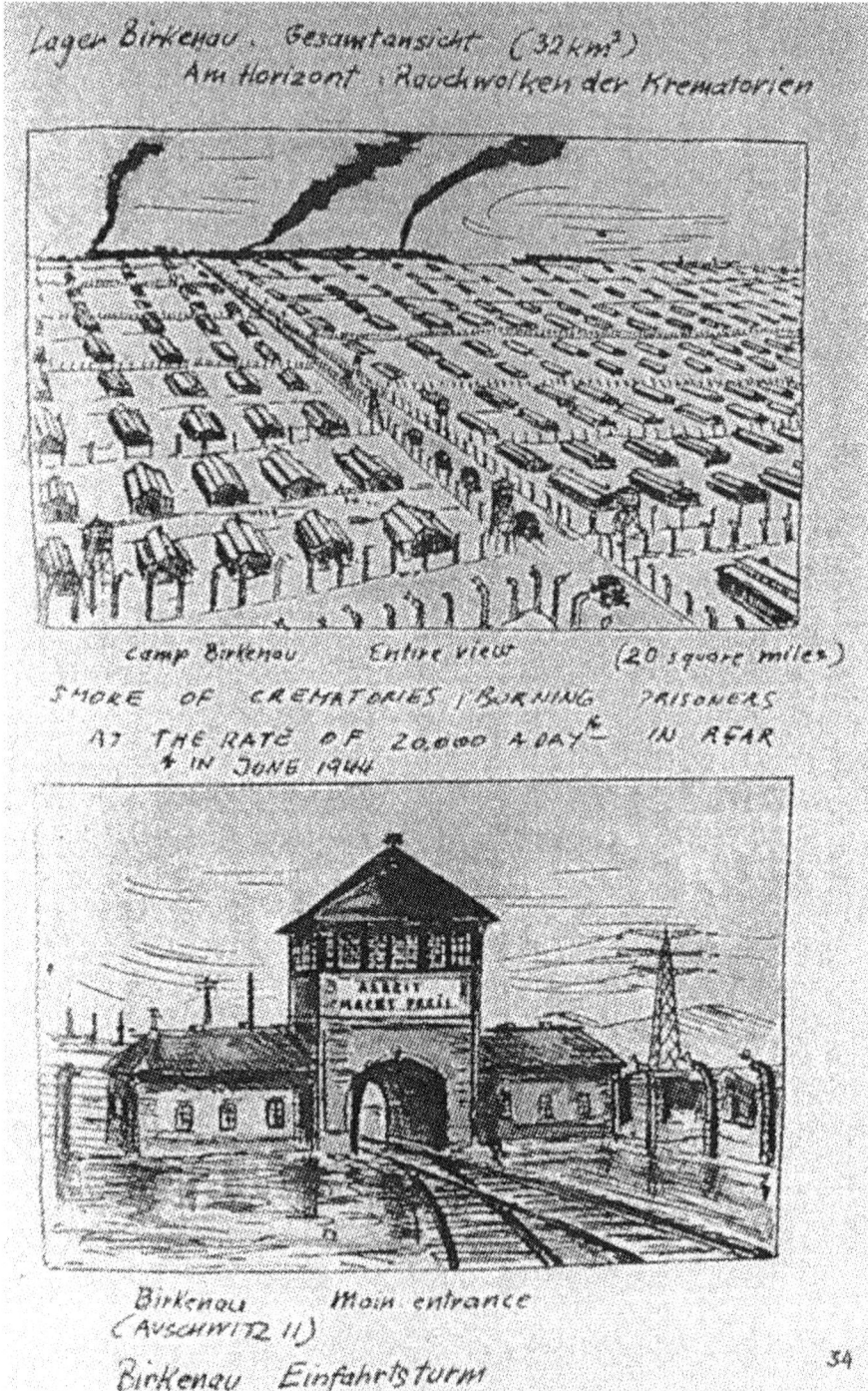

Fig. 11.18 Alfred Kantor, *"Birkenau,"* from: *Das Buch des Alfred Kantor* (The Book of Alfred Kantor, 1971) Jüdischer Verlag.

Notes

1. Owen Beattie and John Geiger, *Der eisige Schlaf: Das Schicksal der Franklin-Expedition* (Cologne 1989).

2. See Detlef Hoffmann, "Perspektiven und Probleme von Spurensicherung. Wozu kann demokratische Erinnerungsarbeit dienen?" in Alfred G. Frei, ed., *Friedrich Hecker in den USA: Eine deutsch-amerikanische Spurensicherung* (Konstanz 1993), 135–152. See also the very important, methodical success-oriented criminological literature, like: Hans Groß and Friedrich Geerds, eds., *Handbuch der Kriminalistik* (Berlin 1977), vol. 1, par. 14: "Spurenkunde," 476–489; for detailed information on the analysis of various traces: Klaus Dieter Pohl, *Handbuch der naturwissenschaftlichen Kriminalistik unter besonderer Berücksichtigung der forensischen Chemie* (Heidelberg 1981), 2–16: "Der Unfallort trägt—wie übrigens praktisch auch jeder andere Tatort—die Spur des Tathergangs." (2). Günter Bauer, *Auf den Spuren des Verbrechens: Grenzen und Möglichkeiten der Kriminalistik* (Lübeck 1973), subsumed under the headings "Spurensicherung," "Beweismittel" (50–61). I wish to thank Bärbel Schmidt, who informed me about this literature.

3. The complete *Tales and Poems* of Edgar Allan Poe (London 1982; first edition by Random House, Inc., New York 1938), 154.

4. From among the endless number of publications on this subject I will single out Bruce Chatwin, *The Songlines* (London 1987). Many stories of this kind can be found in the ten volumes of *Das malerische Deutschland,* published around 1840 Georg Wigand, ed., in Leipzig. See also Utz Haltern, "Landschaft und Geschichte," in Bernard Korzus, ed., *Exhibition catalog: Das malerische und romantische Westfalen: Aspektes eines Buches* (Münster 1974), 199–210.

5. "Mit sorgfältiger Berücksichtigung der neuesten Forschungen im Gebiet der Geologie." The theater leaflet is printed in Detlef Hoffmann and Almut Junker, *Laterna Magica: Lichtbilder aus Menschenwelt und Götterwelt* (Berlin 1982), 73.

6. Franz Unger, *Die Urwelt in ihren verschiedenen Bildungsepochen: 14 landschaftliche Darstellungen mit erläuterndem Text* (Wien 1851), quoted after the 2nd ed. 1852.

7. See Ulrich Thieme and Fritz Becker, *Allgemeines Lexikon der bildenden Künste von der Antike bis zur Gegenwart* (Leipzig 1929), vol. 22, 145.

8. The report starts in *Illustrierte Zeitung* 436 (1851), and ends in no. 455 (20 March 1852).

9. With this pictures he follows Bernhard Cotta, *Geologische Bilder* (Leipzig 1852, 2nd ed. 1854).

10. Rudolf Ludwig, *Das Buch der Geologie oder die Wunder der Erdrinde und der Urwelt: Naturgeschichte der Erde in allgemein verständlicher Darstellung für alle Freunde dieser Wissenschaft mit Berücksichtigung der Jugend ...*, parts 1 and 2 (Leipzig 1855).—For detailed information on the whole complex: Detlef Hoffmann, "Malerische Wissenschaft," in Historisches Museum, *Exhibition catalog Laterna Magica—Vergnügen, Belehrung, Unterhaltung* (Frankfurt/ M. 1981), 63–99; see also Hoffmann and Junker, *Laterna Magica,* 75f.

11. "Das niedere Land, welches die Zeit bereits abtrotzte und zu einer Stätte der mannigfaltigsten Entwicklungen erhob, ist wieder eine Beute des alles verschlingenden Wassers geworden ... Auf einem riffigen Boden, ebenso ein Bauwerk wie eine Wohnstätte der Korallen und anderer Meeresgeschöpfe, ... sehen wir die Mannigfaltigkeit des untermeerischen thierischen Lebens ... ausgebreitet ... Mit gierigen Blicken betrachtet sie als willkommene Beute ein seltsames Ungeheuer von crocodilartiger Gestalt ... Es ist der Nothosaurus gigantheus ... Die unendliche Schwermut, welche sich über der Gegend ausbreitet, ... wird durch den Schleier der Nacht ... noch ungemein erhöht." Unger, *Die Urwelt,* 22f.

12. Some of them are to be found in Melchior Neumayr, *Erdgeschichte* (Leipzig and Vienna 1895).

13. My Oldenburg colleague Mamoun Fansa informed me about the catalog of the Schweizerisches Landesmuseum, edited by Markus Höneisen, *Die ersten Bauern: Pfahlbaufunde Europas* (Zürich 1990), which sums up the science so far on this topic. Here especially see Josef Speck, "Zur Geschichte der Pfahlbauforschung" (9–20). I first learned about the buildings on stilts during a lecture given by Francois de Capitani.

14. "Vortreffliche Einblicke in die Kultur der neolitischen Periode gewähren uns die reichen Funde aus den Schweizer Pfahlbaustationen, die überhaupt seit ihrer Entdeckung eine der allerwichtigsten Quellen der vorgeschichtlichen Forschung bilden. Die Pfahlbauten standen über dem Wasser...."

15. "Aller Abfall des täglichen Lebens, aller schadhaft gewordene Hausrat, Produkte oft langer und mühsamer Arbeit, versank in die Wassertiefen des Sees und wurde vom Grundschlick innig umschlossen, daß nichts von ihm verloren ging, nicht einmal die einstige Gestalt. Kein Wunder, daß schon die Entdecker dieser untergegangenen Welt reiche Ernte machten und daß sich in den Folgejahrzehnten, als immer neue Dörfer hervortauchten aus dem Seegrund, schier unübersehbar die Schätze häuften." Carl W. Neumann, *Das Werden des Menschen und der Kultur* (Leipzig 1932), 192.

16. "Man hat nun die Frage aufgeworfen, warum wohl die Urbevölkerung der Schweiz ihre Wohnungen in Seen angelegt habe. Offenbar lässt sich in dieser Hinsicht annehmen, daß die Schweizer P. ebenso wie die gleichen Ansiedlungen der oben genannten noch jetzt lebenden Völker als eine sichere Zuflucht vor wilden Thieren und Menschen dienen sollten. In der Schweiz waren es vielleicht, wie man annimmt, gallische Volksstämme (Kelten), welche diese Wohnstätten erbauten. Kein Geschichtsschreiber meldet von ihnen, und als Caesar in Helvetien eindrang, fand er, wie es scheint, schon keine Pfahlbauern mehr vor." *Meyers Konversationslexikon*, 3rd ed. (Leipzig 1878), vol. 13, 805, s. v. "Pfahlbauern."

17. "Für Beatties Forschungen war eine Analyse der Haare besonders wichtig. Man verwandte dafür 10 cm lange Haarsträhnen aus der Nackenpartie. Das Haar war lang genug, um über die Höhe der Bleiaufnahme während der ersten acht Monate der Franklin-Expedition Auskunft geben zu können." Beattie/Geiger, *Der eisige Schlaf*, 123.

18. The following is based on the report and pictures published in *Stern*, 19 August 1993, titled "Die letzten Tage des Ötzi. Wissenschaftler enträtseln das geheimnisvolle Leben des Gletschermannes," 46–63.

19. "Gepeinigt von schmerzhaften Rippenbrüchen, wird "Ötzi" kurz vor seinem Tod hoch über dem Südtiroler Tisental von einem Wettersturz überrascht."

20. Michael Heim and Werner Nosko, *Die Ötztalfälschung: Anatomie einer archäologischen Groteske* (Reinbek 1993).

21. Konrad Spindler, *Der Mann aus dem Eis: Die Ötztaler Mumie verrät die Geheimnisse der Steinzeit* (Munich 1993).

22. "Ötzi: Der Mann aus der Steinzeit. Wie er war. Wie er lebte. Wie er starb," *Geo*, October 1996, 69ff. Institutions argue about the rights to exhibit the reconstruction. The Southern Tyrol provincial government in Bozen, which owns the mummy and thus holds the copyrights, prohibited the Neanderthal-Museum in Mettmann (Rheinland, Germany) from exhibiting the *Geo* reconstruction of Ötzi by threatening the museum with a 30 000 German Marks (15 000 €) penalty for breach of contract. *(Frankfurter Allgemeine Zeitung (FAZ)*, 5 December 1996). On 11 December 1996 the *FAZ* reported on a settlement out of court.

23. Johann Gustav Droysen, *Historik: Historisch-kritische Ausgabe*, ed. by Peter Leyh (Stuttgart 1977), 447f.

24. See Jan Assmann, *Das kulturelle Gedächtnis: Schrift, Erinnerung und politische Identität in frühen Hochkulturen* (Munich 1992), 20. Assmann is interested in the time index, which interprets with the present time the various layers of past.

25. "Die Fahndung nach Genen in mehr als ein Jahrhundert altem Blut ist auch für die Experten des Münchner Instituts (für Rechtsmedizin) wissenschaftliches Neuland. Denn nach 163 Jahren ist die DNS zu einem verblichenen, angefressenen und zerschlissenen Dokument geworden. Sie wurde von Enzymen gespalten, von Mikroorganismen verdaut, von Sauerstoff oxidiert. Von den oft meterlangen Molekülsträngen sind nur winzige Bruchstücke erhalten." "Schönster Krimi aller Zeiten," *Der Spiegel* 48 (25 11 1996): 254–273, here 255. I know that doubts were voiced on the examination carried out by *Spiegel,* especially concerning the question of whether the examined trousers belonged to Kaspar Hauser. See *Die Zeit* 49 (29 11 1996). In the context of my argumentation this is of minor importance.

26. See Margaret Larkin, *Die sechs Tage von Yad Mordechai* (Jerusalem, n.d.), for further information about the event.

27. "Von dieser Stelle aus leitete König Wilhelm die Schlacht am 18. August 1870."

28. Ulrich Pohlmann and Marjen Schmidt, "Das Münchner Daguerre-Triptychon: Ein Protokoll zu Geschichte seiner Präsentation, Aufbewahrung und Restaurierung," *Fotogeschichte* 14 (1994): 3–13.

29. See the exhibition catalog Herbert Beck, ed., *Natur und Antike in der Renaissance* (Frankfurt/ M. put out by Liebighaus 1985), specially chapter 7. "Das genaue Abbild der Natur—Riccios Tiere und die Theorie des Naturabgusses seit Cennini," 198–277.

30. I have outlined the following reflections in my article "Abdruck, Form, Symbolisierung. Überlegungen zum nonverbalen Gedächtnis," *Kulturwissenschaftliches Institut, Jahrbuch* 1992/93 (Essen 1994): 177–183.

31. Hannah Arendt, *The Human Condition* (Chicago 1958), 95. "Um in die Welt der Dinge einzugehen, um als Taten, Tatsachen und Ereignisse oder als Gedanken, Gedankenformen und Ideen sich in der Welt anzusiedeln, müssen sie erst gesehen, gehört, erinnert und dann verwandelt, nämlich verdinglicht werden, um überhaupt Gegenstandscharakter zu gewinnen—wie ein gedichteter Vers, eine geschriebene Seite, ein gedrucktes Buch, ein Bild oder ein Skulptur, wie alle Denk- und Mahnmäler des menschlichen Geistes. Die Faktizität des gesamten Bereichs menschlicher Angelegenheiten hängt davon ab, einmal, daß Menschen zugegen sind, die gesehen und gehört haben und darum erinnern werden, und zum anderen davon, daß eine Verwandlung des Nichtgreifbaren in die Handgreiflichkeit eines Dinghaften gelingt. Ohne Erinnerung und die Verdinglichung, die aus der Erinnerung selbst entspringt, weil die Erinnerung der Verdinglichung für ihr eigenes Erinnern bedarf (warum sie denn auch, wie die Griechen sagen, die Mutter aller Künste ist), würde das lebendig Gehandelte, das gesprochene Wort, der gedachte Gedanke spurlos verschwinden." "Die verwandelnde Vergegenständlichung ist der Preis, den das Lebendige zahlt, um nur überhaupt in der Welt bleiben zu können." Hannah Arendt, *Vita activa oder Vom tätigen Leben* (Munich 1960), 86 and 87f.

32. Wirklichkeit und Verläßlichkeit der Welt"—so Hannah Arendt—"beruhen darauf, daß die uns umgebenden Dinge eine größere Dauerhaftigkeit haben als die Tätigkeit, die sie hervorbrachte, und daß diese Dauerhaftigkeit sogar das Leben ihrer Erzeuger überdauern kann," ibid., 88.

33. Die Methode, durch die dies erreicht wird, kann nur eine indirekte sein. Man muß durch das Studium aller Arten von Urkunden, die sich mit diesem Bild nach historisch-kritischer Methode in Verbindung bringen lassen, einen Indizienbeweis führen für die Tatsache, daß ein im einzelnen aufzuweisender Vorstellungskomplex an der Gestaltung des Bildes mitgewirkt hat." Edgar Wind, "Warburgs Begriff der Kulturwissenschaft und seine Bedeutung für die Ästhetik" (1931), in *Aby M. Warburg, Ausgewählte Schriften und Würdigungen* (Baden-Baden 1992), 401–417, see 406 and 407.

34. "Zu einem begrifflich geleiteten Erinnerungsvorgang, durch den er Eintritt in die Reihe derer, die die "Erfahrung" der Vergangenheit lebendig erhalten.

35. Warburg war davon überzeugt, daß er in seiner eigenen Arbeit, das heißt im reflektierenden Akt der Bildanalyse, eine Funktion ausübte, die das Bildgedächtnis der Menschen im spontanen Akte der Bildsynthese unter dem Zwang des Ausdrucksstriebes vollzieht: das Sichwiedererinnern an vorgeprägte Formen. Edgar Wind, "Warburgs Begriff der Kulturwissenschaft," see p. 406 and 407.

36. "Von vornherein muß man sich aber klar sein, daß jede bildliche Darstellung einer Handlung von sich aus dahin tendiert, diese Handlung als Gebärde aufzufassen, weil nämlich die bildliche Darstellung aus dem Verlauf der Handlung nur einen Moment zu erfassen im Stande ist. Und weiterhin läßt sich gerade an unserem Beispiel verfolgen, daß wohl die im Stadium des 'Suchens' entstehende Darstellung mehr die Handlung, die zum Typus entwickelte Darstellung dagegen vorzüglich die Ausdrucksgebärden zum Ausdruck bringen."

37. "Die bildende Kunst wählt nun aus diesen transitorischen Gebärden, die in der Fülle des Raumes und in der Fülle der Zeit vonstatten gehen, bestimmte Gebärden zu Darstellung des Ausdrucks aus ... Die Ausdrucksformeln der künstlerischen Gebärdensprache sind also im Ver-

hältnis zur Gebärdensprache des Lebendigen, die doch auch schon 'Ausdrucksform' ist, nur (oder besser: sogar) gleichsam Ausdrucksformen zweiter Potenz."

38. Fritz Saxl, "Die Ausdrucksgebärden in der bildenden Kunst" (1932), in *Warburg, Ausgewählte Schriften,* 419–431, see 423–425.

39. See Hilmar Pabel, *Jahre unseres Lebens: Deutsche Schicksalsbilder* (Stuttgart 1954), 18. See also Viktoria Schmidt-Linsenhoff, "Die Verschlußzeit des Herzens: Zu Hilmer Pabels Fotobuch 'Jahre unseres Lebens' 1954," *Fotogeschichte* 12 (1992): 53–64, in particular 56.

40. See Janet Blatter and Sybil Milton, *Art of the Holocaust* (New York 1981), 85.

41. Bertold Brecht, *Kriegsfibel* (1955), 2nd ed. (Berlin 1968, 59): "Hier sitz ich, halte meinen armen Kopf …" (Here I sit holding my poor head …).

42. Michael Mansfeld, *Denk ich an Deutschland* (Munich 1959), 40.

43. Jürgen Möllemann was a politician of the Free Democratic Party (FDP) (the translator).

44. "Only external combining of picture and content through a comparative point." Friedrich Vischer, "Das Symbol" (1887), in Friedrich Vischer, *Ausgewählte Werke in acht Teilen,* 8. Teil: *Prosaschriften II,* Leipzig o. J. (ca. 1920), 312–347, in particular 325.

CHAPTER 12

Ruins: A Visual Expression of Historical Meaning

MOSHE BARASCH

1

Early in the second half of the eighteenth century, Sir William Chambers was appointed architect to the Crown Princess Augusta, the mother of King George III, with the task of reshaping Kew Gardens, later to become one of the greatest botanical gardens in the world. He tried to give the garden a particular character, and to do so he erected buildings that were to become famous all over Europe. Both in style and in cultural connotations Chambers' attitude was syncretistic. In addition to a Chinese pagoda eight stories tall, he inserted into the "wilderness" of Kew Gardens a mosque, some Greek temples, and a Roman ruin.[1]

In shaping such a seemingly paradoxical product—an artificial, newly erected ruin—Chambers did not remain isolated. The fashion of constructing artificial ruins that began in England soon spread over the European continent, and as we know, even in garden cultures as strongly opposed to the English model as that of France, newly built ruins were soon to be found.

The fashion of creating artificial ruins has been studied and variously interpreted. Without attempting a review of these discussions, each of which stresses the specific conditions and trends prevailing at a certain time and in a given national culture, we should like here to emphasize the wider, if less manifest problem behind any individual explanations, correct and justified as they may be. The problem simply is the basic attitude to ruins.[2] When eighteenth-century architects, Sir William Chambers included, erected artificial ruins in

---

Notes for this section begin on page 221.

the gardens they laid out, they meant to convey something by this odd procedure. Such a "message" need not have been conceived in conceptual terms, nor need the architects necessarily have been aware of it. Often they may have been moved by an intention to create a mood rather than to convey an abstract notion. But the intentional creation of a mood is, of course, no less a "message" than the explicit articulation of a concept. What, then, was it that the ruin said?

When trying to disentangle the different trends of thought that went into that "message," we cannot help feeling perplexed, and even confused. The ruin, whether natural or represented in a painting, whether the result of long-lasting decay or deliberately built, tends to evoke two altogether different, and perhaps even overtly conflicting, ideas or moods. Hence it must be experienced on two different levels.[3]

On the simplest and most direct level, the ruin is an actual, tangible testimony to the past. What we now call a ruin once formed part of a building, and, in a more expanded form, of a city, a culture, an age. But at the same time the ruin also testifies to something else. It shows, by the very fact of its being a ruin, that the building (or the city, the culture, the age) of which it once formed part, now belongs to the past. The decay that makes a building into a ruin is, of course, as essential a feature of the ruin as is the original shape that still is discernible, even in the decrepit and decayed condition of the object. The ruin is thus the presence of the past as past in the world in which we live today. In this respect, the ruin is a true historical monument.

But yet another contradiction, related to the first one but not identical with it, is suggested by the ruin. To be sure, it is not as distinct and as tangible, but it can still be apprehended, and as a rule it is made manifest in pictorial representations. The ruin as such is an emblem of decay and disintegration. But by incorporating the architectural vestige into nature, the process of transforming a complete building into a ruin also makes it a basis of naturally thriving, sometimes vigorously growing, vegetation. The fact that pictorial renderings emphasize the vegetation, a motif that stands in such sharp contrast to the dilapidation and collapse of the original building, shows that the ruin was conceived not only as a symbol of transience, but also of renewal and regeneration (albeit in a different medium). In itself, this conflict between human planning and building (the architectural form that is the core of the ruin) and the power of nature (the disintegration of the building and the vegetation invading and covering it) may perhaps not be considered part of the historical meaning. We shall attempt to show, however, that artists have transformed this conflict, too, into an explicit historical emblem.

In the following comments I shall try to clarify how the visual imagination of medieval and Renaissance culture made use of these conflicts immanent in our perception of ruins to create patterns of historical consciousness.

2

It is of interest to follow the interlocking of two processes: in one the ruin is crystallized as an articulate pictorial motif; in the other, the consciousness of history, of the past as distinguished from the present, attains concise visual expression. It was the ambiguity inherent in the ruin, the suggestion of both old and new at the same time, that made the image of the decaying building partly covered by thriving vegetation an appropriate configuration for the expression of the idea of history. The complex phenomenon of these interlocking processes marks the transition from the medieval to the modern world.

In the minds of present-day travelers touring the historical sites and cities of Europe, the ruin has come to be closely connected with the Middle Ages. Mighty columns, even if smashed and toppled (still preserving their majesty even in their fall), may evoke in our minds the image of Antiquity, but houses and walls, decayed and fragmented, overgrown with vegetation while still standing upright, will frequently be labeled "medieval." When we ask how medieval culture understood ruins, we therefore cannot help being surprised to find that in a precise sense of the word, medieval art did not represent ruins at all. Buildings, of course, frequently appeared, yet all the edifices shown are in a perfect state, standing proud and unharmed. In fact, as we know, city dwellers in the Middle Ages must have been thoroughly familiar with the sight of ruins, with buildings in different stages of breakdown and dilapidation. Yet when medieval writers and artists described or represented their cities, few signs of decay can be discovered in what they tell and show us. This can probably be seen best in the medieval literary and visual renderings of the city of Rome.

Particularly good examples are the depictions of the Capitol or the Colosseum. It is tempting, says Gregorovius, the well-known nineteenth-century historian of the city of Rome, to cast a glance "on the tragic world of ruins of the Capitol."[4] The most daring imagination, he believes, cannot evoke "the dark greatness" of those ruins. In the twelfth century, this "world of ruins" was a maze of rubble and heroic vestiges and a sure haven for criminals and other fugitives; even to the police of the city of Rome this fearful and dangerous area was out of bounds. It was, however, not only suspicious fugitives who lived intimately with the great monuments that stood in ruins. In the Middle Ages, Rome's densely populated area, the *abitato,* as it was called in the sixteenth century, invaded the lower city, the *citta bassa,* and its many remains of great monuments. The mighty vaults were exploited for housing, storing, and shops. People literally lived in, and with, ruins.[5]

At the same time, however, mainly in the twelfth century, the *Mirabilia urbis Romae,* the best known guide book to the city of Rome and its "marvels," was written, and soon also illustrated. In the *Mirabilia,* the areas and buildings that we know to have lain in ruins at the time, such as the Capitol and the

Colosseum, are described as if they were perfect edifices untouched by time and destruction. Nothing in the literary descriptions or the visual images reminds us of dereliction. Were we to rely only on these descriptions and images, we could not suspect that at the time the *Mirabilia* was composed these majestic sites were already fields of ruined stones.

The absence of ruins from medieval art is all the more remarkable as the culture of the Middle Ages inherited the vision of ruins (though in a particular context) from as authoritative a source as the Bible. The Lord has "brought to ruin" (Isaiah 23:13) the palaces and towers of the Assyrians. "Thou hast made a city an heap; of a defenced city a ruin …" (25:2).[6] Ezekiel sees in his vision: "Upon his ruin shall all the fowls of the heaven remain …" (31:13).[7]

In the New Testament this tradition of expressive imagery continues. Quoting "the prophets," the author of the Acts of the Apostles imagines (15:16) the redemption: "After this I will return, and will build again the tabernacle of David, which is fallen down; and I will build again the ruins thereof.…"

3

In the present essay I shall not try to explain this strange fact, the absence of ruins in medieval art. An understanding of this absence involves, I believe, an insight into some important aspects of medieval culture as a whole. To propose an explanation of our problem, and to support it with the analysis it demands, would require a separate study, and I hope in the future to come back to it. Here I only wish to describe the major stages by which the image of the ruin emerged in medieval art, and to analyze the specific context and meanings in which this process took place. It will be obvious, I hope, that the image of the ruin did not crystallize as a result of looking at the reality surrounding the medieval artist, but was rather created to express in visual terms an abstract concept: specifically, what was conceived as the central process of human history.

The first stage is probably the most problematic one for the student of the visual arts. Though medieval art, as we have said, does not offer a proper portrayal of ruins, we find in it many images of cities destroyed and walls demolished, a theme that is close to the ruin in character. Such representations, though not restricted to one subject, are found mainly in the illuminated manuscripts of the Apocalypse, particularly in the illuminations to Revelations 14:8, 18:1–3, and 18:20. The very fact that these images somehow became linked to the Apocalypse places them in an ominous context and probably determines the mood that they express. We shall consider a few of them, asking what the pictorial formulas are for representing the destruction that is their content. We shall also ask whether or not a more or less clear line of development can be detected in these formulas.

The earliest stage of medieval representation of destruction is represented here by examples from two well-known manuscripts: a page from the Bamberg Apocalypse (Fig. 12.1), and a page from the Beatus manuscript in the Morgan Library in New York (Fig.12.2). In both of them, though they were made in different countries (the first in Germany, the other in Spain), the formulas of destruction, of buildings or city walls tumbling down, are almost identical.

The Bamberg Apocalypse, done in 1001–1002 in the famous scriptorium at Reichenau, represents a peak of the concise, compressed depiction characteristic of the Ottonian style. One of the illuminations (Fig. 12.1)[8] illustrates Revelations 18:20.

The text of the verse reads: "Rejoice over her, thou heaven, and ye holy apostles and prophets: for God hath avenged you on her." In our context the crucial word is "avenged." How is God's vengeance shown? The emotional character of the scene, as the artist wished to render it, is best expressed by the figures on the right, perhaps the inhabitants of the city of Babylon. They perform familiar gestures from scenes of lamentation and despair; pulling at their hair, clutching their cheeks, and perhaps covering their eyes to avoid seeing the images of destruction. But what precisely is it that they see? What is specifically shown is the process of the city walls falling apart. This frightening event is made visible by using a firmly cast, definite formula: the frontal part of the city wall (the one closest to the spectator) is placed upside down, the big watch

Fig. 12.1 Bamberg Apocalypse, Bamberg, Staatliche Bibliothek, Msc. Bibl. 140, fol. 45r.

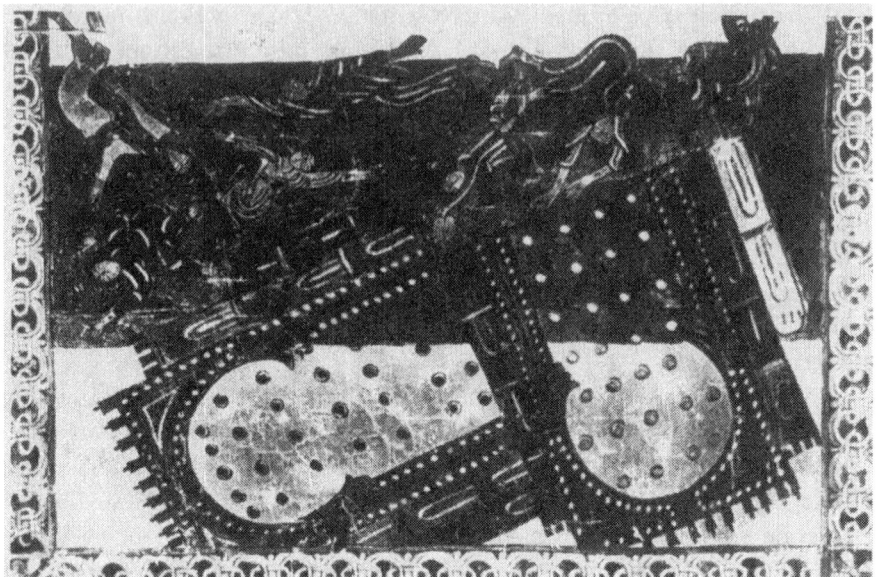

Fig. 12.2 Beatus Manuscript, Morgan Library, Ms. 6434, fol. 176v.

tower in the middle of that wall pointing downwards, and three huge blocks indicate the power of destruction. Note, however, that neither the city wall nor the tower is disintegrating; they are not even cracked. The destruction is shown mainly by the relationship between this tower and the adjoining parts of the wall, and the rest of the city. Destruction is the upsetting of the overall order.

Our next example, the Morgan Beatus, an earlier manuscript, was written and illuminated Spain in the early tenth century. The illumination I have selected (Fig. 12.2)[9] illustrates Revelations 14:8: "And there followed another angel, saying: Babylon is fallen, is fallen, that great city, because she made all nations drink of the wine of the wrath of her fornication." The city of Babylon is represented by an abbreviated urban image, two mighty towers with crenellations, and huge gates within them. In our context, the student's attention is caught mainly by two features, the shape of the towers and gates, and their place in space. The horseshoe line of the gates clearly reflects forms actually employed in oriental or Moorish architecture. In the tenth century such gate-forms could be seen on European soil mainly in Spain. By carefully drawing these shapes, the artist shows his keen observation of reality and his awareness of formal configuration. The decoration of the towers, mainly the narrow crenellations (so fragile that they look like ornamentation rather than parts of an architectural structure), and the dotted lines (recalling small-scale precious objects) also have an Islamic flavor. All this suggests the artist's meticulous observation of how an object looks in reality, and his wish to represent it faithfully.

The other feature that attracts our attention, however, is opposed to the first one. While in the depiction of architectural shapes and wall decorations the artist intended to follow what could actually be seen, the representation of the events of "falling," and the image of the "fallen" city, disregard regular experience and are altogether conceptual in character. The fallen gates and towers are complete in themselves, altogether unharmed; we can say that they are "perfect," to use Thomas's term. The act of crashing down has not left any traces. Nothing in the gates and towers is broken or even merely cracked; the crenellations that seem so slender and fragile have miraculously survived the fall and remain intact. That Babylon is "fallen," we learn here only from the angle of the towers—they are not in their normal upright position; instead, one tower is diagonal to the frame of the page, and the other is almost completely upside down. They are furthermore detached from each other, and placed in such a way that they partly overlap. The destruction of the city, then, is not understood as the decay or disintegration of the material substance, but as the sudden upsetting of the overall order that welds individual walls, towers, and gates into the structure of a city. The breaking up of the whole structure into its individual parts (which remain complete in themselves) is the pictorial formula for destruction.

In summarizing the general meaning of the ruin, particularly as it emerges from the images produced in medieval art, we perceive the destruction of buildings as a visual formula for just punishment, the wages of sin. In the literature of the period we occasionally find testimony to the fact that what we now understand by "ruin," the disintegration of a building, especially a once monumental structure, was perceived not so much as an illustration of the punishment of sin, or as an expression of the general sense of transience, but rather as a testimony to the greatness of the past. This partial transformation of perceptions took place mainly during, and in the wake of, what we call the Renaissance of the twelfth century, when the idea of experiencing past greatness in front of a decayed building was first expressed in medieval literature. To be sure, medieval thought, in both its literary and visual expressions, never altogether abandoned a didactic attitude or even melancholic contemplation when considering partly destroyed buildings of a distant past, particularly when they were the ruins of monumental pagan edifices. Yet an attentive reader cannot fail to notice that, at least in some important texts composed in the twelfth and early thirteenth centuries, the documentary value of the crumbling building receives more attention than before, and sometimes even becomes the central issue of the description. Instead of being a mere formula of preaching, it is transformed into the revelation of a historical event of long-lasting effect. It will be enough for us to mention the famous poems on Rome that Hildebert of Lavardin composed early in the twelfth century. What he sees in the ruins of Rome is not so much the destruction—that is, the wages of (pagan) sinfulness—but the original grandeur to which the remains of the buildings attest.[10]

4

In the late Middle Ages, beginning with the fourteenth century, the ruin appears in a new iconographic context. This change in meaning also involved a more complex configuration as a pictorial motif. I should like to illustrate this new stage with a visual example, an illumination of a manuscript produced in Paris in the early fourteenth century, in the workshop of Jean Pucelle. Part of the so-called Belleville Breviary, it is now kept in the Bibliothèque national de France in Paris (Fig. 12.3).[11]

We do not know much about the life of Jean Pucelle, except that he was well established in Paris between 1319 and 1324. His position in the history of early fourteenth-century imagery, however, is assured.[12] Pucelle, a great "Italianist" in Parisian manuscript illumination, had broad European horizons. In addition to introducing into his workshop the motifs and principles of early Trecento painting, he also borrowed, and brought to full effect, important features of manuscript illumination from English scriptoria. Of particular importance, also for our present subject, is the historiated bas-de-page, a feature found in English psalters of the late thirteenth century. In this context it is worth noting that two of his major authenticated manuscripts were written by English scribes.[13]

In the so-called Belleville Breviary, written and probably also illuminated between 1323 and 1326, the important development of the bas-de-page that may be linked to Jean Pucelle's work can be clearly observed. In this work the bas-des-pages no longer display mere drolleries, the fanciful and sometimes

Fig. 12.3 Belleville Breviary, Bibliothèque national de France (Paris), Ms. Lat. 10483–4.

rather coarse humorous scenes in earlier illuminated manuscripts by this artist and other, but rather show, to use Panofsky's formulation, "elements of a serious and continuous narrative." It was, however, not only continuous narrative that was introduced here, but also the symbols of elevated moralistic and theological meanings. Thus in the Psalter section of the Breviary we see the representation of the seven sacraments, flanked by illustrations of the Deadly Sins on the left side and the Christian virtues on the right.

The bas-des-pages illuminations of the Belleville Breviary's Calendar section take up a central theological theme that also exercised the imagination of earlier medieval artists. It is the complex, dialectical relationship between the Old and the New Testaments. As is well known, medieval artists searched for visual configurations to express this relationship. Perhaps the most prominent, found in statues and stained glass windows, is the image of the apostles of the New Testament standing on the shoulders of the Old Testament prophets. In our specific context we should stress that, whatever the individual artistic motifs employed, in none of them did the ruins of buildings play any part. If I am not mistaken, it was the original contribution of Jean Pucelle—made, we remember, in the early fourteenth century—to use the image of a ruined building as a visual emblem to express this ambiguous theological relationship.

Between the Calendar and the Psalter of the Belleville Breviary, several miniatures described in the explanatory text are missing. Some of them depicted the demolition of a building representing a synagogue. In its present condition, the Calendar comprises only the months of November and December. The bas-de-page of the month of December is especially revealing. Here (Fig. 12.3) we see an Old Testament prophet ripping out a stone of the fabric of the synagogue (standing for the Old Testament, or the Old Law), and passing it on to the apostle so that it may serve as building material for the Church. The apostle, however, does not build a material building. The Church is a spiritual structure.

The student familiar with the medieval rendering of destroyed cities and shattered buildings and their meaning cannot help being surprised by what he sees in this illumination. I should like to stress here two points, the formal pattern of the ruin and its spiritual connotation. First, the edifice of the synagogue from which the prophet is pulling out the stone takes on a new appearance. It does not look like a mighty edifice suddenly destroyed, as if struck by lightning; instead the destruction of the synagogue building is perceived as an extended, continuous process by which the building undergoes slow decay. The gradual disintegration of the structure is the condition for the articulation of the image of the ruin. The other point I should like to stress is that the new building that is to be erected is not shown. While the one composing element in the image of the ruin, the past, is convincingly presented to the spectator's eye, the other element, the indication of the future, is not shown at all. In Jean Pucelle's illumination, the Church, instead of erecting a new building, is pulling away the veil from the synagogue with one hand and holding what seems to be a book in the other. Only one dimension of time, the past, is rendered here; the other, the future, is understood by the initiated. However, no pictorial formula was available to the illuminator to represent the transition into the future.

5

The ruin appeared as a fully developed pictorial motif only in the Renaissance. Several historical conditions and intellectual trends that may have assisted the emergence of the ruin motif have occasionally been mentioned. The interest in ancient monuments that was so significant in some circles at the time comes to mind; one may also recall the "realistic" trends in Quattrocento painting that could have led artists to portray the ruins they actually saw. However, it should be emphasized that the theological connotation of the transition from the Old to the New Testament remained the major context for ruin representation and provided the iconographic frame for the full articulation of the modern image of the ruin.

In the art of the fifteenth century the ruin is particularly frequently represented in one specific scene, that of the Nativity. So common is the rendering of the motif in this particular scene—at least in certain regions and some, rather important, artistic traditions—that one can hardly imagine a Nativity without a mighty ruin. In the present essay we lack space to discuss the iconography of the Nativity—a central theme in Christian art—but it may be possible to make some brief observations on the theme, as seen from the point of view of the creation of historical emblems.

The Nativity, it goes without saying, was represented at all stages of Christianity and in all parts of the Christian world. It was only in Western art, however, that ruins were included, and prominently presented, in depictions of the Nativity. Thus in Byzantine art, and in the art of the areas dominated by Byzantine influences, the many representations of the Nativity do not include ruins. Often the event takes place in a cave, or in some other natural environment.[14]

In the art of the West during this period, as is well known, the Nativity is usually rendered not in natural surroundings, but in some man-made structure. Yet even here, as we see in early Flemish art, for instance, it is in a dilapidated shack that the birth of Christ takes place. Such wooden huts, though decaying, cannot be considered as ruins. It is essentially only in the last decades of the fifteenth century that the proper architectural ruin, the vestige of a mighty building, becomes part and parcel of the Nativity scene in art.

As illustrations we shall briefly consider two works by van der Weyden and Dürer, examining them for what they may disclose about our subject. My first example is the central panel of Roger van der Weyden's so-called "Columban"

Altarpiece (Fig. 12.4), now in Munich. Painted around 1458 or 1459, the altar represents the Adoration of the Magi. Rogier still retains something of the image of the wooden hut; the customary holes in the roof are visible through the roof-covering, some kind of straw. Yet the whole scene takes place in a fantastic architectural location, framed by two Antique arches in a state of decay—an image of ruins as we now know them. The composition of the painting offers no clue as to why these ruins are there at all; the other buildings, to the right of the arch and in the background, are quite intact. Clearly, the ruined arches are presented as emblems.

Of particular interest in our context is the arch to the right, behind the group of the Magi. This impressive architectural fragment represents not only a venerable decayed monument, an ancient arch, but also shows that the decay was an extended process: where the arch is broken, it is overgrown with vegetation. The vegetation slowly invading the remains of a mighty building manifests the gradual demolition of the structure, and thus indicates the long passage of time that turns it into a ruin. This arch in Rogier's painting is remarkable for yet another reason. On top of the ruined, yet still powerful arch,

Fig. 12.4 Rogier van des Weyden, *Die Anbetung der Könige* (Adoration of the Magi) St. Columba Altarpiece. Bayerische Staatsgemäldesammlungen, Alte Pinakothek, Munich.

a little tree is growing, spreading its branches to the sky. The other arch, to the left of the group, also bears a tree, perhaps shaken by a storm.

We should keep in mind that vegetation in general, and trees—either altogether isolated or growing on unlikely ground, in particular—were an old symbol of rebirth.[15] The juxtaposition of a ruin, the remains of a once great building that is now in a state of decay, and of abundant vegetation, particularly the unlikely sight of a tree growing on top of an arch, manifests to the eye what was conceived as the essence of history. It illustrates quite vividly the historical meaning of the Nativity: the decline of the old and the beginning of the new age.

I should like to conclude this brief survey of a complex theme with its appearance in the work of Albrecht Dürer. Dürer seems to have been particularly attracted to this subject in rendering the Nativity scene or the Adoration of the Magi. On several occasions, in paintings as well as in graphic works, he developed and fully articulated the juxtaposition, or combination, of the two emblematic motifs of the architectural ruin and sprouting vegetation. It will suffice here to look at one of his early paintings, the central panel of the so called Paumgärtner Altarpiece, now in Munich, painted roughly around 1500 (Fig. 12.5).[16]

Concentrating only on our motif, we notice the mighty arch, obviously constructed of huge stone slabs; above it, in the upper part of the painting, the crumbling remains of a brick wall are seen, and from that wall luxuriant vegetation and small trees spreading their branches emerge. In other works, especially in engravings and woodcuts, Dürer presented several variations on this motif. The crumbling yet mighty architectural ruin, it should again be stressed, appears only in his scenes of the Nativity or the Adoration of the Magi. That half-decayed arch, partly covered with sprouting vegetation, is not seen in the representation of any other subject.

The appearance of a mighty ruin in depictions of the Nativity seems to have been derived neither from literary, nor probably from oral, traditions. Medieval narrations of the birth of Christ, as we know, are frequently adorned with a great many narrative and descriptive details, including details about the place where Christ was born. From these we learn, for example, that the birth took place in a "passage between two houses," and that the roof of that passage was leaking.[17] However, in none of these descriptions, is an architectural ruin or arch ever mentioned. Nothing, then, in these stories prepares the reader for the majestic arch that even now, though in ruins, still documents the greatness of the building in the past. The awe-inspiring ruin in the representations of the Nativity is the artist's invention to express the idea that the greatness of the Old Testament is now destroyed and overgrown by thriving vegetation, a manifestation of new life. The Christian faith, overcoming the Old Law, is the conceptual framework for the emergence of the pictorial motif of the ruin. The ruin as a pictorial motif was born as a visual form of expressing historical meaning.

Fig. 12.5 Albrecht Dürer, Paumgärtner Altarpiece, Bayerische Staatsgemäldesammlungen, Alte Pinakothek, Munich.

Notes

1. Marie Gothein, *Geschichte der Gartenkunst,* 2 vols. (Jena 1926), vol. 2, 382.

2. See for example Aleida Assmann, Monika Gomille, and Gabriele Rippl, eds., *Ruinenbilder* (Munich 2002); Sabine Forero-Medoza, *Temps des ruins: Le gout des ruines et les formes de la conscience historique à la Renaissance* (Seyssel 2002).

3. For an interesting philosophical contemplation of the ruin, see Georg Simmel's essay "Die Ruine," in idem, *Philosophische Kultur: Gesammelte Essays,* 2nd ed. (Leipzig 1919), 125–133.

4. Ferdinand Gregorovius, *Rom im Mittelalter,* 8 vols. (Munich n.d. [1921]), vol. 2, 72ff.

5. Richard Krautheimer offers a great deal of information in his *Rome: Profile of a City*, 312–1308 (Princeton 1980), chapter 10, esp. 243ff.

6. The *Vulgata*, the Latin translation of the Bible canonical in the Middle Ages, here employs the term *ruina*. Thus the first quotation ends "suffoderunt domos eius, posueram eam in ruinas." The latter quotation reads: "quia posuisti civitatem in tumulum, urbem fortem in ruinam,... In ruina eius habitaverunt omnia volatilia caeli, et in ramis eius fuerunt universae bestiae regionis."

7. Here the Latin translator did not use the term *"ruina,"* yet it is obvious that this is what he meant.

8. Bamberg, Staatliche Bibliothek, Ms. A II 42, folio 45 r.

9. Morgan Library, Ms. 6434, fol. 176 verso. Best reproduced in John Williams, *A Spanish Apocalypse: The Morgan Beatus Manuscript* (New York 1991).

10. Peter von Moos, *Hildebert von Lavardin: 1056–1133* (Stuttgart 1965), 241ff.

11. Paris, Bibl. Nat., Ms. Lat. 10483–4.

12. Kathleen Morand, *Jean Pucelle* (Oxford 1962), seems to be the only monographic study of the artist. But see also Erwin Panofsky, *Early Netherlandish Painting: Its Origins and Character* (Cambridge, Mass. 1953), 29ff. The old study by G. Vitzthtum von Eckstadt, *Die Pariser Miniaturmalerei von der Zeit des Hl. Ludwig bis zu Philipp von Valois und ihr Verhältnis zur Malerei in Nordwesteuropa* (Leipzig 1907), is still instructive.

13. Panofsky, *Early Netherlandish Painting*, 11; Morand, *Jean Pucelle*, especially 3ff. The English influence was already emphasized by von Eckstadt.

14. For a good survey of later "Eastern" representations, see Gabriel Millet, *Recherches sur l'iconographie de l'Evangile aux XIVe, XVe et XVIe siecles*, 2nd ed. (Paris 1960), 93–169.

15. Panofsky, *Early Netherlandish Painting*, 286ff.

16. Georg Ladner, "Vegetation Symbolism and the Concept of Renaissance," originally published in M. Meiss, *De artibus opuscula XL: Essays in Honor of Erwin Panofsky* (New York 1961), 302–322, and reprinted in Georg Ladner, *Images and Ideas in the Middle Ages*, 3 vols. (Rome 1983), vol. 2, 727–763.

17. Views concerning the precise date of the this work vary. While the traditional date, long accepted, is as early as 1498, more recent scholarship places it as late as 1504. For our present purpose, the precise date is of no great importance. For the passage, see Th. Graesse, ed., *Jacobi a Voragine: Legenda aurea* (Dresden 1846), 41.

CHAPTER 13

Three Versions of Wallenstein
Differences of Meaning Production between Historiography, Biography, and Novel

Eberhard Lämmert

Our schoolteachers have handed down to us an image of Wallenstein as one of the most fascinating personages of the Thirty Years' War, and even if one knows little more than that he was of Bohemian origin and an imperial generalissimo for a while, this apparently suffices to remind us that treason was also involved. Dozens of dramatic plays, the first of which was even published during his lifetime, and the ambitions of historians, extending into this century, to confront the reliable with the unreliable sources, have in our collective memory firmly associated the notion of "treason" with his name. Treason—carrying a double connotation, i.e., of Judas in religious and of Ephialtes in humanistic terms—is regarded by our cultural tradition as a most heinous crime, the historical valence of Wallenstein, whether in scientific literature or belles lettres, so crucially depends on whether his multilateral negotiating tactics and military wavering are attributed to treacherous motives or more noble intentions. In the latter case, however—which is characteristic of an enduring deposit in our collective memory—the efforts of authors to remove the accusation of treason from Wallenstein's action, or non-action, discernible owing to either circuitous or the passionate pleading of the arguments, respectively. That the issue of treason involved in our dealing with this historical figure would ever assume such importance can in part be explained by denominational divisions in Germany, which have continued into the twentieth-century. It is therefore symptomatic that, as these differences have diminished in recent times, so the heat of the controversy has also cooled.

Notes for this section begin on page 237.

In the present case study, we have to take into account the bequest, or maybe burden, of this collective memory, as we examine three texts and ask how the meaning-producing features, as presented in a scientific, portraying, and literary text, respectively, are developed. The episode that occurred late in the fall of 1631, which above all else raised the question of potentially treasonous behavior on the part of Wallenstein, takes up about ten to fifteen pages in each of the three voluminous books studied here. On 1 November, Hans Georg von Arnim, a marshal in service with Saxony and allied with the Swedish king, invaded Bohemia after the imperial troops had unexpectedly withdrawn from Lusatia. Wallenstein, who had been relieved of his duties as imperial general at the Imperial Diet of Regensburg two years previously, had just agreed, after much pleading by the Emperor Ferdinand, to take over the supreme command of the imperial troops again, but was still negotiating the conditions. He suddenly withdrew from Prague to his Bohemian estates. Soon after, on 15 November, Arnim took Prague—without meeting any resistance. Eventually, after several delays, a carefully prepared meeting took place on 30 November between Wallenstein and Arnim in the Bohemian town of Kaunitz. What was discussed at that meeting, and whether Wallenstein had previously directly asked Arnim to invade Bohemia from Saxony and occupy Prague, which had been evacuated without a battle, is at the heart of this much debated controversy and of considerable import to the assessment of Wallenstein's subsequent actions.

Three accounts of this event will be examined below, in terms of the views they convey, as well as of the means employed in presenting their evaluations. The first work, by Josef Pekař, is *Wallenstein, 1630–1634: Tragödie einer Verschwörung*. The life's work of a Prague historian, it was first published in 1895 and again, in 1934, in thoroughly revised form in Pekař's native Czech. In 1937, the 1934 edition was translated into German under the author's supervision. The second work is *Wallenstein: Sein Leben erzählt*, by Golo Mann—a biographical account published by the sexagenarian author in 1971. The third work, *Wallenstein*, was written by Alfred Döblin, then thirty years old. Conceived during the First World War, the book came out in 1920 and was republished in 1965 by Walter Muschg.

Pekař's book turned out so voluminous because it was designed "to present to the reader all the data allowing him to make up his own mind." This recalls a virtue warmly recommended by Johann Christoph Gatterer to his colleagues when the new world history began to be written, a virtue that Rousseau had already propagated, in turn praising Thucydides for it. For Pekař's work this means that Wallenstein is hardly mentioned, except in the epilogue and even there only briefly, and that the book is mainly about the contemporary sources. And a large part of this endeavor goes, in turn, toward a careful checking of the credibility of the sources cited.

Pekař's work primarily involves two sources, namely two sizable accounts of Bohemian emigrants, one by Anton Schlief, a colonel in service with Saxony, and the other by Jaroslov Sina Rašin, in service with Sweden. Both men had been called upon to report to a commission established by the Viennese imperial court after 1634 to examine—and vindicate—Wallenstein's murder. A characteristic of Pekař's approach to these sources is that he always begins by asking a question of these sources, then compares the data of the reports and checks their consistency, and finally arrives at a judgement that does not by any means always result in a statement of facts totally free of doubt. Following are some illustrative examples.

Pekař wonders about the motive that might have driven Wallenstein to ask Arnim to occupy Prague after his incursion into Bohemia. "Should it have been necessary to further heighten the deeply felt anxiety of the court in the wake of the Saxons' invasion of the kingdom so as to make even more apparent the humiliation, showing the world what had happened to Vienna when it dispensed with Wallenstein's leadership? The duke made sure it did—at a time when he let it transpire that he was willing to save the situation by taking over the generalship. Supposedly, it was he himself who encouraged Arnim to enter Prague."[1] Pekař had the last part of the sentence printed widely spaced to emphasize that this is the object of his study of the historical sources.

There can be no doubt that after his victory over Tilly at Breitenfeld, the Swedish king offered troops to Wallenstein, affording him an opportunity to become king of Bohemia with the support of the Bohemian emigrants. It is also common knowledge that Wallenstein took over the imperial high command for a second time only on condition that he would be completely free to decide on the recruitment and deployment of his troops. Pekař studies the subsequent reports of Schlief and Rašin that Arnim had only wanted to secure winter quarters in Bohemia and would never have entered Prague, "if the Fridtländer had not called and informed him that he could take the city without losing even one man," as Schlief writes.[2] Rašin also states before the commission that Wallenstein "has offered to the Swedish king and Arnim to take Prague."[3] In Pekař's view, these statements confirm his previous conclusions, drawn after a careful review of the correspondence between Arnim and his elector, that "Arnim did not initially think of Prague. He dared take this crucial step only after learning that Prague was defenseless, after receiving the almost incredible news that the imperial occupation troops had evacuated the capital and residency of the kingdom."[4] Here Pekař adds a note, quoting from the report of the Swedish governor in Dresden, Laurens Nicolai, that Arnim himself had hinted that his forces would not have been sufficient for a military conquest of Prague.[5]

After detailed analysis of what each of these witnesses could have known from firsthand experience as well as of any interests that might have been involved in each of the statements, Pekař finally concludes that Schlief's assertion that Wallenstein asked Arnim via an ominous note to invade Bohemia is to be dismissed, but that his and Rašin's claim that Wallenstein enticed von

Arnim to enter Prague has been substantiated to the extent "that among the emigrants it has been explained and believed that without Wallenstein's persuasion Arnim would not have dared attack Prague."[6] Later, however, Pekař bluntly accuses the same Rašin of lying because he relates other agreements between Wallenstein and Arnim in greatly changed order.[7]

Pekař proceeds in a similar way to identify the content of a dialogue between Arnim and Wallenstein at Kaunitz. Again he begins by "presenting to us ... the picture presented by those two persons considered crucial by us."[8] Then follows his conclusion: "We may accept as undoubted fact that at Kaunitz the duke confirmed that he would stick to his revolutionary plans and that perhaps, as Arnim claims, he also said he would arrange everything so as to make the Emperor and his entire court painfully aware that he had offended a cavalier."[9] Some of these statements, including the plan to negotiate peace with the Saxons, are deemed by Pekař, the historiographer, to be a pretext needed by Wallenstein for a political justification acceptable to both sides. Arnim, by contrast, is held to have genuinely tried to work out a peace agreement at Kaunitz, driven by the fear that "the German empire should not fall victim to foreign nations, in concrete terms: the Swedes and the French."[10]

Pekař concludes his investigation with a telling statement: "What we have here, as one can see, is merely the guesswork of a scientific investigator attempting to find the only passable way out of a labyrinth."[11] To emphasize that his weighing of carefully accounts method is the only scientifically appropriate one, Pekař, after scrutinizing a corpus of sources, never fails to critically review more recent research on the subject, usually expressing dissent.

Pekař's *Wallenstein* seems a typical, even superb scholarly work of the historical school, one might be inclined to judge. The investigative presentation, which Droysen likened to that of a criminal case, takes up much space compared to the narration, and the motives thus identified as guiding the action of Wallenstein and his comrades are presented in thetic rather than narrative form. Another characteristic of Pekař's account is that it relies on a rich selection of modal auxiliaries and qualifying adverbs such as "should," "assumes to know," "possibly," etcetera, which he employs to define the varying degrees of certainty reached.

The reader is therefore all the more surprised at the lapidary judgements Pekař makes in his brief epilogue. It begins thus: "What have we found? A weakling prostrated by physical ailment, confused by superstition, and driven by titanic schemes of revenge and megalomania, a timid traitor and foolish intrigant."[12] He notes some glaring contradictions reflecting both merciless insatiability and a mystical yearning for peace. Ultimately, however, everything is subsumed in Wallenstein's Bohemian sense of mission, which eventually even outweighed his plans for the German empire. Pointedly Pekař adds that "the grand literature on Wallenstein, to the extent that it has been written by German scholars," has "hardly or not at all understood the Bohemian option."[13]

His own investigations would "present the history of Wallenstein as a reflection of the political rivalry between the German, though ultimately Saxon, and the Bohemian approach to the future, a struggle between German and Bohemian ideas on the reshaping of Europe."[14] It should not be forgotten that in the subtitle of his book Pekař announces the *Tragödie einer Verschwörung* (tragedy of a conspiracy). By listing a number of indicative assumptions not free from pathos, he affirms this unequivocally, not in the 700 pages of his study but in this brief epilogue: that a chapter of the Bohemian tragedy that required conspiracies with Sweden, Saxony, and the emigrants was due for analysis. "The Friedland conspiracy thus becomes part of the national history," and "behind the personal conflict of the Friedländer looms a greater, more powerful drama, the tragedy of a people struck on its head...."[15]

Although there is no direct contradiction between the scholarly study and the final confession of the historian, they are in strange contrast in view of the unequivocal tone of the statement. It may be that this epilogue was the result of a lecture given by the author, but more significant in my opinion is the aspect that, retroactively, the scholarly study was to be fitted with an overarching meaning construction, even though the concrete interpretation of various sources had shown that, by the standards of traditional source criticism, many of the details were merely suppositional.

What does Pekař's epilogue do, though, to give a meaning to his overall work? By placing it within a general and persistent struggle between German and Bohemian conceptions of Europe, it does something not at all explicitly mentioned in the previous 700 pages of his text: it now refers to something different and greater than what the reader has been offered so far. By presenting the story of Wallenstein as he has conceived of it, i.e., as a paradigm of the "Bohemian tragedy," Pekař transforms the text, replete with ample proofs of the truth, into an allegorism of a centuries-old Bohemian "destiny" that can be recognized in such tragedies.

The attempt at constructing a meaning consists here in the transfer of established facts relating to the years 1630 to 1634 to another, more general level where Wallenstein is not the only, or even the most important, subject. To convey this meaning, everything said so far will, when viewed in the new light, necessarily lose its unique character; now it will need to be conceived of as recurrent in its essential aspects, for only then can it be completely meaningful to the contemporary reader around 1937 and after.

In his study entitled *Wallenstein und seine Anhänger am Wiener Hof zur Zeit des Zweiten Generalats 1631 bis 1634,* the Finnish historian Pekka Suvanto has probed Pekař's data again and found unwarranted enlargements as well as abbreviations in the reproduction of the sources, generally lending support to Wallenstein's anti-imperial plans.[16] To be sure, Pekař deserves full marks for the care with which he examines his sources—note, for example, how Heinz Rieder, in his book on Wallenstein thirty years on, accepts the statements of

Schlief and Rašin verbatim as factual accounts: projecting that "Bohemian tragedy," resulting in the Thirty Years' War, onto a new, possibly imminent one in 1937 contributed in some way toward the dramatic composition of these exemplary, source-critical investigations. At the same time, though—and this is how the disagreement between the work's main part and the epilogue should be seen—the passion for the study of sources, considered the hallmark of historical scholarship since the nineteenth-century, has imposed on the author and the main body of his work a diction in which rhetoric reflecting the processing of evidence and justification has largely been substituted for narration.

How is the same event presented by a historian who indicates even in the subtitle of his work that he wants to recount a life? Golo Mann entitles the chapter in question "Höchste Verwirrung" (The Biggest Confusion), but begins with a very unambiguous quotation from a letter by Wallenstein to Arnim in December 1631: "For finally, when most countries are reduced to ashes, peace will need to be made, as these examples of war that has continued these 14 years have amply demonstrated." Golo Mann continues lapidarily: "That was his mood and his will. He spoke to the point, instead of making pompous speeches like most of the others, which did not help. He had profited enough from war, now he was tired, increasingly plagued by gout; he wished peace for himself and the others. He could not escape on his own. There had to be peace so that he would have peace."[17]

By opening the chapter with a visionary statement contained in a later letter by Wallenstein together with commentary reflecting Wallenstein's personal view, Golo Mann turns Wallenstein's desire for peace, which Pekař had several times interpreted as a tactical move to engineer the Kaunitz meeting, into the main if not the only motive for seeking and holding this conversation. As for his gout, Wallenstein did actually make his visitor at Kaunitz wait an entire day, claiming indisposition. What is interesting is that Golo Mann not only presents Wallenstein's intentions as they are stated later by Wallenstein himself in his letter, but also confirms them by using a form of narrative that blurs any distance between the author and his protagonist: By way of "interior monologue," the narrator Golo Mann lets his own judgement become an idea of Wallenstein's. This manner of speech, better known by the French term *style indirect libre,* or passive medium, is employed by the narrator to let his hero, in the third person, reflect in the narrative preterite tense so that the reader can no longer distinguish between the thoughts of Wallenstein and their rendering by the narrator. This is one of the subtlest devices of modern narrative art, suggesting to the reader an emotional empathy, and thus identification, with the protagonist. Moreover, the narrator, by endowing only one of the figures of his text with such "thinking speech," places this figure in command of the historical setting, as the successful example of Conrad Ferdinand Meyer's *Jürg Jenatsch* shows.

Taking a whole page, Golo Mann then reflects on the need for a general peace treaty, repeating Wallenstein's reproaches to the emperor that he had not contemplated such a peace treaty even before the Swedish invasion, and suddenly concludes: "Thus, his anger was not about his dismissal of 1630, which the Spanish had tried to prevent, but about the politics of the House of Habsburg."[18] This refers especially to Ferdinand's papally inclined advisers. Two pages later, after an account of the Emperor Ferdinand's desperate attempts to persuade Wallenstein, a rhetorical question is posed: "Did Wallenstein want satisfaction for the humiliation suffered at Regensburg, a legend anyhow: could he want for something even more pathetic?"[19] The Prince of Peace thus enthroned could not possibly have wanted such a thing: such is the reading of this pejorative mode of the narrator.

All compositional forms of this text suggest that in this chapter, Wallenstein will be elevated to becoming Prince of Peace, a sage focused on his own peace of mind and the peace of the world, preparing to have the appropriate political instruments ready for the purpose. Accordingly, Wallenstein, even on the same page, has to show surprise at Arnim's invasion of Bohemia, just like all the other parties involved, for Arnim's action is now presented as his "very own decision."[20] Previously, Golo Mann presented Arnim as "this pious intrigant, Germanic in his attitude, anxious to secure the independence of the German Protestants, possibly the nation."[21] Thus, two more or less noble-minded characters seek a dialogue at Kaunitz: Wallenstein, the angel of peace, and von Arnim, the guardian of the nation's honor. Anything that might interfere with this picture, such as the persistent rumor of a note sent by Wallenstein to Arnim prior to the invasion of Bohemia, is presented as "pure invention";[22] von Arnim would have been "foolish" if he "could have had Prague so cheaply and had not taken it."[23]

Why, though, did Wallenstein leave the city beforehand? Mann's answer is as laconic as it is characteristic of the personalization of history: Wallenstein "did not feel in any way inclined to find himself in Prague face to face with his former employee, having been defeated, and made a prisoner of war, however chivalrous the ceremony might have been. Hence his retreat ... and he hardly enjoyed exchanging his comfortable domestic life in Prague for an improvised residence."[24] Again we witness a historically significant step because, according to the narrator's vision of his heroes' characters, two noble personages should not have to measure each other's strength in the wrong place.

As if to dig a moat to protect his own interpretation, which is reflected in every sentence, on almost every page, Golo Mann repeats his attacks against "a foolish reading,"[25] for instance, that with this attitude Wallenstein wanted to keep hurting the Emperor Ferdinand, or that his actions had the malevolent purpose "of giving the Saxons a free hand in Bohemia."[26] However, since Golo Mann cannot explain away the sources reflecting the opinions about such behavior, he elevates his protagonist a little further: "Was he like the philosopher's god who is with both combatants at the same time? People seemed to believe that. The Friedländer was responsible for the weather everywhere, the fair and especially the foul; for inscrutable, inscrutably insidious reasons known only unto his own dark soul."[27] We note here, almost 100 years to the day since Conrad Ferdinand Meyer's *Jürg Jenatsch,* that the whole scenario of the narration is all too clearly set for a demonizing elevation of the hero so that ultimately even betrayal, of one side or the other, would barely damage the "lonely one," as he is called on the next page. Accordingly, in conclusion it is said about all accounts of the crucial conversation at Kaunitz that the reporters had to belittle the comprehensive peace proposals for the sake of the Viennese court, but that Arnim had of course understood that Wallenstein was interested in more than just a constructive separate peace with Saxony. Golo Mann notes laconically: "Everything else written on Kaunitz Castle in the books is third or fourth-hand talk, not worthy of further investigation."[28]

Golo Mann's rhetoric favors laconic statements of fact. He has the conception and clear purpose of a narrator. The beginning and end of a particular life are fixed, its significance, climax, and the hero's character are determined accordingly, and the sources may come in useful, or they may not. Pure narration takes the form of a chain of indicative sentences whose credibility is contingent on a cultural norm or trust in the narrator as an individual. This applies to myth, to all stories of creation, and, still, to the embedding of historical events in a general philosophy of history, which is why narration has been declared the very paradigm of ideologizing discourse by the French structuralists and their successors, and has been more carefully termed an allegorical and hence typifying form of reproduction of events past by Anglo-Saxon analysts.[29] What Pekař imposed on his text with hindsight, so to speak—namely, that it also had an allegorical quality—is true of any purely narrative text. For this reason, unlike a chronicle, it cannot dispense with possible meaning constructions, and the direct intervention of the narrator is one means of limiting the narration to fit a specifically intended meaning. In contrast to more modern narrators, Golo Mann makes ample use of this privilege of the auctorial narrator.

Golo Mann's text also demonstrates that narration cannot do without the personalization of historical processes. At the end of his chapter, proof is provided of this when the authors allegorizes of the web of relations among Wallenstein, the Saxons, the Swedish king, and the Bohemian emigrants, as well as Habsburg, as an aerial figuration, so that rather than hiding his view of it, he explains it in terms of an imaginary vision. "Shadowy," concludes the narrator, "as Wallenstein's relations with the enemies of the House of Habsburg had been in ... the late fall of 1631, something remained of them nevertheless. Torn threads in the air. Clouds high above the earth, separate but floating in such proximity that they could have been perceived as one or as many, whatever,... The same is true of the peacemaker's character."[30]

This one sentence in itself refutes the thesis put forward by Golo Mann himself, and which is still widely respected, namely that the historian always "deals with the unique."[31] To be exact, an application of meaning to a strictly unique occurrence would be impossible, unless it came in the form of a miraculous story. Incidentally, this is also an argument against the assertion of an absolute contrast between the ideographic and the nomothetic sciences to which Golo Mann, unlike Hans-Ulrich Wehler, wants to adhere at the end of his self-defense of the narrated Wallenstein.

Golo Mann himself called his Wallenstein biography an "all-too-authentic novel,"[32] using the term novel explicitly with respect to its narrative form. This recalls Victor von Scheffel's defiant stance a good century earlier when he transformed his habilitation thesis into the narrative prose *Ekkehard,* intending to present to its readers a "condensed" picture of the life of "extinct generations of the 10th century"[33] instead of a "literature of scholars for scholars unnoticed by the majority of the nation."[34] As Victor von Scheffel did with his *Ekkehard,* whom he moreover blends from four historically attested abbots bearing this name, so Golo Mann endowed his *Wallenstein* with a historical impulse, a yearning for peace that transcends his time and leads to his eventual undoing. As a result, not only the emperor's advisers but Ferdinand II himself are placed on the shady side of history. Even though recent research is again emphasizing Wallenstein's peace concept, what counts in this book is the composition which seeks to enlist the reader's sympathy with his fate: Wallenstein's perspective is with him to the end, affecting not least his inner life and inspiring it with a telos, a goal that transcends it: the peace of Europe.

What happens to narration, on the other hand, when there is a change or break in perspective is shown by Alfred Döblin's novel *Wallenstein,* written nearly half a century earlier. In this work, too, the episode I have selected begins with a compact characterization of the protagonist in a picturesque setting. One dramaturgic aspect is immediately obvious: the Kaunitz meeting takes place before Wallenstein leaves his Prague residence and the Saxons enter the city. Döblin accomplishes two things by this: the meeting suggests a crucial decision is in the offing, and the entire passage leads up to a climax, the occupation of Prague by Arnim's troops. Thus a mass scene unfolds from an intimate moment, or put differently: the strings held by two players set in motion thousands of soldiers and citizens.

Losing no time, therefore, Döblin immediately presents a stark introductory scene that serves as the pivot of subsequent events: Wallenstein receives his former subordinate in a "heated, heavily carpeted bedroom,"[35] poking about with his cane, restless. His speech is jerky; he gets up close to the other's face but remains in control of events at all moments—with entirely different intentions, though, from those in Golo Mann. Here we see a wire-puller supreme who treats his friends as enemies and his enemies as friends in order to exploit all of them for his own ends. Abruptly, he demands of Arnim that he invade Bohemia so as to provoke a Bohemian rebellion and, with the help of the Swedish king, envelop the emperor; then he secures from him additional guarantees for himself. Arnim, pale-faced and deferential throughout, does not even turn into an opponent. Döblin's entire novel, for reasons of aesthetic economizing, reserves this place for someone else: the luminous figure, increasingly shaped to contrast with the somber figure of Wallenstein as the novel develops, is to be the Emperor Ferdinand II, who is purging himself into becoming an ascetic. As it is he who embodies the true contrast to the hybrid subjectivity of the unscrupulous entrepreneur Wallenstein, the author finally lets him merge voluntarily into the collective of his people, and in this way totally separates him from the historical model.

In a much more pronounced and unconcerned manner than Döblin the analytically inclined or narrating historian, Döblin the army surgeon, even in his preliminary notes of 1917/18, contrasts the contemporary concept of the human individual as a late bourgeois with the expressionist-utopian "new human individual" who renounces all power, wishing to live anonymously as an equal among others. But in Döblin, too, an abundance of historical detail remains. In a proliferous "fantasy of facts" he introduces traditional requisites and names wherever they fit, and in this way colors his story even more richly with facts than Pekař, the carefully probing historian, or Golo Mann, who is extremely concerned with inner logic. A multitude of figures and sudden turnabouts in perspective result from this diversity of concrete objects and individual acts. An entire page is taken up by Wallenstein arranging his retreat from Prague; then, in a small paragraph, we are told of the capture of Prague by the Saxons, and again the perspective is reversed: "Above the battlements of the gate on the Altstädter bridge, withered human heads were shown stuck on posts and pikes, whose bodies had been severed from them."[36] Mercilessly, the next sentence lists the names of the rebels, executed in 1621, whose heads had lined the Moldau bridge for eighteen years, not omitting the fact that the nests that finches had built in the skulls' cavities were destroyed and the heads then placed, together with the posts, in magnificent coffins. It is stated as unquestioned fact:

"Suddenly the country was free.
The governor fleeing.
Friedland, the main culprit, fleeing.
The citizens ran out of their houses, looked at the Ring, ran to the bridge. It was there as it had always been, the heads were missing. Should one rejoice?"[37]

The next sentence is dominated by "an unlikely figure": "... the whitebearded Count Thurn stood amid a crowd of howling frenzied Bohemians in the flooded Hradcany square."[38] A narrative cascade follows, in which each sentence tells of new places and people, throws open new questions, lets surge "enormous parades that assemble spontaneously in all parts of the town," accompanied by "howling and singing" and the waving of "the old flags": "a tumultuous procession" pushing into the Veitsdom, brandishing hats and weapons, a priest triumphant and wide-eyed with ecstasy, the masses poised to pillage." Döblin continues: "Then Arnim proceeds to occupy a number of deserted houses and castles"—first those belonging to Wallenstein, incidentally—and "looters begin to be shot."[39] Confusion, disappointment, and angry calls for justice and revenge in front of the castle are followed by intimidation, the disarming of citizens, men being taken from the crowd and randomly incarcerated. But the Saxon occupiers remain uneasy: there is unrest among the Bohemians, suggesting a sortie. Thus in the end, the Saxons are "glad when the rowdy crowds began to attack the Jews' town."[40]

With the scenery, the mode of presentation also changes: in momentary impressions, and passages where events are narrated, one sentence at a time is spoken by certain people; the next sentence shifts to another scene, a different perspective. Though there is an abundance of historical names of persons and places, a general description is given nevertheless of a collective ecstasy of liberation, including its reversion to pillage and the latter's suppression by the liberators. And finally, as is typical of such excesses, the occupiers look on indifferently as the people vent their anger on those near them who happen to be weaker.

From the fragments of tradition, Döblin creates a panorama with historical features, and in this way accomplishes something that von Scheffel had already described as a definite advantage over professional historiography: here, the ordinary folks, the actual people of whom the historian, especially one who relies on the sources, is unable to write even one authentic word because practically they do not exist as individuals, fill the scene, as they did in reality, with their deeds and suffering, thus affirming a fate of their own. Only a "fantasy of facts" makes the story appear "as it was" and grants a continuing existence to those denied individual treatment by the historian, who is bound by the written documents before him.

It would be far from the truth, though, to think that Döblin reproduced the seventeenth century in this way! He takes the scene and raises it to a level where it becomes a setting for the type of human mass behavior that can be observed during sudden changes of ruling power. Döblin narrates innumerable details that are not significant in themselves but together place before us a grander picture in which individuals become visible, if only for seconds and in passing, while a great number of violent perpetrators and an even greater number of those suffering from their violence dominate the scene.

Only an abrupt change in perspective and hastily lined up, momentary impressions—and certainly not a persistent interest in one person—can make such mass scenes come alive. This is a mode of presentation that enables Döblin, like Tolstoy and Zola before him and Heinrich Mann shortly after, to narrate stories of mass movements and conflicts between collectives. However, the salient difference from a presentation of particular societal movements, currents, or even accumulated conflict is that this strongly pictorial, multiperspectival mode of presentation also grants to the collective event a semblance of spontaneous self-motion. In 1986, Axel Hecker showed in his well-argued dissertation that the narrator Döblin does "practically not admit any possibility for explicit causal explanations" of the events presented in his Wallenstein; "the occurrences start somewhere and end somewhere. Everything seems to be merely present."[41] In this way, any impression of actions based on overarching laws or factual constraints is avoided, and since no comments are offered, any ostentatious interpretation of the events—such as Pekař sought to give in hindsight and Golo Mann intermittently—is absent from this text, in spite of the introduction of much historical material.

In contrast to Golo Mann's biography, Döblin's *Wallenstein* novel does not tell a story of the Thirty Years' War. The war serves the author, as Adolf Muschg has already noted,[42] merely as material for an aesthetic experiment in "lifeless reality": "rapid sequences, chaos reflected in mere catchwords," and a complete withdrawal on the part of the author from the visible and invisible reality. A preferable term, though, would be "fantasy of facts," the futuristic concept formulated by Döblin as early as 1913.[43] Regarding his plan for *Wallenstein,* he emphasizes that he had only dark schooltime memories of the Thirty Years' War, of "something hopeless and bleak involving many battles." He states that in 1916, in connection with an advertisement in a paper concerning a festival performance in honor of Gustav Adolph to take place in Kissingen, he had a sudden vision of Gustav Adolph crossing the Baltic with a fleet of vessels. "There was a surging all around me, ships sailed across the vast grassy green water; through the trees, I saw them travel on glass, the air was the water. This overwhelming, but totally incoherent image never left me. In spite of my aversion to the chaos of this period, I felt compelled to read some historical books about it. No, better not read, and this is the crucial point, but find out what I actually wanted from these books, and why this image, this dazzling vision of cogs and corvettes crossing the sea, did not leave me. I wanted to let this surging that surrounded me, this never-ending sailing, become language; figures were emerging from it. I 'read' the books, and a vast number of others later, as a flame 'reads' wood. I never came across a 'fact'; like a magnet, my emotions scanned the pages and extracted what fitted. An inclination to breathe life into an inanimate dead mass? Not at all. No dead mass came before my eyes; the Thirty Years' War is still a sealed book to me as it was 20 years ago."[44]

Reading the novel only confirms this. It is a book that builds on, but is not about, the Thirty Years' War, however many of its details may be true. Contrary to what might be desirable from the historian's point of view, the meaning of an artistic work on the Thirty Years' War need by no means lie in its faithful reconstruction and in recovering it from the past for a contemporary observer. It need not even be suitable for an allegory: the novel may simply be a source for a completely differing view. Even to fulfill this intention, though, it is necessary that a semblance of what potential readers might otherwise know about this war—the names and fragments of a commonly shared memory—lend credence to the principal theme of the soulless present and its potential salvation. For this purpose, it is unimportant whether Döblin chooses the figure of Wallenstein, or whether the author Georg Kaiser picks the burghers of Calais out, to confront a general clanking of arms as an incarnation of the old man with a visionary yearning for death as a prototype of the new man. It is the unsolved conflicts of the present, and the experience of the unchecked violence of accelerating mass movements in the final and revolutionary years of the war around 1918, that provide the motive for this narrative literature—the latter eventually outgrowing even the figure of its title hero—and guide its development. This is a meaning construction based on sources very different from those that supply the raw material of actors, dates, and events.

To the extent that the historic Wallenstein is used in this way, though, he remains, especially in transformations of this kind, in reserve for new interpretations. A ready witness to human conflict, he can be called up for allegorical application and stored in the collective memory, enabling it to create an ever new and truthful image of the human individual by drawing on the requisites of the greatest stage provided by literature, which is history.

Let us now return to the situation of the historians whose texts we have already studied. At the end of the nineteenth century, Pekař was concerned mainly with Ranke's brilliant work, which by 1880, eleven years after its first appearance, had already seen a fourth printing. Half a century later, one would not like to reverse the opinion voiced by Ranke, then just thirty years old, that "the intention of a historian ... [depended] on his opinion."[45] But his interest in the specific tension that existed between Wallenstein's disposition and the ideas he put forward, and in his ingenious diplomatic moves in favor of peace for the emperor and the empire, clearly guided even with the older Ranke in his sketching not only of Wallenstein's personality, but also of the political, denominational, and military constellations surrounding him. Pekař's declared intention was against this to substitute the image of a Bohemian Wallenstein for the allegedly patriotic German prince. This image of a condottiere who, together with his people, is capable of, though still too weak for, rebellion, who is superior to everyone but ultimately deserted by all—this memorial to his compatriots, newly erected by Pekař between 1933 and 1937, provides the key to a conscientious, even meticulous search for detail. For among the majority of German historians, whom he joins and at the same time confronts with his own conception of *Wallenstein,* that search's allegedly unbiased objectivity is the necessary, and in his case strenuously practiced, ritual of validation of a book written not only, but also "by a scholar for scholars."

What about Golo Mann? The author who, with his *Deutsche Geschichte des 19. und 20. Jahrhunderts,* broke the spell and rearranged the basic facts of this story within a European context, assigned the French Revolution and Karl Marx to their proper places, and spoke in favor of Franco-German dialogue and a general understanding among the nations? He also made his *Wallenstein* a mouthpiece carrying the message of peace by modeling the Friedländer as being neither a patriot nor a traitor of the German Reich, but a character foreboding the necessity of a European peace ending not only the religious wars in the heart of Europe, but also those of France and Denmark. In the mid-1960s, this was a step that no German among the major Wallenstein scholars had taken, although a Finn, Pekka Suvanto, had done so previously, and with the same determination. To give his work credibility, Golo Mann chooses mostly conventional means, such as added characteristics and assessments offered by the auctorial narrator, but also, in particularly powerful scenes, forms of "interior monologue," an art that had been progressively developed by the European novelists of the nineteenth century.

It has probably been noted by now that the inclusion of perspectives, especially of unsolved conflicts of the present, in the presentation of the past is not a sufficient criterion for separating belletristic from historiographic literature. Meaning construction of past processes hardly ever takes place without regard to present circumstances. The eager reception research has long claimed with respect to the interest it arouses in readers is equivalent to authors' greedy apperception of the subjects they choose. While scholars may additionally be subject to academic constraints that drive them to load their findings with controversial or competing meanings, other authors have been confronted with similar problems under pressure to be original since the European Sturm und Drang period. Droysen saw good reason for ultimately assigning to his "diskussive Darstellung," (discussing presentation) which is also supposed to contribute to solving present-day conflicts, an important role among the various styles of historical writing. It is thus not his fault that, subsequently, this presentational mode—whereby research results are assessed in terms of their significance at the time for the solution of contemporary problems in any age or period—is not given preference. By contrast, in an ambitiously professionalizing historical science, it is the "analytic presentation," at best capable only of preparing such an approach, that has tended to be the criterion for measuring historians' accuracy and, ultimately, their professional performance. The reverse effect of this concentration on source analytical and source critical work manifests itself as early as the nineteenth century, for example in Treitschke, in that it repeatedly provokes unreflected shifts from supposedly objective findings to ideological interpretations. The regularity of this phenomenon was exposed fully only by the probing epistemological discourse conducted in the 1970s. As a result of this joint effort by historians, epistemologists, linguists, and literary scholars, it can no longer be taken for granted that an approach to truthful views can be developed of past circumstances—whether by means of reflective, narrative, or even analytical procedures—without some intention of meaning construction being involved. It seems advisable therefore to be conscious of this from the outset.

Since meaning production will always contain an imaginary moment, despite the most meticulous source evaluation, a distinction emerges between the historical and belletristic literatures in that the proposed meaning of a text can, in the latter case, detach itself more easily, perhaps even completely in the end, from its historical object. In the final analysis, it would by no means be the worst accomplishment of historical science to act as supplier to a general kind of anthropology, a more comprehensive knowledge of the human individual. To this end, though, within each presentation concerned with accuracy of detail, the historian would also need to place at least the seed of meaningful generalization.

Ultimately, nothing conclusive can be said about the meaning produced by texts since neither the author nor the interpreter can ever conclude it. Every reader takes up the thread again—something that is likely to happen in turn to this triple reading of the story of Wallenstein. For readers cannot help deriving, in a general or specific sense, new meanings from the texts before them, even though they may be guided, or even urged, by the collective rule of existing "meaning constructions." This restores to a good old saying of Terentianus Maurus, usually quoted only in shortened form, its full meaning: *"Pro captu lectoris habent sua fata libelli."* (The fate of books depends on the discernment of the reader.)[46]

Translated from the German by Adelheid E. Baker

Notes

1. Josef Pekař, *Wallenstein, 1630–1634: Tragödie einer Verschwörung*, 2 vols. (Berlin 1937), 147.
2. Ibid., vol. 1, 149.
3. Ibid., 150.
4. Ibid., 149.
5. Ibid., fn. 116 in vol. 2, 68; cf. also fn. 102, 66.
6. Ibid., 152.
7. Ibid., 156f.
8. Ibid., 153.
9. Ibid., 169.
10. Ibid., 178.
11. Ibid., 179.
12. Ibid., 692.
13. Ibid., 701.
14. Ibid., 706.
15. Ibid., 709.
16. Studia Historica, publ. by Historical Society, vol. 5 (Helsinki, 1963), esp. 109.
17. Golo Mann, *Wallenstein: Sein Leben erzählt von Golo Mann* (Frankfurt/ M. 1971), 772.
18. Ibid., 773.
19. Ibid., 775.
20. Ibid., 775.
21. Ibid., 774.
22. Ibid., 774.
23. Ibid., 777.
24. Ibid., 777.
25. Ibid., 778.

26. Ibid., 778.
27. Ibid., 778.
28. Ibid., 28.
29. On this, cf. Hayden White, "Das Problem der Erzählung in der modernen Geschichteschreibung", in Pietro Rossi, ed., *Theorie der modernen Geschichtsschreibung* (Frankfurt/ M. 1987), 57–106, 63ff.
30. Golo Mann, *Wallenstein,* 783.
31. Golo Mann, "Plädoyer für die historische Erzählung" in Jürgen Kocka and Thomas Nipperdey, eds., *Theorie und Erzählung in der Geschichte* (= *Theorie der Geschichte: Beiträge zur Historik,* vol. 3) (Munich 1979), 40–56, 40.
32. Mann, "Plädoyer," 45.
33. Josef Viktor Scheffel, "Ekkehard. Eine Geschichte aus dem 10. Jahrhundert," in Friedrich Panzer, ed., *Scheffels Werke,* vol. 3 (Leipzig and Vienna 1919), "Vorwort," 20f.
34. Ibid., 29f.
35. Alfred Döblin, *Wallenstein,* ed. Walter Muschg (Olten and Freiburg im Breisgau 1965), 548.
36. Ibid., 550f.
37. Ibid., 551.
38. Ibid., 551.
39. Ibid., 552.
40. Ibid., 552.
41. Axel Hecker: *Geschichte als Fiction: Alfred Döblins "Wallenstein"—eine exemplarische Kritik des Realismus.* (Epistemata, vol. 21) (Würzburg 1986), 308.
42. Ibid., "Nachwort des Herausgebers," 745.
43. Alfred Döblin, "An Romanautoren und ihre Kritiker. Berliner Programm" (May 1913), in idem, *Die Zeitlupe: Kleine Prosa,* ed. Walter Muschg (Olten and Freiburg im Breisgau 1962), 15–19; cf. Muschg, "Nachwort," 743.
44. Alfred Döblin, "Der Epiker, sein Stoff und die Kritik," in idem, *Die Zeitlupe,* 22f.
45. Leopold von Ranke, "Geschichten der romanischen und germanischen Völker von 1494 bis 1514," in idem, *Sämtliche Werke* (Leipzig 1867–1890), vols. 33–34, "Vorrede," iv.
46. Terentianus Maurus, *De litteris syllabis et metris* (Hildesheim 2002), v. 258.

CHAPTER 14

The Arts of Jewish Memory in a Postmodern Age

JAMES E. YOUNG

Given our present skepticism of national memory and the self-aggrandizing versions of the past it bequeaths us in our memorial institutions, it might seem a little strange to regard the museum as "a kind of key paradigm in contemporary postmodern culture," as Andreas Huyssen has characterized it.[1] But in fact, Huyssen's point is very well-taken: an ever larger proportion of our cultural time is now being devoted not only to collecting the past and arranging it around ourselves, but also to arranging ourselves around the past. Indeed, as Huyssen has also suggested, the forms of memory seem to multiply in direct proportion to our age's forgetfulness. Given the propensity of memorial icons to displace as much memory as they would embody, it could even be said that the impulse to memorialize events like the Holocaust might actually spring from an opposite and equal desire to forget them.[2]

With these thoughts in mind, I would like to explore the forms and meanings of a few of the transformations in Jewish memory now under way in what we have come to describe, a little too loosely perhaps, as a "postmodern age." Specifically, I want to look at a few postmodern responses to the emblematically modern event of the Holocaust, meditate on their significance, and then speculate on what forms Jewish memory and our relationship to it might take in a postmodern age.

Like the larger cultures around it, Jewish culture is increasingly obsessed with the past. Indeed, memory of historical events and the narratives delivering this memory have always been central to Jewish faith, tradition, and identity. For if the Jewish God is known only insofar as he reveals himself historically, as Yerushalmi and others suggest, then to remember history and to interpret its

Notes for this section begin on page 253.

texts assumes religiously obligatory proportions.[3] Throughout the Torah, Jews are enjoined not only to remember their history but to observe the rituals of faith through remembrance. To this day, history continues to assert itself as the primary locus of Jewish identity, memory as a primary form of Jewish faith. Moreover, in cultivating a ritually unified remembrance of the past, we continue to create a common relationship to it.

Like the other parts of our cultural lives, however, Jewish memory in this age is also increasingly bent on problematizing itself, on reflecting self-consciously on its role in a political and social world. As the past becomes ever more usable, its uses attract ever more critical attention. Now, a postmodern aesthetics of memory is already a slippery thing to define. At first blush, in fact, postmodern memory work sounds a little like Nietzsche's prescription for what he called "critical history": works that destabilize the idea of history through memory that interrogates itself; works that take conventional forms and turn them inside out into perpetually unfinished, self-doubting, self-reflexive works in process; works that ask us to look beyond themselves to the consequences they hold for our lives.[4]

That is, rather than locking the past into unreflexive analogue, postmodern memory—like critical history—asks where such analogues take us: do we use memory of the past to affirm, even reify certain political and economic realities? Or do we use it to undermine such realities? Or, more to Nietzsche's original point: At what point does memory of the past enable life? And at what point does it disable life?

In their response to these questions, the postmodern arts of memory might be characterized by their formalization of themes like absence, ambiguity, anomie, aporia, and arbitrariness (to begin with the "A's"). Other postmodern preoccupations have included uncertainty, undecidability, exhaustion, entropy, and blankness. Indeed, ways of representing an absence and the silences between words has become one of the postmodern project's consuming passions, literarily enacted by the likes of Edmond Jabes and Emanuel Levinas, among others. And as these writers began to challenge literary conventions and taxonomies (with counterrealisms, fabulations, and surfictions), other Jewish and non-Jewish memory artists have begun to interrogate their own forms and traditions.[5]

If one of the hallmarks of postmodern literature has been its compulsive inquiry into its own possibility of production, then Jewish memory in a postmodern age has been no less preoccupied with the possibility of its production. But such self-interrogation also confronts us with other, even more problematic dilemmas. We now ask, for example, to what extent can Jewish memory parody itself and still be Jewish? Can Jewish memory problematize itself and still retain its liturgical authority? Just as postmodern writers used to ask at the end of every work, "Why write? Why read?" we now ask "Why remember? And to what specific historical, social, political, and religious ends?"

Unlike the utopian, revolutionary forms with which modernists hoped to redeem art and literature, postmodern literature and art is pointedly anti-redemptory. The postmodern memory artist in particular would say that not only is art not the answer, but that after the Holocaust, there can be no more Final Solutions. Some of this skepticism was a direct response to the enormity of the Shoah, which seemed to exhaust not only the forms of modernist experimentation and innovation, but also the traditional meanings still reified in such innovations. The breach itself now demanded some kind of representation—but how to do it without automatically recuperating it? Indeed, the postmodern enterprise is both fueled and paralyzed by the double-edged conundrum articulated first by Adorno: not only does "cultural criticism share the blindness of its object," but even the critic's essential discontent with civilization can be regarded as an extension of that civilization.[6] Just as the avant-garde might be said to feed on the illusion of its perpetual dying, postmodern memory work seems to feed perpetually on the impossibility of its own task.[7]

Following Walter Benjamin's lead in his "Theses on the Philosophy of History," Saul Friedländer wonders whether all historical interpretation, whether the very act itself, is somehow fraught with redemptory potential.[8] That is, he asks whether the very act of making meaning in events like these—which is the unavoidable consequence of all historiography—somehow redeems them with significance. As a historian, Friedländer also questions the efficacy of ironic and experimental responses to the Shoah, insofar as their transgressiveness seems to undercut any and all meaning, verging on the nihilistic. Yet he also suggests that a postmodern aesthetics might "accentuate the dilemmas." Even on Friedländer's terms, this is not a bad thing: an aesthetics that re-marks its own limitations, its inability to provide eternal answers and stable meaning. Partly ironic, partly straightforward, works in this vein acknowledge both the moral need to bear positive witness and the impossibility of doing so in art and literature. In short, postmodern responses devote themselves primarily to the dilemmas of representation, their difficulty and their irresolvability.

As postmodern Jewish memory-work challenges the conventional assumptions underpinning our very definitions of "national memory," it also challenges our own disciplinary biases and structures, forcing us to enlarge our critical modes of inquiry—and in so doing to enlarge our definition of Jewish memory and history. At the same time, non-Jewish artists have also begun to generate and add to Jewish memory in ways unthinkable a generation ago. As I hope to show by the end of this piece, even the notion of an exclusively "Jewish Memory" in a postmodern age will begin to break down—or to put it more optimistically, it has now begun to open up to include the memory of other groups whose histories have been shaped by Jewish memory.

If part of this century's early modern project was to sever people from the forms and traditions anchored in an archaic past, to liberate ourselves from tradition and its archaic meanings, then the postmodern project has been to recognize both our inescapable debt to traditional forms and our rejection of them, studying the ways they continue to define us, even in dialectical opposition. As a result, Jewish memory in a postmodern age will challenge itself, its origins, and its meanings—and thereby renew itself as the primary site of Jewish identity.

Jewish memory in a postmodern age has begun to look less like collective memory and more like collected memory. Instead of a single meaning ascribed to disparate memories, many meanings are now being allowed to exist side by side. In fact, even the same Jewish memory in a postmodern age may have multiple meanings, depending on who receives it, under what conditions, and to what ends. Even the art of collecting these memories is now being noticed and incorporated into such memory-telling. In this way, Jewish memory in a postmodern age generates disparate, occasionally competing meanings for the same historical events. Rather than a singular master-narrative of memory—that which has traditionally been recited as liturgy—there are now many forms of memory, each owing a debt to the particular Jewish community doing the memory-work. Lest this sound like a formula for Balkanizing of Jewish memory by splintering Am-Israel into so many special interest groups, I would suggest that Jewish memory has never been monolithic but has always been multivoiced, inclusive of competing memory precisely in that it is openly contested.

So what is a Jewish memorial postmodernity? What does it look like? How do we talk about it? Such memory work comes in many forms and media: film and music, installation and performance art, comic, museums, and monuments as well as antimuseums, antimonuments, and what we might call "uncanny histories of the Holocaust." Rather than continuing in the abstract, I would like to turn here to a handful of the memory works themselves: Jochen Gerz's "Invisible Monument" of Saarbruecken; Horst Hoheisel's "Denk-Stein Sammlung" in Kassel; Daniel Libeskind's Jewish Extension to the Berlin Museum; the handshake between Yitzhak Rabin and Yasser Arafat. Finally, I'd like to look briefly at one "uncanny history of the Holocaust," as I find it, in Art Spiegelman's *Maus,* and then extrapolate from it to suggest the outlines of what I want to call a "received history" of the Holocaust.

Some readers will notice that not all of these artists are Jewish. But in another of the strange twists of the post-Holocaust era, non-Jewish Germans have begun to remember Jewish victims of the Nazis in explicitly Jewish forms of remembrance. The postmodern aesthetic preoccupation with absence has clearly set the stage for much of the memory work in Germany centered around a now absent people. In fact, perhaps no single emblem better represents the conflicted, self-abnegating motives for memory in Germany today than the vanishing monument. German memory-artists are heirs to a double-edged postwar legacy: a deep distrust of monumental forms in light of their systematic exploitation by the Nazis and a profound desire to distinguish their generation from that of the killers through memory.[9] Beyond these questions, they are also faced with an essentially German set of memorial conundrums: How to remember events they would rather forget? How to build a new and just nation on the bedrock memory of your people's crimes? In the countermonuments that ensued, a generation of German memory-artists have begun to renegotiate the tenets of their memory work, whereby monuments are born resisting the very premises of their being.[10]

Jochen Gerz's Invisible Monument in Saarbruecken

In keeping with the bookish, iconoclastic side of Jewish tradition, the first "memorials" to the Holocaust period came not in stone, glass, or steel, but in narrative. The Yizkor Bucher "memorial books" recall both the lives and the destruction of European Jewish communities according to the most ancient of Jewish memorial media: the book. Indeed, as the preface to one of these books suggests, "Whenever we pick up the book we will feel we are standing next to [the victim's] grave, because even that the murderers denied them."[11] The shtetl scribes hoped that when read, the Yizkor Bucher would turn the site of reading into memorial space. In response to what has been called "the missing gravestone syndrome," the first sites of memory created by survivors were thus interior spaces, imagined gravesites.

Without realizing it, perhaps, conceptual artist Jochen Gerz has recently recapitulated not only this missing gravestone syndrome but also the notion of the memorial as an interior space. I refer not to his and Esther Shalev-Gerz's vanishing monument in Harburg but to his more recently dedicated, invisible monument in Saarbruecken, which takes the countermonument to, shall we say, new depths.[12] Celebrated in Germany for his hand in Harburg's Gegen-Denkmal, Gerz was appointed a guest professor at the School of Fine Arts in Saarbruecken. In a studio class he devoted to conceptual monuments, Gerz invited his students to participate in a clandestine memory-project that he regarded as a kind of guerilla memorial action. The class agreed enthusiastically, swore themselves to secrecy, and listened as Gerz described his plan: Under the cover of night, eight students would steal into the great cobblestone square leading to the Saarbruecker Schloss, former home of the Gestapo during Hitler's Reich. Carrying book bags laden with cobblestones removed from other parts of the city, the students would spread themselves across the square, sit in pairs, swill beer, and yell at each other in raucous voices, pretending to have a party. All the while, in fact, they would be stealthily prying loose some seventy cobblestones from the square and replacing them with the like-sized stones they had brought along, each with a nail embedded underneath so that they could be located later with a metal detector. Within days, this part of the memorial mission had been accomplished as planned.[13]

Meanwhile, other members of the class had been assigned to research the names and locations of every former Jewish cemetery in Germany, over 2,000 of them, now abandoned, destroyed, or vanished. When their classmates returned from their beer-party, their bags heavy with cobblestones, all set to work engraving the names of missing Jewish cemeteries on the stones, one by one. The night after they finished, the memory guerillas returned the stones to their original places, each inscribed and dated. But in a twist wholly consistent with Gerz's previous countermonument, the stones were replaced face down, leaving no trace of the entire operation. The memorial would be invisible, itself only a memory, out of sight and therefore, Gerz hoped, in mind.

But, as Gerz also realized, if the memorial was no longer visible, then public memory would depend on knowledge of the memorial action becoming public. To this end, Gerz wrote Oskar Lafontaine, at that time minister-president of the Saarland and vice president of the German Social Democratic Party, apprising him of the deed and asking him for parliamentary assistance to continue the operation. Lafontaine responded with DM 10,000 (5000 €) from a special arts fund and a warning that the entire project was patently illegal. The public, however, had now become part of the memorial. Once the newspapers got wind of the project, a tremendous furor broke out over the reported vandalization of the square; editorials asked whether yet another monument like this was necessary; some even wondered whether the whole thing had been a conceptual hoax designed merely to provoke a memorial storm.

As visitors flocked to the square looking for the 70 stones among over 8,000, they too began to wonder "where they stood" vis-à-vis the memorial: Were they standing on it? In it? Was it really there at all? On searching for memory, Gerz hoped, they would realize that such memory was already in them. This would be an interior memorial: as the only standing forms in the square, the visitors themselves would become the memorials they sought.

The politicians' positions were less equivocal. As Jochen Gerz rose to address the Saarbruecken Stadtverband to explain his project, the entire CDU contingent stood up and walked out. The rest of the parliament remained and voted the memorial into public existence. Indeed, they even voted to rename the plaza "Square of the Invisible Monument," its name becoming the only visible sign of the memorial itself. Regardless of whether the operation ever really took place, the power of suggestion had already planted the memorial where it would do the most good: not in the center of town, but in the center of the public's mind. In effect, Jochen Gerz's "2,160 Stones: A Monument against Racism" returns the burden of memory to those who come looking for it.

Horst Hoheisel's Denk-Stein Sammlung

In Kassel, another German artist has also turned to traditional Jewish memorial media to remember Jewish victims of the Nazis. Having already designed a negative-form monument in Kassel to commemorate a pyramid fountain destroyed by Nazis in 1938 as "the Jews' fountain," Horst Hoheisel turned to the next generation with a new project.[14] With permission from the local public schools, the artist visited the classrooms of Kassel with a book, a stone, and a piece of paper. The book was a copy of *Namen und Schicksale der Juden Kassels* (The Names and Fates of Kassel's Jews). In his classroom visits, Hoheisel would tell students the story of Kassel's vanished Jewish community: how they had once thrived there, lived in the very houses where these schoolchildren now lived, how they had sat at these same classroom desks. He then asked all the children who knew any Jews to raise their hands. When no hand appeared, Hoheisel would read the story of one of Kassel's deported Jews from his memory book. At the end of his reading, Hoheisel invited each of the students to research the life of one of Kassel's deported Jews: where they had lived and how, who their families were, how old they were, what they had looked like. He asked them to visit formerly Jewish neighborhoods and get to know the German neighbors of Kassel's deported Jews.

After this, students were asked to write short narratives describing the lives and deaths of their subjects, to wrap these narratives around cobblestones, and to deposit them in one of the archival bins the artist had provided every school. After several dozen such classroom visits, the bins began to overflow and new ones were furnished. In time, all of these bins were transported to Kassel's central terminal, where they were stacked on the rail platform whence Kassel's Jews were deported. It is now a permanent installation, what the artist is calling his Denk-Stein Sammlung (memorial stone archive). It continues to grow as new bins are filled around the city and transported to the station.

This memorial cairn—a witness-pile of stones—marks both the site of deportation and the community's education about its murdered Jews, their absence now marked by the still evolving memorial. Combining narrative and stone in this way, the artist and students have thus adopted the most Jewish of memorial forms as their own—thereby enlarging their memorial lexicon to include that of the absent people they would now recall. After all, only they are now left to write the epitaph of the missing Jews, known and emblematized primarily by their absence, the void they have left behind.

Daniel Libeskind's Jewish Extension to the Berlin Museum

When city planners in Berlin began making plans for a Jewish Museum there some forty years after the Holocaust, they found themselves mired almost immediately in an intractable quandary: Just how does a city "house" the memory of a people no longer at "home" there? How does a city like Berlin invite a people like the Jews back into its official past after having driven them so murderously from it? In fact, such questions may suggest their own, uncanny answers. A "Jewish Museum" in a nation that not so long ago voided itself of Jews, making them alien strangers in a land they had considered "home," will not by definition be *heimlich* but must be regarded as *unheimlich*—or as our translation would have it, uncanny. The dilemma facing the designer of such a museum thus becomes: How then to embody this sense of *Unheimlichkeit,* or uncanniness, in a medium like architecture, which has its own long tradition of *Heimlichkeit,* or homeliness?

In their initial conception of what they then regarded as a Jewish "extension" to the Berlin Museum, city planners hoped to recognize the role Jews had once played as co-creators of Berlin's history and culture and acknowledge that the city was fundamentally haunted by its Jewish absence. At the same time, the very notion of an "autonomous" Jewish Museum struck them as problematic. The museum wanted to show the importance and far-reaching effect of Jewish culture on the city's history, to give it the prominence it deserved. But many also feared dividing German from Jewish history, inadvertently recapitulating the Nazis' own segregation of Jewish culture from German. This would have reimposed a distinct line between the history and cultures of two peoples—Germans and Jews—whose fates had been inextricably mingled for centuries in Berlin. From the beginning, planners realized that this would be no mere reintroduction of Jewish memory into Berlin's civic landscape but an excavation of memory already there, though long suppressed.

Freud may have described such a phenomenon best: "This uncanny is in reality nothing new or alien, but something which is familiar and old-established in the mind and which has become alienated from it only through the process of repression.... The uncanny [is] something which ought to have remained hidden but has come to light."[15] Thus might a memorial installation like Berlin's Jewish Museum generate its own sense of a disquieting return, the sudden revelation of something concealed or buried. The uncanniness of such a project comes when one expects that at any moment something will burst forth, even when it never does, thus leaving one always ill at ease, even a little frightened with anticipation—hence, the constant, free-floating anxiety that seems to accompany all the uncanny arts of memory in Germany.

The Jewish wing would be both autonomous and integrative, the trick being to link a museum of civic history with the altogether uncivil treatment of that city's Jews. How to do this in a form that would not suggest reconciliation and continuity? How to reunite Berlin and its Jewish part without suggesting a seamless rapprochement? Enter architect Daniel Libeskind, born in Lodz in 1946 to the sole survivors of a Jewish family wiped out in the Holocaust, now an American citizen living in Berlin. Of the 165 designs submitted from around the world for the museum competition that closed in June 1989, Daniel Libeskind's struck the jury as the most outrageous, most problematic, and most unbuildable of all. It was awarded first prize and thereby became the first work of Libeskind's ever to be commissioned. Before beginning, however, Libeskind replaced the very name of the project—"Extension of the Berlin Museum with the Jewish Museum Department"—with his own more poetic rendition, "Between the Lines." In his words, the building would consist of "a straight line, but broken into many fragments; [and] a tortuous line, but continuing indefinitely."[16] According to the architect, these lines would have a dialogue but would also fall apart.

Libeskind began by overlaying the map of Berlin with an anamorphic star of David, through which he then shot a jagged bolt of lightening. Through this twisted structure, which looks like the broken pieces of a Magen David (shield of David, or as it is more commonly known, the Star of David), Libeskind ran a straight-cut void that sliced through the rest of the building: an empty, unused space bisecting the entire museum. According to Libeskind, "The new extension is conceived as an emblem where the not visible has made itself apparent as a void, an invisible…. The idea is very simple: to build the museum around a void that runs through it, a void that is to be experienced by the public" (63). Like most of Libeskind's simple ideas, this one is also not so simple. But he does allow his drawings to work through the essential paradoxes at the heart of his project: how to give a void form without filling it in? How to give architectural form to the formless and to challenge the very attempt to house such memory?

Libeskind does not want to suggest that this void was imposed on Berlin from without, but that it was created in Berlin from within. It was not the bombing of Berlin that created the void, he says, but the vacuum and inner-collapse of moral will that allowed Berlin to void itself of Jews. According to Libeskind, this void will also represent a space empty of Jews that echoes an inner space empty of the love and values that might have saved Berlin's Jews. At the same time, he hopes, his zig-zag line will suggest the broken backbone of Berlin society.

His drawings for the museum thus look more like the sketches of the museum's ruins, a house whose wings have been scrambled and reshaped by the jolt of genocide. It is a devastated site that would now enshrine its broken forms. In this work, Libeskind asks whether architecture, which can be representative of historical meaning, can also represent unmeaning and the search for meaning. The result is an extended building broken in several places. The straight void-line running through the plan violates every space through which it passes, turning otherwise uniform rooms and halls into misshapen anomalies, some too small to hold anything, others so oblique as to estrange anything housed within them. The original design also included inclining walls, at angles too sharp for hanging exhibitions. Museological and economic realities intruded, however, straightening the walls and taking out several of the voids that had been intended for the museum's exterior.

All the attention this design has received, both laudatory and skeptical, has generated yet another historical irony. Where the city planners had hoped to return Jewish memory to the house of Berlin history, it now seems that Berlin history will have to find its place in the larger haunted house of Jewish memory. The Jewish wing of the Berlin Museum will now be the prism through which the rest of the world will know Berlin's own past.

The Handshake

The mere introduction of these countermemorial forms into the canon of traditional Jewish memorial texts both expands this canon and problematizes it in significant ways. The very notion of Jewish memory in a postmodern age may now depend on broadening this memory to include not only the spatial counter-arts of memory and the Jewish memory-work accomplished by non-Jews, but also the memory of those whom Jewish history now affects. As the Germans have been forced to expand their national memory with that of their victims, Jews are now being asked to enlarge Jewish memory so that it encompasses not only Jewish history but also the lives of those, whom affected by Jewish history. Here I would like to turn not to the ways memory has shaped historical events, but to the ways that contemporary history may now be reshaping Jewish memory.

As a watershed event, the September 1993 handshake between Israelis Prime Minister, Yitzhak Rabin and PLO Chairman Yasser Arafat on the White House lawn may not have rivaled the near-mythic images of Israel's victories in its 1948 War of Independence and 1967 Six Day War. But the significance of this handshake for Jewish memory may be infinitely farther reaching—in profoundly double-edged ways. In the peace treaty sealed by the handshake, Jews were asked to simultaneously remember events we had not regarded as our own and forget events that had been too much a part of our past. Until the Zionist revolution, the very idea of Jewish history, not to mention the covenant itself, was intertwined with the assumption that Jews are an acted-upon people: "I am the Lord your God who brought you out of Egypt," i.e., you know me by what I have done for you (and to you). "Remember what Amalek did to you," i.e., remember what the enemies of Israel have always done to you. In 1948 this changed when Israel transformed itself from the leaf shuddering in the wind to the wind itself. Even so, it has taken Israel almost two generations to get used to both this active role in history and the responsibilities that come with it.

For the first time, we are being asked to remember the pain and suffering that accompanied the Palestinians' displacement from their homeland and our negation of their national aspirations. This hurts not just because both ancient and recent Jewish pasts make us so sensitive to the pain of others, but also because we are now being asked to recognize our part in causing this pain: that is, we are being asked to recognize the consequences our history, and memory of it, may have for others around us. In effect, we are also being asked to consider the possibility that Jewish memory now includes the histories of both Jews and those directly affected by Jewish history.

Just as we have made our persecutors integral to Jewish history and memory, we will now remember as part of our history those who have been victimized by it. Neither is this altogether foreign to Jewish tradition: recall the token drops of wine we spill every Passover in memory of the plagues that befell our pursuers. It turns out to be much harder for Jews remember the pain we caused in the pursuit of our own national homeland.

In this, we are also being asked to expand Jewish memory to include triumphs, not because this they would redeem destruction, but because it would complicate the notion of triumph by highlighting the suffering it caused to others.

At the same time, Jews are also being asked to forget the years of terror and negation perpetrated on Jews by Palestinians. As long as we remember too well, that outstretched hand will always be a bloody one and thus forbidden. In effect, Jewish memory in a postmodern age may be a radical departure from the very rules by which we have understood ourselves as Jews—a people constituted by our relation to a vociferously remembered past. Indeed, we are being asked not only to forget this past but, in a twist on the Passover refrain, to remember the Palestinians' past as if it were our own. This is not a mere appropriation of another people's past, but a recognition of the part one's own people have already played in it.

Ironically, it may also be true that once the histories of Israel's enemies are incorporated into Jewish memory, Israeli history and memory will be expanded even further: it will include not only the histories of Palestinians whose lives have been shaped by Israeli history, but also the diasporic histories of Israel's own immigrants, heretofore denied them in the Zionist negation of Jewish life in exile. In this vein, we might now ask that Israeli memory include the history of events that drove *olim hadashim*—new immigrants—to Israel's shores. As an immigrant nation, Israel will necessarily be a nation of immigrant memories, as well.

Art Spiegelman's *Maus* as Received History

Finally, in addition to exploring the plastic and spatial, national and official counter-arts of memory, we might look at the possibilities for countermemorial narratives as well. Narrative, that most Jewish of memory-texts, also seems to be most resistant to postmodern tampering, partly because it is already such a self-referential medium and partly because once it challenges its own conventions, it turns quickly into something other than narrative. In the next section of this meditation, therefore, I would like to look briefly at the ways Art Spiegelman's *Maus* suggests a form of memory work I call "received history."

As conceptual artists like Jochen Gerz and Horst Hoheisel and the architect Daniel Libeskind have turned to unusual forms and media for memory, artist Art Spiegelman has turned to his own special medium, a co-mixture of image and narrative that he calls "commix." As most readers know by now, *Maus: A Survivor's Tale* is not about the Holocaust so much as about the survivor's tale itself, his father's telling of it and the artist-son's recovery of it. In Spiegelman's own words, "*Maus* is not what happened in the past, but rather what the son understands of the father's story."[17] To this end, the artist's commixture of image and narrative constitutes the imaginative record of his father's telling. Throughout *Maus*, Spiegelman thus confronts his father with the record of his telling, even incorporating his father's response to Art's record into later stages of *Maus*. Like any good postmodern memory-art, *Maus* thus feeds on itself, recalling its own production, even the choices the artist makes along the way (would he draw his French wife who converted to Judaism as a frog or an honorary Maus?)—all with the aim of highlighting the inseparability of his father's story from its effect on Artie as he listens.

While the commix per se is not a postmodern medium, the way Spiegelman uses it is. For example, when Spiegelman is asked, "Why mice?" he answers, "I need to show the events and memory of the Holocaust without showing them. I want to show the masking of these events in their representation." In this way, he can tell the story and not tell it at the same time. As ancient Passover Haggadoth used to put birds' heads on human forms in order not to show humans and to show them at the same time, Spiegelman has put mouse heads on the Jews. By using mice masks, the artist also asks us not to believe what we see. They are masks drawing attention to themselves as such, never inviting us to mistake memory of events for events themselves.

Other aspects of Spiegelman's specific form and technique further incorporate the process of drawing *Maus* into its finished version. By drawing his panels in a 1:1 ratio, for example, instead of drawing large panels and then shrinking them down to page size, Spiegelman reproduces his hand's movement in scale—its shakiness, the thickness of his drawing pencil line, the limits of miniaturization, all to put a cap on detail and fine line, and so keep the pictures underdetermined. In addition, the box-panels convey information in both vertical and horizontal movements of the eye, as well as in the analogue of images implied by the entire page appearing in the background of any single panel. The narrative sequence of his boxes, with some ambiguity as to the order in which they are to be read, combines with and then challenges the narrative of his father's story—itself constantly interrupted by Art's questions and own neurotic preoccupations, his father's pill-taking, the bitter father-son relationship, his father's new and sour marriage. As a result, Spiegelman's narrative is constantly interrupted by—and integrative of—life itself, with all its dislocutions, associations, and paralyzing self-reflections. It is a narrative echoing with the ambient noise and issues surrounding its telling. The roundabout method of memory-telling is captured here in ways unavailable to straighter narrative. It is a narrative that tells both the story of events and its own unfolding as narrative.

And as if all this weren't enough, we now have *Maus* on CD-Rom, where the text-panels are accompanied by complete geneaologies of their origins. Where did a particular story or set of images come from, how did they first enter the artist's consciousness? It's all here: press the interactive screen on one of the colored boxes and up comes a complete (pre-)history of that panel. Vladek's tape-recorded voice tells one version, with Art's interruptions; the artist's early sketches, done as his father spoke, tell another. Photographs and drawings from Art's library that inspired certain images appear one after the other, even video footage of Art's trip to Poland and Auschwitz. By making visible the memory of this memory-text's production, the CD-Rom version of *Maus* reveals the interior, ever-evolving life of memory—and even makes this life too part of the text.

Conclusion

As part of my recent work on memorials, I have also begun to examine my own role within the spaces of memory, the ways in which historical meaning and memory are shaped in the dialogical relationship between memorial and visitor. I have found in this work that what is remembered and understood of the Holocaust depends very much on who is remembering, who is listening, and to what end. During this same search for the known and unknown narratives of the Holocaust, I met hundreds of survivors. All of them had different stories to tell, some of them polished and slick from many other tellings, some of them raw and barely articulable. In addition to giving a human cast to the literary and institutional memory I was studying, they also forced me to examine my own stance vis-à-vis their histories: I asked questions, and they asked back, quite unlike the silent monuments. At first, their questions rolled off the all-too-correct decorum of my scholarly inquiry. This was not about me, I assured them, but about the need to understand Holocaust history and its consequences for the survivors' contemporary lives. But of course, it was also about me and the ways their stories had begun to shape my own inner and professional life.

With this in mind, I would like to adapt the kind of received history we find in *Maus* to another, purely narrative kind of memory work. In such a project, I would like to tell the stories of survivors whose lives and my uncovering of them intertwine in a double-stranded narrative of the Holocaust and my generation's relationship to it: what I am characterizing here as "received histories."

On the one hand, every history is received in some manner, either assembled from bits and pieces of others' records or told in the words of the participants themselves. But not many histories betray the usually hidden dimensions of the historian's reception of events; even fewer historians have tolerated the sound of their own voice, a subjectivity they believe undercuts their work's sense of disinterested authority. But in transversing what he calls the "twilight zone between history and memory," Saul Friedländer redefines the space between history and memory as something "between the past as a generalized record which is open to relatively dispassionate inspection and the past as part of, or background to, one's own life…"[18]

As historians come increasingly to draw in the lines of their particular telling, the receiver of history might now paint in the texture of its reception: under what circumstances was it received? Who told it, when, in what social and political context? What did the teller read that morning in the newspapers? And what preoccupied the listener that day? At what point did the listener's attention lapse upon being reminded of his or her own recent past, or that of others nearby? How did the listener's response to a particular story shape the teller's story as it unfolded? Where do their life stories end and mine begin? How are we marked by the histories we receive? And how does that marking become part of the historical text?

In this alternative to conventional history telling, we might restore both the telling and reception of historical lives to the historical record. Such work aims to reinvest the narrated past with the animacy of its telling, the consequences of its reception for teller and listener. In this way, we might make the listeners' and readers' responses to history a part of that history's record. As such, these received histories could include the author's journey to the past, the distance between the lives of tellers and listeners, the points of engagement. They will also include the "inaudibles" of history: the momentary reflexes and associative responses in both teller and listener, the pauses between memories as they come, the interruptions in telling that come with the impinging realities of daily life. By restoring to these histories the times and places, the social and political circumstances surrounding a given story's telling, we might enlarge the text of history with its own coming into being.

For the uncanny historian, this means a historiography whose narrative skein is disrupted by the sound of the historian's own, self-conscious voice. In the words of Friedländer, such "commentary should disrupt the facile linear progression of the narration, introduce alternative interpretations, question any partial conclusion, withstand the need for closure."[19] These interruptions would also remind readers that this history was told and remembered by someone in a particular time and place, that it is the product of human hands and minds. In this kind of double-voiced history, no single, overarching meaning emerges unchallenged; instead, narrative and counternarrative generate a frisson of meaning in their exchange, in the working-through process they now mutually reinforce.

Finally, in this process, we might also begin to reflect on our own academic commodification of Holocaust history, and on all the ways that the next generation simultaneously feeds on the past and disposes of it in their work. While academic critics have been quick to speculate on the motives of filmmakers, novelists, and popular historians, we have remained curiously blind to our own instrumentalization of memory, to the ways an entire academic industry has grown up around the events of the Holocaust. It is time to step back and take an accounting: where does all this history and its telling lead, to what kinds of knowledge, to what ends? This is, I believe, the crux of Jewish memory in a postmodern age: memory not only marks its own coming into being but also points to the places—both real and imagined where it inevitably takes us.*

Notes

1. Andreas Huyssen, "The Monument in a Post-modern Age," in James E. Young, ed., *The Art of Memory: Holocaust Memorials in History* (Munich 1994), 11.

2. I explore this notion at much further length in James E. Young, *The Texture of Memory: Holocaust Memorials and Meaning* (New Haven and London 1993), 1–15, 27–48.

3. Yosef Hayim Yerushalmi, *Zakhor: Jewish History and Jewish Memory* (Seattle and London 1982), 9.

4. See Friedrich Nietzsche, *The Use and Abuse of History,* trans. Adrian Collins (New York 1985), 20–22.

5. In addition to the artists under discussion in this essay (Gerz, Hoheisel, Liebeskind, and Spiegelman), I would include the artists Christian Boltanski, Rachel Whiteread, Ellen Rothenberg, Vera Frenkel, and Susan Jahoda; the photographers David Levinthal and Shimon Attie; the filmmaker Abraham Ravett; and the musician Steve Reich.

6. Theodore W. Adorno, *Prisms,* trans. Samuel and Shierry Weber (Cambridge, Mass. 1981), 27, 19.

7. For a brilliant elaboration on the "ever-dying" of the avant-garde, see Paul Mann, *The Theory-Death of the Avant-Garde* (Indianapolis and Bloomington 1991).

8. Saul Friedländer, *Memory, History, and the Extermination of the Jews of Europe* (Indianapolis and Bloomington 1993), 55.

9. For elaboration of this theme, see Matthias Winzen, "The Need for Public Representation and the Burden of the German Past," *Art Journal* 48 (winter 1989): 309–14.

10. For more in this vein, see James E. Young, "The Counter-monument: Memory against Itself in Germany Today," *Critical Inquiry* 18 (winter 1992): 267–96, expanded further in *The Texture of Memory,* 17–48.

11. From "Forwort", in *Sefer Yizkor le-kedoshei ir (Przedecz) Pshaytask Khurbanot ha'shoah,* 130, as quoted in Jack Kugelmass and Jonathan Boyarin, eds., *From a Ruined Garden: The Memorial Books of Polish Jewry* (New York 1983), 11.

12. See my "The Counter-monument: Memory against Itself in Germany Today," noted above.

13. For the details of this project, I am indebted to personal correspondence and conversations with Jochen Gerz, as well as these articles, among others: Barbara v. Jhering, "Duell mit der Verdrängung," *Die Zeit* (14 February 1992); Amine Haase, "Mahnmale gegen Faschismus und Rassismus," *Kunst und Antiquitäten* 1, no. 2 (1992): 12–14; Jacqueline Lichtenstein and Gerard Wajeman, "Jochen Gerz: Invisible Monument," *artpress* (April 1993): E1–E6.

14. For more on Hoheisel's "negative-form" monument, see Young, "The Counter-monument: Memory against Itself in Germany Today," noted above. For the details of this current project, I am indebted to conversations and correspondence with Horst Hoheisel.

15. Sigmund Freud, "The Uncanny," in *The Standard Edition of the Complete Psychological Works of Sigmund Freud,* trans. James Strachey, 24 vols. (London 1955), vol. 17, 241.

16. Daniel Libeskind, "Between the Lines," in Kristin Feireiss, ed., *Daniel Libeskind: Erweiterung des Berlin Museums mit Abteilung Judisches Museum* (Berlin 1992), 67.

17. From the author's interview with Art Spiegelman.

18. Eric J. Hobsbawn, *The Age of Empire: 1875–1924* (London 1987), quoted in Friedländer, *Memory, History, and the Extermination of the Jews of Europe,* vii.

19. Ibid., 132.

*An earlier version of this essay appeared in Bryan Cheyette and Laura Marcus, eds., *Modernity, Culture, and 'the Jew'* (Oxford 1998), 211–225. Parts of this essay have also appeared in James E. Young, *At Memory's Edge: After-images of the Holocaust in Contemporary Art and Architecture* (New Haven and London 2000).

Bibliography

Adorno, Theodore W. *Prisms*. Trans. Samuel and Shierry Weber. Cambridge, Mass. 1981.
Althaus, Paul. *Vom Sinn und Ziel der Geschichte*. Bonn 1947.
Ammann, Ludwig. *Die Geburt des Islam: Historische Innovation durch Offenbarung* (Essener kulturwissenschaftliche Vorträge. Vol. 12). Göttingen 2001.
Anderson, Perry. *Zum Ende der Geschichte*. Berlin 1993.
Ankersmit, Frank R. *Narrative Logic: A Semantic Analysis of the Historian's Language*. The Hague 1983.
———. "Antwoord aan Nauta." *Theoretische Geschiedenis* 20 (1993): 523–534.
———. *De historische ervaring*. Groningen 1993.
———. "Tocqueville and the sublimity of democracy. Part 1." *The Tocqueville Review* 14 (1993): 173–201.
———. "Tocqueville and the sublimity of democracy. Part 2." *The Tocqueville Review* 15 (1994): 193–218.
———. *History and Tropology*. Berkeley 1994.
———. "Ervaring, waarheid en representatie." In I. Bulhof, ed. *De representatiekrisis*. Kampen 1995.
———. "Van taal naar ervaring." In S. Alexandrescu, ed. *Richard Rorty*. Kampen 1995.
———. "Die postmoderne Privatisierung der Vergangheit" ("The Postmodernist 'privatization' of the past"). In H. Nagl-Docekal, ed. *Geschichtstheorie nach der grossen Erzählung*. Frankfurt/M. 1995.
———. "Historism: An attempt at synthesis." *History and Theory* 34 (1995): 143–162.
———. "Can we experience the past?" In R. Torstendahl and I. Veit-Brause, eds. *Historymaking: The Intellectual and Social Formation of a Discipline*. Stockholm 1996.
———. "Historische Sinnbildung durch Erzählen: Eine Argumentationsskizze zum narrativistischen Paradigma der Geschichtswissenschaft und der Geschichtsdidaktik im Blick auf nichtnarrative Faktoren." *Internationale Schulbuchforschung* 18 (1996): 501–543.
———. "The sublime Dissociation of the Past: Or How to Be(come) What One is No Longer." *History and Theory* 40 (2001): 295–323.
———. "Language and historical experience." See chap. 8 of this vol.; published in German as "Sprache und historische Erfahrung." In Klaus E. Müller and Jörn Rüsen, eds. *Historische Sinnbildung*. Reinbek 1997.
———. "Representatie, waarheid en ervaring." In J. Klukhuhn, ed. *Postmodermism revisited*. Utrecht 1995.
Arendt, Hannah. *The Human Condition*. Chicago 1958.
Aron, Raymond. *Introduction à la philosophie de l'histoire: Essai sur les limites de l'objectivité historique*. Paris 1948.
Assmann, Aleida. *Erinnerungsräume: Formen und Wandlungen des kulturellen Gedächtnisses*. Munich 1999.
———. Monika Gomille and Gabriele Rippl, eds. *Ruinenbilder*. Munich 2002.

Assmann, Jan. *Das kulturelle Gedächtnis: Schrift, Erinnerung und politische Identität in frühen Hochkulturen.* Munich 1992.

———. *Ägypten: Eine Sinngeschichte.* Munich 1996.

Augustinus, Aurelius. *Bekenntnisse.* Stuttgart 1989.

Balke, Friedrich et al., eds. *Zeit der Ereignisse – Ende der Geschichte.* Munich 1992.

Balthasar, Hans Urs von. *Das Ganze im Fragment.* Einsiedeln 1963.

Bandau, I. "Fiktion." In Joachim Ritter, ed. *Historisches Wörterbuch der Philosophie.* Vol. 2. Basel 1972.

Barthes, R. "To write: An intransitive verb." In R. Macksey and E. Donato, eds. *The Languages of Criticism and the Sciences of Man.* Baltimore 1970.

Bates, Elizabeth. *Language and Context: The Acquisition of Pragmatics.* New York 1976.

Bauer, Günter. *Auf den Spuren des Verbrechens: Grenzen und Möglichkeiten der Kriminalistik.* Lübeck 1973.

Beattie, Owen, and John Geiger. *Der eisige Schlaf: Das Schicksal der Franklin-Expedition.* Cologne 1989.

Beck, Herbert, and P.C. Bol, eds. *Exhibition catalogue Natur und Antike in der Renaissance.* Frankfurt/ M. 1985.

Bell, J. C. "The historic Sense." *Journal of Educational Psychology* 5 (1917): 317–318.

Bell, W. *Foundations of Futures Studies.* New Brunswick 1997.

———, ed. *The Democratic Revolution in the West Indies.* Cambridge, Mass. 1967.

Benjamin, Walter. "Über den Begriff der Geschichte." In idem, *Gesammelte Schriften,* ed. Rolf Tiedemann and Hermann Schweppenhäuser. Vol. I. 2. Frankfurt/ M. 1991.

Berdjajew, Nikolaus. *Der Sinn der Geschichte: Versuch einer Philosophie des Menschengeschicks.* Introduction by Graf Hermann Keyserling. Translated from the Russian by Otto Freiherr von Taube. Darmstadt 1925.

Berger, Klaus. *Wissenschaft als Beruf: Zur Kritik literaturwissenschaftlicher und verwandter Sinnproduktion.* Frankfurt and Bern 1983.

Berger, Peter L., and Thomas Luckmann. *Die gesellschaftliche Konstruktion der Wirklichkeit: Eine Theorie der Wissenssoziologie.* Frankfurt/ M. 1979.

Bernhart, Joseph. *Sinn der Geschichte.* Freiburg im Breisgau 1931.

Bernheim, Ernst. *Geschichtsforschung und Geschichtsphilosophie.* Göttingen 1880.

———. *Lehrbuch der Historischen Methode und der Geschichtsphilosophie.* 3rd and 4th completely revised and extended editions. Leipzig 1903.

Bitterli, Urs. "Amerikanische Entdeckungsreisen im Wandel." In André Stoll, ed. *Sypharden, Morisken, Indianerinnen und ihresgleiche: Die andere Seite der hispanischen Kultur.* Bielefeld 1995.

Blatter, Janet, and Sybil Milton. *Art of the Holocaust.* New York 1981.

Blumenberg, Hans. *Die kopernikanische Welt.* Frankfurt 1965.

———. *Die Lesbarkeit der Welt.* Frankfurt/ M. 1981 (3rd ed. 1993).

Brecht, Bertold. *Kriegsfibel.* 2nd ed. Berlin 1968 [1955].

Brown, Roger. *A First Language.* 5th ed. Cambridge, Mass. 1976.

Bubner, Rüdiger. *Geschichtsprozesse und Handlungsnormen: Untersuchungen zur praktischen Philosophie.* Frankfurt/ M. 1984.

Burckhardt, Jacob. *Weltgeschichtliche Betrachtungen: Über geschichtliches Studium.* Darmstadt 1970.

Carr, David. *Time, Narrative and History.* Bloomington 1986.

———. "Narrative and the Real World: An Argument for Continuity." *History and Theory* 25 (1986): 117–131.

———. "Phenomenology and historical knowledge." In Ernst Wolfgang Orth and Chan-Fai Cheung, eds. *Phenomenology of Interculturality and Life-World* (Phänomenologische Forschungen, Sonderband). Freiburg im Breisgau 1998.

———. "The Reality of History." Chap. 7 of this volume.

Cavalli, Alessandro. *Il tempo dei giovani.* Bologna 1985.

———. "Zeiterfahrungen von Jugendlichen." In R. Zoll, ed. *Zerstörung und Wiederaneignung von Zeit.* Frankfurt/ M. 1988.

———. "I giovani e la memoria del Fascismo e della Resistenza." *Il Mulino* 45 (1996): 51–57.
Certeau, Michel de. *L'Absent de l'Histoire*. Paris 1973.
Chatwin, Bruce. *The Songlines*. London 1987.
Cheyette, Bryan, and Laura Marcus, eds. *Modernity, Culture, and 'the Jew.'* Oxford 1998.
Chomsky, Noam. *Aspects of the Theory of Syntax*. Cambridge, Mass. 1965.
Collingwood, Robin G. *An Autobiography*. Oxford 1939.
———. *Philosophie der Geschichte*. Stuttgart 1955.
———. *The Idea of History*. London 1969.
Cotta, Bernhard. *Geologische Bilder*. Leipzig 1852 (2nd ed. 1854).
Curtius, Ernst Robert. "Alkaloid Spaniens: Zu Miguel de Unamunos 70. Geburtstag am 29. September." *Berliner Tageblatt*. 30 September 1934.
Danto, Arthur. *Analytical Philosophy of History*. Cambridge 1965.
Deleuze, Gilles. *Logik des Sinns*. Frankfurt/ M. 1993.
Demandt, Alexander. *Metaphern für Geschichte, Sprachbilder und Gleichnisse im historisch-politischen Denken*. Munich 1978.
DeVitt, Michael, and Kim Sterelny. *Language and Reality*. Oxford 1987.
Dewey, J. *Art as Experience*. Carbondale 1987.
Diels, Hermann, and Walther Kranz. *Die Fragmente der Vorsokratiker*. 2 vols. 15th ed. Dublin and Zürich 1971.
Diemer, Alwin. *Grundriß der Philosophie*. 2 vols. Meisenheim am Glan 1962.
Dierse, Ulrich. "Geschichtsphilosophie." In Joachim Ritter, ed. *Historisches Wörterbuch der Philosophie*. vol. 3. Darmstadt 1974.
Diller, H. "Der griechische Naturbegriff." *Neue Jahrbücher für Antike und deutsche Bildung* 2 (1939): 241–257.
Dilthey, Wilhelm. *Der Aufbau der geschichtlichen Welt in den Geisteswissenschaften* (= *Gesammelte Schriften*. vol. 7). Ed. Bernhard Groethuysen. Vol. 7. Leipzig and Berlin 1927 (5th ed. Stuttgart 1968).
———. *Einleitung in die Geisteswissenschaften: Versuch einer Grundlegung für das Studium der Gesellschaft und Geschichte* [1883]. 5th ed. Stuttgart and Göttingen 1959.
Döblin, Alfred. "An Romanautoren und ihre Kritiker: Berliner Programm" [May 1913]. In idem, *Die Zeitlupe: Kleine Prosa*, ed. Walter Muschg. Olten and Freiburg im Breisgau 1962.
———. "Der Epiker, sein Stoff und die Kritik," in idem, *Die Zeitlupe*.
———. *Wallenstein*. Ed. Walter Muschg. Olten and Freiburg im Breisgau 1965.
Droysen, Johann Gustav. *Historik: Historisch-kritische Ausgabe*. Ed. Peter Leyh. Stuttgart 1977.
Dux, Günter. *Die Logik der Weltbilder. Sinnstrukturen im Wandel der Geschichte*. Frankfurt/ M. 1982.
———. *Die Zeit in der Geschichte: Ihre Entwicklungslogik vom Mythos zur Weltzeit*. Frankfurt/ M. 1989.
———. *Liebe und Tod im Gilgamesh-Epos: Geschichte als Weg zum Selbstbewußtsein des Menschen*. Vienna 1992.
———. *Geschlecht und Gesellschaft: Warum wir lieben*. Frankfurt/ M. 1994.
———. "Die ontogenetische und historische Entwicklung des Geistes." In idem and Ulrich Wenzel, eds. *Der Prozeß der Geistesgeschichte: Studien zur ontogenetischen und historischen Entwicklung des Geistes*. Frankfurt/ M. 1994.
———. *Historisch-genetische Theorie der Kultur*. Weilerswist 2000.
———. "How meaning came into the world and what became of it." Chap. 2 of this volume.
Eckstadt, Vitzthtum G. von. *Die Pariser Miniaturmalerei von der Zeit des Hl. Ludwig bis zu Philipp von Valois und ihr Verhältnis zur Malerei in Nordwesteuropa*. Leipzig 1907.
Eliade, Mircea. *Cosmos and History*. New York 1956.
Eliot, T. S. *Selected Prose*. Ed. John Hayward. Harmondsworth 1953.
———. *The Sacred Wood*. London 1960.
Endt, E. *Herman Gorter: Documentatie 1864–1897*. Amsterdam 1986.
Enright, D. J., and Chickera, Ernest de, eds. *Englisch Critical Texts*. London 1968.
Erlich, Victor. *Russian Formalism: History—Doctrine*. 2nd, rev. Ed. The Hague 1965.
Eucken, Rudolf. *Der Sinn und Wert des Lebens*. Leipzig 1907.

Fichte, Johann Gottlieb. *Das System der Sittenlehre* (*Werke* vol. 4). Ed. I. H. Fichte. Berlin 1971.
Forero-Medoza, Sabine. *Temps des ruins: Le gout des ruines et les formes de la conscience historique à la Renaissance.* Seyssel 2002.
Forster, E. M. *Aspects of the Novel* [1927]. London 1964.
Foucault, Michel. *The Order of Things.* Trans. A. Sheridan. New York 1970.
Franz, Otmar, ed. *Vom Sinn der Geschichte.* Stuttgart 1976.
Freud, Sigmund. "Erinnern, Wiederholen, Durcharbeiten" [1914]. In idem, *Gesammelte Werke, Bd. X: Werke aus den Jahren 1913–17,* ed. Anna Freud et al. Frankfurt/ M. 1973.
———. "The Uncanny." In *The Standard Edition of the Complete Psychological Works of Sigmund Freud.* Trans. James Strachey. Vol. 17. London 1955.
Freyer, Hans. *Theorie des objektiven Geistes. Einleitung in die Kulturphilosophie.* Berlin 1928.
Friedländer, Saul. *Memory, History, and the Extermination of the Jews of Europe.* Indianapolis and Bloomington 1993.
———, ed. *Probing the Limits of Representation. Nazism and the "Final Solution."* Cambridge 1992.
Fukuyama, Francis. *Das Ende der Geschichte: Wo stehen wir?* Munich 1992.
———. "The End of History?" *The National Interest* 16 (1989): 3–35.
Gadamer, H.G. *Wahrheit und Methode.* Tübingen 1960.
Galtung, Johan. *Peace By Peaceful Means.* London 1996.
———, Tore Heiestad, and Erik Rudeng. "On the Last 2,500 Years in Western History. And Some Remarks on the Coming 500." In Peter Burke, ed. *New Cambridge Modern History.* Vol. 13. Cambridge, Mass. 1979.
Gebhardt, Jürgen. *Politik und Eschatologie: Studien zur Geschichte der Hegelschen Schule in den Jahren 1830–1840.* Munich 1963.
Gerhardt, Volker. "Sinn des Lebens." In Joachim Ritter, ed. *Historisches Wörterbuch der Philosophie.* Vol. 9. Darmstadt 1995.
Gibson, Kathleen. "Has the Evolution of Intelligence Stagnated Since Neanderthal Man?" In George Butterworth and Julie Rutkowska, ed. *Evolution and Developmental Psychology.* New York 1985.
Ginzburg, C. "Ekphrasis and quotation." *Tijdschrift voor filosofie* 50 (1988): 3–19.
Gothein, Marie. *Geschichte der Gartenkunst.* Vol. 2. Jena 1926.
Gotlib, Ian H., and Blair Wheaton, eds. *Stress and adversity over the life course: Trajectories and turning points.* Cambridge 1997.
Gorter, Herman. *Verzen* (1890). Amsterdam 2004.
Graesse, Th., ed. *Jacobi a Voragine. Legenda aurea.* Dresden 1846.
Graeve, Hans. *Die offene Zukunft. Orientierung in der Gegenwart aus den Lehren der Geschichte.* Gräfelding 1996.
Gregorovius, Ferdinand. *Rom im Mittelalter.* Vol. 2. Munich n.d. [1921].
Groß, Hans and Friedrich Geerds, ed. *Handbuch der Kriminalistik.* Berlin 1977.
Haase, Amine. "Mahnmale gegen Faschismus und Rassismus." *Kunst und Antiquitäten* 1/2 (1992): 12–14.
Habermas, Jürgen. *Theorie des kommunikativen Handelns,* 2 vols. Frankfurt/ M. 1981.
Halbwachs, Maurice. *Das kollektive Gedächtnis.* Stuttgart 1967.
———. *Das Gedächtnis und seine sozialen Bedingungen* (French 1925). Frankfurt/ M. 1985.
Haltern, Utz. "Landschaft und Geschichte." In *Exhibition catalog. Das malerische und romantische Westfalen: Aspektes eines Buches.* Münster 1974.
Haufe, Eberhard, ed. *Schillers Werke: Nationalausgabe.* Vol. 25. Weimar 1979.
Hecker, Axel. *Geschichte als Fiction: Alfred Döblins "Wallenstein"—eine exemplarische Kritik des Realismus.* Epistemata, Vol. 21. Würzburg 1986.
Hegel, Georg Wilhelm Friedrich. *Vorlesungen über die Philosophie der Geschichte* (= *Werke.* Vol. 12). Ed. Eva Moldenhauer and Karl Markus Michel. Frankfurt/ M. 1970.
———. *Vorlesungen über die Philosophie der Geschichte.* Frankfurt 1976.
Heim, Michael and Werner Nosko. *Die Ötztalfälschung: Anatomie einer archäologischen Groteske.* Reinbek 1993.

Heuß, Alfred. *Verlust der Geschichte.* Göttingen 1959.
Heussi, Karl. *Vom Sinn der Geschichte: Augustinus und die Moderne.* Jena 1930.
Heyde, Johannes Erich. "Vom Sinn des Wortes Sinn: Prolegomena zu einer Philosophie des Sinnes." In Richard Wisser, ed. *Sinn und Sein: Ein Philosophisches Symposium.* Tübingen 1960.
Hillebrandt, Alfred, ed. *Upanishaden: Die Geheimlehre der Inder,* 27th–30th ed. Düsseldorf 1975.
Hoffmann, Detlef. "Malerische Wissenschaft." In Historisches Museum Frankfurt, ed. *Laterna Magica: Vergnügen, Belehrung, Unterhaltung. Exhibition catalog.* Frankfurt/ M. 1981.
———. "Perspektiven und Probleme von Spurensicherung: Wozu kann demokratische Erinnerungsarbeit dienen?" In Alfred G. Frei, ed. *Friedrich Hecker in den USA: Eine deutsch-amerikanische Spurensicherung.* Konstanz 1993.
———. "Abdruck, Form, Symbolisierung. Überlegungen zum nonverbalen Gedächtnis." In *Kulturwissenschaftliches Institut, Jahrbuch 1992/93.* Essen 1994.
———, and Almut Junker. *Laterna Magica: Lichtbilder aus Menschenwelt und Götterwelt.* Berlin 1982.
Holenstein, Elmar. *Von der Hintergehbarkeit der Sprache.* Frankfurt/ M. 1980.
Höneisen, Markus. *Exhibition catalog. Die ersten Bauern: Pfahlbaufunde Europas.* Zürich (Schweizerisches Landesmuseum) 1990.
Hornung, E. *Der Eine und die Vielen: Ägyptische Gottesvorstellungen.* Darmstadt 1971.
Huizinga, Johan. *Verzamelde werken,* 9 vol. Haarlem 1948–53.
———. "De kunst der Van Eyck's in het leven van hun tijd." In *Verzamelde werken.* Vol. 1. Haarlem 1948.
Humboldt, Wilhelm von. "Über die Aufgabe des Geschichtsschreibers" [1821]. In idem, *Werke in fünf Bänden,* ed. Andreas Flitner, Klaus Giel. Vol. 1. Darmstadt 1960.
Huntington, Samuel. *The Clash of Civilizations and the remaking of the world.* New York 1996.
———. *Der Kampf der Kulturen: Die Neugestaltung der Weltpolitik im 21. Jahrhundert.* Trans. Holger Fliessbach. Vienna 1996.
Husserl, Edmund. *Cartesianische Meditationen und Pariser Vorträge (= Husserls gesammelte Werke Edmund Husserl.* Vol. 1). Ed. Stefan Strasser. Den Haag 1959. 159ff.
———. *Vorlesungen zur Phänomenologie des inneren Zeitbewußtseins.* Ed. Martin Heidegger. 2nd ed. Tübingen 1980.
Huyssen, Andreas. "The Monument in a Post-modern Age." In James E. Young, ed. *The Art of Memory: Holocaust Memorials in History.* Munich 1994.
Illustrierte Zeitung, 436 (1851); 455 (20 March 1852).
Immelmann, Thomas. *Der unheimlichste aller Gäste: Nihilismus und Sinndebatte in der Literatur von der Aufklärung bis zur Moderne.* Bielefeld 1992.
Jaeger, Friedrich. "Der Kulturbegriff im Werk Max Webers und seine Bedeutung für eine moderne Kulturgeschichte." *Geschichte und Gesellschaft* 18 (1992): 371–393.
———. *Bürgerliche Modernisierungskrise und historische Sinnbildung: Kulturgeschichte bei Droysen, Burckhardt und Max Weber (Bürgertum. Beiträge zur europäischen Gesellschaftsgeschichte.* Vol. 5). Göttingen 1994.
Jansonius, F. "De stijl van Huizinga." *Bijdragen en mededelingen betreffende de geschiedenis der Nederlanden* 88 (1973): 195–215.
Jhering, Barbara v. "Duell mit der Verdrangung." *Die Zeit* (14 February 1992).
Johnson, Samuel. "Preface to Shakespeare" [1765]. In *English Critical Texts.* D. J. Enright and Ernest de Chickera, eds. London 1968.
Joyce, James. *Ulysses* [1922]. Harmondsworth 1969.
Kamerbeek Jr., J. "Huizinga en de beweging van tachtig." *Tijdschrift voor geschiedenis* 67 (1954): 317–335.
Kant, Immanuel. "Von der Deduktion der reinen Verstandesbegriffe." In idem, *Kritik der reinen Vernunft.* Vol. 3 of *Gesammelte Werke.* Ed. Königlich Preußische Akademie der Wissenschaften, Berlin 1968.
———. "Idee zu einer allgemeinen Geschichte in weltbürgerlicher Absicht" [1784]. In idem, *Werke in sechs Bänden,* ed. Wilhelm Weischedel. Vol. 6. Darmstadt 1975.
———. *Deines Lebens Sinn.* Ed. Wolfgang Kraus. Zürich 1987.

Kemperink, M. G. *Van observatie tot extase*. Utrecht 1988.
Kittsteiner, Heinz Dieter. "Walter Benjamins Historismus." In Norbert Bolz and Bernd Witte, eds. *Passagen: Walter Benjamins Urgeschichte des neunzehnten Jahrhunderts*. Munich 1984.
Klaus, Georg, and Manfred Buhr, eds. *Philosophisches Wörterbuch*. 2nd ed. Leipzig 1965.
Koelmel, Wilhelm. "Typik und Atypik. Zum Geschichtsbild der kirchenpolitischen Publizistik (11.–14. Jahrhundert)." In Clemens Bauer and Laetitia Boehm, eds. *Speculum Historiale: Geschichte im Spiegel von Geschichtsschreibung und Geschichtsdeutung (Festschrift Johannes Spoerl)*. Munich 1965.
Köhler, Oskar, ed. *Vom Sinn und Unsinn in der Geschichte*. Freiburg 1985.
Kon, Igor S. *Die Geschichtsphilosophie des 20. Jahrhunderts. Kritischer Abriß*. Vol. 1: *Die Geschichtsphilosophie der Epoche des Imperialismus*. Translated into German by v. W. Hoepp. 2nd ed. Berlin 1966.
Koselleck, Reinhart. "'Historia Magistra Vitae': Über die Auflösung des Topos im Horizont neuzeitlich bewegter Geschichte." In Hermann Braun, ed. *Natur und Geschichte: Karl Löwith zum 70. Geburtstag*. Stuttgart 1967.
———. *Vergangene Zukunft: Zur Semantik geschichtlicher Zeiten*. Frankfurt/ M. 1979.
Krautheimer, Richard. *Rome: Profile of a City, 312–1308*. Princeton 1980.
Krug, Wilhelm Traugott. *Allgemeines Handwörterbuch der philosophischen Wissenschaften*. 2nd ed. vol. 3, Leipzig 1833.
Krul, W. E. *Historicus tegen de tijd: Opstellen over leven en werk van Johan Huizinga*. Groningen 1990.
———. "In de schaduwen van morgen." In R. T. Segers, ed. *Visies op cultuur en literatuur*. Amsterdam 1991.
Kugelmass, Jack, and Jonathan Boyarin, eds. *From a Ruined Garden: The Memorial Books of Polish Jewry*. New York 1983.
Kulke, Hermann. "Geschichtsschreibung als Heilung eines Traditionsbruches?" In *Report 2/94 der Forschungsgruppe Historische Sinnbildung*. Bielefeld 1994/95.
Ladner, Georg. "Vegetation Symbolism and the Concept of Renaissance." Originally published in M. Meiss, ed. *De artibus opuscula XL: Essays in Honor of Erwin Panofsky*. New York 1961. Reprinted in Georg Ladner. *Images and Ideas in the Middle Ages*. Vol. 2. Rome 1983.
Lang, B. *Act and Idea in the Nazi Genocide*. Chicago 1990.
Laotzu. *Tao te king*. Trans. Richard Wilhelm. Düsseldorf 1982. (For a translation into English, the reader is referred to the rendering by Wing-tsit Chou, *The Way of Lao Tzu*, New York 1963).
Larkin, Margaret. *Die sechs Tage von Yad Mordechai*. Jerusalem n. d.
Laub, D. "Bearing witness, or the vicissitudes of listening." In S. Felman and D. Laub, eds. *Testimony. Crises of Witnessing in Literature, Psychoanalysis and History*. New York 1992.
Lauth, Rudolf. *Die Frage nach dem Sinn des Daseins*. Munich 1953.
Le Goff, Jacques. *Geschichte und Gedächtnis*. Frankfurt/ M. 1992.
Leed, Eric J. *No Man's Land: Combat and Identity in World War I*. Cambridge 1979.
Leinhardt, Gaea et al. "A Sense of History." *Educational Psychologist* 29, no. 2 (1994): 79–88.
Lenneberg, Eric H. *Biologische Grundlagen der Sprache*. Frankfurt/ M. 1972.
Lessing, Theodor. *Geschichte als Sinngebung des Sinnlosen* [1919]. Munich 1983.
Levi-Straus, Claude. *The Savage Mind*. Chicago 1966.
Libeskind, Daniel. "Between the Lines." In Kristin Feireiss, ed. *Daniel Libeskind: Erweiterung des Berlin Museums mit Abteilung Jüdisches Museum*. Berlin 1992.
Lichtenstein, Jacqueline, and Gerard Wajeman. "Jochen Gerz: Invisible Monument," *artpress* (April 1993): E1–E6.
Liebermann, P. *Uniquely Human: The Evolution of Speech, Thought and Selfless Behavior*. Cambridge, Mass. 1991.
Lock, Andrew. *The Guided Reinvention of Language*. London 1980.
Lotze, Herman. *Mikrokosmos, Ideen zur Naturgeschichte und Geschichte der Menschheit: Versuch einer Anthropologie*. Vol. 3 (1864) of 3 vols. (1856–64), 6th ed. Leipzig 1923.
Lovejoy, Arthur O. *The Great Chain of Being*. Cambridge, Mass. 1966 [1936].
Löwith, Karl. *Von Hegel zu Nietzsche* [1941]. 2nd ed. Stuttgart 1950.

———. *Weltgeschichte und Heilsgeschehen. Die theologischen Voraussetzungen der Geschichtsphilosophie* [1953]. 6th ed. Stuttgart 1973.
Luckmann, Thomas. *Lebenswelt und Gesellschaft*. Paderborn 1980.
Ludwig, Rudolf. *Das Buch der Geologie oder die Wunder der Erdrinde und der Urwelt: Naturgeschichte der Erde in allgemein verständlicher Darstellung für alle Freunde dieser Wissenschaft mit Berücksichtigung der Jugend ...* , parts 1 and 2. Leipzig 1855.
Luhmann, Niklas. *Soziale Systeme*. Frankfurt/ M. 1984.
Lyotard, Jean Francois. *Le Différend*. Trans. Van Den Abbeele. Minneapolis 1987.
Mahler, Margaret et al., eds. *Die psychische Geburt des Menschen*. Frankfurt/ M. 1989.
Mann, Golo. "Die Grundprobleme der Geschichtsphilosophie von Plato bis Hegel." In Leonhard Reinisch, ed. *Der Sinn der Geschichte: 7 Essays von Golo Mann. Karl Löwith. Rudolf Bultmann. Theodor Litt. Arnold J. Toynbee. Karl R. Popper. Hans Urs von Balthasar*. 4th ed. Munich 1970.
———. *Wallenstein: Sein Leben erzählt von Golo Mann*. Frankfurt/ M. 1971.
———. "Plädoyer für die historische Erzählung" in Jürgen Kocka and Thomas Nipperdey, eds. *Theorie und Erzählung in der Geschicht*e (= *Theorie der Geschichte: Beiträge zur Historik*. Vol. 3). Munich 1979.
Mann, Paul. *The Theory-Death of the Avant-Garde*. Indianapolis and Bloomington 1991.
Mansfeld, Michael. *Denk ich an Deutschland*. München 1959.
Marquard, Odo. "Zur Diätetik der Sinnerwartung. Philosophische Bemerkungen." In *Sinn im Wissenschaftshorizont* (*Mainzer Universitätsgespräche,* SS 1983). Ed. Günter Eifler et al. Mainz 1984.
Marx, Karl. "Zur Kritik der Hegelschen Rechtsphilosophie. Einleitung [1844]." In *Marx-Engels-Werke*. Vol. 1. Berlin 1969.
——— and Friedrich Engels. *Die deutsche Ideologie* [1845]. In *Marx-Engels-Werke*. Vol. 3. Berlin 1969.
Maturana, Humberto R. *Der Baum der Erkenntnis*. Bern 1987.
———, and Francisco J. Varela. "Autopoietische Systeme: eine Bestimmung der lebendigen Organisation." In: *Erkennen: Die Organisation und Verkörperung von Wirklichkeit*. Ed. Humberto R. Maturana. Braunschweig 1982.
Maurus, Terentianus. *De litteris syllabis et metris*. Hildesheim 2002.
Mayntz, R. *Soziale Diskontinuitäten, in Soziale Dynamik und politische Steuerung*. Frankfurt/ M. 1997.
Megill, Allan. "Jörn Rüsens's Theory between Modernism and Rhetoric of Inquiry," *History and Theory* 33 (1994): 39–60.
Mehlis, Georg. *Lehrbuch der Geschichtsphilosophie*. Berlin 1915.
Meinecke, Friedrich. *Von geschichtlichen Sinn und vom Sinn der Geschichte*. 5th unrevised ed. Stuttgart 1951.
Meinhardt, H. "Idea." In Joachim Ritter, ed. *Historisches Wörterbuch der Philosophie*. Vol. 4. Darmstadt 1976.
Meyer, Martin. *Ende der Geschichte?* Munich 1993.
Meyers Konversationslexikon. Vol. 13. 3rd ed. Leipzig 1878.
Millet, Gabriel. *Recherches sur l'iconographie de l'Evangile aux XIVe, XVe ey XVIe siecles*, 2nd. ed. Paris 1960.
Mink, Louis. "History and Fiction as Modes of Comprehension." In Brian Fay, Eugene O. Golob, and Richard T. Vann, eds. *Historical Understanding*. Ithaca 1987.
Moos, Peter von. *Hildebert von Lavardin: 1056–1133*. Stuttgart 1965.
Morand, Kathleen. *Jean Pucelle*. Oxford 1962.
Müller, Klaus E. "Identität und Geschichte: Widerspruch oder Komplementarität? Ein ethnologischer Beitrag." *Paideuma* 38 (1992): 17–29.
———. "Prähistorisches Geschichtsbewußtsein." In Jörn Rüsen, Michael Gottlob and Achim Mittag, eds. *Die Vielfalt der Kulturen*. Frankfurt/ M. 1998.
Nagl-Docekal, Herta. "Ist Geschichtsphilosophie heute noch möglich?" In idem, ed. *Der Sinn des Historischen. Geschichtsphilosophische Debatten*. Frankfurt/ M. 1996.

Namer, G. *La Commémoration en France: de 1945 à nos jours.* Paris 1987.
Neumann, Carl W. *Das Werden des Menschen und der Kultur.* Leipzig 1932.
Neumayr, Melchior. *Erdgeschichte.* Leipzig and Vienna 1895.
Niethammer, Lutz. *Posthistoire. Has history become to an end?* London 1992.
Nietzsche, Friedrich. *Werke in drei Bänden.* Ed. Karl Schlechta. Vol. 3. Munich 1962.
———. "Aus dem Nachlass der Achziger Jahre." In idem, *Werke.* Vol. 3.
———. *Die Fröhliche Wissenschaft* [2nd ed. 1887]. In idem, *Werke.* Vol. 3.
———. *The Use and Abuse of History.* Trans. Adrian Collins. New York 1985.
———. "Unzeitgemäße Betrachtungen. Zweites Stück: Vom Nutzen und Nachteil der Historie für das Leben." [1874] In idem, *Werke.* Vol. 3, and in idem. *Sämtliche Werke: Kritische Studienausgabe,* eds. Giorgio Colli and Mazzino Montinari. Vol. 1. Munich 1988.
Nora, P. *Les lieux de memoire.* Vol. 1. Paris 1984.
Nordau, Max. *Der Sinn der Geschichte.* Berlin 1909.
Norman, Andrew P. "Telling It Like It Was: Historical Narratives on Their Own Terms." *History and Theory* 30 (1991):119–135.
Ort, Ernst Wolfgang. "R. H. Lotze: Das Ganze unseres Welt- und Selbstverständnisses." In Josef Speck, ed. *Grundprobleme der großen Philosophen (Philosophie der Neuzeit IV).* Göttingen 1995.
Overbeck, Franz. *Christentum und Kultur, from the literary bequest* [1919]. Ed. C. A. Bernoulli. Darmstadt 1963.
Pabel, Hilmar. *Jahre unseres Lebens. Deutsche Schicksalsbilder.* Stuttgart 1954.
Panofsky, Erwin. *Early Netherlandish Painting: Its Origins and Character.* Cambridge, Mass. 1953.
———. "Renaissance - Selbstbezeichnung oder Selbsttäuschung?" In idem, *Die Renaissance der Europäischen Kunst.* Frankfurt/ M. 1979.
Parfit, Derek. *Reasons and Persons.* Oxford 1984.
Parker, Sue Taylor. "Higher Intelligence as Adaptations for Social and Technological Strategies in Early Homo Sapiens" In George Butterworth, ed., *Evolution and Developmental Psychology.* Whitstable 1985.
———, and Constance Milbrath. "Higher Intelligence, Propositional Language, and Culture as Adaptations for Planning." In Kathleen R. Gibson and Tim Ingold, eds. *Tools, Language and Cognition in Human Evolution.* Cambridge 1993.
Pekař, Josef. *Wallenstein, 1630–1634: Tragödie einer Verschwörung.* Berlin 1937.
Pelters, Wilm. *Lessings Standort: Sinndeutung der Geschichte als Kern seines Denkens.* Heidelberg 1972.
Piaget, Jean. *The Moral Judgment of the Child.* Glencoe 1948.
———. *The Construction of Reality in the Child.* New York 1954.
Plato. *The Dialogues of Plato.* Translated with analyses and introductions by B. Jowett. 4 vols. Oxford 1953.
———. *The Republic of Plato.* Translated with intoduction and notes by Francis MacDonald Cornford. London 1945 [1941].
Platt, Kristin, and Mihran Dabag, eds. *Generation und Gedächtnis. Erinnerungen und kollektive Identitäten.* Opladen 1995.
Poe, Edgar Allan. *Tales and Poems.* London 1982 [first edition by Random House, Inc., New York 1938].
Pohl, Klaus Dieter. *Handbuch der naturwissenschaftlichen Kriminalistik unter besonderer Berücksichtigung der forensischen Chemie.* Heidelberg 1981.
Pohlmann, Ulrich, and Marjen Schmidt. "Das Münchner Daguerre-Triptychon: Ein Protokoll zu Geschichte seiner Präsentation, Aufbewahrung und Restaurierung." *Fotogeschichte* 14 (1994): 3–13.
Pope, Alexander. "An Essay on Criticism [1711]." In *English Critical Texts.* D. J. Enright and Ernest de Chickera, eds. London 1968.
Quincey, Thomas de. *Confessions of an Opium-Eater.* Harmondsworth 1971.
Quine, W. O. *From a Logical Point of View.* 2nd rev. ed. New York 1963.
Ranke, Leopold von. *Geschichten der romanischen und germanischen Völker von 1494–1514.* In idem, *Sämtliche Werke.* Vol. 33–34. Leipzig 1855.

———. *Das Briefwerk*. Ed. Walther Peter Fuchs. Hamburg 1949.
———. *Über die Epochen der neueren Geschichte: Historisch-kritische Ausgabe (Aus Werk und Nachlaß*. Vol. 2). Ed. Theodor Schieder and Helmut Berding. Munich 1971.
Rauh, Horst Dieter. *Im Labyrinth der Geschichte. Die Sinnfrage von der Aufklärung zu Nietzsche*. Munich 1990.
Reiner, Hans. *Der Sinn unseres Daseins*. 2nd ed. Tübingen 1964.
Rickert, Heinrich. *Die Grenzen der naturwissenschaftlichen Begriffsbildung. Eine logische Einleitung in die historischen Wissenschaften*. Freiburg 1902.
———. *Die Probleme der Geschichtsphilosophie: Eine Einführung*. 3rd rev. Ed. Heidelberg 1924.
Ricoeur, Paul. *Temps et Recit*. Vol. 1. Paris 1983.
———. *Oneself as Another*. Trans. K. Blamey. Chicago 1992.
———. "Geschichte und Rhetorik." In *Der Sinn des Historischen*. Ed. Herta Nagl-Docekal.
Rorty, Richard, ed. *The Linguistic Turn*. Chicago 1964.
Rossanda, Rossana. "Sartre und die politische Praxis." In idem., *Über die Dialektik von Kontinuität und Bruch*. Frankfurt/ M. 1975.
Rusch, Gerhard. *Erkenntnis, Wissenschaft, Geschichte: Von einem konstruktivistischen Standpunkt*. Frankfurt/ M. 1987.
Rusconi, G.E. *Resistenza e postfascismo*. Bologna 1995.
Rüsen, Jörn. *Grundzüge einer Historik*. Vol. 1: *Historische Vernunft: Die Grundlagen der Geschichtswissenschaft*. Göttingen 1983. Vol. 2: *Rekonstruktion der Vergangenheit: Die Prinzipien der historischen Forschung*. Göttingen 1986. Vol. 3: *Lebendige Geschichte: Formen und Funktionen des historischen Wissens*. Göttingen 1989.
———. *Zeit und Sinn. Strategien historischen Denkens*. Frankfurt/ M. 1990.
———. *Konfigurationen des Historismus, Studien zur deutschen Wissenschaftskultur*. Frankfurt/ M. 1993.
———. "Vom Umgang mit den Anderen—zum Stand der Menschenrechte heute." *Internationale Schulbuchforschung* 15 (1993): 167–178.
———. "Historische Methode und religiöser Sinn -Vorüberlegungen zu einer Dialektik der Rationalisierung des historischen Denkens in der Moderne." In *Geschichtsdiskurs*. Vol. 2: *Anfänge des modernen historischen Denkens*. Eds Wolfgang Küttler/ Jörn Rüsen/ Ernst Schulin. Frankfurt/ M. 1994, reprinted in idem, *Geschichte im Kulturprozeß*. Cologne 2002.
———. "Was ist Geschichtskultur? Überlegungen zu einer neuen Art, über Geschichte nachzudenken." In idem, *Historische Orientierung: Über die Arbeit des Geschichtsbewußtseins, sich in der Zeit zurechtzufinden*. Cologne 1994.
———. "Historisches Erzählen." In idem, *Zerbrechende Zeit: Über den Sinn der Geschichte*. Cologne 2001.
———. "History: Overview." In Neil J. Smelser and Paul B. Baltes, eds. *International Encyclopedia of the Social & Behavioral Sciences*. Amsterdam 2001.
———. "Following Kant: European idea for a universal history with an intercultural intent." *Groniek: Historisch Tijdschrift* 160 (2003): 359–368.
———. "Holocaust memory and German identity." In idem, *History: Narration – Interpretation – Orientation*. New York 2004.
———, ed. *Western Historical Thinking. An Intercultural Debate*. New York 2002.
———, ed. *Time and History in the Variety of Cultures*, New York, forthcoming.
Saussure, Ferdinand de. *Course in General Linguistics*. Ed. C. Bally and A. Sechehaye. New York 1959.
Saxl, Fritz. "Die Ausdrucksgebärden in der bildenden Kunst" [1932]. In Dieter Wuttke, ed. *Warburg, Ausgewählte Schriften*. Baden-Baden 1979.
Scheffel, Josef Viktor. "Ekkerhard. Eine Geschichte aus dem 10. Jahrhundert." In Friedrich Panzer, ed. *Scheffels Werke*. Vol. 3. Leipzig and Vienna 1919.
Schieder, Theodor. "Vom Sinn der Geschichte." In Otmar Franz, ed. *Vom Sinn der Geschichte*. Stuttgart 1976.
Schiller, Friedrich. "Was heißt und zu welchem Ende studiert man Universalgeschichte?" [1789]. In Kurt Rossmann, ed. *Deutsche Geschichtsphilosopie: Ausgewählte Texte von Lessing bis Jaspers*. Munich 1969.

Schluchter, Wolfgang. *Die Entwicklung des okzidentalen Rationalismus.* Tübingen 1979.

Schmidt, Siegfried J. "Gedächtnis—Erzählen—Identität." In Aleida Assmann and Dietrich Harth, eds. *Mnemosyne: Formen und Funktionen der kulturellen Erinnerung.* Frankfurt/ M. 1991.

Schmidt-Linsenhoff, Viktoria. "Die Verschlußzeit des Herzens: Zu Hilmer Pabels Fotobuch 'Jahre unseres Lebens' 1954." *Fotogeschichte* 12 (1992): 53–64.

Schopenhauer, Arthur. *Die Welt als Wille und Vorstellung.* Ed. Arthur Hübscher. Vol. 2, 2nd ed. Wiesbaden 1949.

Schütz, Alfred. *Der sinnhafte Aufbau de sozialen Welt: Eine Einleitung in die verstehende Soziologie.* Frankfurt/ M. 1974 [Vienna 1932].

Schütz, Alfred, and Thomas Luckmann. *Strukturen der Lebenswelt.* 2 vols. Frankfurt/ M. 1979, 1984.

Simmel, Georg. "Die Ruine." In idem, *Philosophische Kultur: Gesammelte Essays,* 2nd ed. Leipzig 1919.

———. "Das Abenteuer" [1910]. In idem, *Philosophische Kultur: Über das Abenteuer, die Geschlechter und die Krise der Moderne. Gesammelte Essays.* Berlin 1983.

———. *Die Probleme der Geschichtsphilosophie* [1892]. In idem, *Gesamtausgabe.* Vol. 2. Frankfurt/ M. 1998.

Snell, Bruno. *Die Entdeckung des Geistes.* Hamburg 1955.

Speck, Josef. "Zur Geschichte der Pfahlbauforschung." In Markus Höneisen, ed. *Exhibition catalogue. Die ersten Bauern.* Zürich 1990.

Spence, Donald P. *Narrative Truth and Historical Truth. Meaning and Interpretation in Psychoanalyis.* New York 1982.

Spindler, Konrad. *Der Mann aus dem Eis: Die Ötztaler Mumie verrät die Geheimnisse der Steinzeit.* Munich 1993.

Spranger, Eduard. *Lebensformen: Geisteswissenschaftliche Psychologie und Ethik der Persönlichkeit.* 8th ed. Tübingen 1950.

Steenblock, Volker. "Historische Vernunft—Geschichte als Wissenschaft und als orientierende Sinnbildung: Zum Abschluß von Jörn Rüsens dreibändiger 'Historik'." *Dilthey-Jahrbuch für Philosophie und Geschichte der Geisteswissenschaften* 8 (1992/3): 367–380.

Strauß, Botho. "Wollt ihr das totale Engeneering?" *Die Zeit* 20, no. 52 (December 2000): 59–61

Stückrath, Jörn. "The Meaning of History: A Modern Construction and Notion?" Chap. 4 in this volume.

Suvvanto, Pekka. "Wallenstein und seine Anhänger am Weiner Hof zur Zeit des Zweiku Generalats 1631 bis 1634," *Studia Historica,* publ. by Historical Society, Vol. 5. Helsinki 1963.

Swift, Jonathan. *A Tale of a Tub. Written for the Universal Improvement of Mankind* [1704]. Ed. Lewis Mellville. London 1968.

Taylor, Charles. *Multikulturalismus und die Politik der Anerkennung.* Frankfurt/ M. 1993.

Thieme, Ulrich and Fritz Becker. *Allgemeines Lexikon der bildenden Künste von der Antike bis zur Gegenwart.* Vol. 22. Leipzig 1929.

Thürnau, Donatus. "Sinn." In Hans Jörg Sandkühler, ed. *Europäische Enzyklopädie zu Philosophie und Wissenschaften.* Vol. 4. Hamburg 1990.

Unger, Franz. *Die Urwelt in ihren verschiedenen Bildungsepochen: 14 landschaftliche Darstellungen mit erläuterndem Text.* Vienna 1851, 2nd ed. 1852.

Unseld, Siegfried, ed. *Zur Aktualität Walter Benjamins.* Frankfurt/ M. 1972.

van Deijssel, Lodewijk. *Verzamelde opstelle: Tweede bundel.* Amsterdam 1897.

Vischer, Friedrich. "Das Symbol" [1887]. In Friedrich Vischer. *Ausgewählte Werke in acht Teilen.* Vol. 8: *Prosaschriften II.* Leipzig n. d. ca. 1920.

Weber, Max. "Die 'Objektivität' sozialwissenschaftlicher und sozialpolitischer Erkenntnis." In idem, *Gesammelte Aufsätze zur Wissenschaftslehre,* ed. Johannes Winckelmann. 3rd ed. Tübingen 1968.

———. *Wirtschaft und Gesellschaft.* Cologne 1964.

———. *Gesammelte Aufsätze zur Religionssoziologie.* Vol. 1. Tübingen 1968.

———. "Wissenschaft als Beruf" (1917). In idem. *Gesammelte Aufsätze zur Wissenschaftslehre,* ed. Johannes Winckelmann. 3rd ed. Tübingen 1968.

———. "Die protestantische Ethik und der Geist des Kapitalismus." In idem, *Gesammelte Aufsätze zur Religionssoziologie.* Vol. 1. Tübingen 1968.

———. "Kritische Studien auf dem Gebiet der kulturwissenschaftlichen Logik." In idem, *Gesammelte Aufsätze zur Wissenschaftslehre,* ed. Johannes Winckelmann, 7th ed. Tübingen 1988.

Welsch, Wolfgang. *Vernunft. Die zeitgenössische Vernunftkritik und das Konzept der transversalen Vernunft.* Frankfurt/ M. 1996.

Wentscher, Max. *Herman Lotze.* Vol. 1: *Lotzes Leben und Werk.* Heidelberg 1913.

Wenzel, Ulrich. *Vom Ursprung zum Prozess.* Opladen 2000.

———. "Dynamismus und Finalismus: Zur Strukturlogik der aristotelischen Naturphilosophie" In Günter Dux, *Der Prozeß der Geistesgeschichte.* Frankfurt/ M. 1994.

White, Hayden. "The Question of Narrative in Contemporary Historical Theory." In idem, *The Content of the Form.* Baltimore 1987.

———. "Das Problem der Erzählung in der modernen Geschichtsschreibung." In Pietro Rossi, ed. *Theorie der modernen Geschichtsschreibung.* Frankfurt/ M. 1987.

———. "Historical emplotment and the problem of truth." In *Probing the limits of representation.* S. Friedlander, ed. Cambridge, Mass. 1992.

———. "Writing in the middle voice." *Stanford Literature Review* 9 (1992): 185–188.

Wieland, Wolfgang. *Die aristotelische Physik.* Göttingen 1970.

Wigand, Georg, ed. *Das malerische Deutschland.* 10 vols. Leipzig ca. 1840.

Williams, John. *A Spanish Apocalypse: The Morgan Beatus Manuscript.* New York 1991.

Wills, Gary. *Lincoln at Gettysburg: The Words That Remade America.* New York 1992.

Winch, Peter. "Understanding a Primitive Society." *American Philosophical Quarterly* 1 (1964): 307–324.

Wind, Edgar. "Warburgs Begriff der Kulturwissenschaft und seine Bedeutung für die Ästhetik" (1931). In Dieter Wuttke, ed. *Aby M. Warburg, Ausgewählte Schriften und Würdigungen.* 3rd ed. Baden-Baden 1992.

Wineburg, Samuel S. "Introduction: Out of our Past and Into Our Future—The Psychological Study of Learning and Teaching History." *Educational Psychologist* 29, no. 2 (1994): 57–60.

Winzen, Matthias. "The Need for Public Representation and the Burden of the German Past." *Art Journal* 48 (Winter 1989): 309–314.

Yerushalmi, Yosef Hayim. *Zakhor: Jewish History and Jewish Memory.* Seattle and London 1982.

Young, James E. "The Counter-monument: Memory against Itself in Germany Today." *Critical Inquiry* 18 (winter 1992): 267–296, expanded further in idem, *The Texture of Memory: Holocaust Memorials and Meaning.* New Haven and London 1993.

———. *The Texture of Memory: Holocaust Memorials and Meaning.* New Haven and London 1993.

Notes on the Contributors

Frank R. Ankersmit, Dr., Professor of Intellectual History and Historical Theory at the University of Groningen in the Netherlands. General research topics: historical theory, political philosophy, and aesthetics. His many publications include *History and Tropology* (1994), *Aesthetic politics: Political philosophy beyond fact and value* (1997), and *Historical Representation* (2001); his *Sublime Historical Experience* (Stanford, Calif. 2005)

Aleida Assmann, Dr., Professor of English Literature and Literary Theory at the University of Konstanz, Germany. Main areas of interest: history and theory of writing, historical anthropology, intermediality, and cultural memory. Her publications include *Erinnerungsräume: Formen und Wandlungen des kulturellen Gedächtnisses* (1999) and *Zeit und Tradition: Kulturelle Strategien der Dauer* (1999). She is also the editor of several anthologies of comparative literature and cultural studies, including *Weisheit* (1991) and *Texte und Lektüren* (1996).

Moshe Barasch (†), Dr., Professor Emeritus of the History of Art at the Hebrew University of Jerusalem. His research interests include iconography from late Antiquity to Baroque and the theory of art. His publications included *Das Gottesbild: Studien zur Darstellung des Unsichtbaren* (1998), *The language of art: Studies in interpretation* (1997), and *Blindness: The history of a mental image in Western thought* (2001).

Alessandro Cavalli, Dr., Professor of Sociology at the University of Pavia (Italy). He has been a visiting professor in Heidelberg, Louvain-la-Neuve and was a Fellow of the Collegium Budapest and a Member of the Council of the Academia Europaea and of the Accademia delle Scienze of Turin. General research topics: history of sociological thought, generations, youth and education, social organization of time, memory, sociology of emergencies. His publications include *Giovanni oggi* (1984), *Georg Simmel e la modernità* (1994), *Youth in Europe* (1995), and *Incontro con la sociologia* (2001).

David Carr, Dr., Professor of Philosophy at Emory University, Atlanta, Georgia, USA. He is the author of *Phenomenology and the Problem of History* (1974), *Time, Narrative, and History* (1986), *Interpreting Husserl* (1987), and *The Paradox of Subjectivity* (1999).

Günter Dux, Dr., Professor at the Institute for Sociology, University of Freiburg, Germany. Director of the Research-Center for Social and Cultural Change. Main interests: general social theory; sociology of knowledge and theory of culture. He has published numerous books and articles. His latest book is *Die Moral in der prozessualen Logik der Moderne: warum wir sollen, was wir sollen* (2004).

Johan Galtung, Dr. hc mult, Professor of Peace Studies at the University of Hawaii (USA), the University of Witten/Herdecke (Germany), the European Peace University (Austria), and the University of Tromsoe (Norway); Director of TRANSCEND: A Peace and Development Network. General research topics: conflict, peace and development theory, macrohistory, epistemology and civilization theory. His books include *Theory and Methods of Social Research*, vols. 1–14 (1970), *Essays in Peace Research*, vols. 1–6 (1975), *Peace by Peaceful Means* (1996), and with Sohail Inayatullah *Macrohistory and Macrohistorians* (1997). See www.transcend.org.

Detlef Hoffmann, Dr., Professor of Art History at the Carl von Ossietzky University in Oldenburg. From 1971 till 1981 Curator of the Historisches Museum, Frankfurt am Main. He studies the cultural history of playing cards, research on memorials in former concentration camps, and traces of traumatic events in art of the twentieth-century. His many publications deal with art and cultural history from the eighteenth to the twentieth-century, especially the history of photography, playing cards, comics, and industrial archeology, and with the theory and practice of museum studies. One is *Das Gedächtnis der Dinge: KZ-Relikte und KZ-Denkmäler 1945–1995* (1998).

Eberhard Lämmert, Dr. Dr. h.c., Professor at the Institut für Allgemeine und Vergleichende Literaturwissenschaft at the Freie Universität Berlin. General research topics: theory of literature, narratology, history of the freelance writer, history of humanities. Relevant publications (among others): *Geschichtsschreibung und Geschichtsdarstellung im Roman seit dem 18. Jh.* (1987), *Wer sind wir? Europäische Phänotypen im Roman des 20. Jh.* (Ed.) (1996), *Die erzählerische Dimension. Eine Gemeinsamkeit der Künste* (Ed.) (1999).

Paul Ricoeur†, Dr., Professor emeritus of the University of Paris-X (Nanterre) and of the University of Chicago. Main interests: language, history, and philosophy. His work was essentially concerned with that grand theme of philosophy: the meaning of life. His most widely read works are the three volumes of *Time and Narrative* (1984), *From Text to Action* (1991), *Oneself As Another* (1992), and *The Rule of Metaphor* (2003). His latest was *La memoire, l'histoire, l'oubli* (2003), *Sur la traduction* (2003), and *Pacours de la reconaissance* (2004).

Jörn Rüsen, Dr., Professor for General History and Historical Culture at the University of Witten/Herdecke (Germany) and President of the Institute for Advanced Study in the Humanities at Essen. Fields of research: theory and methodology of history, history of historiography, modern intellectual history, historical consciousness, historical learning; processes of sense-generation, strategies of intercultural comparison and communication, general issues of cultural orientation in modern societies. His many publications include *Historische Vernunft* (1983), *Zeit und Sinn* (1990), *Geschichte im Kulturprozeß* (2002), *Kann Gestern besser werden?* (2003), and *History: Narration – Interpretation – Orientation* (New York and London 2005).

Jörn Stückrath, Dr., Professor at the University of Lüneburg, Germany. General research topics: historical consciousness, didactics of literature. His publications include *Zur Geschichte und Theorie der historischen Rezeptionsforschung* (1978), *Metageschichte. Hayden White und Paul Ricoeur* (1997, ed. et al.), and *Literaturwissenschaft: Ein Grundkurs* (8th ed.2004, ed. et al.).

James E. Young, Dr., Professor of English and Judaic Studies at the University of Massachusetts, Amherst, and currently Chair of the Department of Judaic and Near Eastern Studies. He is the author of *At Memory's Edge: After-images of the Holocaust in Contemporary Art and Architecture* (2000), *The Texture of Memory* (1993), and *Writing and Rewriting the Holocaust* (1988).

Index of Names

A

Adolph, Gustav, 234
Adorno, Theodor W., 241
Ankersmit, Frank, 4, 12, 14
Antonionis, Michelangelo, 194
Arafat, Yasser, 242, 248
Arendt, Hannah, 195, 196
Aristotle, 37
Aristotelian, 29, 34, 95, 110
Arnim, Hans Georg von, 224, 225, 226, 228, 229, 230, 231
Aron, Raymond, 15
Assmann, Aleida, 4
Auerbach, Erich, 146, 147
Augusta (Crown Princess), 209
Augustine of Hippo, 10, 15, 67, 83

B

Balthasar, Hans Urs von, 73
Barasch, Moshe, 4
Barthes, Roland, 145, 148
Beagle Boys, 183
Beattie, Owen, 184, 189
Benjamin, Walter, 80, 241
Benveniste, Émile, 145
Berdjajew, Nikolaus, 65
Bernhart, Joseph, 65
Bernheim, Ernst, 65, 75
Bismarck, Otto von, 104
Blumenberg, Hans, 155
Bossuet, 67, 73
Braudel, Fernand, 12
Brecht, Bertolt, 198
Browne, Dik, 52
Buber, Martin, 95
Büchner, Georg, 74

Buhr, Manfred, 67, 69, 82
Burckhardt, Jacob, 12, 66, 67, 74, 121
Burri, 178

C

Cavalli Alessandro, 4
Carr, David, 4
Cartesian, 33, 95
Celan, Paul, 148
Certeau, Michel de, 12
Chambers, Sir William, 209
Chaucer, Geoffrey, 160
Collingwood, R. G., 12, 31, 120, 133
Columbus, Christopher, 51, 52, 53
Comte, Auguste, 83
Cotta, Bernhard, 185
Croce, 67
Curtius, Ernst Robert, 163

D

Daguerre, Louis Jacques Mande, 194
Danto, Arthur, 133, 134
De Quincey, Thomas, 165
Dedalus, Stephan, 166
Demandt, Alexander, 73
Derrida, Jacques, 108, 109, 117, 149
Descartes, 119
    see also Cartesian
Dewey, John, 117
Diemer, Alwin, 69, 71
Dilthey, Wilhelm, 65, 75, 83, 84, 109, 118, 126, 133
Döblin, Alfred, 224, 231–235,
Droysen, Johann Gustav, 66, 190, 226, 236
Dryden, John, 160

Dufour, Guillaume-Henri (General), 188
Dupin, August, 185
Dürer, Albrecht, 196, 200, 218, 220
Durkheim, Emile, 180
Dux, Günther, 4

E

Eckermann, 99
Eliade, Mircea, 127
Eliot, T. S., 164–167
Enlai, Zhou, 99
Ephialtes, 223

F

Faure, Edgar, 99
Felman, Shoshana, 148
Ferdinand II. (Empereur), 224, 229, 231, 232
Feuerbach, Ludwig, 65
Fichte, Johann Gottlieb, 29
Forster, E. M., 164
Foucault, Michel, 113, 134
Francis of Assisi, 95
Freising, Otto von, 73
Freud, Sigmund, 13–14, 16, 246
Freudian, 174
Friedländer, Saul, 241, 252
Fritta, Bedrich, 198
Fukuyama, Francis, 96
Furet, François, 12

G

Gadamer, Hans-Georg, 109, 114, 117, 138, 141, 165
Gadamerian, 115
Gallie, Walter B., 118
Galtung, Johan, 4, 5
Gatterer, Johann Christoph, 224
George III. (King of England), 209
Gerz, Jochen, 242, 243–244, 250
Goethe, Johann Wolfgang von, 83, 99, 101, 115
Gorgias, 131
Gorter, Herman, 142, 143
Gregorovius, Ferdinand, 211

H

Habermasian, 90
Hägar the Horrible, 52, 55
Halbwachs, Maurice, 10, 11, 166
Hauser, Kaspar, 190, 191
Hecker, Axel, 233
Hegel, Georg Wilhelm Friedrich, 17, 65, 66, 67, 73–74, 76, 77, 78, 79, 80, 82, 83, 95, 113, 118, 126, 161, 162
Hegelian, 45, 74, 80, 81–82
Hegelianism, 83
Heidegger, Martin, 163
Heim, Michael, 190
Heraklitos, 95
Herder, Johann Gottfried, 65, 66, 115, 121, 137
Heussi, Karl, 65, 69
Hildebert of Lavardin, 215
Hitler, Adolf, 243
Hoffmann, Detlef, 4
Hoffmann, Paul, 185, 186
Hoheisel, Horst, 242, 244–245, 250
Homer, 159
Horace, 159
Huizinga, Johan, 115, 116, 120, 121, 139, 140–144, 145
Humboldt, Wilhelm von, 66, 72
Huntington, Samuel P., 45
Hus, Johann, 193
Husserl, Edmund, 11
Husserlian, 10
Huysman, Joris-Karl, 142
Huyssen, Andreas, 239

I

Isabella of Spain, 51, 52, 53

J

Jabes, Edmond, 240
Jameson, Frederic, 115
Jansonius, F., 143
Joyce, James, 146, 166
Judas, 223

K

Kafka, Franz, 21
Kaiser, Georg, 235
Kamerbeek, Jr., Jan, 144
Kant, Immanuel, 21, 66, 67, 72, 74, 78, 82, 91
Kantian, 111, 116, 117, 149
Kantianism, 114
    Neo-Kantian, 36

Keller, Ferdinand, 187, 189
Kemperink, M. G., 140
Khomeini, 95
Kierkegaard, Søren, 161–163, 165
Koselleck, Reinhart, 9, 14, 68, 127, 155
Krug, Wilhelm Traugott, 72–73
Krul, W. E., 141
Kulke, Hermann, 126
Kuwasseg, Joseph, 185, 186

L

Lafontaine, Oskar, 244
Lang, Berel, 145
Lao-tzu, 34
Laub, Dori, 148
Lauth, Rudolf, 69, 72, 76
Lämmert, Eberhard, 4
Leibnitz, Gottfried Wilhelm, 11, 73, 77
Leibnitzian, 76, 81
Lessing, Theodor, 55, 78, 79–80, 82, 85
Leucippus of Miletus, 29
Levi, Primo, 148
Levinas, Emanuel, 240
Levi-Strauss, Claude, 127
Libeskind, Daniel, 242, 245–247, 250
Lincoln, Abraham, 131–132
Lock, Andrew, 21
Lotze, Hermann, 65, 66, 69, 75–84
Lovejoy, Arthur, 33
Löwith, Karl, 67, 69, 82, 162
Luhmann, Niklas, 21
Lukasiewicz, Jan, 119
Luther, Martin, 133, 134
Lyotard, Jean-François, 108

M

MacCay, Windsor, 192
Mallarmé, Stèphane, 140
Mann, Golo, 67, 82, 224, 228–231, 232, 234, 235–236
Mann, Heinrich, 233
Mansfeld, Michael, 198
Marquard, Odo, 70
Marx, Karl, 35–36, 66, 95, 235
Mates, Benson, 119
Maurus, Terentianus, 237
Mehlis, Georg, 69, 84
Meinecke, Friedrich, 83
Meineckian, 81
Meyer, Conrad Ferdinand, 228, 230

Meyer, Eduard, 12
Michelangelo, 170
Michelet, Jules, 12, 121,
Mink, Louis, 125
Möllemann, Jürgen, 200
Mörike, 70
Müller, Klaus E., 127
Muschg, Walter, 224

N

Napoleon, 99
Napoleonic, 191
Neumann, Carl W., 187
Newton, Isaac, 134
Nicolai, Laurens, 225
Nietzsche, Friedrich, 17, 18, 72, 74, 84–85, 161, 162, 163, 165, 240
Nordau, Max, 65, 75
Nosko, Werner, 190

O

Overbeck, Franz, 161, 162–163, 165

P

Pabel, Hilmar, 196, 199
Panofsky, Erwin, 217
Pekař, Josef, 224–227, 228, 230, 232, 234, 235
Pericles, 131
Piaget, Jean, 28
Plato, 29–31, 32, 33, 67
Poe, Edgar Allen, 185
Pope, Alexander, 158–160, 165
Proust, Marcel, 146
Pucelle, Jean, 216, 217

Q

Quine, W. O., 94

R

Rabin, Yitzhak, 242, 248
Rafael, 115
Ranke, Leopold von, 42, 181, 235
Rašin, Jaroslov Sina, 225, 226, 228
Rau, Horst Dieter, 68
Rickert, Heinrich, 65, 75, 83, 84
Ricoeur, Paul, 3, 124
Rieder, Heinz, 227

Rorty, Richard, 108, 149
Rousseau, Jean-Jacques, 83
Rüsen, Jörn, 4, 124, 133
Ruskin, John, 115

S

Sandberg, Herbert, 202
Saussurian, 113
Saxl, Fritz, 196, 201
Scheffel, Victor von, 231, 233
Schelling, Friedrich Willhelm Joseph, 9
Schiller, Friedrich, 66, 67, 160
Schlief, Anton, 224, 225, 228
Schluchter, Wolfgang, 36
Schopenhauer, Arthur, 66, 74, 84
Shalev-Gerz, Esther, 243
Simmel, Georg, 65, 75, 158, 173
Smetek, Wislaw, 190
Snell, Bruno, 37
Spamer, Otto, 186
Spenglerian, 45
Spiegelman, Art, 242, 249–251
Spindler, Konrad, 190
Spinoza, Baruch, 95
Spranger, Eduard, 83
Strempel, Horst, 200
Stückrath, Jörn, 4
Suvanto, Pekka, 227, 236
Swift, Johnathan, 156–158

T

Thales of Miletus, 34
Thucydides, 131, 224
Thurn, Heinrich Matthias von (Count), 232
Tilly, Johann Tserclaes von, 225
Timaeus, 29–30, 32–33, 34–35, 37
    see also Plato
Titian, 115
Tolstoy, Leo, 233
Tomás de Torquemada, 95
Toynbeeesque, 92
Treitschke, Heinrich von, 236
Troeltsch, Ernst, 67
Tynjanow, Jurij, 166

U

Unamuno, Miguel de, 163
Uncle Scrooge, 183
Unger, Franz, 185, 186
Urban II. (Pope), 97

V

Van Deijssel, Lodewijk, 139–140, 141
Van der Weyden, Rogier, 218–219
Van Eyck, 116, 142
Vico, Giovanni Battista, 126
Virgil, 159
Vischer, Friedrich Theodor, 202
Vladek, 251

W

Wallenstein, Albrecht Wenzel Eusebius von, 223, 224, 225, 226, 227, 228, 229, 230, 231, 232, 233, 234, 235, 236, 237
Walter von der Vogelweide, 196
Warburg, Aby, 192, 195, 202
Warhol, Andy, 159
Weber, Max, 12, 36, 43, 47, 49, 82, 91
Weberian, 36, 175
Webster, Daniel, 132
Wehler, Hans-Ulrich, 231
White, Hayden, ix–x, 125, 139, 144–148
Wiley, Miller, 51
Wilhelm, Richard, 34
William I. (German Emperor), 193
Wills, Gary, 131–132
Wind, Edgar, 195
Wittgensteinian, 149
Woolf, Virginia, 146

Y

Yerushalmi, Yosef Hayim, 239
Young, James E., 4

Z

Zola, Emile, 233

www.ingramcontent.com/pod-product-compliance
Lightning Source LLC
Chambersburg PA
CBHW071335080526
44587CB00017B/2840